On Courts and Democracy

Judge J. Skelly Wright

On Courts and Democracy

Selected Nonjudicial Writings of J. Skelly Wright

Edited by

ARTHUR SELWYN MILLER

Contributions in American Studies, Number 75

Greenwood Press
Westport, Connecticut • London, England

Library of Congress Cataloging in Publication Data

Wright, J. Skelly.
On courts and democracy.

(Contributions in American studies, ISSN 0084-9227 ; no. 75)
Bibliography: p.
Includes index.
1. Law—United States—Addresses, essays, lectures.
I. Miller, Arthur Selwyn, 1917- . II. Title.
III. Series.
KF213.W74M56 1984 349.73 83-22810
ISBN 0-313-23938-X (lib. bdg.) 347.3

Library of Congress Catalog Card Number: 83-22810
ISBN: 0-313-23938-X
ISSN: 0084-9227

First published in 1984

Greenwood Press
A division of Congressional Information Service, Inc.
88 Post Road West, Westport, Connecticut 06881

Printed in the United States of America

10 9 8 7 6 5 4 3 2 1

Contents

	Preface	vii
	Introduction: Radical Democracy and Judicial Review: J. Skelly Wright's Approach to Public Law THOMAS C. GREY	xi
1.	The Role of the Supreme Court in a Democratic Society—Judicial Activism or Restraint?	3
2.	Professor Bickel, the Scholarly Tradition, and the Supreme Court	33
3.	Politics and the Constitution: Is Money Speech?	73
4.	Money and the Pollution of Politics: Is the First Amendment an Obstacle to Political Equality?	97
5.	Judicial Review and the Equal Protection Clause	137
6.	Public School Desegregation: Legal Remedies for De Facto Segregation	167
7.	Color-Blind Theories and Color-Conscious Remedies	195
8.	The Courts and the Rulemaking Process: The Limits of Judicial Review	231
9.	Beyond Discretionary Justice	257
	Bibliography	283
	Index	287

Preface

This book is a companion volume to my simultaneously published biography of Judge J. Skelly Wright, *A "Capacity for Outrage": The Judicial Odyssey of J. Skelly Wright.* Nine of his more important contributions to legal periodicals have been brought together in this volume. Since these essays deal with many of the themes of his judicial career—racial segregation, money and politics, the role of courts in a democracy, affirmative action plans, and the extent to which judges should overrule the bureaucracy—this collection complements the biography. The title, *On Courts and Democracy,* encapsulates what may be found in the several articles. Judge Wright is a staunch democrat (with a small "d") and stoutly believes in most of the basic assumptions of American democracy: that the United States in fact is a democracy; that wise, or at least better, decisions will come from government if the channels of communication in the nation are unclogged; that people generally not only want to know but have the capacity to learn in adequate detail all of the intricacies of proposed public policies; that the elected representatives of the people will both listen to and heed what the people say; that there is such a thing as "the" people in the United States; that in a bureaucratized nation, such as the United States, secrecy is aberrational; that government does not engage in propaganda designed to influence the popular mind; and that more than formal equality is necessary, because equality before the law is inconsistent with unequal property rights (wealth).

This is not the place to analyze either the validity of those assumptions or the extent to which Judge Wright believes in them. That was done, to some degree at least, in the biography of the judge. It is enough now to say that his is a faith in the essential goodness of people and in the capacity of law to help people reach decisions that further both the specific and the general good.

Preceding each of Judge Wright's essays is a brief introductory statement, discussing the article and indicating what is to be expected in it. An introduction by Professor Thomas C. Grey opens the collection.

Professor Grey, who clerked for Judge Wright in 1969-1970, has superbly synthesized the principal messages of the several articles. Following the articles is a bibliography that lists all of the Judge's nonjudicial writings. It reveals that Wright has been more prolific off the bench than any other judge in modern times—and possibly in American history. As Professor Grey tells us, these nonjudicial writings are often a means of taking Judge Wright's views to the professoriate generally as well as to law students.

A final note: The concluding bibliography reveals that Judge Wright started slowly in his off-bench writings but gathered speed through the years. He is far more prolific today than he was thirty years ago. All of the articles reproduced here were written in the past twenty years, many in the last few years. As Judge Wright grows older, he retains an enormous capacity for hard and sustained work and a willingness to make his views known beyond the realm of professional lawyers. This book, then, should be read in conjunction with his biography.

ACKNOWLEDGMENTS

I am indebted to several people for making this collection possible. Judge Wright readily agreed to my proposal for the volume. His secretary and indispensable assistant, Martha Scallon, furnished me with copies of all except a very few of Judge Wright's articles (the missing ones are from the 1950s, before Miss Scallon began to work for Judge Wright). Tom Grey has added greatly to the merit of the collection with his finely constructed introductory analysis. I am grateful to each of them.

COPYRIGHT ACKNOWLEDGMENTS

—Arthur Selwyn Miller

Key West, Florida
August 1983

Introduction: Radical Democracy and Judicial Review: J. Skelly Wright's Approach to Public Law

THOMAS C. GREY*

This book collects the more important of Judge J. Skelly Wright's extra-judicial writings, generalizations drawn from nearly 35 years experience on the federal bench. Judges' speeches and papers usually supply either shop-talk or truisms. These essays, all originally given as speeches, fall into neither category. In them, Skelly Wright has forcefully set out his controversial views on politically charged legal issues—busing, affirmative action, campaign spending, and business regulation.

The traditional judicial avoidance of off-bench pronouncements on such subjects is soundly self-interested. Every pronouncement limits future judicial freedom, exposing the judge to the challenge "but earlier you said. . . ." Judges have to commit themselves whenever they decide cases; why invite extra trouble?

By a familiar process, guild self-interest has been transformed into professional propriety on this point. Judges' natural predisposition to keep their powder dry has become an ethical norm, behind which judicial nominees can retreat, for instance, when legislators ask questions probing their views on abortion or capital punishment at confirmation hearings. The argument is that to answer such questions (or, more generally, to state controversial legal opinions off the bench) will prejudice litigants whose later cases require decision of the contested point; a judge who has revealed his view is pre-committed and hence not impartial. But if we carried the implications of this argument through, we would not let judges write opinions, which likewise pre-commit them for the future more than would a bare ruling. And yet we do not take this step, thinking it useful that the officials whose job it is to apply the law in doubtful cases should sometimes state what they think the law is, thus giving guidance to litigants and lawyers and at the same time exposing judicial views and arguments to criticism.

Traditional arguments of propriety against the kind of writing collected here hence do not have much force. Still, being a judge is hard enough

*Professor of Law, Stanford University

work; why would one spend the time and invite the trouble involved in extrajudicial commentary? Generally, judges do not win fame or prestige by writing law review articles. Spoken from the bench, judicial pronouncements come clothed with a certain aura of majesty that the same utterances lack when they come from a lecture podium. The judicial opinion accompanies a judgment that can set in motion the whole force of government. By contrast, the lecture or article summons up, not the sheriff or the jailer, but only spirits from the vasty deep of legal doctrine. Many mediocre legal essays have been cited and quoted for generations and preserved in casebooks because their judicial authors hooked them to decisions and published them in the reports.

In the face of these disadvantages, Skelly Wright has persisted in pressing his controversial legal views off as well as on the bench; this book is the fruit of that continued effort. I suspect that his motives have been mostly pedagogic. Judge Wright takes the business of legal education very seriously and realizes that he cannot count on his judicial opinions alone to get across his views to law students. Professors have unfair advantages over judges in the law school classroom. There a judicial opinion, originally written in a particular tactical situation and directed to resolve a particular dispute rather than to organize a body of doctrine, lies defenseless, to be picked over at leisure. It has already been drained of life-giving facts by the editing of one law professor; now it will be further abused by another, who can blow its doctrinal asides up into vast hollow structures which then collapse, punctured by ingenious hypotheticals that would never have occurred to the judge who decided the original case or the lawyers who litigated it. Unlike most judges, Skelly Wright does not assume that all this takes place in an "ivory tower" and has no effect once the students who undergo it escape into the "real world"; he understands that presuppositions planted early persist long, affecting the practice even of the most practical. Thus he sets forth to meet the professors on their own ground, the lecture halls of the law schools and the pages of the law reviews.

In his extrajudicial work as in his opinions, he has drawn on the help of the recent law school graduates who have served as his clerks. They supply much of the citation material that fills the footnotes of these essays; more than that, they try to satisfy the judge's constant urge to keep in touch with the ideas of the generation entering the law from the bottom; and they supply whatever fortification he gets from youthful enthusiasm. They (or we, as it was my good luck to be a Wright clerk) get in return the chance to be underlaborers on the continuing articulation of Skelly Wright's vision of what American law should be—the vision that animates and unifies the several essays in this book and that has made him so important a figure on our legal scene over the last generation.

The short way of describing that vision would be to say that Skelly Wright sees American public law through the eyes of a radical democrat.

This is a characterization that not all who know his work will readily accept. Surely, it will be said, his most distinctive feature is his extreme judicial activism, an activism always ready to override or squeeze past the mandates of the politically responsive parts of the governmental system.

There is certainly something to the ascription of judicial activism to Skelly Wright. He *is* ready to invoke the spirit of the law when sticking to the letter of precedent or statute would, in his view, kill or stifle some healthy development in the body politic. He has said, in Chapter 2, below, that the ultimate test of a judge's work is its goodness. Yet "judicial activism" does not capture the heart of Skelly Wright's vision, nor does his adherence to so vague and indeterminate a value as "goodness." What appears good to him as a judge is the law that a fair and uncorrupted democratic political process would produce. His activism is triggered when political procedures are corrupt or unfair. In John Ely's phrase, Skelly Wright's is a "representation-reinforcing" public law theory.

We can confirm this by looking at the issues on which Judge Wright has and has not been an activist. On this question, Chapter 5, below, provides a convenient summary, supporting evidence for which is amply supplied by the other chapters of this book as well as by the whole course of his judicial career.

Take first the issue of race, the issue that brought Skelly Wright to national attention as a district judge in New Orleans in the 1950s and that produced perhaps his most activist judicial effort—*Hobson v. Hansen,* the Washington, D.C., school case—in the late 1960s. In these two situations, the judge did intervene most forcefully in the workings of a political system. But in each case it was a system that disenfranchised the black complainants: in Louisiana as a result of the traditional Jim Crow system supported by federal non-enforcement of the fifteenth amendment, and in the District of Columbia as a result of denial of home rule.

Apart from these dramatic situations, Judge Wright has been no uncompromising "activist" on racial questions. Where the political system has supplied race-consensus remedies for the results of the historical oppression of black Americans, he has been quite happy to defer to it (see Chapter 7, below). Thus he is no activist on behalf of those injured by affirmative action; they have sufficient recourse in the political system. On the other side, he has criticized the Supreme Court's attempt to confine the reach of the equal protection clause to cases of purposeful discrimination; it is precisely the record of long exclusion of blacks from fair participation in politics that, in Judge Wright's mind, justifies an activist constitutional requirement that present *de facto* discrimination, even without provable present racial animus, should be remedied so far as is reasonable.

Skelly Wright's version of the first amendment likewise flows more from a belief in egalitarian democracy than from any special judicial self-assertiveness. His main scholarly writings in this area have criticized the

Supreme Court's nullification, in the name of freedom of expression, of reasonable legislative efforts to check the power of money in politics (Chapters 3 and 4, below). Those injured by these campaign spending regulations can take care of themselves in the political process; indeed, it is their very ability to use concentrated economic power on their behalf, beyond what political equality would allow, that is the occasion for the legislation they challenge. Judge Wright thus accepts Alexander Meiklejohn's notion that the first amendment has as its main purpose the reinforcement of popular self-rule, not the protection of any elite, economic or cultural, against democracy. On this view, judicial activism is required mainly to check the tendency of governments and temporary majorities to protect entrenched positions by suppressing that critical debate in politics that is the condition for democratic change. The judge must interpret the first amendment with some bias against the status quo.

Skelly Wright's work in administrative law fits the same pattern as his first amendment writing. He has pressed to open the administrative process to groups whose interests are affected by bureaucratic decisions but who have been excluded from the process of making those decisions. Thus he is activist on questions of standing, and on questions of what substantive interests the agencies must take into account. In a day when the bureaucracy is a "fourth branch," and in many ways the most important branch, of government, the interests of the average citizen are too easily left out of account in dealings between potentially captive bureaucrats and the powerful economic units that they regulate. Decisions of this kind are too frequent and too invisible for the voters to make congressional oversight a fully effective guarantee of democratic decision. On the other hand, Judge Wright does not believe that the courts should engage in any especially activist review of administrative action when corporations complain that they are being overregulated; here, as in the first amendment area (and as with the white majority in questions of racial affirmative action), ordinary legislative politics provides an adequate, if not an excessively responsive, remedy (see Chapters 8 and 9).

Skelly Wright's general public law theory is based on the premise that judicial activism is appropriate where, for some structural reason, the ordinary political process will not represent the interests of the people according to the democratic doctrine of one person, one vote; one vote, one unit of influence. This is a premise he shares with the mainstream of theorists of the judicial role in public law over the last half century, from Justice Harlan Fiske Stone to Dean John Ely.

Wright's distinctive contribution to this tradition has been a special focus on the relation between political equality—government of, by, and for the people—and economic power. The working of the market economy produces substantial economic inequality. Political egalitarianism, or democracy, does not condemn this as such, but a *realistic* political egalitarianism recognizes that concentration of wealth is likely to give its possessor, in effect, more than one vote, while poverty is likely to leave its victim with, in effect, less. The judiciary has a special mission, so I read Skelly Wright as saying, to provide a continuing modest corrective against the natural tendency of economic inequality to undermine the ideal of political democracy.

To say that Skelly Wright is a "realistic" political egalitarian provides an opening to the last main topic he addresses in these essays: the question of what attitude the judge should take to authoritative legal materials. One might crudely say that the "formalist" judge tends to emphasize subordination to those materials, while the "realist" tends to see them only as laying down broad guidelines within which to exercise creativity in decision. (The axis "realism-formalism" is different from the axis "activism-restraint"; Justice Oliver Wendell Holmes was a "restrained realist," while Justice Hugo Black, for example, was a "formalist activist.") It seems natural to say of Skelly Wright that, along with his modified activism, he inclines toward the "realistic" view of the judicial role. He knows better than most that in the cases coming before appellate courts there is usually a sound lawyer's argument for deciding either way. He is fully a master of those flexible techniques of leeway and interpretation in dealing with precedent and statute that Karl Llewellyn, chief among the American legal realists, catalogued so carefully.

Further, Judge Wright is a realist in another sense, the sense brought out in calling him a "realistic" political egalitarian. He tries to base his exercise of the judge's inevitable lawmaking function on the full reality of the situation to which the law will apply, as best he can discern it. He is not inclined to assume that things in the world are as they are said to be in the ideal constructs of high-school civics and in some traditional public law commentary. He knows, for example, that not all political interests are represented according to their numerical weight and intensity in the actual political process—after all, he grew up in Louisiana, where blacks were scarcely represented politically at all, and where oil money did not just talk but (Bob Dylan's word) screamed in the legislative ear. He has criticized the basing of constitutional doctrine on civics-book presumptions, most notably in what is probably his best-known article, included below as Chapter 2. This same realism animates his critique of using "race-blind" equal protection doctrine to block remedies against historically generated racial inequality (Chapter 7).

But in another sense, Skelly Wright is not a legal realist. There is a kind of "realism" that rests on ultimate skepticism about values, perhaps best expressed in our legal tradition in the thought of Justice Holmes. Holmes, who said he had his "can't helps" but could not assert that they were better than the next person's, accepted democracy as a kind of least evil among forms of government. In the absence of values as such, human wants, desires, or preferences had to prevail, and peace was most likely to be preserved if the preferences of the many (however vulgar) prevailed over those of the few. Judicial restraint naturally accompanies this view of politics, since if there can be no reasoning about values, the "reasoning branch" of government, the judiciary, has no call to upset settlements achieved by elected politicians.

A judiciary operating on this brand of realism would never have declared Jim Crow unconstitutional, an action that brought strife to a relatively peaceful Southern scene in the name of equality and led to crosses being burned on the lawn of a Southern federal judge (Wright) who took the project seriously. Holmesian skepticism, then, is not Skelly Wright's variety of realism. Equality, not peace and quiet (or law and order), is his ultimate test of political goodness. He has an affirmative concept of democracy, seeing it not as uneasy practical truce in the war of all against all but as the ongoing effort to embody the ideal of equal human dignity in working institutions. Reason, including the reason of the judge, need not accede to the status quo when the question is whether this ideal is being reasonably pursued. Nor of course is this guiding ideal a merely subjective or idiosyncratic one; rather, it has been the proclaimed ideal of American politics from our national beginnings. Skelly Wright has made it his lifelong project, on the bench and, as this book illustrates, off the bench, to do what he could to hold our legal practices to the requirements of this our own theory.

On Courts and Democracy

1

The Role of the Supreme Court in a Democratic Society—Judicial Activism or Restraint?

During the past three decades, since the 1954 Supreme Court decision requiring racial desegregation of public schools, scholars have debated the extent to which judges should substitute their views for those of the officers of the nominally democratic branches of government. Often this intellectual quarrel has taken the form of casting "judicial activism" against "judicial restraint." Justice Felix Frankfurter was the leader of the restraint school; he and his followers argued for a limited role of courts in the governing process. They inveighed against members of the Supreme Court, particularly Chief Justice Earl Warren and Justices Hugo Black and William Douglas.

Judge Skelly Wright was also one of their targets. Because of a number of his controversial rulings, he has been and still is considered to be the preeminent judicial activist of the modern era. In this opening essay of this collection, Judge Wright enters the fray with a spirited defense of the activist position. To be sure, he is not uncritical: He advocates an activism that would further the concepts of equality and human dignity. His main point comes in the concluding paragraph. The courts, he maintains, must act when legislatures neglect their constitutional responsibilities to further the values of constitutionalism.

Judge Wright's defense of the innovative decisions of the Supreme Court under Chief Justice Earl Warren is one that not only approves of the specific decisions of that Court but also maintains that such judicial action is wholly proper. Judicial review gives American society an opportunity for a "sober second thought" about public policies. Wright analyzes the criticisms of judicial activism, acknowledging that some of them are at least partially meritorious, but comes down strongly in defense of the courts acting to protect the spirit of the Constitution.

One of the Warren Court's severest critics tells us that during the Chief Justice's tenure the Supreme Court has "wrought more fundamental changes in the political and legal structure of the United States than during any similar span of time since the Marshall Court had the unique opportunity to express itself on a [clean slate]."[1] This has distressed those who counsel judicial restraint.

Remembering that certain past Supreme Courts, particularly those of the twenties and early thirties, also tried to play an active role in shaping our society, the apostles of restraint warn that even though we may approve the results that the Warren Court has decreed, we still must chastise the Court for assuming an activist role.[2] For even if the changes are desirable, they say the Court is not the proper institution to initiate them. Rather, the sorts of judgments the Court has made are the province of the legislatures; and, of course, the Court must not legislate. After all, it was the illicit role of a super legislature that the Nine Old Men are said to have assumed.

These critics are particularly upset because, just as many of the ill-fated "activist" decisions of the past were decided by recourse to the open-ended concept of substantive due process,[3] so many of the Warren

---

1 Kurland, *The Supreme Court 1963 Term, Foreword: Equal in Origin and Equal in Title to the Legislative and Executive Branches of Government*, 78 HARV. L. REV. 143 (1964).

2 *See, e.g.*, Freund, *New Vistas in Constitutional Law*, 112 U. PA. L. REV. 631 (1964); Freund, *The Supreme Court Under Attack*, 25 U. PITT. L. REV. 1 (1963).

3 *See, e.g.*, Adkins v. Children's Hospital, 261 U.S. 525 (1923); Coppage v. Kansas, 236 U.S. 1 (1915); Adair v. United States, 208 U.S. 161 (1908); Lochner v. New York, 198 U.S.

Court's path-breaking decisions have been rendered pursuant to the equally open-ended concepts of equal protection and procedural due process.[4] It is into these generalized constitutional commands that the Justices are most likely to read their own personal predilections and thus render ad hoc justice. Consequently, both the old Court and the Warren Court are criticized for much the same reasons.

There is, however, an obvious difference between the two Courts. The Nine Old Men were trying to halt a revolution in the role of government as a social instrument,[5] while the Warren Court is obviously furthering that effort. Its most significant pronouncements have decreed change in the status quo, not its preservation.[6] Rather than invalidate legislative efforts at social progress, its decisions have ordered alteration of widespread and long accepted practices, including many which had not been legislatively sanctioned in the first place. In Professor Berle's phrase, the Warren Court has functioned as a "revolutionary committee."[7]

---

45 (1905). For a discussion of the Court's retreat from this area, see McCloskey, *Economic Due Process and the Supreme Court: An Exhumation and A Reburial*, 1962 SUP. CT. REV. 34, 36-45.

4 *See, e.g.*, Harper v. Virginia Bd. of Elec., 383 U.S. 663 (1966); Reynolds v. Sims, 377 U.S. 533 (1964); Schneider v. Rusk, 377 U.S. 163 (1964); Douglas v. California, 372 U.S. 353 (1963); Griffin v. Illinois, 351 U.S. 12 (1956); Brown v. Board of Educ., 347 U.S. 483 (1954). *See also* Miranda v. Arizona, 384 U.S. 436 (1966); Escobedo v. Illinois, 378 U.S. 478 (1964); Gideon v. Wainwright, 372 U.S. 335 (1963), all of which, though couched in terms of fifth and six amendment guarantees, have strong equal protection overtones. *See* Kamisar, *Equal Justice in the Gatehouses and Mansions of American Criminal Procedure*, in Y. KAMISAR, F. INBAU & T. ARNOLD, CRIMINAL JUSTICE IN OUR TIMES 69 (A. Howard ed. 1965).

5 Surely one of the hallmarks of the old Court was the frequency with which it struck down recently enacted legislation, both state and federal. Hammer v. Dagenhart, 247 U.S. 251 (1918), struck down the Child Labor Act which had been passed in 1916. Bailey v. Drexel Furniture Co., 259 U.S. 20 (1922), invalidated the Child Labor Tax Act, passed only three years before in a legislative effort to circumvent the results of *Dagenhart*. In Schechter Poultry Corp. v. United States, 295 U.S. 495 (1935), the Court scuttled the National Industrial Recovery Act, passed only two years before, and in Carter v. Carter Coal Co., 298 U.S. 238 (1936), the Bituminous Coal Conservation Act of 1935, enacted the previous year, met a similar fate. The Agricultural Adjustment Act of 1933, was almost as short-lived when it was killed by United States v. Butler, 297 U.S. 1 (1936). Furthermore, while the Court was busy saving the states from a federal government which it felt was acting beyond its constitutional powers, it also attempted to save the states from themselves. In Morehead v. New York *ex rel.* Tipaldo, 298 U.S. 587 (1936), for instance, the Court, following its illustrious predecessors that had decided Lochner v. New York, 198 U.S. 45 (1905), and Adkins v. Children's Hospital, 261 U.S. 525 (1923), struck down New York's 1933 minimum wage law for women as violative of substantive due process.

6 *See* cases cited note 4 *supra*. *See also* Griswold v. Connecticut, 381 U.S. 479 (1965); New York Times Co. v. Sullivan, 376 U.S. 254 (1964); Abington School Dist. v. Schempp, 374 U.S. 203 (1963); Engel v. Vitale, 370 U.S. 421 (1962).

7 A. BERLE, THE THREE FACES OF POWER vii (1967).

Simply to say, however, that the Warren Court has frequently ordered change while the old Court tried to halt it does not itself establish that the one has done a good job and the other a bad one. Nor does it establish that either Court should have acted at all. It is my contention that the Warren Court has not simply decreed the right results, but also that it was right to have decreed them. Its active role in shaping our society has been a necessary and proper one. It is, then, necessary to distinguish its performance from that of certain "activist" Courts of the past whose performances were certainly injudicious. In order to do this, the sort of arguments that are made to support the doctrine of judicial restraint will be examined briefly, and both their validity and their bearing on an assessment of the work of the Warren Court must be considered.

I

The Arguments for Restraint

Three types of arguments are made against the courts playing an active role in shaping our society. One stresses the illegitimacy of the courts so acting, another emphasizes the adverse effects on democratic processes when the court so acts, while the third denies the ability of the courts to do it well. The last argument will be considered first.

A. *Limitations of Institutional Competency*

The stress here is not on the illegitimacy of the Court's behaving like a legislature, but on its incapacity to do so effectively. To begin with, we are told that the Court cannot act until a case is brought to it, and that anything said in the course of the opinion that is not crucial to the decision itself is mere dictum and without the force of law. Moreover, the judgment in a particular case binds only the parties. Consequently, the Court can never confront a broad social issue or solve it in a comprehensive fashion.[8] In addition, the Court does not have the requisite fact-finding machinery and therefore cannot acquire the pertinent knowledge upon which intelligent social action must be based.[9]

Moreover, judicial review is a blunt instrument. The Court cannot make the subtle, delicate, and in a sense arbitrary, distinctions and discriminations which the legislature can, and frequently must, make.

---

[8] *See* Mr. Justice Holmes' statement on this point in Southern Pac. Co. v. Jensen, 244 U.S. 205, 221 (1917).

[9] *See* Alfange, *The Relevance of Legislative Facts in Constitutional Law*, 114 U. Pa. L. Rev. 637 (1966).

If, for instance, the Court had held discrimination in public accommodations to be unconstitutional, it could not very well have exempted, as the Civil Rights Act of 1964 does, owner-occupied rooming houses with fewer than five boarders.[10] Furthermore, it could never have undertaken the temporal and geographical line-drawing that characterizes the Voting Rights Act of 1965.[11] Similarly, it was long believed that the Court could not decree that its constitutional judgment, like most legislation, be given only prospective effect. Most important of all, perhaps, is the fact that the Court, having the power neither of the purse nor the sword, must rely on the legislative and executive branches of government to enforce its directives.[12]

These considerations are, of course, very persuasive arguments for judicial restraint. We have seen the consequences of their disregard. For instance, without any fact-finding machinery whatever, the old Court in *Lochner v. New York* felt confident in surmising that there was "*no* reasonable foundation for holding [a state statute limiting the hours of work for bakers to sixty hours a week] to be necessary or appropriate as a health law to safeguard the public health or the health of the individuals who are following the trade of a baker."[13] Indeed, virtually all the old economic due process cases holding federal and state statutes unconstitutional resulted, at least in part, from the Court's fact-finding incapacity.

Moreover, these considerations of institutional incapacity may apply with particular force where the Court is itself decreeing broad changes in the status quo. For the Court not only faces its usual fact-gathering disabilities involved in making its initial judgment; it must also be prepared to oversee and administer the operation of the decree itself. And the Court's affirmative mandate may require the state to expend money which the legislature is unwilling to appropriate.[14]

In certain areas the Court has tried to surmount these obstacles. It has, for instance, tried to inform itself more fully by requesting amicus briefs and, on occasion, such as in the second *Brown v. Board of Education* case,[15] it has invited the Attorney General to file a brief

---

10 42 U.S.C. § 2000a(b)(1) (1964).

11 42 U.S.C. § 1973 (Supp. I 1965).

12 *See* Deutsch, *Neutrality, Legitimacy, and the Supreme Court: Some Intersections Between Law and Political Science*, 20 STAN. L. REV. 169, 186 (1968).

13 198 U.S. 45, 58 (1905) (emphasis added).

14 *See, e.g.*, Gideon v. Wainwright, 372 U.S. 335 (1963); Griffin v. Illinois, 351 U.S. 12 (1956). *See also* State v. Rush, 46 N.J. 399, 217 A.2d 441 (1966).

15 349 U.S. 294 (1955).

even though the United States was not a party to the case.[16] It has also limited several of its constitutional decisions in the criminal law area to prospective effect only.[17] In *Miranda v. Arizona*[18] it tried to deal with an issue at wholesale by establishing a veritable constitutional code of police procedure. And it has delegated the administrative responsibility for enforcing *Brown* and the reapportionment cases to the lower federal courts.[19] These courts have in turn looked to experts for guidance. The Fifth Circuit in the *Jefferson County* school integration case, for instance, judicially adopted the HEW desegregation guidelines.[20]

Interestingly, many of the critics who point out that the Court is not institutionally competent to make "legislative" determinations become even less sanguine when the Court tries to overcome its institutional limitations. The critics, however, cannot have it both ways—criticizing the Court for making legislative judgments in the guise of adjudication because it cannot legislate wisely, then becoming even more scornful when the Court legislates more candidly in order to do so more effectively.[21]

But whatever one may think of the Court's attempts to mitigate the effects of its institutional incapacities, what is clear about these incapacities is that, where relevant, they counsel deference to the legis-

---

16 The Court also invited the Attorneys General of all states requiring or permitting racial discrimination in public education to present their views on the question of relief. Brown v. Board of Educ., 347 U.S. 483, 495-96 (1954).

17 Stovall v. Denno, 388 U.S. 293 (1967); Johnson v. New Jersey, 384 U.S. 719 (1966); Tehan v. United States *ex rel.* Shott, 382 U.S. 406 (1966); Linkletter v. Walker, 381 U.S. 618 (1965).

18 384 U.S. 436 (1966).

19 Bluntly, litigation in these fields has reached the point where, in many cases, the Supreme Court lays down the principle but sends the case itself back to a district or a state court with instruction to draw an appropriate decree . . . .

A. Berle, *supra* note 7, at 53.

20 United States v. Jefferson Co. Bd. of Educ., 372 F.2d 836 (5th Cir. 1966). *See* N.Y. Times, Mar. 11, 1967, at 24, col. 2.

21 The point is somewhat analogous to one made in a recent article by Professor Deutsch:

> If the difficulty with entrusting political decisions to the Court is its political unresponsiveness, ought we not welcome a "greater sensitivity to . . . shifts in the political temper?" If, on the other hand, we distrust decisions based on transitory shifts in the electorate's mood, is not the solution precisely an institution "unresponsive to the democratic process?" What we cannot do—once we agree that judicial review involves a duty to render decisions that necessarily entail political consequences—is to have it both ways, simultaneously denying legitimacy to decisions of a politically unresponsive institution and to decisions of one that responds to shifts in political sentiment.

Deutsch, *supra* note 12, at 187.

lature but do not require it. Where the choice is between the Court struggling alone with a social issue and the legislature dealing with it expertly, legislative action is to be preferred. All too often, however, the practical choice has been between the Court doing the job as best it can and no one doing it at all.[22] Faced with these alternatives, the Court must assume the legislature's responsibility. If the legislature simply cannot or does not act to correct an unconstitutional status quo, the Court, despite all its incapacities, must finally act to do so. For "nature abhors a political vacuum as much as any other kind,"[23] and if the legislatures do not live up to their constitutional responsibilities, the Court must act to fill the vacuum.

B. *Adverse Effects on Popular Responsibility*

An altogether different argument for judicial restraint is based on the presumed tendency of judicial review to weaken the democratic processes. Here the emphasis is not on the ineffectiveness of judicial action, but on the debilitating side effects such action is likely to have on the other branches of government. For if the Court steps in to correct the constitutional errors of the legislative and the executive branches of government, those institutions will come to rely on it to do so and will cease to discharge their own responsibilities to remain within the boundaries of the Constitution.

James Bradley Thayer laid the keystone for this argument over sixty-five years ago:

> [L]egislatures are growing accustomed to this [judicial] distrust and more and more readily inclined to justify it, and to shed the considerations of constitutional restraints . . . turning that subject over to the courts . . . . The people, all this while, become careless as to whom they send to the legislature . . . [and come to depend on] these few wiser gentlemen on the bench . . . to protect them against their more immediate representatives. . . . [T]he [consequent exercise of the power of judicial review], even when unavoidable, is always attended with a serious evil, namely, that the correction of legislative mistakes comes from the outside,

22 It is regrettable, of course, that in deciding this case this court must act in an area so alien to its expertise. It would be far better indeed for these great social and political problems to be resolved in the political arena by other branches of government. But these are social and political problems which seem at times to defy such resolution. In such situations, under our system, the judiciary must bear a hand and accept its responsibility to assist in the solution where constitutional rights hang in the balance.

Hobson v. Hansen, 269 F. Supp. 401, 517 (D.D.C. 1967). *See also* Cox, *The Supreme Court 1965 Term, Foreword: Constitutional Adjudication and the Promotion of Human Rights*, 80 Harv. L. Rev. 91, 122 (1966).

23 D. Brogan, The Crises of American Federalism 43 (1944).

> and the people thus lose the political experience, and the moral education and stimulus that comes from fighting the question out in the ordinary way, and correcting their own errors. The tendency . . . is to dwarf the political capacity of the people, and to deaden its sense of moral responsibility.[24]

Despite the insight of Thayer's observation, in the last analysis his advice is mistaken. When the Court is asked to review a statute it can do one of three things: find it constitutional, find it unconstitutional, or, one way or another, avoid dealing with the constitutional question altogether. Leaving aside the last possibility, Thayer seems to say that, except in a compelling case,[25] the Court should uphold the statute's constitutionality and hope for its repeal by a more enlightened legislature.

As Professor Black has perceptively observed, however, when the Court upholds a statute's constitutionality it "legitimates" it.[26] When a statute expresses the most enlightened sentiments of the community, this legitimating function may serve the important and creative purpose of adding impetus and dignity to measures hesitantly enacted. But unfortunately the Court's seal of constitutional approval has the same effect where the statute is a repressive one. When the Court validates such a statute, it adds moral fuel to the political fire and makes a legislative repeal even less likely. Of course lawyers know that, theoretically at least, the Court's finding a statute constitutional implies nothing about its wisdom. Nevertheless, until the Supreme Court validates it, the opposition's argument that it is unconstitutional, or simply unwise, may induce the majority to take a second look. Once the Supreme Court warrants the statute, the opposition is undercut.

It is perhaps instructive to notice that even where the Court has expressed moral disapproval of a statute, while upholding its constitutionality, the legislature has often vigorously asserted its acknowledged prerogative and has paid scant attention to the Court's attempt at moral suasion. For instance, after the Court reluctantly upheld the compulsory flag salute rule in *Minersville School District v. Gobitis*,[27] the West

---

24 J. Thayer, John Marshall 103-04, 106-07 (1901), *as discussed in* A. Bickel, The Least Dangerous Branch 21-22 (1962).

25 "[The Court] can only disregard the Act when those who have the right to make laws have not merely made a mistake, but have made a very clear one,—so clear that it is not open to rational question." Thayer, *The Origin and Scope of the American Doctrine of Constitutional Law*, 7 Harv. L. Rev. 129, 144 (1893). Few such compelling cases exist. For an analysis of Thayer's rule of the "clear mistake," see A. Bickel, *supra* note 24, at 35-46.

26 C. Black, The People and the Court 34-86 (1960).

27 310 U.S. 586 (1940).

Virginia legislature enacted a comparable statute for the state as a whole, and other states quickly joined the repressive band wagon. Finally the Court was forced to reverse this trend by reversing itself and overruling *Gobitis* three years later in *West Virginia State Board of Education v. Barnette*.[28]

Although Thayer did not stress the alternative of avoidance, Professor Bickel has suggested, not that the Court validate such unconstitutional statutes, but that, in part for the reasons Thayer canvassed, it stay its hand and avoid a constitutional determination altogether.[29] By avoiding decision on the constitutional merits, the Court gives the representative branches a chance to correct their own constitutional mistakes. Of course, when the Court avoids review and thus denies the claim of a valid constitutional right, the moving party's right goes unvindicated. But perhaps Professor Bickel is right to the extent that where the moving party's claims, although perhaps valid, are less than overpowering, avoidance by the Supreme Court is the lesser of two evils.[30]

Furthermore, Bickel's advice may be particularly meaningful when the Court contemplates the recognition of a constitutional duty rather than the invalidation of a particular statute. To begin with, whether such a duty has come to exist in our society—whether, in other words, the status quo is now unconstitutional—may be a judgment more difficult to make than declaring a specific statute unconstitutional. In addition, it would be a very serious matter for the people to come to rely on the Court as the most important force for change in our society. That the legislature might come to enact laws without adequately considering their constitutionality, leaving it to the Court to correct its mistakes, would be very unfortunate; but if the people and the legislatures were to come to expect the Court to do their work for them, it

---

28 319 U.S. 624 (1943).

29 A. Bickel, *supra* note 24, at 69-72, 110-98. *See* Bickel, *The Supreme Court 1960 Term, Foreword: The Passive Virtues*, 75 Harv. L. Rev. 40 (1961).

30 [T]he equities on the side of the moving party will vary in intensity. . . . This is not an argument relevant to the issue of principle itself. It can only make more palatable the use of a device of avoidance that works against the moving party. . . . There are crucial differences . . . between the role of the Supreme Court in constitutional cases and the function of courts of general jurisdiction. The latter sit as primary agencies for the peaceful settlement of disputes. . . . They must, indeed, resolve all controversies within their jurisdiction, because the alternative is chaos. [By contrast, the Supreme Court's] interventions are . . . exceptional and limited, and they occur, not to forestall chaos, but to revise a pre-existing order that is otherwise viable and was itself arrived at by more normal processes. Fixation on an individual right to judgment by the Supreme Court is, therefore, . . . question-begging.

A. Bickel, *supra* note 24, at 173.

would be far worse. Finally, as previously mentioned, the Court may be institutionally ill-equipped to decree and oversee substantial social reform.

In the last analysis, however, these considerations again simply require that the Court not act precipitately. If substantial rights are at stake which the legislative process cannot or will not vindicate, the task of doing so unfortunately, but inevitably, passes to the courts. It is this task which the Warren Court has reluctantly, but properly, assumed with respect to the implementation of our constitutional ideal of equality.

C. *The Court as an Undemocratic Institution*

A final argument for judicial restraint goes neither to the Court's efficiency nor to the effect of judicial review on other branches of government, but rather to the Court's legitimacy as a policy maker in a democratic society. Here the Court's required self-restraint is said to follow from its undemocratic structure. The syllogism goes something like this: Ours is an essentially democratic society. The Supreme Court, in its reviewing capacity, is an undemocratic, "inherently oligarchic,"[31] and "deviant institution in the American democracy."[32] Therefore, except in the most compelling situations, it should allow the representative bodies to act, or not act, as they choose.[33]

There are at least two things that should be said about this argument. First, both of its premises are shaky. It is, to begin with, unclear just what is meant by a "democratic society." Perhaps we can agree on this familiar definition:

> [A] democratic political system is one in which public policies are made, on a majority basis, by representatives subject to effective popular control at periodic elections which are conducted on the principle of political equality and under conditions of political freedom.[34]

---

31 *See* AFL v. American Sash & Door Co., 335 U.S. 538, 555 (1949) (Frankfurter, J., concurring).

32 A. BICKEL, *supra* note 24, at 18.

33 Dennis v. United States, 341 U.S. 494, 555-56 (1951) (Frankfurter, J., concurring). *See generally* A. BICKEL, *supra* note 24, at ch. 1. *But see id.* at 258 (contradicting ch. 1); L. HAND, *The Contribution of an Independent Judiciary to Civilization,* in THE SPIRIT OF LIBERTY 172 (1952); Choper, *On the Warren Court and Judicial Review,* 17 CATH. U.L. REV. 20, 36-41 (1967); McCleskey, *Judicial Review in a Democracy: A Dissenting Opinion,* 3 HOUST. L. REV. 354 (1962). *Contra,* C. BLACK, *supra* note 26, at 155-222; E. ROSTOW, THE SOVEREIGN PREROGATIVE: THE SUPREME COURT AND THE QUEST FOR LAW 118-21 (1962); Beth, *The Case for Judicial Protection of Civil Liberties,* 17 J. POL. 100 (1955); Mason, *The Supreme Court: Temple and Forum,* 48 YALE REV. 524 (1959); Rostow, *The Democratic Charter of Judicial Review,* 66 HARV. L. REV. 193 (1952).

34 H. MAYO, AN INTRODUCTION TO DEMOCRATIC THEORY 70 (1960).

Although under this definition the Court is certainly not a democratic institution—staffed as it is by men with lifetime appointments and "hedged about by an unusually intricate impeachment process and an absolute guaranty against diminution of compensation"[35]—it is equally clear that many of our other governmental institutions are also undemocratic. To the extent the definition suggests that policy making should be responsive to majority will, the Senate itself could not qualify, for its composition, whereby the votes of 18,000,000 Californians count no more than those of 180,000 Alaskans, can hardly be said to be conducive to majority rule. And the House, at least before its districts were ordered apportioned by population in *Wesberry v. Sanders*,[36] was not truly representative either.

Moreover, the internal rules of the legislatures make popular—that is to say majority—control even less likely. The enormous power of the committee chairman stems from seniority which is often more the product of the disenfranchisement of the opposition than of ability or even popularity. Or, to take an even more extreme example of minority leverage, consider the Senate's rules of debate. Under these rules, a filibuster can be broken only if two-thirds of the Senate votes to close off debate. And if cloture is not voted, the debated bill will almost certainly not be enacted. Consequently thirty-four Senators representing fewer than 15,000,000 people can kill legislation that may be desired by an overwhelming majority.[37]

These are just a few of the anti-majoritarian features of our most representative bodies. In addition, consider the heads of the administrative agencies who wield tremendous power and are not directly responsible to any electorate.[38] Finally, and most important of all, a thoroughgoing majoritarianism is inconsistent with the very idea of limited—that is to say constitutional—government. For the Constitution itself sets out certain areas as simply beyond the reach of the present majority.[39] Is the Constitution itself then a deviant document in our democracy?

---

35 McGowan, *The Supreme Court in the American Constitutional System, The Problem in Historical Perspective*, 33 NOTRE DAME LAW. 527, 539 (1958).

36 376 U.S. 1 (1964).

37 *See* M. SHAPIRO, FREEDOM OF SPEECH: THE SUPREME COURT AND JUDICIAL REVIEW 17-34 (1966); Deutsch, *supra* note 12, at 185-86.

38 *See* C. BLACK, *supra* note 26, at 179-80; E. ROSTOW, *supra* note 33, at 152.

39 The very purpose of a Bill of Rights was to withdraw certain subjects from the vicissitudes of political controversy, to place them beyond the reach of majorities and officials and to establish them as legal principles to be applied by the courts. One's right to life, liberty, and property, to free speech, a free press, freedom of worship and assembly, and other fundamental rights may not be submitted to vote; they depend on the outcome of no elections.

West Virginia Bd. of Educ. v. Barnette, 319 U.S. 624, 638 (1943).

This argument for judicial restraint not only overplays the Court's deviancy but also overstresses its immunity from democratic processes. To begin with, the Justices are appointed by the President, the one elected official whose constituency is the nation as a whole. On the average a new appointment is made every twenty-two months.[40] And, as Justice Frankfurter reminds us, "Judges are men, not disembodied spirits"[41] who are blind to the political reality around them. Moreover, if the Justices are not themselves sufficiently attuned to the times, Congress can bring reality home to them through its power over the Court's appellate jurisdiction. Indeed, if the Court is too far out of touch with the people, the Congress and the executive can annul its directives simply by refusing to execute them, or the people can do so by constitutional amendment. In sum, although the Court is not politically responsible, it is likely to be politically responsive.[42]

Even more important, however, is the fact that the legitimacy of a particular institution in our society depends not on its intrinsic representational structure, but rather on its institutional authorization from, and acceptance by, the community. As Dean Rostow has said, whatever the intention of the Framers, judicial review

> . . . has been exercised by the Court from the beginning . . . . And it stands now . . . as an integral feature of the living constitution, long since established as a working part of the democratic political life of the nation.[43]
>
> The weight of . . . history is evidence that the people do expect the courts to interpret, declare, adapt and apply these constitutional provisions, as one of their main protections against the possibility of abuse by Presidents and legislatures.[44]

No conclusions can be drawn as to whether the Court should play a vigorous or a subdued role simply because its judgments may not reflect majority will. No one has ever suggested that the Senate should act cautiously for similar reasons, or even that it should defer to its more representative co-chamber, the House. Although the undemocratic, nonrepresentative structure of the Court is not informative as to how the Court should play its role within its proper province, it does tell us something about the limits of the province itself. It is this province that requires definition.

---

40 *See* Dahl, *Decision-Making in a Democracy: The Supreme Court as a National Policy-Maker*, 6 J. Pub. L. 279, 284-86 (1957).

41 Frankfurter, *Some Observations on the Nature of the Judicial Process of Supreme Court Litigation*, 98 Proc. Amer. Phil. Soc. 233, 237 (1954).

42 *See* A. Bickel, *supra* note 24, at 16-19; Deutsch, *supra* note 12, at 169, 186.

43 Rostow, *The Supreme Court and the People's Will*, 33 Notre Dame Law. 573, 576 (1958).

44 *Id.* at 590.

II

Judicial Review in a Democracy

Despite what has just been said, there can of course be no doubt that ours is essentially a society where the exercise of power draws its legitimacy from the consent of the people.[45] Moreover, the sort of society we are going to have is to be determined by the people. Our faith is not simply in our ability to choose wise rulers, but in our ability to rule ourselves wisely. Learned Hand was not alone when he said that he would find it irksome to be ruled by a bevy of platonic guardians even if he knew how to choose them.[46]

The Court, then, is not to function as a nine-man bevy, reviewing legislation from the same, but presumably more enlightened, perspective as the legislature. When the majority, speaking through the legislature, has decided that the legislation is desirable, it is not for the Court to strike it down simply because it thinks otherwise. Yet whenever the Court strikes down legislation, it says to the majority that it may not have its own way. If the Court is to refrain from doing this simply because the Justices find the status quo preferable, when and on what basis is it to strike down legislation? What are the Court's institutional characteristics that enable it to bring to the appraisal of legislation a new and different perspective unavailable to the legislature? How can the Court presume to say to the present majority that it cannot have its own way because its wishes are contrary to its own fundamental principles?

But just as an individual may be untrue to himself, so may society be untrue to itself. The Court's reviewing function, then, can be seen as an attempt to keep the community true to its own fundamental principles. Maintaining these "enduring general values" of the community is a task for which the Court's structure makes it peculiarly well suited. Professor Bickel suggests that judges have, or should have, the leisure, the training, and the insulation to follow the ways of the scholar in pursuing the ends of government. This is crucial to sorting out the enduring values of a society. And it is not something that institutions can do well on occasion, while operating for the most part with a different set of gears.[47]

Moreover, in considering questions of principle, courts are presented with the reality of their application. Statutes deal typically with

---

45 A. Bickel, *supra* note 24, at 29-30.

46 L. Hand, The Bill of Rights 73-74 (1958).

47 A. Bickel, *supra* note 24, at 25-26.

abstract or sometimes dimly foreseen problems. Courts are concerned with the flesh and blood of an actual case. This tends to modify, perhaps to lengthen, everyone's view. It also provides an extremely salutary proving ground for all abstractions; it is conducive, in a phrase of Holmes, to thinking things, not words, and thus to the evolution of principle by a process that tests as it creates.[48] "Their insulation and the marvelous mystery of time give courts the capacity to appeal to men's better natures, to call forth their aspirations, which may have been forgotten in the moment's hue and cry."[49] This is what Justice Stone called the opportunity for "the sober second thought."[50] Charles Black put it more concisely when he termed judicial review "the people's institutionalized means of self-control."[51]

This conception of judicial review, casting the Court as the guardian of enduring principle and as a check on overzealous legislatures, depicts the Court as an essentially conservative rather than creative force in our society—hardly the "revolutionary committee" Professor Berle has called the Warren Court.[52] The political and social realities of the twentieth century, however, have required government to essay an affirmative role in its service to its citizens. The Court, as part of government, must participate in that affirmative role.

This, of course, does not minimize the importance of protecting fundamental individual rights from governmental invasion. The original Bill of Rights was essentially negative, putting beyond the reach of government the world of the spirit and raising procedural barriers to governmental intrusion. The definition of these barriers in opinions such as Brandeis's dissent in *Olmstead*[53] or his concurrence in *Whitney*,[54] which have since carried the day, has been crucially important in charting the direction in which our society has moved. But today, as Archibald Cox put it:

> [T]he political theory which acknowledges the duty of government to provide jobs, social security, medical care, and housing extends to the field of human rights and imposes an obligation to promote liberty, equality, and dignity. For a decade and a half recognition of this duty [of the Court] has been the most creative force in constitutional law.[55]

---

48 *Id.*

49 *Id.* at 26.

50 Stone, *The Common Law in the United States*, 50 HARV. L. REV. 4, 25 (1936).

51 C. BLACK, *supra* note 26, at 107.

52 *See* A. BERLE, *supra* note 7.

53 Olmstead v. United States, 277 U.S. 438, 471 (1928) (dissenting opinion).

54 Whitney v. California, 274 U.S. 357, 372 (1927) (concurring opinion).

55 Cox, *supra* note 22, at 93.

The more traditional rationales of judicial review do not quite fit when the Court's role is so utterly different. Yet the specter of the Court ruling the people persists and is, if anything, even more ominous where the Court is telling the government what it must do, not simply what it cannot do. What, then, is the Court's legitimate role in delineating constitutional duties? Again, the legitimacy of the Court's decrees must be derived from the community itself. Just as society may not be true to its enduring principles, so may it not be fully aware of its emerging ones. And just as the Court should maintain the one set of principles, so should it support and encourage the adoption of others.

The law need not, as Learned Hand suggested, "be content to lag behind the best inspiration of its time until it feels behind it the weight of such general acceptance as will give sanction to its pretension to unquestioned dictation."[56] Rather, the Court must foster the best inspiration of the time and help it win general acceptance.

Nevertheless, inspiration is "best," not simply because the individual Justices think so, but because it accords with the ideals of the community itself. Today the most important of those ideals is political equality, and the Warren Court is correct in perceiving it as the dominant theme of American political development. The accuracy of this perception gives the Court's equal protection pronouncements their legitimacy.[57]

It was the inaccuracy of the old Court's perception of community ideals that made its performance so bad. For what the Nine Old Men tried to put beyond the reach of government, both state and federal, was "the momentous issue of the welfare state itself"[58]—an issue so political that it cannot and should not be determined by a court.[59] It is certainly not an issue about which there is a consensus in the community, moral or otherwise. It is in fact *the* issue around which politics in this country has generally been divided. "Principles" bearing on the issue, though fervently believed by those professing them, are utterly conflicting. Unlike the ideal of political equality, they represent the creeds of particular political parties, but are not the enduring principles of our society itself. The issue of the welfare state must, and will, be "determined by 'dominant opinion' with or without judicial approval."[60] Yet this was just the issue which the old Court told the people they could not determine for themselves by trying to place the min-

56 L. Hand, *supra* note 33, at 15-16.

57 *See* Cox, *supra* note 22, at 98.

58 McCloskey, *supra* note 3, at 51.

59 Finkelstein, *Judicial Self-Limitation*, 37 Harv. L. Rev. 338, 345 (1924).

60 McCloskey, *supra* note 3, at 51.

imum wage, the federal income tax, and government price control beyond the majority's reach.

To some critics, the Warren Court's implementation of political equality has also seemed a novel and illegitimate judicial theme.[61] Equality, however, is not a novel ideal at all.[62] It is only that the range of its required application is becoming broader and more evident as the community becomes aware of the extent to which the world of the poor and of the Negro differs from that in which the bulk of the public lives. The apparent novelty of the Court's recent equal protection decisions stems "from the Court's partial recognition, reflecting a new awareness on the part of the public, that the freedom embodied in constitutional guarantees as they have historically been limited is, for the economically and socially disadvantaged, no freedom at all."[63]

In this context, and in the era of positive government, it is incumbent on the Court to protect unpopular minorities not simply from governmental persecution, but from governmental neglect as well. For just as there are certain groups in society that have proved politically advantageous to oppress, so there are others whose interests are consistently bypassed by the political process in the rush toward the great society. This explains the necessity for affirmative decrees.

Because the Warren Court, unlike the old Court, has affirmatively applied the true principles and ideals of our community to protect those whose interests go unprotected elsewhere, it has acted properly. An examination of a few of its more significant decisions demonstrates my point.

III

A Look at Some Cases

A. *The Desegregation Cases*

In *Brown v. Board of Education*[64] and its progeny,[65] the Court was not applying an emerging but unrecognized moral principle; rather, it

---

61 *See especially* Kurland, *supra* note 1, at 144.

62 Kurland's charge of "novelty" is rebutted by Choper, *supra* note 33, at 29. Choper thoroughly approves of the Warren Court's heightened concern for equality before the law. "Contrary to the plaint of hostile critics, I suggest that the Court's recent turn to egalitarianism is a salutary movement, quite properly fulfilling its role in a democratic society." My own analysis of the Court's role draws on Choper's article.

63 Deutsch, *supra* note 12, at 226.

64 347 U.S. 483 (1954).

65 *E.g.*, Johnson v. Virginia, 373 U.S. 61 (1963) (courtroom seating); State Athl. Comm'n v. Dorsey, 359 U.S. 533 (1959) (statute prohibiting integrated athletic competition); Gayle v. Browder, 352 U.S. 903 (1956) (segregation on buses); Holmes v. City of

was enforcing a promise that the nation had made to the Negro in 1868 and had broken nine years later in the Compromise of 1877. Reconstruction had not proved good for business, and when the disputed presidential election put the Northern Republicans to the choice between their humane and their economic ideals, they chose the latter. "[They] abandoned the Negro to protect the tariff, 'hard' national money, the national banking system, and lush business subsidies."[66] This sell-out of the Negro was constitutionalized by the Fuller Court in the *Civil Rights Cases*[67] and *Plessy v. Ferguson*.[68] "Just as the Settlement saved the South from political reconstruction, these decisions saved it from constitutional reconstruction."[69] Thus, the "separate but equal" doctrine of *Plessy*, not the desegregation commanded by *Brown*, was the legislative, unprincipled, non-judicial judgment. Furthermore, the "separate but equal" compromise standard imposed by *Plessy* was an unadministrable, almost meaningless one. The Southern states never lived up to it, and the courts never effectively enforced it.

In the almost sixty years between *Plessy* and *Brown* the gap between our ideal of racial equality and our racial practices had widened even more. At the time *Brown* was decided, there was no reason to think Southern legislatures would ever act to narrow the gap. In fact, the Negro was not even a participant in the processes of the Southern states. Nor had the national Congress proved receptive to Negro claims. Despite the express authorization for federal legislation in section 5 of the fourteenth amendment, Congress had not worried about Negro rights for almost seventy-five years. There was little prospect that it was about to become concerned once again. And, of course, it did not until *Brown* awakened the nation's conscience.

It was, then, right and proper that the Court acted in *Brown* to treat our "sweating national shame."[70] The decision made the nation face up to its commitments to the Negro which it had found convenient to ignore. There seems no question that but for *Brown*, legislative response would have been a long time coming.

Atlanta, 350 U.S. 879 (1955) (municipal golf courses); Mayor of Baltimore v. Dawson, 350 U.S. 877 (1955) (outlawing segregation in public beaches and bathhouses); Muir v. Louisville Park Theatrical Ass'n, 347 U.S. 971 (1954) (city lease of park facilities).

66 Mendelson, *The Politics of Judicial Supremacy*, 4 LAW & ECON. J. 175, 179 (1961). *See also* V. DESANTIS, REPUBLICANS FACE THE SOUTHERN QUESTION 47-51 (1959); C. WOODWARD, REUNION AND REACTION 12-13 (1956):

67 109 U.S. 3 (1883).

68 163 U.S. 537 (1896).

69 Mendelson, *supra* note 66, at 180.

70 Black, *The Supreme Court 1966 Term, Foreword: "State Action," Equal Protection and California's Proposition* 14, 81 HARV. L. REV. 69 (1967).

Indeed, even the Court's critics applaud the *Brown* decision. Only Professor Wechsler, who thoroughly approves its result,[71] is troubled by it.[72] He does not think that a rationale for *Brown* can be worked out which meets his demand for "neutral principles," a standard of constitutional adjudication he would require in every case.[73]

Although, as Wechsler concedes, the concept of neutral principles is an illusive and enigmatic one,[74] his disquietude with *Brown*, and with the white primary[75] and restrictive covenant[76] cases, seems to be that the claims of Negroes have been singled out for special, kindly treatment. He feels that if comparable claims had been made by members of other groups, the Court would not have vindicated them. Thus, because Negroes receive special treatment, the decisions do not express neutral principles.[77]

Special protection of Negroes' rights, however, is not necessarily a breach of neutrality. So long as the Court would have aided any group comparably situated in our society it acts with the requisite neutrality. Just because no other group, given the appalling history of slavery, black codes and compelled segregation, may in fact be comparably situated does not alter the neutrality. Indeed, the three constitutional amendments required to give the Negro equal legal rights attest to the fact that no other group *is* comparably situated.

In other words, so long as the Court acts to protect any group whose legitimate interests are consistently and shamefully neglected by the political processes, it acts neutrally. The Court, then, protects Negroes not simply because they are Negroes, or because the Justices think them especially worthy people, but because their legitimate interests continue to go unprotected elsewhere.

By the same principle, I submit that compensatory legislation favoring Negroes would not be unconstitutional even though it made

---

71 Wechsler, *Toward Neutral Principles of Constitutional Law*, 73 HARV. L. REV. 1 (1959). These cases, Wechsler feels, "have the best chance of making an enduring contribution to the quality of our society of any that I know in recent years." *Id.* at 27.

72 *Id.* at 31-34. For discussions of Professor Wechsler's article, see Deutsch, *supra* note 12, at 178-98; Golding, *Principled Decision-Making and the Supreme Court*, 63 COLUM. L. REV. 35 (1963); Miller & Howell, *The Myth of Neutrality in Constitutional Adjudication*, 27 U. CHI. L. REV. 661 (1960); Mueller & Schwartz, *The Principle of Neutral Principles*, 7 U.C.L.A.L. REV. 571 (1960); Pollak, *Racial Discrimination and Judiciary Integrity: A Reply to Professor Wechsler*, 108 U. PA. L. REV. 1 (1959); Brown, Book Review, 62 COLUM. L. REV. 386 (1962).

73 *See* Wechsler, *supra* note 71.

74 *Id.*

75 Smith v. Allwright, 321 U.S. 649 (1944).

76 Barrows v. Jackson, 346 U.S. 249 (1953); Shelley v. Kraemer, 334 U.S. 1 (1948).

77 Wechsler, *supra* note 71, at 27-34.

racial classifications and even though similar legislation favoring whites would violate equal protection.[78] As the Supreme Court has taught us, in the racial area "equal protection" does not involve simply the *rationality* of classifications, for even the illicit segregation statutes had conceivable rational bases, such as minimizing tension in the schools. Rather, the function of equal protection here is to shield groups or individuals from stigmatization by government. Whether or not particular legislation stigmatizes is largely a sociological question requiring consideration of the structure and history of our society as well as examination of the statute itself. Legislation favoring Negroes, then, would be constitutional because it is rational *and* because in *our* society it would not stigmatize whites. On the other hand, even if the "equality" demanded by the separate but equal doctrine had been lived up to, the doctrine itself, imposed by a white society, unconstitutionally stigmatizes Negroes in that society. Similarly, the miscegenation statutes, even though "neutral" on their faces, forbidding whites as well as Negroes from interracial marriage or cohabitation, unconstitutionally stigmatize Negroes in the same way.[79] This is largely what equal protection, at least in the area of racial classifications, is all about. It requires judicial vindication, for the legislature can hardly be expected to protect the rights of those it seeks to vilify.

B. *The Reapportionment Cases*

In 1962 the Court overruled *Colegrove v. Green*,[80] and held in *Baker v. Carr*[81] that a justiciable claim was stated in a complaint asserting that the inequality in voting districts, caused by the failure of the Tennessee Legislature to reapportion by population, resulted in a denial of plaintiffs' fourteenth amendment rights. The Court, however, did not indicate what the constitutional standards of apportionment were to be. In fact, it held that the justiciable issue was the determination whether "a discrimination reflects *no* policy, but simply arbitrary and capricious action."[82] It seemed, therefore, as though a state legislative apportionment scheme had only to meet the test of minimum rationality—that is, that the differentiation among voters had to reflect an intelligible policy consistently applied.

Perhaps at the time of *Baker* the Court did not know precisely

78 *But see* Bittker, *The Case of the Checkerboard Ordinance: An Experiment in Race Relations*, 71 Yale L.J. 1387 (1962).

79 *See* Loving v. Virginia, 388 U.S. 1 (1967); McLaughlin v. Florida, 379 U.S. 184 (1964)

80 328 U.S. 549 (1946).

81 369 U.S. 186 (1962).

82 *Id.* at 226.

where it was going, but its decisions in *Gray v. Sanders*[83] in 1963 and *Wesberry v. Sanders*[84] in early 1964 gave some indication of its direction. When it decided *Reynolds v. Sims*[85] and its companion cases[86] later in 1964, it was clear that the Court had arrived—not at a standard of minimum rationality, but at that of "one man—one vote—one value."[87] This, the Court held, was the constitutional standard required by the equal protection clause for both houses of a bicameral state legislature.

Concededly, the "immediate preoccupation" of those who produced the mandate of equal protection was not the malapportionment of state legislatures, but the relevant constitutional language of equal protection. Such language "deals not only with racial discrimination, but also with discrimination not based on color."[88] Like the Framers of the Constitution, the draftsmen of the fourteenth amendment chose "language capable of growth"[89] in order to "permit reasonable future advances."[90] Consequently

> it was open to the Court, in the "tradition of a broadly worded organic law . . . necessarily intended for permanence," to treat the matter of legislative apportionment within the confines of the equal protection clause.[91]

What is interesting about the decisions for our purposes is not the propriety of "one man—one vote," but that the Court was again aiding a group that was unable to achieve effective legislative recourse. Although in the *Reapportionment Cases* the Court was seeking to protect the rights of urban majorities rather than those of minorities, these urban groups were not political majorities with respect to the issue of apportionment because of the malapportionment itself.

---

83 372 U.S. 368 (1963).

84 376 U.S. 1 (1964).

85 377 U.S. 533 (1964).

86 *See* WMCA, Inc. v. Lomenzo, 377 U.S. 633 (1964); Maryland Comm. for Fair Representation v. Tawes, 377 U.S. 656 (1964); Davis v. Mann, 377 U.S. 678 (1964); Roman v. Sincock, 377 U.S. 695 (1964); Lucas v. Forty-Fourth Gen'l Ass'y, 377 U.S. 713 (1964).

87 For an excellent discussion and defense of the "one man—one vote" principle, see Auerbach, *The Reapportionment Cases: One Person, One Vote—One Vote, One Value,* 1964 SUP. CT. REV. 1. *See also* McCloskey, *The Supreme Court 1961 Term, Foreword: The Reapportionment Case,* 76 HARV. L. REV. 54 (1962). For criticism of the Court's work in this area, see Kurland, *supra* note 1, at 149-57; Neal, *Baker v. Carr: Politics in Search of Law,* 1962 SUP. CT. REV. 252.

88 Bickel, *The Original Understanding and the Segregation Decision,* 69 HARV. L. REV. 1, 60 (1955).

89 *Id.* at 62-63.

90 *Id.* at 61.

91 Choper, *supra* note 33, at 30 (footnotes omitted).

For change, compulsion was required. There was little likelihood that the representatives from the malapportioned districts would voluntarily redraw the boundary lines of the very districts kind enough to put them in office. And though Congress doubtless could have acted pursuant to section 5 of the fourteenth amendment, there was no prospect that it would. After all, the representatives in the House itself were put there by malapportioned congressional districts. Consequently, where no referendum procedure existed, the majority was utterly powerless against the entrenched rural minority.[92] As with *Brown*, it was only the Court that could effectively remedy the situation.

Although the reapportionment decisions have met with widespread popular approval, the judicial restrainers have not treated them kindly. Mr. Justice Harlan, dissenting, termed them "an experiment in venturesome constitutionalism."[93] Professor Kurland refers to their "unbending simplicity"[94] and Professor Freund calls their governing principle simplistic.[95] In 1963 Professor Bickel doubted that *Baker v. Carr* was likely "to play a substantial and enduring role in shaping our society."[96]

However, as Professor Auerbach has pointed out, it is

> paradoxical for the advocates of judicial self-limitation to criticize the Court for helping to make majority rule effective, because the case for self-restraint rests on the assumption that the Court is reviewing the legislative acts of representatives who are put in office and can be turned out of office by a majority of the people. Since malapportionment destroys this assumption, judicial intervention to remove this obstacle to majority rule may be less intolerable than the self-perpetuation of minority rule.[97]

Of course it may also be paradoxical "for the judicial activists, who extol the Court as the protector of minorities, to praise it [here] for helping to erase the power of minorities to curb majority rule in our state legislatures."[98] But even if it is desirable to require a consensus greater than that reflected by a simple majority before any affirmative legislation action can be taken, such a decision should not

---

92 As the Court stated in *Reynolds*, "No effective political remedy to obtain relief against the alleged malapportionment of the Alabama Legislature appears to have been available." 377 U.S. 533, 553 (1964) (footnote omitted).

93 *Id.* at 625 (dissenting opinion).

94 Kurland, *supra* note 1, at 156.

95 Freund, *supra* note 2, at 638.

96 Bickel, *Reapportionment and Liberal Myths*, 35 COMMENTARY 483 (1963).

97 Auerbach, *supra* note 87, at 2.

98 *Id.*

be made by the legislators whose political fates may depend on that decision.[99] Furthermore, there is no good reason to think that the rural minority which gains power through malapportionment needs such added protection. "Past experience gives us reason to think that protection of minorities will expand as the electoral base of our representative institutions becomes broader and more democratic."[100]

> Up to now few, if any, of our states have been governed by "transitory majorities representing the more populous districts." . . . [M]alapportionment has often given a coalition of conservative urban forces, farm groups, and small-town businessmen, the power to frustrate state welfare efforts.[101]

Indeed, malapportionment is undoubtedly one of the reasons why the states have not lived up to their constitutional responsibilities to the Negro and to the poor.[102]

Finally, it is not inappropriate that the guarantor of democracy in state government is itself a federal institution. For it was to counter the threat of factional domination of state legislatures that the Federalists wrote into the Constitution the command of article IV, section 4: "The United States shall guarantee to every state in this Union a Republican form of Government." They intended this clause to grant the federal government the power to restore republicanism, or what we now would refer to as representative democracy.[103] Even if the guarantee clause does not state a justiciable standard,[104] it does establish a model of federalism which contemplates the federal government safeguarding the democratic processes in the states.[105]

C. *Other Voting Cases*

The *Reapportionment Cases* are not the only ones where state limitations on the right to vote have come under equal protection scru-

---

99 *Id.* at 67.

100 *Id.* at 49 (footnote omitted). *See also* S. HOOK, THE PARADOXES OF FREEDOM 66 (1962).

101 Auerbach, *supra* note 87, at 49-50 (footnote omitted).

102 *See generally* Willbern, *The States as Components in an Areal Division of Powers,* in AREA AND POWER; A THEORY OF LOCAL GOVERNMENT (A. Maass ed. 1959); COMMISSION ON INTERGOVERNMENTAL RELATIONS, REPORT TO THE PRESIDENT FOR TRANSMITTAL TO THE CONGRESS 39-40 (1955).

103 *See* THE FEDERALIST No. 10 (Madison); THE FEDERALIST No. 43 (Madison); *see also* Diamond, *The Federalist's View of Federalism,* in ESSAYS IN FEDERALISM 21 (Institute for Studies in Federalism ed. 1961); THE FEDERALIST No. 39 (Madison).

104 Baker v. Carr, 369 U.S. 186, 227 (1962); Colegrove v. Green, 328 U.S. 549, 552 (1946). *See* Bonfield, *The Guaranty Clause of Article IV, Section 4: A Study in Constitutional Desuetude,* 46 MINN. L. REV. 513 (1962).

105 *See* Note, *Theories of Federalism and Civil Rights,* 75 YALE L.J. 1007, 1023-24 (1964). *See also* Auerbach, *supra* note 87, at 84-87.

tiny by the Warren Court. In *Carrington v. Rash*[106] the Court held that the state could not disenfranchise actual residents simply because they resided pursuant to military assignment. And in *Harper v. Virginia Board of Elections*[107] the Court invalidated the long familiar state laws making payment of the poll tax a prerequisite of voting. In so doing, the Court applied an egalitarian principle of our community that emerged long after the drafting of the clause under which the law was struck down. For in 1868, when the fourteenth amendment was enacted, property requirements as a condition for voting were widespread.[108] Nevertheless, as Mr. Justice Douglas told us in *Harper,* "In determining what lines are unconstitutionally discriminatory we have never been confined to historic notions of equality . . . . Notions of what constitutes equal treatment for purposes of the Equal Protection Clause *do* change."[109] That the Court was correct in its assessment of our emergent principle of absolute equality between rich and poor with respect to the franchise seems abundantly clear. In fact in section 10 of the Voting Rights Act of 1965,[110] Congress had declared its view that the poll tax was unconstitutional.

Again those hit hardest by the laws struck down in *Carrington* and *Harper*—those, in other words, disenfranchised by them—could obviously not seek recourse through the legislative processes in which they were not permitted to participate. And legislators elected without their participation were not likely to worry greatly about their interests or be anxious to extend the franchise to them. In *Carrington* and *Harper,* then, as in the *Reapportionment Cases,* it was up to the undemocratic Court to promote our democratic values.

D. *The Criminal Procedure Cases*

In the area of criminal procedure, as with race relations, an appalling gap has existed between our principles and our practices. For while the constitutional provisions safeguarding the accused have proved politically viable as slogans in Fourth of July oratory, their effective implementation apparently has not. In this area also the Supreme Court has acted to compel the community to live up to its pro-

---

106 380 U.S. 89 (1965). The case is discussed in Van Alstyne, *The Fourteenth Amendment, the "Right" to Vote, and the Understanding of the Thirty-Ninth Congress,* 1965 SUP. CT. REV. 33.

107 383 U.S. 663 (1966).

108 In fact, the Supreme Court had twice before upheld state poll tax laws. Butler v. Thompson, 341 U.S. 937 (1951); Breedlove v. Suttles, 302 U.S. 277 (1937).

109 383 U.S. at 669 (emphasis in original).

110 42 U.S.C. § 1973(h)(a) (Supp. I, 1965).

fessed ideals. And once again those whom the Court has sought to protect are politically impotent.

Criminal defendants as such are not likely to be a popular group. And since those most subject to arrest and to the abuses of the criminal process are the poor, the Negro, and the poor Negro, even less legislative concern is to be expected. Their plight at the hands of the police is not likely to inspire legislative empathy,[111] and their rights, constitutional and otherwise, will almost surely go unprotected without judicial intervention. The political voice of the urban poor has not been a loud one until very recently, and malapportionment has further muffled its effectiveness in state legislatures. Especially since assurance of the indigent defendant's constitutional rights would require the state legislatures to appropriate money, the probability of continuing political stagnation was even greater.

Again the egalitarian ideal informed much of the Court's work in this area. *Griffin v. Illinois* held that a state violates equal protection by refusing to furnish a transcript of the trial to any indigent accused who alleges serious errors on appeal.[112] *Gideon v. Wainwright* required the states to supply trial counsel at public expense to paupers accused of felonies.[113] *Douglas v. California* extended the *Gideon* holding to paupers appealing to the initial court of review.[114] In the criminal process, then, as with the franchise, it has become unconstitutional to draw any lines between rich and poor. In the area where the ultimate coercive power of the state is brought to bear on the individual, such absolute equality is both constitutionally appropriate and required by our professed ideals. To realize this ideal fully, it may be necessary in

---

111 Skinner v. Oklahoma, 316 U.S. 535 (1942), is perhaps illustrative of this point. At issue there was a statute which authorized involuntary sterilization for those convicted of three felonies involving moral turpitude. But exempted from the statute's coverage were "offenses arising out of the violation of the prohibitory laws, revenue acts, embezzlement, or political offenses . . . ." Could it be that the legislators could conceive of themselves, their families and their friends as potential violators of the exempted laws but not of those criminal laws much more likely to bear on the poor such as assault or robbery? The Court struck down the Oklahoma sterilization law as violative of equal protection because the lines it drew were found to be "artificial." But if the Court had not been dealing with "legislation which [involved] one of the basic civil rights of man"—the right to procreate—such artificial line-drawing would probably have been sustained. *See* discussion of Railway Express Agency v. New York, 336 U.S. 106 (1949), at p. 26, *infra*. Perhaps *Skinner's* equal protection ground of decision was simply a way of avoiding the substantive due process (or cruel and unusual punishment) question which lurked in the background, *i.e.*, is involuntary sterilization even constitutional? *But see* Choper, *supra* note 33, at 33.

112 351 U.S. 12 (1956).

113 372 U.S. 335 (1963).

114 372 U.S. 353 (1963).

future decisions to require the states to provide "equality" for the poor with respect to bail and the facilities for investigation.

That the Court should take the lead is not surprising. The preservation of the integrity of the judicial process, unlike reapportionment, is a task for which the judiciary has a special competence and a special responsibility. It is only by seeing the criminal process as it functions in actual cases that the areas where constitutional rights are threatened, and the remedies required to vindicate them, become evident.

In addition, in the area of criminal procedure the interest of federalism per se—that is, the interest in the states as laboratories for social experimentation—has never seemed a particularly keen one. Furthermore, when the Court has decreed uniform protection for specific constitutional rights, the method of their protection has remained largely a matter of state concern. After *Gideon,* for instance, it remains the prerogative of the state legislatures to install either a public defender system or one of appointed counsel from the bar as a whole. In *Miranda,*[115] though the Court virtually promulgated a prearraignment code, it expressly invited legislative response and state formulation of alternative schemes that would provide equally adequate safeguards for the fifth amendment rights at stake.[116]

Perhaps under the prod of prior Supreme Court cases, many of the states had already adopted the various reforms which the Court subsequently decreed for the nation as a whole. In fact, at the time of *Gideon* only five states did not provide trial counsel for the indigent accused of a felony.[117] Even within the states, however, the needed reforms were frequently initiated by the state courts rather than the legislature.[118] Moreover, those states which had not acted before the Supreme Court's declarations were not likely to do so in the near future. For although *Wolf v. Colorado* held in 1949 that the federal fourth amendment right to be free from unreasonable searches and seizures applied to the states,[119] *Mapp v. Ohio* did not apply the federal exclusionary rule to the states until 1961, twelve years later.[120] In *Wolf*

---

115 384 U.S. 436 (1966).

116 *Id.* at 490.

117 Israel, *Gideon v. Wainwright: The "Art" of Overruling,* 1963 Sup. Ct. Rev. 211, 212 n.7.

118 *See, e.g.,* People v. Cahan, 44 Cal. 2d 434, 282 P.2d 905 (1955).

119 338 U.S. 25 (1949).

120 367 U.S. 643 (1961). *See* Allen, *Federalism and the Fourth Amendment: Requiem for Wolf,* 1961 Sup. Ct. Rev. 1, for an excellent discussion of *Wolf* and *Mapp* and events taking place in the interval between them.

the Court had left the newly declared federal right of privacy "to the tender mercies of the states for its enforcement,"[121] although in the federal system it had been recognized as early as 1914, in *Weeks v. United States*,[122] that only the exclusionary rule provided a constitutionally adequate safeguard for the protection of that right. Any state that did not realize this by 1961 probably simply did not want to, and never would.

In the criminal law area, the Court has faithfully discharged its reviewing responsibilities. It has decreed equality between rich and poor in an area where the community's principles required it, but where the legislatures had not translated these principles into practice. At the same time it has, where practical, left room for both legislative initiative and legislative response.

Conclusion

"Once loosed, the idea of Equality is not easily cabined."[123] Nevertheless, the Court's equal protection decisions have avoided the twin dangers posed by the judicial implementation of the egalitarian ideal. First, the Court has recognized that our egalitarianism is not, and is not likely to become, one of maximum *material* equality among people. We still believe in material rewards for individual accomplishment. It is only, therefore, in certain limited areas that equality between rich and poor is a moral principle of our society. Where such equality is a part of our ideals, however, the Court is right to decree its realization even if the political branches have been unwilling to pay for its implementation. The Court was correct in singling out the criminal process and the franchise for such treatment, since in these areas the relationship of the individual to his government should not depend on the ability to pay.

A second danger which the Court must continue to avoid is the choking of the political process with the equal protection clause. For almost all legislation is advantageous to some groups and disadvantageous to others, and often in a somewhat arbitrary way. Nevertheless, this sort of give and take within the political process, particularly where economic regulation is challenged, should not become the concern of the Court.[124] Unlike the old Court, the current Court has specifically eschewed responsibility in this area.

---

121 Allen, *supra* note 120, at 5.

122 232 U.S. 383 (1914).

123 Cox, *supra* note 22, at 91.

124 *See* A. Bickel, *supra* note 24, at 221-28.

Railway Express Agency v. New York is illustrative.[125] Railway Express challenged a New York City traffic ordinance forbidding advertising on the sides of trucks, the theory being that it distracted drivers of other vehicles. Those trucks whose advertisements were connected with the owner's business, however, were exempted from the ordinance. Railway Express, which sold advertising space on its delivery trucks, argued that simply because one is touting one's own product does not make his sign any the less a distraction to other drivers. Railway Express of course was right. The statute *did* draw an arbitrary, unreasonable distinction. Mr. Justice Douglas, however, was also right in rejecting the argument, saying, "It is no requirement of equal protection that all evils of the same genus be eradicated or none at all."[126] One can confidently surmise that in the New York City council the small business interests were sufficiently powerful to block the regulation altogether unless they were granted exemption from it. Granted, they won special "irrational" dispensation. But surely the legislation did not discriminate *against* Railway Express. Interpreted otherwise, equal protection could become as debilitating to welfare legislation as the ill-fated doctrine of substantive due process once was.

The Court must continue carefully to distinguish those groups whose rights are consistently trammelled and whose interests are consistently neglected in the political arena, from those groups whose interests are occasionally submerged in legislative compromise. This the Court has done. It has applied and extended the principles and ideals of our society to those "insular" minorities[127] which, either because they are unpopular or because the vindication of their rights is expensive, are persecuted or neglected by the legislatures. In so doing, it has tried to secure the integrity of the legislative processes themselves. These are tasks for which the courts, the "deviant" institutions in our democratic society, are required.[128]

---

125 336 U.S. 106 (1949).

126 *Id.* at 110.

127 United States v. Carolene Prods. Co., 304 U.S. 144, 152-53 n.4 (1938). *See also* Chambers v. Florida, 309 U.S. 227, 238 (1940).

128 By contrast, the old Court was in large measure protecting states' rights, not individual rights. For the argument underlying the Court's *Child Labor Case*, Hammer v. Dagenhart, 247 U.S. 251 (1918), and its progeny (*e.g.*, Bailey v. Drexel Furniture Co., 259 U.S. 20 (1922); Hill v. Wallace, 259 U.S. 44 (1922); United States v. Butler, 297 U.S. 1 (1936)), was that the tenth amendment's reservation of powers to the states constituted an independent restriction on otherwise constitutional acts of the federal government. Yet the Court's use of substantive due process had already emasculated the states' power to deal with these social and economic problems. *See* cases cited in note 4 *supra*. Rather than fill a legislative vacuum, the Nine Old Men decreed one. And they did so in an area where Congress should have been left a free hand.

In three 1966 cases[129] interpreting Congress's powers to enforce equal protection pursuant to section 5 of the fourteenth amendment, the Supreme Court has given Congress almost free rein where the Fuller Court had curtailed it in the *Civil Rights Cases*.[130] As Professor Cox has said, "If the Congress follows the lead that the Court has provided, [these cases] . . . will prove as important in bespeaking national legislative authority to promote human rights as the Labor Board decisions of 1937 were in providing national authority to regulate the economy."[131] Congressional action, however, is a big "if." For as Cox also warns, "the need for judicial action is strongest in the areas of the law where political processes prove inadequate, not from lack of legis-

---

To begin with, the Court's interpretation of the tenth amendment was simply wrong. Before M'Culloch v. Maryland, 17 U.S. (4 Wheat.) 316 (1819), a plausible argument could have been made that that amendment did prevent the implied expansion of federal power pursuant to the necessary and proper clause. But *M'Culloch* decided in 1819 that it did not prevent such an expansion of power. Then, 100 years later, in the *Child Labor Case*, the Court adopted the implausible position that the reserved powers of the states comprise an independent restriction on otherwise clearly constitutional acts of the federal government. As has been conclusively demonstrated, the tenth amendment was declaratory of the division of powers between state and nation and "was not intended as a yardstick, or independent restriction of federal power." Cramton, *The Supreme Court and the Decline of State Power*, 2 LAW & ECON. J. 175, 186 (1959). As its sponsor, James Madison, put it in 1791: "Interference with the power of the States was no constitutional criterion of the power of Congress. If the power was not given, Congress could not exercise it; if given, they [*sic*] might exercise it, although it should interfere with the laws, or even the Constitution[s] of the States." 2 ANNALS OF CONGRESS 1897 (1791). And in overruling the *Child Labor Case*, the Court came back to this view when it said: "The [tenth] amendment . . . states but a truism that all is retained which has not been surrendered." United States v. Darby, 312 U.S. 100, 124 (1941).

In addition to being wrong about the tenth amendment, the Court was wrong in so vigorously protecting states' rights from the national government. Where states' (as opposed to individual's) rights are at issue,

> . . . the justification for *judicial review* . . . , for the final constitutional word to be spoken by a "deviant institution" in a democracy, is weak. The states, whose constitutional rights are allegedly being assaulted, are well represented in the councils of national government (especially the Congress) and are in a peculiarly strong position to protect themselves against national encroachment. Here, the political process may generally be depended upon to produce a fair judgment. If a majority of the states' representatives (. . . [the] members of Congress) determine that federal power has not been exceeded, then the Court should overturn the decision, if at all, only if it is so clearly in error as not to be "open to rational question."

Choper, *supra* note 33, at 39-40 (emphasis in original) (footnotes omitted).

129 Katzenbach v. Morgan, 384 U.S. 641 (1966); South Carolina v. Katzenbach, 383 U.S. 301 (1966); United States v. Guest, 383 U.S. 745 (1966). *See generally* Cox, *supra* note 22.

130 109 U.S. 3 (1883).

131 Cox, *supra* note 22, at 91.

lative power but because the problem is neglected by politicians."[132] If the legislatures continue to neglect their constitutional responsibilities, we can only hope the Court will continue to do the best it can to fill the gap.

---

[132] *Id.* at 122.

2

Professor Bickel, the Scholarly Tradition, and the Supreme Court

This essay picks up from the previous one and extends its argument. Professor Alexander Bickel was probably Judge Wright's most severe academic critic, who seemed to miss no opportunity to castigate Wright in print for his "activism" and even to ridicule him in his classes at the Yale Law School. The gentlemanly Skelly Wright struck back in this trenchant essay. In it, Wright not only demolishes the criticisms that Bickel leveled at him but goes on to state his conception of the judicial function. With typical insight and characteristic ability to perceive the real issues involved in any dispute, including intellectual debates, Judge Wright states that the "fundamental dispute" is over what constitutes "the good society as well as over judicial method."

Professor Bickel and those who think like him are essentially destructive critics of the judicial system. Their essential message is that "process," not results, is all-important in the governmental system. They are followers of Edmund Burke and would have courts follow Burkean notions in making decisions. Or to put it another way, Bickel was the chief spokesman for the neoconservative clique, most of whom are followers of Justice Felix Frankfurter, that now dominates American legal education.

In some respects, this essay is atypical of Judge Wright's nonjudicial writings. He generally states his views without reference to individuals. But here he quite openly challenges those he calls "self-appointed scholastic mandarins" who make up "the scholarly tradition" as well as mounts a frontal attack upon Professor Bickel's views that were set out in his The Supreme Court and the Idea of Progress *(1970). No more cutting analysis of the "scholastic mandarins" can be found in the literature. He asserts, with characteristic candor, that "the ultimate test of the [Supreme Court's] work . . . must be goodness"—which he does not define, but which to him means something akin to social justice. With that statement Judge Wright repudiates the mandarins' belief in "process"—in, that is, the supreme value of what are called "principled decisions"—and strikes out boldly to fix a position for himself. It is fair to say that no one has been able to refute Wright's basic arguments in this essay.*

IN the fall of 1969 there occurred in Cambridge what Anthony Lewis of *The New York Times* described as "[o]ne of those intellectual events whose reverberations gradually disturb a widening circle . . . . It was an event in the law." [1] What happened was that Professor Alexander Bickel of Yale "was called" to deliver the Oliver Wendell Holmes Lectures at Harvard.[2] Although his lectures were given under the rather grand heading of *The Supreme Court and the Idea of Progress*,[3] they focused almost exclusively on the activity of the Warren Court. With his usual elegance, Professor Bickel argued that the Justices

---

[1] N.Y. Times, Oct. 10, 1969, at 46, col. 5.

[2] It is Professor Bickel himself who refers to the offer of the Holmes Lectureship as a "call"—not inappropriately, since many of the past Holmes Lectures have attained an almost religious authority in the legal community. A. BICKEL, THE SUPREME COURT AND THE IDEA OF PROGRESS xi (1970) [hereinafter cited as IDEA OF PROGRESS].

[3] They now appear in the widely reviewed book of the same title.

of the Warren Court grossly misconceived their proper role in our democratic scheme of government and produced a series of decisions over-interventionist in purpose, sloppy in reasoning, and mistaken in result. Even an occasional reader of the law reviews might well ask "what else is new?"

An apt question. For the Warren years were marked not only by an increasingly activist Court but also by an increasingly dissatisfied and prolific group of legal scholars. Delivering some of their most widely acclaimed indictments of the Warren Court through the prestigious Holmes Lectures [4] and the *Harvard Law Review* Supreme Court Forewords,[5] they have propagated a mode of scholarly criticism which appears and reappears in most professional commentary on the Court.[6] At least in its broad outlines, Professor Bickel's new book falls well within this familiar tradition. It begins with a chapter of history sorting out the sheep and the goats of the scholarly tradition — those who obey the strict constraints of "reason" on the one hand and those who

---

[4] *See* L. HAND, THE BILL OF RIGHTS (1958); Wechsler, *Toward Neutral Principles of Constitutional Law*, 73 HARV. L. REV. 1 (1959).

[5] *See* Bickel, *The Supreme Court, 1960 Term, Foreword: The Passive Virtues*, 75 HARV. L. REV. 40 (1961); Brown, *The Supreme Court, 1957 Term, Foreword: Process of Law*, 72 HARV. L. REV 77 (1958); Griswold, *The Supreme Court, 1959 Term, Foreword: Of Time and Attitudes — Professor Hart and Judge Arnold*, 74 HARV. L. REV. 81 (1960); Hart, *The Supreme Court, 1958 Term, Foreword: The Time Chart of the Justices*, 73 HARV. L. REV. 84 (1959); Henkin, *The Supreme Court, 1967 Term, Foreword: On Drawing Lines*, 82 HARV. L. REV. 63 (1968); Kurland, *The Supreme Court, 1963 Term, Foreword: "Equal in Origin and Equal in Title to the Legislative and Executive Branches of the Government,"* 78 HARV. L. REV. 143 (1964).

[6] The "scholarly tradition" referred to in the title and the "group" of legal scholars of which I speak here are not meant to point to a sharply defined collection of individuals. The first and second parts of this article outline the basic tenets of the "scholarly tradition" and the highlights of its historical development. There need not necessarily be any one individual — Bickel included — who would endorse the "tradition" entirely; but there are, I believe, very many who accept or assume it in a general way. My purpose is not to catalogue legal scholars, but to describe a prevailing climate of opinion, a style and mode of legal analysis, in a fashion that will provoke the reader to reflect on legal commentary with which he is familiar and to attend more closely to its underlying assumptions and approaches.

Of course, the particular concerns of the scholarly tradition have not achieved total dominance. Nor can a division be drawn along strictly generational lines. Leading legal scholars who appear not to be enthusiastic adherents of the tradition under discussion in this article include, for example, Professors Charles L. Black, Jr. and Louis Pollak of Yale, Archibald Cox of Harvard, Caleb Foote of Berkeley, and Arthur S. Miller of George Washington University. The sympathetic accounts of the Warren Court recently published by Professors Black and Cox serve to demonstrate that the gap between academia and the court is not unbridgeable. *See* A. COX, THE WARREN COURT: CONSTITUTIONAL DECISION IN AN AGE OF REFORM (1968); Black, *The Unfinished Business of the Warren Court*, 46 WASH. L. REV. 3 (1970); Cox, *Chief Justice Earl Warren*, 83 HARV. L. REV. 1 (1969).

rely naively and irresponsibly on "faith" on the other. The Professor traces the collapse of the "faith" in judicial decisionmaking held by nineteenth century Justices; the rise of pragmatism and skepticism among the "progressive realists" in the early part of the twentieth century; and then the perversion (by the Warren Court and its supporters) of the brief "age of reason" into a new "age of faith," dedicated this time not to the protection of property but to fair treatment, liberty, and privacy. Stressing the Warren Court's unconcern for the processes of reason and its excessive enthusiasm for social reform, Bickel tells us of systematic failures in the crafting of opinions — judicial "footstomping," and the "invincible impulse to have the cake and eat it, or, in another festive figure, to dance but not pay the piper." [7] And there is also the traditional essay on the virtues of the freely operating political machinery and its frustration by the "imperfectly bridled managerial drive" of the Court. All of this has become standard fare — not necessarily wrong, but hardly "an event in the law."

Yet *The Supreme Court and the Idea of Progress* does go one step beyond the scholarly tradition. At the outset, Bickel concedes that history rarely judges the Court's work by the quality of its reasoning process. He recognizes that the scholarly praise customarily afforded the Marshall Court, despite numerous lapses in craftsmanship, is singularly result-oriented. The Justices of the Warren Court, Bickel suggests, understandably sought to emulate the Marshall Court and earn its place in history for themselves.[8] Thoroughly result-oriented and with a broad program of social reform in mind, they made a "bet on the future," relying "on events for vindication more than on the method of reason for contemporary validation." [9] But even accepting *arguendo* the premise of the Warren Court's supposed strategy, Bickel condemns its execution and results. Unlike his predecessors in the scholarly tradition, he does not praise the historic contribution of the Court's most important work while

---

[7] IDEA OF PROGRESS 61.

[8] Defenders of the Warren Court often rely heavily on an analogy to the Marshall Court. Professor Black has explicitly adopted the premise of evaluation said by Bickel to have inspired the Justices of the Warren Court:

> If the Marshall Court is the paradigm of success, then perhaps the mode through which it became that may be the paradigm of evaluation. . . . Constitutional doctrine succeeds if it expresses what turn out to be at last the authentic impulses of the nation. . . . [The Warren Court] is the only Court so far in American history which has so much as a chance of being one day thought as great as the Marshall Court, for it is the only Court that has made an assertion as large as the Marshall Court made.

Black, *supra* note 6, at 10–12.

[9] IDEA OF PROGRESS 12–13.

criticizing only the process by which it was crafted.[10] Rather, he belittles both. In so doing he goes right for the jugular. The doctrine of *Brown v. Board of Education*,[11] he says, "may be headed for — dread word — irrelevance," and "[a]n even unkinder fate awaits the one-man, one-vote rule of the Warren Court's legislative apportionment cases."[12] "If my probe into a near-term future is not wildly off the mark," he concludes, "the upshot is that the Warren Court's noblest enterprise — school desegregation — and its most popular enterprise — reapportionment — . . . are heading toward obsolescence, and in large measure abandonment."[13]

Bickel's point, then, is that the Court sacrificed all on a bet which is not going to pay off. In a time when irrelevance and obsolescence are indeed "dread words," this assessment is surely enough to make us sit up and take notice. Unlike his predecessors, Bickel challenges the supporters of the Warren Court on their own substantive, result-oriented ground. Yet the ultimate lesson that Bickel would have us learn still reflects the familiar teachings of the scholarly tradition. Bickel argues that it was the Warren Court's failure to heed the strict constraints of reason that headed its work for oblivion.[14]

In this article, I shall discuss both Bickel's verdict on the Warren Court's greatest works and the traditional mode of criticism on which he relies and whose essential assumptions he shares. The scholarly tradition has withstood examination before. In fact, it has gone on to dominate both law teaching and writing on the Court for many years. I do not pretend to have found an entirely new chink in its armor. But times are changing. The assumptions and entailments of the dominant tradition that met with so much acclaim in the atmosphere of the past thirty-five years may begin to find less favor in the 1970's. To that extent, merely revealing them for all to see may work apparent miracles. Perhaps it is not *Brown v. Board of Education* or *Reynolds v. Sims*[15] that is "headed for obsolescence." Perhaps it is, instead, *The Supreme Court and the Idea of Progress* and the tradition of which it is part.

---

[10] Professor Wechsler, for example, has sharply criticized the reasoning behind many of the racial discrimination cases while at the same time observing that these decisions "have the best chance of making an enduring contribution to the quality of our society of any that I know in recent years." Wechsler, *supra* note 4, at 27.

[11] 347 U.S. 483 (1954).

[12] Idea of Progress 151.

[13] *Id.* at 173.

[14] Bickel argues that the success of the Marshall Court was "sui generis" and that any attempt to duplicate it is bound to end unhappily. *Id.* at 41.

[15] 377 U.S. 533 (1964).

I

There have been at least three formative experiences in the growth of the traditional mode of criticism. The first and most important was the great "revolt against formalism" which flourished around the turn of the century.[16] This new intellectual movement decried the old faith that problems are soluble by an almost mechanical deduction from first principles or "absolutes." The rebels denied the very existence of such "absolutes" and, in Judge Learned Hand's words, were resolved to struggle against them and "give them no quarter."[17] In legal scholarship, the movement came to be known broadly as legal realism — the seedbed, as Bickel suggests, of both the modern scholarly tradition and its chosen enemy, known loosely as "result orientation." And, indeed, the heroes of Bickel's historical chapter are the "progressive realists," who constituted one wing of the legal realist movement. At the root of the new creed was the crucial insight, now almost universally accepted, that judges are policymakers who must "make" law by drawing on value choices which have no necessary *a priori* validity. This emphasis on the freedom of judges and the room for disagreement in legal matters was enough to undercut the romantic assumptions of what Bickel terms the "old age of faith."

The progressive realists, however, seem to have taken their analysis a step farther, toward another extreme. They were not satisfied to identify some similarities between judicial and other policymaking. Rather, they held that a judge drawing on an arguable set of value choices is acting *no differently* than any other policymaker.[18] In a world of intellectual uncertainty, they said, the methods and texts of the law provide no special guidance. Thus a legal issue was depicted as similar in its essentials to other policy issues. The value choices involved in the resolution of both were said to be controlled by no standard other than the individual decisionmaker's personal sympathies and beliefs. This equation of legal and ordinary decisionmaking led the progenitors of the scholarly tradition to identify an apparent conflict

---

[16] *See* M. WHITE, SOCIAL THOUGHT IN AMERICA: THE REVOLT AGAINST FORMALISM 59–75 (1949). The account that follows of the legal realist movement — and of the wing of the movement comprising the founders of the modern scholarly tradition — is essentially a critical gloss on Professor Bickel's own account in chapter 2 of *The Supreme Court and the Idea of Progress.* One of the better discussions of legal realism generally is Llewellyn, *Some Realism About Realism — Responding to Dean Pound*, 44 HARV. L. REV. 1222 (1931).

[17] L. HAND, *supra* note 4, at 77.

[18] Even Justice Holmes appeared to equate the "judicial" and "legislative" mode of lawmaking. *See* Kurland, *Toward a Political Supreme Court*, 37 U. CHI. L. REV. 19, 21–22 (1969).

with another root proposition of their creed: the overriding virtue of the democratic political process. They were, after all, progressives as well as realists. Convinced democrats, they asked the question that spawned the traditional mode of judicial criticism: What justifies allocation of important policy decisions to the nonelected members of the judiciary? The question was especially disturbing when the policy issues up for decision were constitutional issues whose judicial resolution might result in frustration of the popular will.

In order to answer the question, Bickel's progressive realists found a way to break the equation between constitutional and ordinary policy issues — by narrowing the institutional role of the courts in deciding constitutional issues. There is, they said, one potential difference between judicial and political decisionmaking. By virtue of their independence, training, and tradition, judges can confine themselves more rigorously and dependably within the constraints of strict reason. So long as judges do no more than apply logic and reason to policy issues, they can avoid duplication of the political branches' function, and their intervention in policy matters involving constitutional considerations is to that extent justifiable. During the tradition's next two formative experiences — the confrontation between the Old Court and the New Deal and the broad reforms by the Warren Court — the meaning and scope of purely "reasoned" decisionmaking became the key to delineation of the proper judicial role.

The progressive realists and their successors in the 1930's and 1940's, while accepting legal reason as a justification for judicial interpretation of the Constitution, believed that its scope was severely limited — indeed, so limited as to exclude the making of any fundamental value choices. They viewed the proper role of the courts as extremely circumscribed and subordinate to the political branches. During the New Deal period they adopted a strict distinction between the narrow "rationality" of a legislative measure under review and its "wisdom." [19] Almost all legislation, they said, was "rational"; and that should be enough to satisfy the Constitution, which they believed set few definite limits on legislative activity. In the end, the New Deal triumphed and that pleased the progressive realists in their capacity as progressives.

The experience of the Warren Court, however, posed new problems. With primarily civil rights and liberties at issue, the heirs of the progressive realists professed that their values led

---

[19] The original and most influential argument for the distinction can be found in Thayer, *The Origin and Scope of the American Doctrine of Constitutional Law*, 7 HARV. L. REV. 129 (1893).

them to side with the Court against the legislature and executive. They found it more difficult to reaffirm enthusiastically the line between "wisdom" and "rationality." In his excellent previous book, *The Least Dangerous Branch*,[20] Bickel commented that the mere "rationality" approach tends to break down when the constitutional issue is one in which action suited to broadly legitimate governmental ends is said to conflict with constitutional protections of civil liberties which limit governmental power. How are the state's broad police powers and the clearly important limitations to be accommodated? "[I]t may not signify a great deal to conclude that such an accommodation is rational. The real question may be whether it is good."[21] Its resolution may not be irrefutably "correct" or "incorrect"; rather, a decision requires a value choice by the constitutional judges. Thus spoke Professor Bickel in *The Least Dangerous Branch*.

In the Warren era, then, the problem of value choices as a part of the reasoned judicial process was posed more poignantly. According to Bickel, the major figure who felt this dilemma more than anyone else — indeed, who symbolizes the dilemma — was Justice Frankfurter. Frankfurter had much to say about the constraints of reason and the virtues of the unrestrained political process, and he commonly "inveighed against the postulation of absolutes."[22] But he often found himself frustrating the actions of legislatures and executives in the defense of "fundamental" values. In the end, says Bickel, Frankfurther "never successfully identified sources from which this judgment was to be drawn that would securely limit as well as nourish it, he never achieved a rigorous general accord between judicial supremacy and democratic theory."[23] Thus even Justice Frankfurter failed in at least one line-drawing endeavor. The leading commentators of the scholarly tradition have tried ever since to succeed where the Justice failed.

II

The scholarly critics of the Court during the Warren era — Bickel included — came to believe that constitutional adjudication could remain a rigorously reasoned process while at the same time making and enforcing constitutional value choices. The *locus classicus* of this new approach is Professor Herbert Wechsler's 1959 Holmes Lecture. Wechsler explicitly recognized that con-

[20] A. Bickel, The Least Dangerous Branch (1962) [hereinafter cited as Least Dangerous Branch].

[21] *Id.* at 39.

[22] Idea of Progress 31.

[23] *Id.* at 34.

stitutional provisions are "directed to protecting certain values" and that value choices are central to constitutional interpretation.[24] But he sought to tame the enterprise by asserting strict demands of principle in the process of decision. His rule of "neutral principles" imposed an essential precondition to the judicial enforcement of a constitutional value choice: the grounds of decision must be general and capable of uncompromising application, regardless of immediate consequences. Professor Wechsler argued that this rule maintained the crucial functional difference between the often unreasoned political process and the reasoned judicial process, thus holding true to the progressive realists' justification for judicial review. The evil, as he saw it, was not the selection of a value whose status was less than revealed truth; rather, it was making a value choice on the basis of its immediate impact. That, he said, is the sort of decisionmaking that should be left to the political process.[25] In *The Least Dangerous Branch*, Bickel gave an extensive argument for this movement from "mere rationality" to "neutral principles," [26] and in *The Supreme Court and the Idea of Progress* he again — though briefly and not without self-contradiction — pledges his allegiance to Professor Wechsler.[27]

Bickel's new book is in the mainstream of the traditional mode of criticism insofar as it applies the rule of "neutral principles" to the Warren Court's work. It also illustrates the gap between theory and practice in Wechslerian criticism. One might expect the torchbearers of neutral principles, having professed to accept significant judicial latitude in making constitutional value choices, to welcome the Court's vigorous defense of our fundamental rights and liberties. But in practice it doesn't seem to work out that way. Wechsler's scholarly followers have repeatedly demonstrated that the rule of "neutral principles" serves

---

[24] H. Wechsler, Principles, Politics, and Fundamental Law xiii (1961). Professor Wechsler made clear that judicial value choices are not only dictated by the nature of the Constitution, but also by the fact that review of the actions of coordinate branches of government amounts to a review of previously made value choices:

> courts in constitutional determinations face issues that are inescapably "political" . . . in that they involve a choice among competing values or desires, a choice reflected in the legislative or executive action in question, which the court must either condemn or condone.

Wechsler, *supra* note 4, at 15.

[25] Wechsler, *supra* note 4, at 15–35. In contrast to "principled" or "reasoned" judicial judgments, Professor Wechsler spoke of "ad hoc" legislative and executive judgments.

[26] Least Dangerous Branch 49–65. Professor Bickel's endorsement of the "neutral principles" approach was not without significant qualification and criticism, however. *See* p. 780 *infra*.

[27] Idea of Progress 81–82.

better as a tool of destructive criticism than as a guide to the more effective protection of constitutional values.[28] Their writings — of which the third chapter of Bickel's book is a good example — often simply catalogue the Warren Court's failure to live up to the ideal of principled decisionmaking. One begins to wonder whether the theoretical concession to judicial protection of fundamental values was not simply illusory or trivial.

Bickel's chapter dissecting a selection of the Warren Court's decisions, like most other work in the scholarly tradition, takes a damned-if-you-do, damned-if-you-don't approach. When the Court attempts to limit its holdings narrowly, the critics charge that the decisions are not sufficiently general and principled. They argue that lines have been drawn between categories of events or individuals which are more relevantly similar than different, and they conclude that the Court is surreptitiously basing its decisions either on a merely pragmatic political assessment of the consequences in the instant case or on some hidden principle it fears to state openly.[29] But when the Court does base its decisions on general principles, the critics say that the Justices cannot possibly have meant what they said. They commonly point to inconsistencies between the articulated principle and past Court decisions, refusing to accept the possibility that those precedents are now to be called into serious question.[30] Alternatively, the critics do their best to extend the principle into disparate and outlying policy areas only to deplore the results it would work there.[31] Rarely do they assist the Court in finding lines that could be drawn in future cases to limit the principle's application. Rather, they seem to assume mistakenly that the Justices will inevitably insist on plowing ahead, uninterested in developing later limitations. Just as rarely do they survey the implications of a principle and say with Professor Charles Black — not one of their number — that if the principle is right and if it would invalidate this or that precedent or common practice, then "so be it." [32] Instead of evaluating the principle as a matter of principle, they focus on results and refuse to admit that the validity of the principle may suggest the validity of its implications. And, most suggestive of their true orientation, these self-appointed scholastic mandarins almost always coat this technique

[28] The body of legal commentary demonstrating the statement in the text is vast. But the *Harvard Law Review* Supreme Court Forewords cited earlier provide adequate illustration. *See* note 5 *supra*.

[29] *E.g.*, IDEA OF PROGRESS 60–63.

[30] *E.g., id.* at 59–60.

[31] *E.g., id.* at 67–68.

[32] This is Bickel's characterization of Professor Black's approach. IDEA OF PROGRESS 67–68. *See* Black, *supra* note 6, at 35–45.

of criticism with a haughty derision of the Court's powers of analysis and reasoning — terming the Court, for example, an inept piano player who need not necessarily be shot but who surely ought to "take piano lessons." [33]

Do these scholarly critics really believe that their strictures of principled adjudication are compatible with enforcement of fundamental rights and liberties? In *The Supreme Court and the Idea of Progress* Bickel may have inadvertently provided an answer. He admits his doubt that the Court has ever fully met the Wechslerian standards and recognizes that he does not know whether the Warren Court fell any farther short than its predecessors. But, he says, such a comparison "does not matter one way or the other, for intellectual incoherence is not excusable and is no more tolerable because it has occurred before." [34] The demands of principle, he says, "are what they are." [35] Perhaps so. But Bickel should have hesitated somewhat longer, I believe, to ask whether he is not demanding the nearly impossible. If past Courts have also systematically failed to meet the requirements of principled decisionmaking, does this not suggest that the requirements themselves — at least as applied by the scholarly critics — are fatally unrealistic?

Surely it is altogether proper for legal scholars to urge the Court to strive for the rational ideal. But it is another thing to demand what Professor Deutsch has termed Wechslerian "total generality" in constitutional decisions.[36] As a matter of fact, I would argue that constitutional adjudication may properly proceed somewhat as does common law adjudication. As Professor Freund has reminded us, Justice Holmes believed that the great growth of the common law came about incrementally: [37]

> It is only after a series of determinations on the same subject-matter, that it becomes necessary to "reconcile the cases," as it is

[33] Kurland, *supra* note 5, at 176. Professor Kurland's Foreword as a whole is a prime example of the usual haughty derision merging into almost scurrilous disrespect. Another, more restrained, example is an article noting Justice Stewart's "hyperbole" that in one voting case his colleagues were engaging in "sixth grade arithmetic"; not to be outdone, the author adds that in more recent cases the Court has been "playing with blocks, and faceless blocks at that." Dixon, *The Warren Court Crusade for the Holy Grail of "One Man-One Vote,"* 1969 SUP CT. REV. 219, 223 (1969).

[34] IDEA OF PROGRESS 47.

[35] *Id.* at 98.

[36] Deutsch, *Neutrality, Legitimacy, and the Supreme Court: Some Intersections Between Law and Political Science*, 20 STAN. L. REV. 169, 188–90 (1968). *See also* Brown, Book Review, 62 COLUM. L. REV. 386, 391 (1962).

[37] P. FREUND, ON LAW AND JUSTICE 76 (1968), *quoting* Holmes, *Codes, and the Arrangement of the Law*, 44 HARV. L. REV. 725 (1931); *see* Deutsch, *supra* note 36, at 232–35. For a criticism of the analogy between common law adjudication and constitutional adjudication, see Kurland, *supra* note 18, at 23–25.

> called, that is, by a true induction to state the principle which has until then been obscurely felt.

Perhaps the most important function of law professors, besides teaching, is to help the courts in this creative process. If it is proper for the Court to make fundamental value choices to protect our constitutional rights and liberties, then it is self-defeating to say that if the Justices cannot come up with a perfectly reasoned and perfectly general opinion *now*, then they should abstain from decision altogether.

Professor Bickel seems to have recognized that the requirements of "neutral principles" are decidedly unrealistic. He makes quite clear that he approves those decisions of the Court made "at retail," depending upon principles of very "small compass." [38] He cites several of the public speech cases, decided "on thinly distinguishable sets of facts," and admits that the decisions were

> often narrow to the point of being virtually *ad hoc*. Yet though they may be deemed good or bad, wise or unwise, they are not analytically vulnerable. While they do not in the aggregate amount to a generalizable proposition, they do not conflict with each other. They are not inconsistent, they are separate. And they are articulated and undisguised.[39]

This is obviously not the "generality" of which the Wechslerian critics speak. Indeed, it probably does not even make sense to call such decisions "principled." Yet Bickel is by no means alone in his conclusion that candid case-by-case balancing of particular elements of particular fact situations is the best that can be done.[40] When forced to adjust Wechsler's rules to the realities of constitutional adjudication, his followers wind up abandoning those rules.

Moreover, Professor Bickel himself has in the past identified

---

[38] IDEA OF PROGRESS 31.

[39] *Id.* at 77.

[40] One student commentator has noted that "a number of enthusiastic [ad hoc] 'balancers' have also been strong advocates of 'principled' decision making. . . . If 'neutral principles' mean anything more than minimal 'rationality' and good faith, then it would appear that they are at the opposite extreme from a resolutely ad hoc weighing of a welter of conflicting interests to produce a one-time only result." He also provides citations to several leading figures of the scholarly tradition who are "enthusiastic 'balancers.'" Note, *Civil Disabilities and the First Amendment*, 78 YALE L.J. 842, 852 n.39 (1969). It is noteworthy that in his previous book Bickel stated that

> the rule of the neutral principles [forecloses] *ad hoc* constitutional judgments which express merely the judge's transient feeling of what is fair . . . . A neutral principle, by contrast, is an intellectually coherent statement of the reason for a result which in like cases will produce a like result.

LEAST DANGEROUS BRANCH 59. This is another indication that Professor Bickel has significantly altered his previous views in his new book.

an even more basic difficulty with Wechslerian analysis. He pointed out that the concentration on the form of judicial decision-making left open the crucial question of substance.

> Which values, among adequately neutral and general ones, qualify as sufficiently important or fundamental or whathaveyou to be vindicated by the Court against other values affirmed by legislative acts? And how is the Court to evolve and apply them? [41]

Wechsler's rule goes a long way toward restricting — indeed, paralyzing — the Court's enforcement of its own value choices. But by failing to provide guidance for which values are to be chosen, Wechsler's approach admits of a high degree of internal ambiguity. How are we to evaluate the "neutrality" of line-drawing except by reference to some sort of value choices? Is it proper, for example, to distinguish de jure from de facto segregation under the fourteenth amendment? Should youths under eighteen be equated with racial minorities for some purposes? Factual surveys may identify the similarities and differences which are relevant; but how are we to decide which of the two is the greater without first making value choices? By the same token, when the Wechslerian critics apply an articulated principle to a new fact situation, deplore the result, and thereupon condemn the principle, they are obviously making an independent value choice in deciding what to deplore and what not to deplore. Yet their method — with the heavy dose of pejoratives that accompanies it — tends to disguise this fact. Wechsler and his followers seem to assume that the simple application of reason will answer the hard questions, yet they never explain how this synthesis of "value free" values comes about.[42]

In *The Supreme Court and the Idea of Progress* Bickel confronts the problems of Wechsler's approach more directly and candidly than do some of his colleagues. In so doing, however, he undercuts the theoretical assumption of the "neutral principle" approach while simultaneously purporting to rely on it. He seems to have undergone a profound crisis of faith in the special judicial capacities upon which Wechsler relied to justify judge-made value choices in the enforcement of fundamental rights.

In *The Least Dangerous Branch*, Bickel characterized the Court's proper role much as Wechsler did: the Court is "predestined" to be "a voice of reason, charged with the creative function of discerning afresh and of articulating and developing

[41] Least Dangerous Branch 55.

[42] According to Professor Wechsler, "The virtue or demerit of a judgment turns . . . entirely on the reasons that support it and their adequacy to maintain any choice of values it decrees . . . ." Wechsler, *supra* note 4, at 19–20.

impersonal and durable principles."[43] "[T]he creative establishment and renewal of a coherent body of principled rules," he said, is crucial to the maintenance of government under law. And it is a function which "our legislatures have proven themselves ill equipped" to perform. Within the political branches of government, "when the pressure for immediate results is strong enough and emotions ride high enough, men will ordinarily prefer to act on expediency rather than take the long view."[44] Clearly, then, Bickel believed that reason and principle would guide the Court in choosing fundamental values to be protected. In *The Supreme Court and the Idea of Progress* he no longer seems to hold that confident belief.

Instead, Bickel now reverts to the original view of the pre-Wechsler progressive realists. The progressive realists, he says, were "skeptical . . . of claims to generality and permanence entered in behalf of social and economic principles."[45] So, too, is he. He has now, "come to doubt in many instances the Court's capacity to develop 'durable principles,' and to doubt, therefore, that judicial supremacy can work and is tolerable in broad areas of social policy."[46] Concepts of justice and injustice, he says, were once thought to have some stable content, but "[t]he words are used in a different sense now because they are no longer rooted in a single, well-recognized ethical precept."[47] "[T]he Constitution . . . states very few plain principles," he goes on, "and few are universally accepted. Principles that may be thought to have wide, if not universal, acceptance may not have it tomorrow, when the freshly-coined, quite novel principle may, in turn, prove acceptable."[48] Bickel now speaks of the unruly "market of norms, values" which cannot be ordered by any institution.

Out of his profound value relativism emerges the view that the Court simply must stay out of most important policy questions. "The judicial process is too principle-prone and principle-bound — it has to be, there is no other justification or explanation for the role it plays." As a result, it is "a most unsuitable instrument for the formation of policy."[49] Thus Bickel resists the temptation to approve judicial protection of civil rights and liberties. He would impose two central substantive rules of limitation on the Court's role: it must, as a general matter, con-

---

[43] LEAST DANGEROUS BRANCH 27, *quoting* Hart, *supra* note 5, at 99.
[44] *Id.* at 25.
[45] IDEA OF PROGRESS 23.
[46] *Id.* at 99.
[47] *Id.* at 84.
[48] *Id.* at 177.
[49] *Id.* at 175.

fine itself to invalidating only totally irrational action and whimsical or arbitrary administrative measures, and it must stay out of "social policy" questions.[50]

Bickel does not define "social policy," but it seems to include almost any matter of more than trivial importance or ordinary complexity. He does, however, give the term some content by mentioning three categories of issues which do not fall within the forbidden area. He would allow the Court freedom in reforming the criminal process, agreeing with Justice Frankfurter that criminal procedure is somehow a technical matter which the public is happy to leave to the judiciary and which may be dealt with simply and without major impact on broader social goals.[51] One wonders whether the Professor has not heard the uproar over such decisions as *Miranda v. Arizona*[52] both within and without the legal community. Be that as it may, what we are concerned with here is not the meaningfulness of Bickel's "social policy" category, but the fundamental orientation toward the judicial process which it reflects. That orientation is revealed quite clearly in Bickel's two other permissible occasions for judicial value choices of more than the narrowest compass: extraordinary breakdowns in the political process, such as the *total* exclusion of an insular group from access to the process, and a "coup d'état," for example, by the military.[53] The Professor's ideal Justices certainly would become adept at sitting on their hands — doing justice in some particular cases, but defining little if any constructive *law* of general application — and the rest of us would be left to our own devices in exercising our constitutional rights and liberties.[54]

---

[50] *See id.* at 35–39.

[51] *Id.* at 32. The idea that reform of criminal procedure is somehow "simple" or "technical" and avoids conflicts with important social goals is quite clearly mistaken, and has been shown to be so in Goldberg & Dershowitz, *Declaring the Death Penalty Unconstitutional*, 83 HARV. L. REV. 1773, 1798–1802 (1970).

[52] 384 U.S. 436 (1966). In fact, Bickel does mention that in recent legislation, Congress "repudiated some of the Court's most recent criminal cases, specifically *Miranda v. Arizona*, dealing with stationhouse confessions, and *United States v. Wade*, dealing with line-ups for eye-witness identification." He goes on to state that "the election of 1968 may have been something of a vote of repudiation of the criminal decisions." IDEA OF PROGRESS 93.

[53] IDEA OF PROGRESS 35. It should be made clear that what is under discussion here are Bickel's substantive rules of limitation on the Court. Just as important to an understanding of his approach is his methodological rule of limitation. "The true distinction," he says, "lies not so much between more and less acceptable principles as between principles of different orders or magnitude and complexity in the application." *Id.* at 177. Thus even in such "social policy" matters as free speech, Bickel would allow very narrow, ad hoc balancing of interests. *See* p. 779 *supra*; note 54 *infra*.

[54] When exercise of constitutional rights and liberties depends upon the will-

That, Bickel says, is as it should be. Corresponding to his new skepticism about the power of reason and principle is a new faith in the pluralistic political process — and in the adequacy of reliance on that process to protect fundamental values. Gone are the references in *The Least Dangerous Branch* to legislative and executive action resulting from pressure and emotion. Since he sees values as items in an undisciplined marketplace, he has only kind words for "[t]he jockeying, the bargaining, the trading, the threatening and the promising, the checking and the balancing" of the political system.[55] Nor should the Court step in to aid minorities which have been severely disadvantaged by dominant political groups.

> In the political process, groups sometimes lose out, but so long as the process is operational and both diffuses power and allows majorities ultimately to work their will, no group that is prepared to enter into the process and combine with others need remain permanently and completely out of power.[56]

The most conservative of post-war political scientists could not have put it better.

Thus, with *The Supreme Court and the Idea of Progress*, the scholarly tradition fathered by the progressive realists has come full circle. The confinement of constitutional value choices to the political process is again the true faith. Unlike the Wechslerians of the late 1950's and 1960's (and unlike his own former self), Bickel makes no theoretical concession to his professed personal enthusiasm for many of the Warren Court's results. Having lost his confidence in "neutral principles," he finds the courts unequipped to define and enforce constitutional rights and liberties. But, as we have seen, the Wechslerians had in practice, if not in theory, strayed not far at all from the fold. Their demands of principle were so rigid that they could rarely be met. So their ultimate prescription of the Court's proper role amounted to almost the same thing: decision on those policy issues known as constitutional issues would actually be left to the legislative and executive branches of government.

---

ingness of the individual to risk prosecution or other serious burden, an after-the-fact ad hoc consideration of particular cases affords him little legal guidance and makes it more likely that he will play it safe by abandoning his rights. This is, of course, the familiar chilling effect. The chilling effect can be dissipated only by judicial articulation of clear and broad rules of constitutional law. *See* Note, *The First Amendment Overbreadth Doctrine*, 83 HARV. L. REV. 844, 852–58 (1970). Thus Bickel's rules of limitation would substantially dampen the exercise of our fundamental freedoms.

[55] IDEA OF PROGRESS 83.

[56] *Id.* at 37.

III

Up to now I have sought to explicate what I mean by the traditional mode of judicial criticism, with only an occasional detour for evaluation. It should be clear, though, that I do not accept the traditional mode. I reject not only its entailment of a rigidly restricted role for the courts, but also its fundamental axioms. The first of these axioms is that a constitutional value choice is the functional equivalent of an ordinary policy decision. Constitutional choices are in fact different from ordinary decisions. The reason is simple: the most important value choices have already been made by the framers of the Constitution.

Followers of the scholarly tradition have argued since the days of the progressive realists that the Bill of Rights and the fourteenth amendment are so vaguely worded as to provide no guidance for decision in modern times.[57] Thus the axiom that a constitutional issue is nothing more than another policy issue. Professor Bickel, for example, stresses the infinite complexity of speech and apportionment questions — note that he does not call them first amendment and fourteenth amendment questions — commenting that

> the answer requires normative choices and prophetic judgments — much as does the solution of other problems of social policy. . . . A coup d'état abolishing elections and representative institutions or excluding an immutably and arbitrarily defined group from the political process would be something else again. And so would a measure flatly forbidding political speech and association. But the former has not been the occasion of the apportionment cases that have come to the Court, nor the latter of the free-speech cases.[58]

He regards constitutional provisions as clearly controlling only the most painfully obvious and paradigmatic instances of unconstitutional action. His unwillingness to take more than the most crabbed, narrow view of constitutional language derives not simply from his position that the Court is a "deviant" institution in a democracy; it derives more fundamentally from his view of the Constitution itself.

Of course, the Constitution is written in broad, majestic language. How else should it have been written? The framers were not so dim-witted as to believe that times would not change, that unforeseen problems would not arise. The reason for framing a constitution is to guarantee a general *sort* of relation between

---

[57] *See, e.g.*, Mendelson, *On the Meaning of the First Amendment: Absolutes in the Balance*, 50 CALIF. L. REV. 821 (1962).

[58] IDEA OF PROGRESS 35.

the government and its citizens. To achieve that end the Constitution must have a purposive permanence. It must serve as a "living" safeguard against certain sorts of excesses on the part of elected officials misled (as Bickel said in *The Least Dangerous Branch*) by inflamed emotions and calculations of immediate consequences. It must, in short, be written in "vague" language. If the framers had intended only to forbid coups d'etat and clearly totalitarian measures, they could have been far more specific.[59]

Clearly, then, constitutional protections of rights and liberties are meant to have meaning beyond what Bickel would allow. The duty of both judges and constitutional scholars is to determine what that meaning ought to be. The question really is how to do it. Here, again, Bickel is a defeatist. He is correct, of course, when he says that filling in the majestic constitutional outlines requires value choices. But the point is that those outlines provide significant and sufficient guidance; the value choices are to be made only within the parameters of the most important value choice embedded in the constitutional language. No matter how imprecise in application to specific modern fact situations, the constitutional guarantees do provide a direction, a goal, an ideal citizen-government relationship. They rule out many alternative directions, goals, and ideals.[60]

The essential requirement of constitutional interpretation should be that it proceed from the top down — not from the bottom up as the traditional mode of criticism would seem to have it. A judge or scholar should begin by expounding his view of the theory and purpose behind the constitutional provision in question. He should not begin by losing himself in the subtlety and complexity of a particular fact situation. This latter approach is nothing more than the "muddling through" said to be characteristic of the political process, which the Constitution is of course meant to bring under some principled control. The proper approach for the judiciary, then, is to state "principled

---

[59] *See generally* Frantz, *Is the First Amendment Law? — A Reply to Professor Mendelson*, 51 CALIF. L. REV. 729 (1963); Frantz, *The First Amendment in the Balance*, 71 YALE L.J. 1424 (1962); Reich, *Mr. Justice Black and the Living Constitution*, 76 HARV. L. REV. 673, 727–50 (1963).

Of course, it might still be argued that the framers were talking only to the executive and legislature when they established more generalized constitutional duties and that the courts are somehow overstepping the bounds of their institutional role when they purport to overhear this conversation. But that argument was settled in *Marbury v. Madison* where it was held that if courts were to decide cases, then they must apply *all* the law to those cases — including the entire Constitution. Moreover, it is obviously self-defeating to have a Constitution designed to protect against the excesses of elected officials and then to entrust its enforcement to those same officials.

[60] *See* note 59 *supra*.

goals"[61] and general rules with a comprehensiveness and degree of clarity sufficient to establish at least a very strong presumption against a range of government actions violative of the articulated purpose. This is not to say that this purposive analysis should emerge full-blown from the heads of the Justices the first time a question is litigated, as the Wechslerians would have it. Obviously, particular fact situations influence the course of the law. If an unanticipated fact situation forces a modification of previously articulated goals and rules, then so be it. But the general thrust of constitutional adjudication should remain firmly grounded in the ideals of the constitutional text. In the end, the Court must tred a middle path between the followers of Wechsler, who would paralyze it by a too rigid insistence on principle, and the followers of Bickel, who would paralyze it by an insistence that principle is impossible.

Naturally there will be differences over the purposes and underlying political theories of the various constitutional protections. But they will be reasoned differences, subject to argument. As Alexander Meiklejohn's[62] and Thomas Emerson's[63] efforts in first amendment interpretation demonstrate, the enterprise is very much a rational one — not at all the unruly clashing of gut value choices that Bickel seems to envision. An assumption of Bickel and his colleagues seems to be that if we accept this mode of constitutional interpretation, we must also accept whatever results judges who apply it may reach, be they "conservative" or "liberal." That, of course, is not the case. When the courts interpret constitutional provisions in ways which we believe wrong, we ought not to shift the focus from the merits of their position to a narrowing of their institutional function. This was the fundamental mistake made by liberal legal scholars in the 1930's.[64] Judicial decisions of which we disapprove can best

---

[61] In his previous book, Bickel distinguished judicial articulation of principled goals from principled rules and went beyond Wechsler in endorsing the former.

> [I]t is the statement of a goal whose attainment will call for a great many prudential judgments [by the other branches], aimed at the goal, to be sure, but not proceeding immediately from principle.
>
> . . .
>
> The role of principle, when it cannot be the immutable governing rule, is to affect the tendency of policies of expediency. And it is a potent role.

LEAST DANGEROUS BRANCH 63–64. Thus he was, at that time, a good deal more willing to take a purposive, top-down approach to constitutional protections.

[62] Meiklejohn, *The First Amendment Is an Absolute*, 1961 SUP. CT. REV. 245 (1961).

[63] Emerson, *Toward a General Theory of the First Amendment*, 72 YALE L.J. 877 (1963).

[64] A possible argument for focusing on institutional role rather than on the constitutional merits is that activism on the part of "liberal" judges somehow encourages or makes more likely activism on the part of "conservative" judges. It should be recognized, first of all, that this is an empirical proposition whose

be challenged on their merits, and in a wholly reasonable manner. Arguments over purposes and theories will be healthy, aiding both judges and the political officials who appoint them. This approach will refocus attention, spawn a new mode of judicial criticism, and allow us to get on with the business of enforcing the purposive commands of the Constitution.

Yet *The Supreme Court and the Idea of Progress* suggests that Professor Bickel would remain unconvinced by this argument. Even if he admitted that a constitutional value choice is not the functional equivalent of an ordinary policy issue, he would still say that the freely operating pluralist political process serves to protect our constitutional rights and liberties adequately. Thus Bickel goes beyond the more usual assertion that, although the Court can enforce the Constitution far better than the other branches, it cannot afford to move too far, too fast since an outraged political majority constitutes an "ever-present threat" to its very existence.[65] His belief seems to rest on two foundations, one theoretical, one empirical, and both mistaken.

Professor Bickel appears to believe that reliance on the political process for protection of most fundamental rights and liberties is somehow inherent in democratic theory. Government by consent of the governed is his frequent touchstone. Judicial decisions are made without the form of popular consent expressed, for example, in the casting of a vote and should therefore be relatively disfavored. But in the theory of *constitutional* democracy, an act of consent such as voting is given in a constitutional context. A vote for a candidate does not give him a carte blanche. Implicit in the vote is an expectation that, if elected, the candidate will conform his actions to the Constitution. Also implicit, given judicial review, is the recognition that there are courts to

validity is not at all obvious. But, more importantly, the argument erroneously assumes that "liberal" and "conservative" positions cannot be the subject of reasoned debate in a judicial context. Judges from all positions on the political spectrum should be "activist" in vindicating rights which they believe are protected by the Constitution. But in so doing, they must be prepared to make reasoned arguments grounded in the constitutional text. If such arguments are — as they should be — more than gut responses, their merits can be debated in rational fashion. It is only through such debate on the merits of constitutional protections that we will arrive at a fuller understanding of what our rights are. When institutional constraints are erected to curb debate on the merits, they tend to straitjacket the Court when new and unforeseen problems requiring judicial resolution arise. A virtually exclusive focus on institutional limits amounts to an endorsement of *no* judicially enforced rights.

[65] *See, e.g.*, Kurland, *supra* note 18, at 22. Of course, Bickel does not abandon this line of argument entirely. IDEA OF PROGRESS 94–95. The potentially outraged majority feared by those who make this prudential case for judicial passivism is similar in its illusory, completely theoretical nature to the "silent majority" so often summoned up as an argument-stopper in the political world.

ensure his obedience. This is particularly important since the individual voter actually participates in, and thus directly consents to, almost none of the governmental decisions that are made in his name. His power to challenge particular decisions in the courts is theoretically necessary to the claim that government officials act with his consent. The Constitution was not originally imposed on us by some court. Rather, it was adopted by the people, may be altered by the people, and must be considered by them in any authorization they give to elected officeholders. It is the people's independent check on popular democracy, and, as such, is best enforced by an independent body with power to check the actions of legislatures and executives. It is very much part of — indeed, it is at the core of — government by the consent of the governed.

Of course, on occasion unconstitutional activity has been sanctioned by direct popular referendum. Moreover, one might posit a case where a congressman was reelected by his constituents on the basis of his support of unconstitutional legislation. But to place majority rule above constitutional guarantees even in these situations is to ignore the inherent power of the majority to bind itself. In this country, the majority made an original decision to protect certain minority rights, and this decision cannot be respected if these rights evaporate whenever it seems expedient to ignore them. Professor Bickel goes on to contend, however, that in fact minorities play an important though indirect role in most governmental decisions, may be presumed to consent to them, and have substantial opportunity to defend their interests without the help of the courts. No minority willing to wheel and deal with other minorities, he says, need despair of eventually vindicating its rights.[66] There are at least two problems with this common position. First, from a constitutional standpoint, is the word "eventually." The Constitution does not say that "no law shall for an inordinately long time" or that "no state shall in perpetuity" deny certain rights. It sets down limitations to be made effective in the present. Nor does the Constitution say that a minority must trade away many of its interests in order to secure support for exercise of its fundamental rights. It does not sanction the putting of prices on these rights. Constitutional provisions are commands meant to control the political process, not simply predictions of how the process will operate.

Bickel's empirical assertion that no minority need remain isolated, that all groups can exert influence on governmental decisions, is also highly doubtful. Perhaps its basic defect is the

---

[66] IDEA OF PROGRESS 37.

fact that power is not distributed equally among the various groups in our society. Bickel explicitly recognizes that the formation of majorities at election time is but one part of our political system. At least equally important is the trading and pressuring that goes on all the rest of the time. The Professor would have us believe that this is just fine: those groups with the most "intense" interests will be the most active in the process, and it is proper that the more "intense" interests be more richly rewarded.[67] This is nonsense. The big winners in the pluralistic system are the highly organized, wealthy, and motivated groups skilled in the art of insider politics. They have the resources to trade for other benefits, and the resources that it takes to press their claims successfully. Perhaps the interest of a great corporation in a tax break is more "intense" than that of a political minority in its first amendment rights — that is, if intensity is defined by how conscious of their interests they are, how articulate and persistent they are in presenting them, and how much political muscle they bring to bear. Intensity, so defined, however, is largely an attribute of the already powerful elite. Unorganized, poor, unskilled minorities simply do not have the sort of "intense" interests in their rights which the pluralistic system regularly rewards.[68] Is this any way to protect their constitutional rights? Under the narrowly constricted judicial role of the scholarly tradition, it is the only way.

IV

The two elements of *The Supreme Court and the Idea of Progress* discussed to this point — the customary critique of judicial opinion writing and the more novel skepticism about legal reason — do not reach its most controversial line of argument, which is of course the substantive attack on the Court's work. Professor Bickel launches the attack by characterizing what he believes to be the four dominant themes underlying the Justices'

[67] *Id.* at 83, 116. Bickel does qualify his rosy view of the pluralist political system with the proviso that the system must be kept "operational." But by "operational" he means merely the presence of formal, legal access to the vote and to a place on the ballot. *Id.* at 37. Despite his recognition that "elections are the tip of the iceberg," *id.* at 83, he sets no requirements for the political process "below." And it is of course in the latter area that "intense" interests tend to hold sway.

[68] Until a few years ago, Bickel's pluralist and wholly complacent view of the political system dominated academic political science. *See, e.g.*, R. DAHL, WHO GOVERNS? (1961), on which Bickel relies. But now there is a rapidly growing body of literature by students of politics that supports the basic approach taken in the text here. *See, e.g.*, P. BACHRACH, THE THEORY OF DEMOCRATIC ELITISM 83–92 (1967); R. WOLFF, THE POVERTY OF LIBERALISM 122–61 (1968).

decisions: egalitarianism, majoritarianism, centralization, and legalization.[69] Yet even here his highly skeptical attitude toward the powers of legal reason and his conservative political philosophy determine his approach and, I believe, lead him astray. He indulges in a sort of argumentative overkill, which only emphasizes the weakness of his criticism.

Bickel apparently feels that he must show the Warren Court to be not simply overly activist, but consciously demonic. His choice of the four "isms" and "izations" to describe the Warren Court's *weltanschauung* introduces his view of the Justices as unreconstructed absolutists, even ideologues. Slaves to simplistic theoretical principles, the Court in Bickel's opinion naively sought "to impose order on the market of norms, values and institutions,"[70] motivated by "[a] certain habit of command, an impatience to take charge of unruly affairs."[71] He depicts the Court as an overconfident planning agency, a master builder whose "tendency was noticeable to circumscribe and displace private ordering, to legalize the society, to rationalize it in the sense in which the great industrial consolidators spoke of rationalizing the economy . . . ."[72] And, portraying the Justices' ideology as a radical one, he suggests that "revolutionaries" formed their surest constituency.[73] The picture he paints of the Court's method of constitutional decisionmaking is a rather lurid one. Purporting to represent reality, in fact it is distorted by Bickel's own allegiance to the *ancien regime*.

When Bickel describes the Warren Court's themes as simplistic, zealously pursued absolutes designed to remake society on the basis of enforced mass equality, he does not attempt to hide his own sharp, single-minded disapproval. "I should say," he says, "that in my view the Court's majoritarianism is ill-conceived, egalitarianism is a worthy ideal but not in all circumstances a self-evident virtue, and centralized, unmitigatedly legalitarian government bears the seed of tyranny."[74] In his view, society should not and cannot be remade by the Court. For the tools of societal transformation inevitably take decisionmaking power from the hands of the many and put it in the hands of the few — for example, the courts ("legalization") or non-local government ("centralization"). The inevitable result, according to

---

[69] IDEA OF PROGRESS 103–17.

[70] *Id.* at 104.

[71] *Id.* at 105.

[72] *Id.* at 104. Bickel is not alone in his emphasis on the supposed conscious, programmatic absolutism of the Warren Court. *See, e.g.*, Jaffe, *Was Brandeis an Activist? The Search for Intermediate Premises*, 80 HARV. L. REV. 986, 1002 (1967).

[73] IDEA OF PROGRESS 94.

[74] *Id.* at 115.

Bickel, is a rigid and stifling uniformity. And the ends of the Warren Court's social engineering program, he believes, compound the damage by systematically levelling personal differences ("egalitarianism") and group-community cohesiveness ("majoritarianism"). In his own ideology, the primary value seems to be the "rich" diversity and freedom of private ordering. In any event, his view is that society is so subtle and complex an organism that it cannot be molded to any theory of man. Reason, legal or otherwise, is too blunt and unsure an instrument.

> [I]n dealing with problems of great magnitude and pervasive ramifications, problems with complex roots and unpredictably multiplying off-shoots — in dealing with such problems, the society is best allowed to develop its own strands out of its tradition; it moves forward most effectively, perhaps, in empirical fashion . . . as it shifts and responds in accordance with experience, and with pressures brought to bear by the political process.[75]

It is only when the Warren Court is viewed from this profoundly conservative perspective, however, that its work appears dangerously radical and absolutist. *The Supreme Court and the Idea of Progress* to the contrary notwithstanding, the Warren Court did not bring us to Armageddon. The Court was not a grand planner or master builder, working from a blueprint of the new society. Bickel's characterization of the Justices' thematic program and approach is, in a word, inaccurate. As one might expect Bickel of all people to realize, these matters are rarely so extreme and polarized as he makes them appear. They are more usually a matter of degree. If the Court's efforts toward greater individual dignity, privacy, and more nearly fair and equal treatment for all were described appropriately in terms of degree,[76] I have little doubt that most of us would accept whatever sacrifices of diversity and private ordering were involved. For the sacrifice was by no means as devastating as Bickel seems to argue. And when we recognize the limited applicability and reformist, corrective nature of the Justices' constitutional principles,[77] the analogy to industrial magnates trying to rationalize the society becomes rather incredible.

When we examine the evidence Professor Bickel himself marshals to support his approach, the radical specter begins to dis-

---

[75] *Id.* at 175.

[76] Professor Black has characterized the basic themes of the Warren Court, for example, in terms of four elements of citizenship, not programmatic absolutes. Black, *supra* note 6, at 8–9.

[77] For a compilation of the many reformist compromises made by the Warren Court, see Blasi, *A Requiem for the Warren Court*, 48 TEX. L. REV. 608, 613–17 (1970).

appear. Take egalitarianism. The conventional wisdom of the scholarly tradition, borrowed from Professor Cox, is that "[o]nce loosed, the idea of Equality is not easily cabined." [78] But what indication is there that the idea ran riot through the Court's decisions? Bickel relies on two lines of cases: those ensuring equal treatment for black people, and those granting a measure of equality for the indigent.[79] But one looks in vain through the cases cited for evidence to make out the charge that the Justices were latter-day socialist levelers. In his Supreme Court Note Foreword last year, Professor Michelman demonstrated what should have been clear to all, that in the indigent cases the Court intervened only when very fundamental interests were at stake.[80] Free access to the vote and to legal assistance surely does not imply a requirement that all monetary barriers fall to the ground. The Court's effort was designed to bring the poor up to a minimum standard. At most, a minimal equality of opportunity — rather than egalitarianism — would be the appropriate characterization, surely one with fewer revolutionary connotations.

"Egalitarianism" may be a more accurate description of the Court's attitude toward cases involving racial discrimination. But if it be egalitarianism, it is directed, and limited, to a very special and historic evil; surely where racial discrimination is at issue any less would be insufficient.[81] Moreover, it should be noted that the Court has not gone head over heels to repair all the harm done by past centuries of slavery, segregation, and discrimination. Rather, it has generally confined itself to ending present continuation of those ancient practices. The cost in terms of leveling personal differences — differences based upon a man's skin color — may be counted in small coins.

"Majoritarianism," says Bickel, "is heady stuff. It is, in truth, a tide flowing with the swiftness of a slogan . . . . The tide is apt to sweep over all institutions, seeking its level everywhere." [82] Harking to the cries of Chicken Little, we expect the skies to fall, the dams to burst open. But where is the deluge? All that Bickel can point to is the one-man, one-vote decisions and the decisions enlarging the electorate and reducing permis-

[78] A. Cox, The Warren Court 6 (1968).

[79] Idea of Progress at 103. Bickel also mentions the voting cases, but they will be discussed under the "majoritarianism" heading. As in the indigent cases, the Court in the voting cases pursued at most an ideal of equality of opportunity — equality only in the most basic fundamentals. *See* p. 793 *infra*.

[80] Michelman, *The Supreme Court, 1968 Term, Foreword: On Protecting the Poor Through the Fourteenth Amendment*, 83 Harv. L. Rev. 7 (1969).

[81] I would agree, as I believe most would, with Professor Black that "[r]acism *is* a special subject in the United States, whether in or outside the law; it is *the* special subject in the United States." Black, *supra* note 6, at 25.

[82] Idea of Progress 111.

sible qualifications for voting.[83] What upsets him is the Court's refusal to allow one's access to the vote or the weight of one's vote to depend upon one's peculiar economic, social, or geographical interests. This emphasis on equal voting rights, according to the Professor, frustrates the true genius of our political system — the pluralist giving and taking, wheeling and dealing of myriad interest groups. But the Court has in no way banned pluralist politics. Interest groups and lobbies can operate as always; they need not secure majority support before they bring pressure to bear on the community's representatives. What the Court has actually done is considerably less dramatic than Professor Bickel's imaginings. It has insisted that when the vote — the ordinary man's one chance to play a role in the direction of public affairs — is at stake, there must be a very heavy presumption against any distinctions that would exclude or disadvantage any group substantially interested in the outcome of the election in question. It is majoritarianism only insofar as the *formal* levers of power are concerned. Since Professor Bickel recognizes that our political system operates largely through informal channels, he must know that the Warren Court did not bring true democracy to America.

The last two themes identified by Bickel are centralization and legalization. Both, he says, undermined the diversity and freedom of local and private decisionmaking. But again the question is, diversity of what? Freedom to do what? And to what extent were these values undermined? Apparently Bickel believes that diversity and private ordering are themselves absolutes, valuable per se. But what joy do we derive from a "diverse" society where some men have the "freedom" to shunt some others to the back of the bus simply because of their race? The Warren Court did not attempt to regulate all spheres of our lives; it simply forbade us to act in certain ways harmful to others. And against these decisions we must balance — as Bickel does not — the many others designed to protect and enlarge no other right than that of privacy and freedom of action.

The one decision to which Bickel often refers in substantiating his centralization charge is *Katzenbach v. Morgan*,[84] enlarging the power of Congress to expand and enforce the guarantees of the fourteenth amendment. That decision did allow Congress to override the "experimentation" by local governments with the rights of disadvantaged minorities. Whether or not such experiments are to be highly valued, their sacrifice to federal control is simply part of a trend in being long before the advent of the

---

[83] *Id.* at 151–73.

[84] 384 U.S. 641 (1966).

Warren Court. The only new element in this incremental step is the purpose for which central power may be exercised. At least, we may demand consistency of Professor Bickel: why is it that the cost of centralization in *Morgan* is so disturbing, while the radical enlargement of congressional commerce clause powers earns only his praise? What is at stake is not really centralization per se, but the particular "rich diversity" whereby some minorities in some localities may be systematically victimized. The cost of losing this sort of diversity hardly equals that summoned up by the specter of totalitarian central government.[85]

Beyond *Morgan*, Bickel presents no other evidence[86] of the great trend toward centralization which, he says, "bears the seed of tyranny."[87] The only other decisions of the Warren Court arguably conforming to the centralization theme are those expanding access of a prisoner to federal court review on habeas corpus and those incorporating Bill of Rights guarantees into the fourteenth amendment.[88] Strangely, Professor Bickel has no harsh words for these developments, crucial to the Court's achievement though they were. In the criminal process, for some reason, he finds no attraction in the old chestnut about the states' capacities as little laboratories for experimentation — experimentation with men's lives, liberty, and privacy.

Legalization, too, is something of a red herring. Professor Bickel's unkind words here are reserved for the decisions "substantially loosen[ing] the definition of a lawsuit . . . open[ing] the door wider to more litigants, and . . . making the lawsuit something of a formality, still an expensive one, but within the reach of just about all who can afford it, at just about any time of their choice."[89] He also refers to a new judicial willingness to protect life and liberty in extraordinary situations.[90] Of course it is true that during the Warren years the champions of racial, economic, and other disadvantaged minorities turned more and more to the lawsuit as an instrument of reform. Again, however, Bickel's opposition to these trends demonstrates his lack of per-

[85] Moreover, Bickel's criticism of *Morgan* is difficult to reconcile with his general distrust of the judicial process. It was, after all, *Congress* which ended state "experimentation" with the electoral rights of minorities and *congressional* power which the Court upheld. Why should the Court strike down congressional action when the legislature moves to protect minority rights, while waiting for a coup d'etat when Congress places those rights in jeopardy?

[86] For a discussion of some quasi-evidence extrapolated from the school desegregation cases, see p. 798.

[87] IDEA OF PROGRESS 115.

[88] *See, e.g.*, Fay v. Noia, 372 U.S. 391 (1963); Mapp v. Ohio, 367 U.S. 643 (1961).

[89] IDEA OF PROGRESS 108.

[90] *Id.* 105–06.

spective on the whole legal system and apparent unconcern for what freedoms and what diversity are at stake. The lawsuit has always been a ready and effective instrument of the rich and powerful, seeking to protect their own interests. Why, then, is it so disturbing when the lawsuit may be almost as readily employed to enforce more fully the Constitution? Moreover, the usual word of moderation is again in order: the lawsuit has yet to replace politics as the primary mode of social change. That legal redress is more available to certain groups in the vindication of certain fundamental rights does not make ours a "legalized" society.

Why is it that Bickel fails to see the possibility of a middle ground when discussing decisions of the Warren Court? He is by no means alone in this approach; many of his colleagues in the scholarly tradition tend to go even more overboard than he. Professor Kurland, for example, recently concluded an article on "Egalitarianism and the Warren Court" with the following observation: "Those too young to remember what happened to Europe immediately prior to World War II, as country after country fell under the thrall of equality, may yet find the allegory of Orwell's *Animal Farm* instructive and frightening." [91] So dispassionate when speaking in the abstract of legal methods and institutions, the scholarly tradition has gone to incredible excess when confronted with its *bête noire*, the Warren Court of the 1960's. The best explanation for these excesses lies in the recognition that the scholarly tradition now is in fact but a part of the western conservative tradition. At least since the French Revolution, it has been characteristic of conservatives to combat the forces of change by misrepresenting their program, by summoning up horrible disasters said to follow from liberal reform, and by depicting the liberals as extreme totalitarians. This reaction has been particularly prevalent when the change involved would enforce for the underprivileged many the rights which have long been enjoyed by the privileged few. The liberal tradition, on the other hand, has been based on a faith in the powers of man to adjust institutions, without making them totalitarian, in the interest of equal justice. The record shows, I believe, that the Warren Court justified the faith of the liberals while belying the conservatives' fears. The contrast between the conservative rhetoric and reality may also reinforce doubts we may have about the more dispassionate theoretical foundation of the scholarly tradition.

---

[91] Kurland, *Egalitarianism and the Warren Court*, 68 MICH. L. REV. 629, 682 (1970).

V

Although Professor Bickel quite clearly reveals his own conservative ideology in his excessive characterization of the Court's work, he nonetheless purports to follow a value-neutral approach. Thus, he attacks the Court's work in the fields of racial segregation and legislative reapportionment not because the results are "wrong" but because the results will not be "historically vindicated." His assertion is that the trend of opinion and events is now conforming not to the Warren Court's plan, but to his own.

Bickel hears

> in increasing volume notes that amount to another tune. There is in being a reaction to the steady unification and nationalization of recent years, a movement toward a decentralization and a diversity of which the as yet unacknowledged prophet — due, I should suppose for a revival — is Brandeis. . . . A striving for diversity is not necessarily in express conflict with the goal of an egalitarian society, but it connotes a different order of priorities. In politics, even as the Warren Court's virtually irresistible slogan — one man, one vote — may still be mouthed on all sides, the cry is for a group participation which presupposes, whether it knows it or not, the Madisonian more than the majoritarian model, and for a process calculated to heed the expression not only of desires and preferences, but of intensities that no ballot can register.[92]

The school desegregation and reapportionment decisions, according to Bickel, constructed constitutional principles which are either irrelevant or a barrier to resolution of the issues of the renascent Brandeisian Age. This is all meant to illustrate his fundamental proposition that, although courts are bound to decide cases on the basis of principle, there are unlikely to be any "durable principles" and that consequently the courts may as well give up.[93]

At the outset it is appropriate to ask whether Bickel's test — which he says the Court's greatest work fails — is a proper one. He seems wholehearted in his acceptance of history as the final judge: "If the [Warren Court's] bet [on the future trend of events] pays off, whatever their analytical failings, the Justices will have won everything."[94] The value-neutrality of this approach must be particularly appealing to the Professor; and it has been accepted by at least one of his most consistent comrades in arms, Professor Kurland. Kurland, however, seems to

---

[92] IDEA OF PROGRESS 116–17.

[93] *See* p. 781 *supra*.

[94] IDEA OF PROGRESS 99.

have given the game away by pointing out an unpleasant implication of the history-as-judge standard of evaluation.

> History . . . has a nasty way of measuring greatness in terms of success rather than in terms of goodness. . . . Roger Taney . . . has gone down in infamy, despite some noteworthy contributions to American constitutional jurisprudence, because he defended the institution of slavery in the *Dred Scott* case when the forces of history proved to be on the other side — the side of the Union Army.[95]

Should a different outcome on the Civil War battlefields really make us approve *Dred Scott*? If Taney's Court had made apartheid its overriding principle, and apartheid had actually come to pass in America, would the judicial result be any more defensible? A bit of the politician's sense of the climate of opinion may be valuable on the Supreme Court; but surely it is not the most important element. The ultimate test of the Justices' work, I suggest, must be goodness, not a cynically defined success. Since Bickel purports to believe that "justice" and "injustice" are no more than passing societal value choices of no inherent and true meaning, he is left with history and chance victories on the battlefield as his only guide — trends and fortuities which, he says, are difficult for a court to predict, yet on which he wholeheartedly relies to scorn the Court's work.

Moreover, even if we accept Bickel's historical test, we can still question its application. Perhaps the Professor ought to have taken his own advice to the Court before so confidently assessing which way the wind is blowing. Thus it may be significant that Bickel's Holmes Lectures were written to be delivered in the spring of 1969 — now almost two years ago. They were probably drafted in 1968. That, indeed, was the year of Brandeisian rhetoric. Senators Kennedy and McCarthy (for whom Professor Bickel did campaign work) spoke eloquently of returning decisionmaking power to localities. Also in 1968, the New York City school decentralization movement had just reached its high water mark. The trend of events and opinion at that time certainly seemed to be running in a rather Brandeisian direction. Two years later, however, Bickel's confident predictions are less convincing. With a new administration in power, the focus of attention seems to have turned. There is still much talk of decentralization, but it is more often meant as a redistribution of power to the states rather than to the local communities of which Bickel speaks. So-called "social issues" — such as crime in the streets and disorder on college campuses — are given first priority by some, while tra-

[95] Kurland, *Earl Warren, The "Warren Court," and the Warren Myths*, 67 MICH. L. REV. 353, 357 (1968).

ditional issues of economic security are stressed by others. The decentralization trend which appeared to be inevitable in 1968 seems to have faltered somewhat. I do not pretend to be an accurate predictor of future public opinion; and, as I have said, I do not believe such a prediction to be terribly relevant to an evaluation of the Warren Court. But I would advise Professor Bickel, who is so agnostic in the making of value judgments, to apply some of that agnosticism to the making of empirical predictions — particularly predictions of so fickle a phenomenon.

Let us, nonetheless, assume *arguendo* that Brandeis *is* due for a revival. Even if Professor Bickel has foreseen the trend of opinion, it is not clear that the school desegregation and voting decisions are either irrelevant to or incompatible with that trend. His technique of argument — a common one among followers of the scholarly tradition — is to read Court decisions for much more than they mean, to extend nascent principles far beyond what was intended by the Court. Yet at the same time that Bickel exhibits this failing in depicting some of the Court's greatest decisions as roadblocks to new reform, he takes far too narrow a view of the same decisions in arguing their irrelevance.[96]

Thus, Bickel identifies two principles or ideals running through the school desegregation cases. The first is a condemnation on fourteenth amendment grounds of state-established racial segregation. The second relates only to education, and seems to view the public school system as pursuing a great, assimilationist mission in American society. To satisfy the former, only the disestablishment of state-sponsored segregation is required. But, to fully satisfy the latter — to achieve actual integration countrywide — more far-reaching measures would be necessary. Professor Bickel's argument is that if the assimilationist ideal is carried to its most extreme conclusion, it will come into direct conflict with the trend of Brandeisian opinion, by requiring centralization of school districts to end de facto segregation and by outlawing tuition grant schemes and private schools. But if the assimilationist ideal is not carried all the way and mere disestablishment prevails, he says, the school desegregation decisions will become irrelevant to the burning issues of the day.[97] It is a heads-I-win, tails-you-lose type of argument.

It is almost too obvious to point out that the extremes of mere disestablishment and total assimilation do not exhaust all possible future uses of the school desegregation cases. Once again, Bickel's tendency to artificially polarize an issue leads him into rather painful excess and undercuts his argument. The slope is

[96] *See* p. 777 *supra*.

[97] Idea of Progress 117–51.

not so slippery as he would have it. The Court could well stop short of requiring centralized school districts, but go beyond mere disestablishment to deal with de facto segregation. Familiar and effective possibilities include judicial review of zoning and new school location decisions by local school authorities.[98] It would not be unprincipled for the Court to recognize that city, town, or county jurisdictions are appropriate for school administration purposes and that the cost of altering these jurisdictions by judicial order would outweigh the assimilationist benefit. The Justices are not blind to the advantages of decentralization. If total assimilation is thought too costly, its nonachievement might nonetheless breathe new life into the separate-but-equal formula of *Plessy v. Ferguson*.[99] Thus the Court might well hold that when zoning and location adjustments fail to achieve acceptably integrated schools, there is a particularly heavy burden on local boards to allocate educational resources equally among all schools. In this fashion, the assimilationist ideal would aid in the resolution of non-southern school problems without erecting a barrier to Bickel's Brandeisian objectives.

The tuition grant and private school problem may be more difficult. But it might be sufficient to command simply that if tuition grants are to be made, the schools which receive the resulting public funds must encourage interracial membership or establish fair racial quotas. Such requirements would not disturb the main, legitimate goal of tuition grants: the sponsorship of diverse educational opportunities and free choice among them. Private schools, not receiving public funds, might be dealt with by forbidding racially discriminatory admission practices under the thirteenth amendment.[100] Again, the most important free choice and diversity values to be served would remain unaffected while gross evasion of school integration would be controlled. I do not necessarily advocate any of these approaches; rather, I suggest them only to show that Bickel's extremist, either-or analysis is but another example of his argumentative overkill.

Description of the school desegregation cases as "irrelevant" is even more implausible than the slippery slope argument. Even if the assimilationist ideal is carried no farther by the Court, it is mere grandstanding to call the principle forbidding de jure

---

[98] *See, e.g.*, Green v. County School Board, 391 U.S. 430 (1968).

[99] 163 U.S. 537 (1896); *see* Hobson v. Hansen, 269 F. Supp. 401, 496–97 (D.D.C. 1967), *aff'd sub. nom.* Smuck v. Hobson, 408 F.2d 175 (D.C. Cir. 1969) (en banc).

[100] *See generally* Note, *The "New" Thirteenth Amendment: A Preliminary Analysis*, 82 HARV. L. REV. 1294 (1969). In the case of "private" schools or tuition grant schemes that can be shown to be designed simply to evade the command of *Brown*, the courts might go a good deal farther. *See* Black, *supra* note 6, at 24.

segregation and its vestiges irrelevant. Events in the South during the difficult fall of 1970 have demonstrated that we are still a long way from effective disestablishment. Perhaps Professor Bickel is bored with the problem, but it is still very much with us, and the line of decisions following *Brown* will continue to be applied in the South long after the executive branch has found it politically expedient to abandon the victims of racial segregation. Some day, we may hope, this horrible scar will be healed and the school desegregation decisions will be cited and applied less often. Even then, however, to call them "irrelevant" is extraordinarily callous and reflects a thorough lack of historical understanding. The post-1937 cases permitting federal social and economic legislation — for which the Professor has nothing but kind words — are now taken for granted and all controversy has been drained out of them; but does that render them "obsolescent"?

Bickel is no more convincing when he attacks the Warren Court's voting decisions. He finds the rule of these cases wanting because it fails to respond to two issues posed by the coming Brandeisian age. The first of the issues is that of proper districting, of gerrymandering: "Given that districts are to be equal, the question is, what is a proper constituency, a proper district?"[101] The second concerns the allocation of voting power within federated administrative jurisdictions such as school districts and metropolitan governments. The voting decisions, says Bickel, are irrelevant to successful resolution of the first and will frustrate solution of the second.[102]

Let us begin with irrelevance. Bickel argues, as usual, that the drawing of district lines is a highly complex and unruly problem of pluralist politics. District boundaries are drawn and can be evaluated only in terms of which minority groups gain power and which lose power thereby. The Court's past emphasis on equality in voting, Bickel says, is of no use in dealing with this distinctly pluralist, group-oriented question. It is true, of course, that one man, one vote does not provide an automatic answer to the district boundary problem. But the basic ideal underlying the reapportionment cases is by no means irrelevant. That ideal, as has been mentioned, is equality of political opportunity: every citizen should have a roughly equivalent opportunity of access to the formal levers of political power.[103] The difficulty, of course, is devising an administrable rule whereby this ideal may be applied to the gerrymandering problem. One far-reaching solution would be to require a system of proportional representation. Such a sys-

---

[101] IDEA OF PROGRESS 151.

[102] *Id.* at 151–73.

[103] *See* p. 793 *supra*; note 79 *supra*.

tem would seem to serve best Professor Bickel's concern with group representation.[104] For no legislative body can catalogue the citizenry into interest groups as well as the citizens can themselves, and no malapportionment program of the sort Bickel advocates can as effectively translate the size of highly fluid interest groups into the proper degree of actual representation as a system that adjusts a group's representation to the support it actually receives in particular elections. Believers in pluralism such as Bickel, however, are rarely willing to carry their logic that far; in fact, they seem to value the supposed stability of the two-party system above their professed enthusiasm for group representation.

Yet even short of required proportional representation, some judicial controls could be imposed on gerrymandering that would serve the pluralists' concerns. The rule of thumb would be largely negative. It would prohibit the most egregiously unfair forms of districting by demanding at the very least that only neutral criteria, such as existing jurisdictional or natural boundaries, be employed.[105] An exception might be allowed for non-neutral boundaries which can be demonstrated to be plainly "benign" such as boundaries providing some representation for a minority group that would otherwise be submerged entirely.[106] I do not pretend that this approach would fully ensure fair districting or full equality of political opportunity. It is capable of principled application, however, and would allow conscientious officials to go farther toward better solutions. The important point, at any rate, is that the voting decisions do not draw a complete blank when applied to the problem.

Just as Bickel is too quick to dismiss any connection between the reapportionment cases and the district boundary problem, he too hastily assumes that a slippery doctrinal slope will frustrate experiments in federated local government. Whether school decentralization is achieved or not, he says, a federated central ad-

---

[104] For an excellent discussion of the pluralist theory of representation and its implications, see Auerbach, *The Reapportionment Cases: One Person, One Vote — One Vote, One Value*, 1964 SUP. CT. REV. 1 (1964).

[105] The Court's most recent reapportionment decisions may prove a barrier to this approach and, if so, should be reconsidered. *See* Wells v. Rockefeller, 394 U.S. 542 (1969); Kirkpatrick v. Preisler, 394 U.S. 526 (1969). Ironically, these decisions — the only ones which seem to bear out Bickel's thesis — came down too late to be included in his book. I am certainly not advocating any significant retreat from the one man, one vote principle. I suggest only that when apportionment disparities are very, very small — say, less than 5% — the state be required to follow "neutral" boundaries of established, historic governmental jurisdictions as much as possible. It will probably remain necessary to cut across such lines to some extent to reduce disparities to this de minimis point.

[106] *See Developments in the Law — Equal Protection*, 82 HARV. L. REV. 1065, 1104–20 (1969). In one case, the Supreme Court has reviewed a boundary line

ministrative board would be desirable. He goes on to argue that the formation of such a board would be "politically infeasible" unless it were malapportioned — giving each neighborhood school district equal representation despite unequal population. Similarly, he argues that metropolitan government of city and suburbs would be "politically infeasible" unless malapportioned, so that neither the city nor the suburbs had permanent majority control.[107] We have reached a strange state of affairs when a spokesman for the scholarly tradition judges constitutional principles according to the "political feasibility" of achieving certain desired results in compliance with them. Nevertheless, it is not divinely ordained that the one man, one vote rule must inexorably apply to such federated administrative bodies. If Professor Bickel can see the desirability of encouraging such developments, so can the Justices. The Court has already made a somewhat cryptic exception, as Bickel recognizes, for "administrative" bodies; but it is an exception which he feels to be unprincipled. There may be, however, a real, judicially cognizable difference between "administrative" and "governing" bodies; the characterization should be a functional one depending on the range of decisions assigned to the official organ.[108] The federated boards which Bickel foresees would presumably have very restricted — primarily money-collection and distribution — responsibilities if decentralized autonomy is to be preserved. Under that condition, the Court might well allow an exception to the one man, one vote rule. In a better world, Professor Bickel might even help in defining the extent of such an exception rather than confine himself to purely destructive criticism.

The attack on the Warren Court's greatest work in *The Supreme Court and the Idea of Progress* has been termed a "block-

---

allegedly drawn in order to ensure Negro representation in Congress. The Court declined to invalidate the boundary, finding insufficient evidence of purely racial motivation. Wright v. Rockefeller, 376 U.S. 52 (1964). The benignity of the boundary was not argued before the Court, and the decision in no way forecloses such an argument.

[107] IDEA OF PROGRESS 170–72.

[108] *See* Avery v. Midland County, 390 U.S. 474 (1968); Dusch v. Davis, 387 U.S. 112 (1967); Sailors v. Bd. of Educ., 387 U.S. 105 (1967). In the most recent of these decisions, the Court said:

> The *Sailors* and *Dusch* cases demonstrate that the Constitution and this Court are not roadblocks in the path of innovation, experiment, and development among units of local government. We will not bar what Professor Wood has called "the emergence of a new ideology and structure of public bodies, equipped with new capacities and motivations" . . . Our decision today is only that the Constitution imposes one ground rule for the development of arrangements of local government: a requirement that units with general governmental powers over an entire geographic area not be apportioned among single-member districts of substantially unequal population.

390 U.S. at 485–86.

buster."[109] Something a good deal less enthusiastic would be more appropriate. At most, the attack on the school desegregation and reapportionment decisions illustrates the flaws in a technique of criticism which always reads a decision for the most or least it might conceivably mean in order to denigrate the Justices' efforts. Spokesmen for the scholarly tradition such as Professors Bickel and Kurland seem to believe that they are engaged in a zero-sum game: if the Warren Court is admitted to have had any virtue, the house of cards built by the progressive realists, along with its recent additions, will collapse into the dust. If the issue is joined on such polarized terms, I believe that it is the Warren Court that must emerge the victor.

Bickel's "blockbusting" attack also illustrates another hidden truth about the scholarly tradition. Shifting ground from "goodness" to "success," he aspires to a neutral, scientific viewpoint; he seeks to demonstrate that the clash between himself and the Warren Court is not one of conflicting value choices, but of fundamental method. Perhaps to some extent it is. However, we may stop to wonder why Bickel chose only to attack the school desegregation and reapportionment cases on the ground of impending obsolescence, while ignoring the one body of decisions which most clearly are at odds with a discernible trend of opinion and events: the criminal procedure cases. He quite clearly provides the answer earlier in the book where he notes his satisfaction with those decisions.[110] Yet if neutrally defined success, and not goodness, were truly at the heart of his creed, he would have to condemn them too. Instead, Bickel manifests interest only in those trends of public opinion of which he personally approves. It is useful, then, to pierce the veil of the scholarly tradition and to see its quarrel with the Warren Court for what it really is. It is, I believe, a fundamental dispute over the good society as well as over judicial method. And Professor Bickel — his protestations of rational skepticism notwithstanding — is quite prepared to assert certain values as paramount. If that is what really is at the core of the current criticism, it should be brought more completely into the open. If the debate is over the true meaning and scope of particular constitutional protections, we should get on with it and avoid for a time the back roads and alleyways of theoretical methodology.

VI

Let it not be forgotten: it was Professor Bickel who brought

[109] This was the characterization of a Harvard Law School professor exhorting his students to attend Professor Bickel's lectures.

[110] IDEA OF PROGRESS 93.

up the subject of "irrelevance" and "obsolescence." His rather audacious commentary on the Warren Court invites an examination of the relevance and vitality of his own mode of judicial criticism. To put it another way: How is the general approach of Professor Bickel and his colleagues in the scholarly tradition likely to relate to the concerns of the new generation of lawyers?

I speak of an identifiable new generation of lawyers because I believe that one of the greatest legacies of the Warren Court has been its revolutionary influence on the thinking of law students. The students of the 1960's were educated in a new "tradition," albeit an incipient one and perhaps only a brief, shining moment. Most of their teachers had first come to see and understand the Court and the Constitution during the New Deal years — an experience which could only serve to corroborate the positions taken by the progressive realists. Thus they generally sought to school their students of the 1960's in a mode of criticism surely appropriate to the Old Court, but of doubtful relevance to the Warren Court. The students could not help but feel the tension since, for them, the Supreme Court *was* the Warren Court. For them, there was no theoretical gulf between the law and morality; and, for them, the Court was the one institution in the society that seemed to be speaking most consistently the language of idealism which we all recited in grade school. Just as they had not lived through the Stalin era and so could not accept the conventional wisdom of the Cold War, so their coming to consciousness in the 1960's left them unscarred by worries of Court packing and judicial obstructionism. Instead, they were inspired by the dignity and moral courage of a man and an institution that was prepared to act on the ideals to which America is theoretically and rhetorically dedicated.

Like Professor Bickel, the new generation of lawyers — the new professors as well as judges and practitioners, I might add — hope that the Supreme Court might resist a coup d'etat. But they see no point in querulous admonitions that the Court should restrain itself from combatting injustice now in order to preserve itself to combat a coup later on. An institution that sits back, always emphasizing its weakness and its reasons for inaction, is unlikely to be in a fighting stance when the tanks roll down Pennsylvania Avenue. The young lawyers know that a country which hoards all of its moral capital in the form of windy rhetoric is likely to die rich — and soon.

Those of us well over thirty may grumble about naiveté and tell ourselves that experience will make the young lawyers more cynical, more cautious, more protective of fragile institutions and tolerant of diversity. Those are the values of the tradition we grew up in. But if it is true that men and women form very basic attitudes, presumptions, and cognitive frameworks in their late 'teens and early twenties, then no amount of experience will substantially dull the inspiration of the 1960's. The students of this decade will never come to value the "unruliness of affairs" for its own sake; for them, there is little charm in an interminable discussion of the complexity and subtlety of life and of how resistant it is to rational solution. They have seen that affairs can be ordered in conformance to constitutional ideals and that injustice — to which *they* are prepared to give powerful meaning — can be routed. They have seen that it can be done: the Warren Court did it and the heavens did not fall.

3

Politics and the Constitution: Is Money Speech?

As an aftermath of the revelations about campaign financing in the Watergate episode, Congress enacted a series of laws designed to curb the power of money in elections. Limits were placed on campaign contributions and campaign expenditures. The law was promptly challenged as an infringement of the first amendment's freedom of speech provision. In 1976, in Buckley v. Valeo, *the Supreme Court invalidated some of the more important statutory provisions. Judge Wright's views that he had expressed when the case was before the Court of Appeals were overruled. Wright responded by taking his case to the academic community with this article.*

Noting that "money is the mother's milk of politics," Judge Wright simply would not agree that the expenditure of money should be equated with speech and thus brought within the ambit of the first amendment. For the Supreme Court to say in effect that money is speech is, to Wright, a misconception of the first amendment. Drawing on the political philosopher Alexander Meiklejohn for support, his view was well expressed in the opinion for the Court of Appeals: "These latest efforts on the part of our government to cleanse its democratic processes should at least be given a chance to prove themselves. Certainly they should not be rejected because they might have some incidental, not clearly defined, effect on first amendment freedoms. To do so might be Aesopian in the sense of the dog losing the bone going after the deceptively larger reflection in the water."

This essay is a clear illustration of Judge Wright's deep knowledge of the political process. And it further indicates his ability to cut through abstractions, such as the first amendment, and perceive what really is at stake in the reforms that Congress enacted. Finally, the article is Wright's first direct criticism of the Supreme Court. In forthright language, he points out where he believes the High Bench went wrong. That in itself is an example, all too rare, of a judge on a lower court daring to disagree with the Supreme Court. He does so courteously but firmly. Judge Wright knows that the professoriate—they who read articles in legal periodicals—themselves have a perhaps subtle but nonetheless important role in the formulation of law through judicial decisions. Hence this article.

Lawyers are often surprised to learn that Alexander Meiklejohn, whose name is so often invoked in epic battles over the meaning of the First Amendment, was not a lawyer. He was a philosopher and educator of the first rank. Perhaps this background positioned him to discern, as he did with unique clarity, the central meaning of freedom of speech under our Constitution. In all events it made him especially sensitive to the Supreme Court's role as teacher to the nation. "[T]he court," he wrote,

> holds a unique place in the cultivating of our national intelligence. Other institutions may be more direct in their teaching influence. But no other institution is more deeply decisive in its effect upon our understanding of ourselves and our government.[1]

In this spirit I wish to examine this Term's most important First Amendment decision, *Buckley v. Valeo*.[2] For I am concerned lest the Court's teaching in that case distort our understanding of ourselves and our government.

I. *Buckley v. Valeo*: Campaign Financing and the First Amendment

Under review in the *Buckley* case was the complex law passed in 1974 to reform the way we finance our federal election campaigns.[3] I

---

1. A. MEIKLEJOHN, POLITICAL FREEDOM: THE CONSTITUTIONAL POWERS OF THE PEOPLE 32 (1960).
2. 424 U.S. 1 (1976).
3. Federal Election Campaign Act Amendments of 1974, Pub. L. No. 93-443, [1974] U.S. CODE CONG. & AD. NEWS 1436 (amending Federal Election Campaign Act of 1971, Pub. L. No. 92-225, 86 Stat. 3) [hereinafter cited without cross-reference as 1974 Act].

focus here on only one part of that reform—the limits placed on campaign contributions and campaign expenditures.[4] Congress imposed rather strict ceilings on contributions to candidates for federal office in order to prevent large contributors from, in effect, buying favorable governmental decisions. Individuals cannot give more than $1,000 to a candidate per election,[5] nor can they give more than $25,000 overall.[6]

Congress also imposed restrictions on campaign expenditures. It limited to $1,000 the independent expenditures an individual or organization could make in support of a "clearly identified" candidate.[7] The term "independent expenditures" means expenditures undertaken without the cooperation or control of the candidate.[8] It was Congress's judgment that large independent outlays might circumvent the contribution limitations and themselves result in a form of political bribery.[9] Congress also placed certain higher limits on how deeply a candidate could dig into his own pocket to finance his campaign.[10]

Sections 101-302 of the 1974 Act dealt with private financing of federal election campaigns. Sections 403-408 made changes in the scheme of public financing of presidential elections. Further amendments were made in 1976. Federal Election Campaign Act Amendments of 1976, Pub. L. No. 94-283, [1976] U.S. Code Cong. & Ad. News (90 Stat. 475) [hereinafter cited without cross-reference as 1976 Act].

4. There were three other major portions of the 1974 law. One portion set new requirements for recordkeeping and disclosure on the part of candidates, their committees, and those individuals who make independent expenditures advocating the election or defeat of identified candidates. 2 U.S.C. §§ 431-437b (Supp. IV 1974) (modified 1976). Another provided for the public financing of both presidential primary and general elections and of party nominating conventions. I.R.C. §§ 9001-9042 (amended 1976). A third part established a Federal Elections Commission to oversee the administration of the law. 2 U.S.C. §§ 437c-438 (Supp. IV 1974) (modified 1976).

The Supreme Court upheld the disclosure requirements and the public financing provisions, but it ruled that the appointment of some of the members of the Commission by congressional leaders violated the separation-of-powers principle of U.S. Const. art. II, § 2, cl. 2, which authorizes the President to appoint "Officers of the United States." 424 U.S. at 84, 108, 140. This defect was remedied by the 1976 Act § 101(a)(1), 2 U.S.C.A. § 437c(a)(1) (Sept. 1976 Pamphlet).

5. 18 U.S.C. § 608(b)(1) (Supp. IV 1974) (modified 1976; to be recodified at 2 U.S.C. § 441a).

6. 18 U.S.C. § 608(b)(3) (Supp. IV 1974) (modified 1976; to be recodified at 2 U.S.C. § 441a). Contributions by political committees were also restricted under the 1974 law. 18 U.S.C. § 608(b)(2) (Supp. IV 1974) (modified 1976; to be recodified at 2 U.S.C. § 441a) (limiting political committees, as defined therein and in 18 U.S.C. § 591(d) (Supp. IV 1974), to a contribution ceiling of $5,000 per candidate per election).

7. 18 U.S.C. § 608(e) (Supp IV 1974) (repealed 1976).

8. Expenditures "authorized or requested by the candidate, an authorized committee of the candidate, or an agent of the candidate," *id.* § 608(c)(2)(B)(ii) (modified 1976; to be recodified at 2 U.S.C. § 441a), were regarded as expenditures by the candidate, 18 U.S.C. § 608(c)(2)(A), (B)(ii) (Supp. IV 1974) (modified 1976; to be recodified at 2 U.S.C. § 441a), and as contributions by the individual or group that made the actual expenditure. 424 U.S. at 46-47 & n.53.

9. *See* S. Rep. No. 93-689, 93d Cong., 2d Sess. 18-19, *reprinted in* [1974] U.S. Code Cong. & Ad. News 5587, 5604-05.

10. In campaigns during a calendar year, a candidate for federal office could not make use of his personal funds or those of his immediate family in excess of the follow-

And finally, Congress enacted overall ceilings on the total amount a candidate and his committees could spend in advancing his candidacy.[11]

Congress passed these provisions in response to political abuses which culminated in the 1972 presidential campaign and its aftermath, commonly called Watergate.[12] Congress found that these excesses were fueled by money collected for political purposes.[13] There can be no question that under the Constitution Congress properly assumed responsibility for combating federal election abuses. Repeatedly the courts have recognized that Congress maintains a strong, vital interest in protecting the political process from distortion and corruption.[14]

Congress, of course, knew there were difficult First Amendment questions involved in limiting campaign contributions and expendi-

ing limits: $50,000 for presidential and vice presidential candidates; $35,000 for senatorial candidates; and $25,000 for candidates for United States Representative. 18 U.S.C. § 608(a) (Supp. IV 1974) (repealed 1976). If the individual were a candidate for United States Representative from a state that is only entitled to one Representative, the relevant limit was $35,000. *Id.* § 608(a)(1)(B) (repealed 1976).

11. The expenditure limits were $10 million for a candidate for the presidential nomination of a political party and $20 million for a candidate for election to the office of President. *Id.* § 608(c)(1) (repealed 1976). Expenditures on behalf of a candidate nominated by a political party for the office of Vice President of the United States were counted toward the $20 million limit for the presidential candidate. *Id.* § 608(c)(2)(A) (repealed 1976). The total expenditure limits for candidates to other federal offices generally varied with the size of the voting age population of the relevant jurisdiction. *Id.* § 608(c)(1)(C)-(F) (repealed 1976). Expenditure limits were to be adjusted yearly to reflect rising prices. *Id.* § 608(d) (repealed 1976).

The 1976 amendments removed all the major contribution and expenditure provisions from Title 18 and placed them, in slightly modified form, in Title 2 of the United States Code. 1976 Act §§ 112, 201. In response to the Supreme Court's *Buckley* decision, however, Congress did make one major modification in these provisions. The expenditure ceilings, which the Court declared unconstitutional, were omitted from 2 U.S.C.A. § 441a (Sept. 1976 Pamphlet), the section that replaces 18 U.S.C. § 608 (Supp. IV 1974)—with one significant exception that corresponds to a curious wrinkle in the *Buckley* decision.

Without even discussing possible problems under the doctrine of unconstitutional conditions, *see generally* Van Alstyne, *The Demise of the Right-Privilege Distinction in Constitutional Law,* 81 HARV. L. REV. 1439 (1968), the Supreme Court left standing the requirement in the 1974 Act § 404(a), 408(c), I.R.C. §§ 9004, 9035 (amended 1976), that presidential candidates who voluntarily accept public funding must agree to abide by the ceilings on total campaign outlays. 424 U.S. at 108-09. These voluntary expenditure ceilings continue under the 1976 Act § 112, 2 U.S.C.A. § 441a(b) (Sept. 1976 Pamphlet), and have been broadened to require that presidential candidates accepting public funding agree to limit spending from personal funds to $50,000 in both the primary campaign and the general election. 18 U.S.C. §§ 301(a), 305(a) (Supp. IV 1974) (to be codified at I.R.C. §§ 9004, 9035).

12. For a detailed account of these abuses, see, *e.g.,* FINAL REPORT OF THE SENATE SELECT COMM. ON PRESIDENTIAL CAMPAIGN ACTIVITIES OF THE U.S. SENATE, S. REP. NO. 93-981, 93d Cong., 2d Sess. (1974) [hereinafter cited as FINAL REPORT]. A comprehensive "Bibliography of Watergate Source Materials" may be found in WATERGATE SPECIAL PROSECUTION FORCE, REPORT 265-73 (1975).

13. *See, e.g.,* FINAL REPORT, *supra* note 12, at 212.

14. *See, e.g.,* United States v. Classic, 313 U.S. 299, 317-20 (1941); Burroughs v. United States, 290 U.S. 534, 545 (1934); *Ex parte* Yarbrough, 110 U.S. 651, 657-67 (1884).

tures.[15] Money does facilitate communication of political preferences and prejudices. It is also clear that money influences the outcome of elections. Generally speaking, the more money spent in behalf of a candidate, the better the candidate's chances of winning. Indeed, a veteran of political campaigns has declared that money is the mother's milk of politics.[16]

But the real questions are these: To what extent does this kind of mother's milk poison the political process? To what extent does it distort the truth-seeking process that lies at the heart of the First Amendment conception?[17] And most importantly, what may the people, acting through Congress, do about it?

The Supreme Court answered these questions by saying that Congress, in passing the campaign reform law, tried to do too much. The Justices left the statute's contribution limits in place, but they struck down all the spending ceilings—on independent expenditures in behalf of a candidate, on personal funds spent by a candidate in his own campaign, and on total outlays by the candidate. Asserting that today "virtually every means" for effectively communicating ideas requires the expenditure of money,[18] the Court found that these provisions placed substantial, direct restrictions on the ability of individuals to engage in protected political expression.[19] The Court concluded that, unlike the contribution limitations, the expenditure ceilings failed sufficiently to serve the governmental interest in preventing corruption;[20] therefore, the burden they placed on "core First Amendment expression" was unconstitutional.[21]

15. *See, e.g.*, FINAL REPORT, *supra* note 12, at 571.

16. TIME, Jan. 5, 1968, at 44 (statement of Jesse Unruh, former Speaker of the California Assembly, now California State Treasurer).

17. The First Amendment conception of which I speak is perhaps best stated by Justice Holmes, dissenting in Abrams v. United States, 250 U.S. 616, 630 (1919):

> [W]hen men have realized that time has upset many fighting faiths, they may come to believe even more than they believe the very foundations of their own conduct that the ultimate good desired is better reached by free trade in ideas—that the best test of truth is the power of the thought to get itself accepted in the competition of the market, and that truth is the only ground upon which their wishes safely can be carried out. That at any rate is the theory of our Constitution. It is an experiment, as all life is an experiment.

18. 424 U.S. at 19.

19. *Id.* at 58-59.

20. Proponents of the expenditure limitations had argued that the ceilings also served to equalize the abilities of individuals and groups to influence the outcome of elections and the abilities of candidates to bring their messages before the public. The Court rejected these objectives as constitutionally illegitimate and unlikely to be achieved by the expenditure limitations. *Id.* at 48-49, 54, 56-57.

21. *Id.* at 47-51, 53-54, 55-59. The Court was also careful to note that the Act had to be tested against the First Amendment's guarantee of freedom of association. *See, e.g., id.* at 15, 22-23, 24-29. The only extended discussion of this First Amendment right, however, appears in the Court's discussion of contribution limitations. *Id.* at 24-29. The

I take issue with the Court's answers, but not primarily because of the result reached in this particular case. Rather, I am deeply concerned with the lesson the Court taught in the course of reaching its result. Throughout its discussion of contributions and expenditures, the Court persisted in treating the regulation of campaign monies as tantamount to the regulation of political expression. The Court told us, in effect, that money is speech.

This, in my view, misconceives the First Amendment. It accepts far too narrow a conception of political dynamics in our society. It accepts without question elaborate mass media campaigns that have made political communication expensive, but at the same time remote, disembodied, occasionally even manipulative. Nothing in the First Amendment prevents us, as a political community, from making certain modest but important changes in the kind of process we want for selecting our political leaders. Nothing bars us from choosing, as I am convinced the 1974 legislation did choose, to move closer to the kind of community process that lies at the heart of the First Amendment conception—a process wherein ideas and candidates prevail because of their inherent worth, not because prestigious or wealthy people line up in favor, and not because one side puts on the more elaborate show of support. Nothing in the First Amendment bars us from those steps, for nothing in the First Amendment commits us to the dogma that money is speech.

II. Money As Speech: The Legal Argument

A. *The Court's Precedents*

No one disputes that the money regulated by the campaign reform legislation is closely related to political expression. And no one disputes that the First Amendment applies with special force to the political arena.[22] The legal question is thus not whether the restrictions on giving and spending are subject to First Amendment scrutiny at all. The question is what degree of scrutiny should apply. There are basically two choices[23]—and I am painting here with a very broad brush. The first is to treat campaign contributions and expenditures

right of free association played only a limited role in the Court's consideration of the three types of expenditure ceilings and in its decision to strike them down. *Id.* at 22-23. The dispositive factor was the Court's view that expenditure ceilings abridge the right of free expression. *See id.* at 39, 47-51, 52-53, 55, 58-59.

22. *See, e.g.*, Monitor Patriot Co. v. Roy, 401 U.S. 265, 272 (1971); Mills v. Alabama, 384 U.S. 214, 218-19 (1966); Garrison v. Louisiana, 379 U.S. 64, 74-75 (1964).

23. *See* 424 U.S. at 15.

as equivalent to pure speech. If this approach is proper, then the giving and spending restrictions enacted in 1974 should be treated in the same way as laws imposing a prior restraint on speech or censoring particular points of view. Such laws are subject to the most rigorous scrutiny known to constitutional law, and rightly so.[24] Nothing distorts the truth-seeking process so much as prior restraint or government censorship. Even ideas utterly false serve the purpose of testing and strengthening views with a better claim to the truth.[25] For this reason only the most intensely compelling governmental interests can sustain such restrictions.

The second legal alternative is to treat political giving and spending as a form of conduct related to speech—something roughly equivalent to the physical act of picketing or to the use of a soundtruck.[26] Alert and careful judicial scrutiny is still warranted, for an ostensibly neutral regulation of conduct may merely disguise an attempt at silencing a particular viewpoint. Nevertheless, a carefully tailored regulation of the nonspeech element—the picketing or the soundtruck—can survive without being required to pass the rigorous test applied to restrictions on pure speech. The regulation is constitutional if it serves an important governmental interest and if that interest is unrelated to suppression of speech.[27]

When the campaign finance reform law came before the United States Court of Appeals for the District of Columbia Circuit—the court on which I serve—we found the second approach to be the proper one. We held[28] that political giving and spending were not pure speech, that they should be treated as speech-related conduct under principles announced in the leading case of *United States v. O'Brien*.[29] And we found the contribution and expenditure limits constitutional.[30] The

24. *See, e.g.*, New York Times Co. v. United States, 403 U.S. 713, 714 (1971); Organization for a Better Austin v. Keefe, 402 U.S. 415, 419 (1971); Freedman v. Maryland, 380 U.S. 51, 57 (1965); Bantam Books, Inc. v. Sullivan, 372 U.S. 58, 70 (1963); Thomas v. Collins, 323 U.S. 516, 530 (1945); Near v. Minnesota, 283 U.S. 697, 713-16 (1931). *See generally* Emerson, *The Doctrine of Prior Restraint*, 20 LAW & CONTEMP. PROB. 648 (1955).

25. *See* J. S. MILL, *Essay on Liberty, in* ON LIBERTY AND CONSIDERATIONS ON REPRESENTATIVE GOVERNMENT 1, 15-21 (B. Blackwell ed. 1946); Bagehot, *The Metaphysical Basis of Toleration*, in 2 THE WORKS OF WALTER BAGEHOT 339, 343, 350 (F. Morgan ed. 1891).

26. *See, e.g.*, Grayned v. City of Rockford, 408 U.S. 104 (1972); Cameron v. Johnson, 390 U.S. 611 (1968); Adderley v. Florida, 385 U.S. 39 (1966); Cox v. Louisiana, 379 U.S. 559 (1965); Kovacs v. Cooper, 336 U.S. 77 (1949). *See generally* Schneider v. State, 308 U.S. 147, 160 (1939).

27. *See* United States v. O'Brien, 391 U.S. 367, 376-77 (1968).

28. Buckley v. Valeo, 519 F.2d 821, 840-41 (D.C. Cir. 1975), *aff'd in part and rev'd in part*, 424 U.S. 1 (1976).

29. 391 U.S. 367 (1968).

30. 519 F.2d at 843-44, 851-60.

law, we thought, was carefully tailored to serve the government's undeniably important interest in purifying elections.[31]

In the *O'Brien* case the Supreme Court approved the conviction of a war protester under a statute that banned the burning of draft cards. O'Brien claimed that in publicly burning his draft card he was merely exercising his right to free expression against the Vietnam War. But the Court held that his act was not pure speech; that an important governmental interest was served by preservation of draft cards; and that his expression-related conduct in burning the draft card was subject to the restrictions Congress had enacted.[32]

O'Brien used the burning of his draft card as a vehicle for expressing his political convictions. So too the use of money in political campaigns serves as nothing more than a vehicle for political expression. It may not have the same overt physical quality that burning a draft card or picketing at the statehouse has, but it remains a mere vehicle. Restrictions on the use of money should be judged by the tests employed for vehicles—for speech-related conduct—and not by the tests developed for pure speech. Our court therefore held that campaign giving and spending, like draft-card burning, were speech-related conduct.

The Supreme Court disagreed. "The expenditure of money," it wrote,

> simply cannot be equated with such conduct as destruction of a draft card. Some forms of communication made possible by the giving and spending of money involve speech alone, some involve conduct primarily, and some involve a combination of the two. Yet this Court has never suggested that the dependence of a communication on the expenditure of money operates itself to introduce a nonspeech element or to reduce the exacting scrutiny required by the First Amendment.[33]

I am bound to say that this passage performs a judicial sleight of hand. The real question in the case was: Can the use of *money* be regulated, by analogy to conduct such as draft-card burning, where there is an undoubted incidental effect on *speech*? However, what the Court asked was whether *pure speech* can be regulated where there is some incidental effect on *money*. Naturally the answer to the Court's question was "No." But this left untouched the real question in the

31. *See id.* at 842-44. The Supreme Court has emphasized the importance of the governmental interest in maintaining federal elections free from corruption. *See, e.g.,* Burroughs v. United States, 290 U.S. 534, 545 (1934); *Ex parte* Yarbrough, 110 U.S. 651, 666-67 (1884).

32. 391 U.S. at 382.

33. 424 U.S. at 16.

case. The Court riveted its attention on what the money could buy—be it communication, or communication mixed with conduct. Yet the campaign reform law did not dictate what could be bought. It focused exclusively on the giving and spending itself.[34] In short, the Court turned the congressional telescope around and looked through the wrong end.

Perhaps I can clarify the difference by an example. Suppose a state enacts a law banning all political advertisements in newspapers during the week preceding an election. Such a law targets the communication itself. It should be subject to rigorous scrutiny. And it should be struck down.[35] If the state attorney general were to argue that the law is justified on the ground that there is a nonspeech element present, simply because somebody has to spend money to place a political advertisement, he would of course lose.

But such a statute is not comparable to the campaign finance law at issue in *Buckley*. The 1974 law targeted the money itself, utterly divorced from the kind of communication—or other campaign services —the money would buy. Congress was not trying to justify suppression of pure speech by seizing on money as a nonspeech element. It was trying to justify a straightforward regulation of the excessive use of money as a blight on the political process. Like draft-card burning, however speech-related, this was a vice Congress had authority to control.[36]

34. Justice White was able to see the distinction clearly. *Id.* at 259-64 (White, J., dissenting in relevant part).

35. *Cf.* Mills v. Alabama, 384 U.S. 214 (1966) (Alabama statute banning publication on election day of editorial supporting candidate violates First Amendment).

36. After rejecting *O'Brien's* applicability to the *Buckley* case on the ground that campaign contributions and expenditures are speech, not conduct, the Supreme Court went on to contend that even if they were speech-related conduct, their regulation by the 1974 law was unconstitutional under *O'Brien*. 424 U.S. at 17. *O'Brien* required that a regulation of speech-related conduct not be aimed at "the suppression of free expression." 391 U.S. at 377. The *Buckley* Court held that the 1974 law was aimed at suppressing communication because Congress meant it, in part, to reduce the quantity of speech on the part of wealthy individuals and interest groups. 424 U.S. at 17.

This rather mechanical application of the *O'Brien* test is unsatisfactory. Congress meant the statute to reduce the quantity of *spending* on the part of wealthy individuals and candidates, but it was unconcerned with the type or quantity of *speech* that might result when people operated within the new limits. More importantly, the "suppressing communication" test is concerned primarily with statutes that are aimed at suppressing a particular viewpoint—statutes which discriminate on the basis of content. *O'Brien* itself makes this interpretation clear. In explaining the test, the *O'Brien* Court took as its example the case of Stromberg v. California, 283 U.S. 359 (1931). 391 U.S. at 382. The California statute in *Stromberg* ostensibly regulated conduct—the use, in certain circumstances, of "any flag, badge, banner, or device," 283 U.S. at 361—but it did not do so evenhandedly. It denied the use of any flag or device to those who intended thereby to demonstrate their "opposition to organized government." *Id.* Demonstrators not opposing organized government could use any flag or banner they wished. *See id.* at 369-70.

Let me approach the question from another angle. The main evil against which rigorous First Amendment scrutiny is designed to guard is content discrimination—discrimination based on the message itself. As the Supreme Court held in unmistakable terms in 1972:

> [A]bove all else, the First Amendment means that government has no power to restrict expression because of its message, its ideas, its subject matter, or its content. . . . [O]ur people are guaranteed the right to express any thought, free from government censorship. The essence of this forbidden censorship is content control.[37]

There has been no showing that the 1974 ceilings on contributions and expenditures discriminate against certain viewpoints.[38] In fact, one could argue that money limitations, if properly drafted and administered, are uniquely manageable as content-neutral controls on political abuses.[39]

Let me reiterate, however, one important qualification. I am not saying that Congress has a free hand so long as it targets money. There

Statutes of this type are invalid because they use the regulation of conduct as a subterfuge for suppressing a certain message. *O'Brien* condemns statutes which are, *in this sense,* aimed at suppressing communication. *See* 391 U.S. at 382. The 1974 law thus did not run afoul of *O'Brien.* As the *Buckley* Court itself recognized, the campaign reform statute did "not focus on the ideas expressed" by those subject to its limits. 424 U.S. at 17. It was content-neutral and, properly understood, did not aim at suppressing communication.

37. Police Dep't v. Mosley, 408 U.S. 92, 95-96 (1972). For a recent discussion of content discrimination, see Karst, *Equality as a Central Principle in the First Amendment,* 43 U. CHI. L. REV. 20 (1975). *See also* T. EMERSON, THE SYSTEM OF FREEDOM OF EXPRESSION 633-34 (1970).

38. The plaintiffs in *Buckley* argued that candidates who challenge incumbents are uniquely burdened by the contribution and expenditure limits. Brief of the Plaintiffs at 149-61, 175-83, Buckley v. Valeo, 519 F.2d 821 (D.C. Cir. 1975). Even if true, this is not quite the same as discrimination based on content of ideas; not all challengers, by any means, represent one particular viewpoint. In any event, the evidence of such a burden is far from conclusive. *See* 424 U.S. at 33-34 (no such showing in record relative to contribution limits of $1,000). *But see id.* at 31 n.33 (suggesting possibility of more serious problem when contribution limits are combined with 1974 Act's limitations on expenditures by groups and individuals, on candidate's use of personal and family resources, and on overall campaign expenditures, but not resolving question).

39. The capacity for abuse is directly related to the size of the contribution or expenditure. Thus ceilings operate in a straightforward manner to curb the capacity for abuse; they are tailored rather precisely to the problem Congress sought to remedy. At the same time, all candidates—popular and unpopular, majority and minority—use money in roughly the same way. It is, to say the least, not immediately apparent how ceilings—so long as they apply evenly across the board—could be designed so as to cast a disproportionate burden on minority or disfavored points of view. Money restrictions, therefore, contrast sharply with laws which seem evenhanded but which in reality make things especially hard for the weak and unpopular—for example, laws banning leafletting, laws curtailing speaking in public places, or indeed, to borrow Anatole France's classic example, laws prohibiting rich and poor alike from sleeping under bridges. A. FRANCE, THE RED LILY 91 (W. Stephens trans. 1894). *See* Kalven, *The Concept of the Public Forum: Cox v. Louisiana,* 1965 SUP. CT. REV. 1, 30.

are delicate links between political giving and spending, on the one hand, and political speech, on the other. Every regulatory scheme concerning campaign finances requires careful judicial review to make sure that Congress maintains a close relation between the important ends sought and the precise means chosen. Some measures may be more clearly justified than others. For example, a far more compelling case can be made for contribution limitations than for the overall candidate spending ceilings, since the former are more closely tied to the paramount goal of preventing political corruption.[40] Thus, I am not suggesting that courts, when faced with regulations like these, be less than vigilant. But the sensitive judicial task is not aided by a blunderbuss formula that equates money and speech.[41]

40. This of course was not the only goal of the 1974 law. In some contexts other goals were equally compelling. For example, as Mr. Justice Marshall eloquently demonstrates in his partial dissent, the limits on spending by a candidate from his personal funds, 18 U.S.C. § 608(a) (Supp. IV 1974) (repealed 1976), were tailored to serve the nation's vital interest in "promoting the reality and appearance of equal access to the political arena," 424 U.S. at 287-90. I agree fully with Mr. Justice Marshall that § 608(a)'s limits should have been conceived as limits on the *contribution* a candidate may make to his own campaign, *id.* at 286-87, and therefore are justified on much the same grounds as those the Court found persuasive with respect to the general contribution limits.

As I shall discuss more fully below, another important objective of the campaign financing reform was to stimulate more direct, personal forms of political speech. Indeed, that those nearing their contribution limits could still engage in more direct communications efforts was an important factor in the Court's decision to uphold the contribution ceilings. I pause here only to ask why that same logic could not have been taken one small step further, with the result that the ceiling on independent expenditures would also have been recognized as constitutional.

The Court upheld the contribution limits because, the opinion explains, those limits constitute only a "*marginal restriction* upon the contributor's ability to engage in free communication." *Id.* at 20-21 (emphasis added). This is so because people who would otherwise give amounts greater than the statutory limits are hardly bottled up once they reach the ceiling. Many avenues of communication remain open to them since, the Court states, they can "expend such funds on *direct political expression.*" *Id.* at 21-22 (emphasis added). In other words, the spender could buy the newspaper ad or TV commercial or handbills directly, instead of giving the money to the candidate for the candidate to choose how to spend it. If he avoided collaboration with the candidate, his spending in this fashion would not count as a contribution. *Id.* at 46-47 & n.53. There would be no limits on his spending to advocate the candidate's election, because the Court struck down the limits on independent expenditures.

But exactly parallel reasoning should have led the Court to sustain the limits on independent expenditures. Properly viewed, those limits constitute nothing but a "marginal restriction." They do nothing but push the spender a little closer still to "direct political expression." Under the statutory provisions for ceilings on independent expenditures, one who has spent his limit—and $1,000 is a generous limit—hardly has his free expression bottled up. Nothing prevents him from devoting future efforts to volunteer activity, door-to-door canvassing, or organizing meetings. And what is this if it is not *direct political expression*? It may not be the form of political expression which the Supreme Court had in mind—expensive things like TV commercials and newspaper ads. But it is no less a real outlet for political expression simply because it is *more* direct.

41. The *Buckley* defendants also contended that the money restrictions were valid under a line of cases permitting government regulation of the time, place, and manner of speaking. *See, e.g.,* Adderley v. Florida, 385 U.S. 39 (1966); Cox v. Louisiana, 379 U.S. 559 (1965); Kovacs v. Cooper, 336 U.S. 77 (1949). The Court rejected this argument.

B. *The Court's Premise*

The premise apparently underlying the Court's treatment of money restrictions as restraints on free expression was that "in today's mass society" the use of money is essential for "effective political speech."[42] But does the First Amendment condemn us to accept helplessly all the implications of the so-called "mass society"? Must we adopt the mass society's definitions of effectiveness? I think not.

Consider this: A half-minute spot commercial can reach into thousands of homes, although with a cursory message. This is the essence of effectiveness in the mass society. And it costs money—lots of it. A lesser amount of money, however, might suffice to purchase the paid staff and supplies necessary to sustain a small army of volunteer canvassers,[43] perhaps enough to reach all the same homes on a meaningful, personal basis.

Which is truly more effective, the spot commercial or the volunteer activity? It depends on whose standards one uses: those implicit in the

424 U.S. at 17-18. The logic of the Court's position, however, is not immediately apparent, for the 1974 law does, on its face, look like a regulation of the manner of speech. The statute says, in effect, speak in a frugal rather than lavish manner.

But the Court did not see the limits in this way: "The critical difference between this case and those time, place, and manner cases is that the present Act's contribution and expenditure limitations impose *direct quantity restrictions* on political communication and association . . . ." *Id.* at 18 (emphasis added). The Court went on in a footnote to emphasize the difference it perceived between the campaign law's money limits and the decibel limits imposed on a soundtruck operator and upheld in *Kovacs*: "The decibel restriction upheld in *Kovacs* limited the *manner* of operating a soundtruck, but not the *extent* of its proper use." *Id.* at 18-19 n.17 (emphasis in original).

The Court, in other words, erected a new distinction between statutes that regulate manner of speech and those that may be said to regulate quantity of speech. Statutes of the former type are permissible; statutes of the latter type are, at a minimum, subject to the most stringent scrutiny.

But the distinction simply does not bear up under analysis. The time, place, and manner cases dealt with restrictions that can just as easily be read as quantity restrictions. In *Kovacs,* for example, the soundtruck operator was surely faced with a quantity restriction. Operating at an unrestricted decibel level, he might have been able to reach all the citizens of his target area by, say, driving down every third street. Operating within the ordinance at a lower volume might have required driving down every street. The quantity of his speech, if one chooses to view it in that fashion, has been reduced by two-thirds. He can reach only a third of the people he could otherwise reach in a given amount of time. Regulations of time and place of expression can generally be seen as working similar quantity restrictions. The Court's rationale for distinguishing the time, place, and manner cases is unconvincing.

42. 424 U.S. at 19.

43. The 1974 law is structured so as to provide added inducements for volunteer activity. An individual who devotes his time without pay is not required to place a monetary value on that time in order to count it against any contribution or independent expenditure ceiling. In other words, a person can volunteer his time without limit. 18 U.S.C. § 591(e) (5)(A) (Supp. IV 1974). Moreover, the first $500 of expenses incidental to such volunteer activity is also exempt from the ceilings. *Id.* § 591(e)(5)(B)-(D), (f)(4)(D), (f)(4)(E). The Court expressly approved these inducements, noting "Congress' valid interest in encouraging citizen participation in political campaigns." 424 U.S. at 36-37.

mass society, or those implicit in the First Amendment. It is certainly possible to argue that the volunteer, face-to-face communication is more effective in a sense highly relevant to the First Amendment: it promotes real interchange among citizens concerning the issues and candidates about which they must make a choice.

The Supreme Court seemed to recognize that "effective political speech" is a multi-dimensional concept. It depends, the Court suggested, on "the number of issues discussed, the depth of their exploration, and the size of the audience reached."[44] Viewed in this light, the effectiveness of political speakers is not necessarily diminished by reasonable contribution and expenditure ceilings. The giving and spending restrictions may cause candidates and other individuals to rely more on less expensive means of communication. But there is no reason to believe that such a shift in means reduces the number of issues discussed in a campaign. And, by forcing candidates to put more emphasis on local organizing or leafletting or door-to-door canvassing[45] and less on full-page ads and television spot commercials, the restrictions may well generate deeper exploration of the issues raised. Finally, even to the extent that smaller audiences result from diminished use of the most expensive and pervasive media—and the campaigning so far gives no substantial indication that this happens—the effectiveness of a given speaker does not decline in relation to that of his opponents. All similarly situated competitors face the same constraints. Within those limits effectiveness still depends on the creativity of the speaker —and on the soundness of his ideas.

44. 424 U.S. at 19 (footnote omitted).

45. Because these activities require a large amount of volunteer effort, some commentators have suggested that contribution and expenditure ceilings discriminate unfairly in favor of those who have a lot of free time. *See, e.g.*, Winter, *Money, Politics and the First Amendment*, in H. PENNIMAN & R. WINTER, CAMPAIGN FINANCES: TWO VIEWS OF THE POLITICAL AND CONSTITUTIONAL IMPLICATIONS 57-58 (1971). This strikes me as a particularly weak claim of discrimination.

In a system dominated by contributions of money, rather than of free time, all but the fabulously wealthy must make hard choices about how they will apply limited financial resources. For most people, making a large contribution means foregoing or postponing something else—an expensive vacation, perhaps, or a new car. In a system where contributions of free time are more important, people are still faced with choices about the application of a limited resource, a temporal resource. A person *can*, if the candidate's success is important enough to him, forego or postpone or rearrange business commitments or outside activities that consume time in order to volunteer for the campaign. I see no reason why the temporal choice should be considered inequitable when the financial choice is not.

If the concern is for those at the margin who really cannot squeeze out additional free time—those who must work long hours simply to provide food and shelter for their families—I would only observe that such people are hardly disadvantaged by contribution and expenditure ceilings. They surely are not the ones whose political spending is cut short by the 1974 law.

If there is a problem latent in expenditure ceilings, it stems not from any disparities in effectiveness among rival campaigns, but from the fact that there are, of course, no dollar limitations on nonpolitical speech. If campaign money ceilings were so low that political speech really were in danger of being drowned out by commercial or other apolitical speech, then those ceilings might well be unconstitutional. But no one has claimed, and no one could credibly claim, that the reasonable ceilings enacted in 1974 pose such a threat.[46] There will be time enough to remedy the problem if at some point the political dialogue truly becomes submerged.[47] In the meantime, we would do well to focus our concern on the danger that certain individual candidates will find *their* speech drowned out by well-heeled opponents who can vastly outdistance them in the spending race—exactly the danger that the overall expenditure limits were meant to minimize.

III. Money As Speech: The Pluralist Underpinnings

Though the equation of money and speech is supported by neither the precedents nor the premise relied on by the Court, the notion may well derive from a more basic source. If so, it is important that we explore it. We can, I believe, identify this source by analyzing carefully the position of the *Buckley* plaintiffs, the opponents of the 1974 law, in order to discern the image .of the political process that underlay their opposition to limitations on giving and spending. The image they embraced makes it natural to conclude that money is speech, but I think we shall see that it differs significantly from the image of the political process the First Amendment bids us to accept.

In their brief before the court of appeals, the plaintiffs argued strongly that money is essential to effectiveness in the political contest.[48] Again and again they asserted their central theme:

> It is . . . too crabbed a notion of the political process to restrain people from demonstrating the intensity of their convictions on particular issues. Indeed, it is hard to see how a democratic nation can have a stable government if it does not permit intensity of feeling as well as numbers of adherents to be reflected in the

46. *See, e.g.,* 424 U.S. at 21-22 (no such problem in connection with contribution limits of $1,000).

47. The Court has shown its readiness to act when reductions in degree result in differences in kind. *Compare* Kusper v. Pontikes, 414 U.S. 51, 59-61 (1973) *with* Rosario v. Rockefeller, 410 U.S. 752 (1973). *See* 424 U.S. at 30.

48. Brief of the Plaintiffs, *supra* note 38, at 102.

> political process. . . . Campaign contributions represent a means by which intensity can be shown . . . .
>
> Of course, those who contribute money to a candidate hope to further their political, social and economic views. . . .[49]

Now it is true that a government which hopes to maintain stability must preserve for its citizens some means of demonstrating intensity of feeling. The plaintiffs, however, evidently interpret intensity not from the standpoint of the potential contributor, but from the standpoint of the candidate or official who is the target of the intensity. I say this because it is brutally obvious that the size of a contribution provides a hopelessly inadequate measure of intensity as felt by the giver. Consider the wealthy man who regularly contributes $5,000 to a particular incumbent, simply to keep open his channels of communication. Compare him to the student who scrapes together $100 for a candidate in whom she passionately believes. Intensity is all with the student, but if one looks only at the dollar totals, this fact is completely obscured. The contribution ceiling in the 1974 law in no way prevents the student from demonstrating her genuine intensity of feeling.

Thus, when the plaintiffs complain that a $1,000 contribution limit thwarts the expression of intensity, they must be viewing intensity from the standpoint of the recipient—the candidate. *He* certainly will feel the heat more intensely from a $5,000 contributor than from a $100 contributor, whatever the subjective feelings of the two contributors themselves. And, the plaintiffs argue, the First Amendment requires that Congress not impede contributors from making candidates feel this kind of intensity.

Consider, then, the picture the plaintiffs' brief paints for us of the way political decisions are made. Campaign monies should be unrestricted because they are a means by which people intensify the pressure to get governmental decisions to come out their way. There is competition among various viewpoints, and candidates and others who want to see certain governmental policies adopted roll up their sleeves and plunge into the competition with all the resources at their command. The prospect of large contributions may, for example, influence a legislator to vote a particular way. Or sizeable media expenditures may swing an important electoral race through advanced techniques of salesmanship. People band together and pool their funds

49. *Id.* at 105. Obviously the plaintiffs' observation is not limited to contributions; it extends to expenditures as well: "[T]hose making the expenditures seek to communicate with the public to promote views they think should become governmental policy or for persons whom they believe will, as public officials, share those views." *Id.* at 100.

in order to bring pressure on the decisionmakers or to elect different decisionmakers in their place. The key to effectiveness is not the soundness of the program advocated, or even the number of voters who support the program, but rather the intensity of the pressure imposed.

This picture of the political process that emerges from the plaintiffs' arguments corresponds closely to a picture familiar to political science as the special interest or pluralist model.[50] This correspondence should not be surprising, even though it has received relatively little attention. Pluralist thinking has dominated political science for years,[51] and it traces its roots to Tocqueville,[52] and even back to Madison's celebrated *Federalist No. 10*.[53] The pluralist view is a powerful conception, and it explains much about how our government works. I do not demean its value when I say nonetheless that it has certain shortcomings. Let me set forth the pluralist outlook in its strongest form, so that we may clearly see the problems.

To the pluralist, the political process consists precisely of the pull-

50. Some writers have made even more explicit the pluralist underpinnings of their attack on campaign finance reform laws. *See, e.g.*, Sterling, *Public Financing of Campaigns: Equality Against Freedom*, 62 A.B.A.J. 197, 200 (1976); Sterling, *Control of Campaign Spending: The Reformers' Paradox*, 59 A.B.A.J. 1148, 1153 (1973). *See also* Fleishman, *Freedom of Speech and Equality of Political Opportunity: The Constitutionality of the Federal Election Campaign Act of 1971*, 51 N.C. L. REV. 389, 462 (1973) ("The fact that people vote with dollars as well as ballots is to be celebrated in a democracy rather than bemoaned.") Compare the unrestrained enthusiasm of one early writer, quoted prominently, with minor, inadvertent alterations, in an important pluralist textbook, W. BINKLEY & M. MOOS, A GRAMMAR OF AMERICAN POLITICS: THE NATIONAL GOVERNMENT 2 (3d ed. 1958):

> [M]en and women who touch practical politics . . . know that men and women now may have as many votes in government as they have interests for which they are willing to sacrifice time and thought and money. . . .
>
> . . . .
>
> . . . . The ruling classes are those who use their craft societies, medical associations, farm bureaus, labor unions, bankers' associations, women's leagues and the like to influence government. Of course, it takes time and intelligence and a little money, but not much. For fifty dollars a year [membership dues] the average family ought to be able to buy half a dozen powerful votes in government, each vote ten times as powerful as the vote guaranteed by the Constitution.

W. WHITE, POLITICS: THE CITIZEN'S BUSINESS 15, 16-17 (1924).

For a dramatically contrasting view, albeit one with serious problems of implementation and limitation, see Nicholson, *Campaign Financing and Equal Protection*, 26 STAN. L. REV. 815, 821, 825-36, 853-54 (1974) (giving of large contributions is form of multiple voting invalid under "one person, one vote" doctrine; courts could, regardless of statutory limits, hold unconstitutional any financing system permitting large contributions).

51. *See, e.g.*, A. BENTLEY, THE PROCESS OF GOVERNMENT (1908); R. DAHL, A PREFACE TO DEMOCRATIC THEORY (1956); R. DAHL, WHO GOVERNS? (1961); E. HERRING, GROUP REPRESENTATION BEFORE CONGRESS (1929); E. LATHAM, THE GROUP BASIS OF POLITICS (1952); C. LINDBLOM, THE INTELLIGENCE OF DEMOCRACY (1965); A. ROSE, THE POWER STRUCTURE (1967); D. TRUMAN, THE GOVERNMENTAL PROCESS (2d ed. 1971).

52. *See* A. DE TOCQUEVILLE, DEMOCRACY IN AMERICA 174-80 (J. Mayer & M. Lerner eds. 1966).

53. THE FEDERALIST No. 10, at 57 (J. Cooke ed. 1961). *See* D. TRUMAN, *supra* note 51, at 4-7. *But see* note 72 *infra*.

ing and hauling of various competing interest groups. Organized groups, not individuals, constitute the only relevant political units.[54] They rise and decline, coalesce and fragment, confront countervailing groups and aid complementary groups. Through lobbying, publicity, campaign contributions, independent expenditures, and other methods —all of which cost money—they bring pressures to bear which ultimately determine the outcome of governmental decisions. They thereby achieve a form of "functional representation," based upon intersecting economic and social groupings, which cuts across our usual conception of political representation based upon "one person—one vote."[55]

The pluralist model tends to be a highly mechanistic conception. The clash of competing groups comes to be seen as the only factor of importance in politics. Force collides with counterforce, pressure meets counterpressure, and the strongest force or the most intense pressure determines the outcome of the governmental process. Some pluralist writers even talk wistfully about the possibility of reducing the political process to a mathematical chart. If only our techniques were sophisticated enough, they suggest, groups pursuing interests could all be measured and then graphed as vectors. And trends in public policy could then be predicted because they automatically conform to the resultant, the mathematical sum of all the private vectors.[56]

Other pluralists go so far as to equate this resultant vector with the "public interest." The very term, they imply, has no meaning apart from the outcome of the pressure group process. Individual assertions as to where the public interest lies are all inherently suspect. Only the group process can be relied upon as "the practical test of what constitutes the public interest."[57]

By this pluralist line of reasoning, the First Amendment's highest function is to let group pressure run its course unimpeded,[58] lest we skew the process that determines for us the public interest. Giving and spending money are important ways for groups to bring pressure—to magnify intensity—and thereby to make the process work. Restrictions on giving and spending can be nothing but unwarranted impediments

54. *See, e.g.*, A. BENTLEY, *supra* note 51, at 208; E. HERRING, *supra* note 51, at 5-6. *See generally* Hale, *The Cosmology of Arthur F. Bentley*, in THE BIAS OF PLURALISM 35-50 (W. Connolly ed. 1969).

55. *See generally* E. HERRING, *supra* note 51, at 8-12.

56. W. BINKLEY & M. MOOS, *supra* note 50, at 6 (quoting Childs, *Pressure Groups and Propaganda*, in THE AMERICAN POLITICAL SCENE 205, 225 (E. Logan ed. 1936)).

57. W. BINKLEY & M. MOOS, *supra* note 50, at 7. *See* Stoke, *The Paradox of Representative Government*, in ESSAYS IN POLITICAL SCIENCE 77, 80-83 (J. Mathews & J. Hart eds. 1937); Wilson, *The Pragmatic Electorate*, 24 AMER. POL. SCI. REV. 16, 33 (1930).

58. *See* Brief of the Plaintiffs, *supra* note 38, at 101-02.

in the path of the process. It follows, in the pluralist view, that all such restrictions are unconstitutional.

Such is the theory. But time has eroded at least the more exuberant forms of pluralist thinking. Recent years have seen scores of books and articles questioning the theory's assumptions or its application.[59] Two major critiques deserve emphasis.

First, pluralists countenance a system which gives undeserved weight to highly organized and wealthy groups.[60] For the pluralist, this imbalance is a virtue to be embraced, not a flaw to be redressed. Under an unrestrained pluralist system, a clustering of people with common interests, even if it is a majority, cannot prevail if it is without organization and without significant funds.[61] And of course we know of instances in our current system where the popular will is thus thwarted —where public opinion polls tell us that a majority prefers a certain policy, and yet that majority seems unable to carry out its wishes against the opposition of a highly organized, narrowly based group able to spend its money freely. Gun control provides an obvious example.[62]

A number of encouraging reform efforts of recent years may be seen as attempts to rectify this systemic imbalance.[63] The public interest law movement, for example, often sees itself as a means for giving diffuse but significant groups a more effective voice.[64] The flowering of so-called citizens' or public interest lobbies is part of the same development. And the campaign reform legislation reviewed in the *Buckley* case can also be seen in this light. In a sense, it *is* an attempt to expand participation in the pluralist pulling and hauling. The

59. For a sampling of the most penetrating critiques of the pluralist viewpoint, see H. KARIEL, THE DECLINE OF AMERICAN PLURALISM (1961); T. LOWI, THE END OF LIBERALISM (1969); G. MCCONNELL, PRIVATE POWER AND AMERICAN DEMOCRACY (1966); Connolly, *The Challenge to Pluralist Theory,* in THE BIAS OF PLURALISM, *supra* note 54, at 3. *See also* S. LAZARUS, THE GENTEEL POPULISTS 167-89 (1964).

60. I have pursued this line of criticism elsewhere in a somewhat different context. Wright, *Professor Bickel, The Scholarly Tradition, and the Supreme Court,* 84 HARV. L. REV. 769, 789 (1971).

61. *See* Note, *The New Public Interest Lawyers,* 79 YALE L.J. 1069, 1070-71 n.3 (1970). Indeed, some critics argue forcefully that the system may prevent such diffuse groups even from achieving effective articulation of their grievances. Their grievances will be seen not as potential issues for the public but merely as troubles afflicting private individuals. *See* Connolly, *supra* note 59, at 14.

62. *See* N.Y. Times, June 5, 1975, at 20, col. 4 (67% of those polled favored registration of all firearms; results consistent with surveys over three decades showing steady support for such gun control legislation); M. HINDELANG, C. DUNN, A. AUMICK & L. SUTTON, SOURCEBOOK OF CRIMINAL JUSTICE STATISTICS—1974 183-88 (1975) (summaries of polls showing similar strong support for gun control and detailing response to particular gun control proposals).

63. *See* S. LAZARUS, *supra* note 59, at 267-74.

64. *See* Note, *supra* note 61, at 1070-71 n.3.

well-organized are deprived of certain financial advantages. The decisionmakers are then better able to respond to the interests of the under-organized, free from imperative obligations to special interest money-providers.

There is a second and more basic critique of the pluralists' view. Their mechanistic conception tends to drain politics of its moral and intellectual content.[65] Rather than seeing the political process as a battle of ideas, informed by values—as the means by which the citizens apply their intelligence to the making of hard public choices[66]—pluralists tend to view politics as a mere clash of forces, a battle of competing intensities, a universe of vectors.

Forces can be measured by science; resultant vectors can be computed by mathematics. Alexander Meiklejohn diagnosed the shortcomings of this kind of thinking with his usual penetrating insight. He wrote:

> In the understanding of a free society, scientific thinking has an essential part to play. But it is a secondary part. We shall not understand the Constitution of the United States if we think of men only as pushed around by forces. We must see them also as governing themselves.[67]

The First Amendment sees people in this way. Although our political practice may often fall woefully short, the First Amendment is founded on a certain model of how self-governing people—both citizens and their representatives—make their decisions.[68] It is a model that restores considerations of justice and morality to the political process—considerations absent from the pluralist approach.[69]

Self-governing people do not simply let the organized groups of the day play out their battle of influence and then vote the way of the prevailing forces. They are more responsible, more independent than that. Instead, they see the group process as a way of calling forth the various positions. They listen to all—the weak and timid voice of the under-organized as well as the sometimes bombastic, sometimes so-

65. *See* T. Lowi, *supra* note 59, at 46-54, 57-58, 68-72, 155-56, 281-82.

66. *See* A. Meiklejohn, *supra* note 1, at 75, 109.

67. *Id.* at 12-13. Meiklejohn has made explicit his critique of pluralist thinking elsewhere. *Id.* at 162-63. *See also id.* at 73-75.

68. *See generally* Whitney v. California, 274 U.S. 357, 375-78 (1927) (Brandeis, J., concurring), *overruled,* Brandenburg v. Ohio, 395 U.S. 444 (1969); Abrams v. United States, 250 U.S. 616, 630 (1919) (Holmes, J., dissenting). "The purpose of constitutional protection of speech is to foster peaceful interchange of all manner of thoughts, information, and ideas. Its policy is rooted in faith in the force of reason." Kunz v. New York, 340 U.S. 290, 302 (1951) (Jackson, J., dissenting).

69. *See* T. Lowi, *supra* note 59, at 289-91.

phisticated, but always elaborate communication of the affluent highly-organized. They do their best to filter out the decibels so that they may penetrate to the merits of the arguments. They retire and consider the positions. And then they choose the course which seems wisest. It may be the course of the noisy or the course of the quiet. At times it may be the course advocated by an apparent minority. But it is a course chosen on the merits.

Thus, what the pluralist rhetoric obscures is that *ideas,* and not intensities, form the heart of the expression which the First Amendment is designed to protect.[70] Money may register intensities, in one limited sense of the word, but money by itself communicates no ideas. Money, in other words, may be related to speech, but *money itself is not speech.* Courts ought to judge restrictions on giving and spending accordingly.

The 1974 campaign reform law moves us closer, even if but a small distance, toward the idealized First Amendment model of self-government sketched out above. Herein lies the key to the statute's importance. Here is why, far from stifling First Amendment values, it actually promotes them. The ceilings on giving and spending take from wealthy citizens, candidates, and organizations only certain limited political advantages totally unrelated to the merits of their arguments—advantages which all too frequently *obscure* the merits of the arguments. In place of unlimited spending, the law encourages all to emphasize less expensive face-to-face communications efforts,[71] exactly the kinds of activities that promote real dialogue on the merits and leave much less room for manipulation and avoidance of the issues.

I can hear the pluralists' rejoinder. You are deeply unrealistic, they might charge. You swallow an 18th-century idealized vision of a process and ignore the play of organized groups and private interests. And indeed if they are right that the "public interest" is nothing more than the outcome of the group process, then we should release our

70. *Cf.* Freund, *Commentary,* in A. ROSENTHAL, FEDERAL REGULATION OF CAMPAIGN FINANCE: SOME CONSTITUTIONAL QUESTIONS 72, 74 (Citizens' Research Found. 1972):

> The right to speak is, I submit, more central to the values envisaged by the First Amendment than the right to spend. We are dealing here not so much with the right of personal expression or even association, but with dollars and decibels. And just as the volume of sound may be limited by law, so the volume of dollars may be limited, without violating the First Amendment.
>
> ....
>
> ....[Large contributors] are operating vicariously through the power of their purse, rather than through the power of their ideas, and again I would scale that relatively lower in the hierarchy of First Amendment values.

71. *See* note 43 *supra.*

grasp on the First Amendment ideal and let the pulling and hauling proceed without hindrance.

But we need not accept the pluralists' proposition. We simply are not so helpless that we must blindly equate the outcome of the group pressure process with the public interest.[72] To return to our gun control example, it is certainly possible to assert—indeed, the case is compelling—that the pluralist process has thwarted the public interest for years.

Realism consists in acknowledging the group process and allowing for it. Group activity is an essential and desirable part of the American system, and indeed the First Amendment recognizes this: it protects the right of assembly and the right of association. But it is simply not true that the play of influence, of competing intensities, is *all there is* to politics. The play of ideas, the sifting of good ideas from bad, of truth from falsehood, of justice from injustice—all these are essential parts of our system as well. One cannot deny this without denying the very essence of the First Amendment. One cannot deny this without letting realism descend to cynicism.

The Framers were not so cynically realistic when they established our form of government. Had they been, we might not have had a First Amendment. A government dedicated to liberty was more a

72. For a thorough development of this point, see Barry, *The Public Interest,* in THE BIAS OF PLURALISM, *supra* note 54, at 159.

Some of the pluralist writers who have equated the public interest with the outcome of the group process are listed in note 57 *supra.* Even so perceptive a pluralist writer as Robert Dahl, although he avoids the simple equation of the earlier writers, joins with other pluralists in concluding, based on his relentlessly empirical approach, that the concept "public interest" is fundamentally meaningless. *See* R. DAHL, A PREFACE TO DEMOCRATIC THEORY, 25-27, 69 n.5 (1956). *Cf.* D. TRUMAN, *supra* note 51, at 50-51 (a totally "inclusive interest" within a nation does not exist).

Dahl elaborates these views in the course of analyzing Madison's famous definition of "faction," which is set forth in *The Federalist No. 10.* Madison's essay is often regarded as a precursor of pluralist thinking, but the passage containing the definition makes it clear that Madison did not regard the "public interest" concept as meaningless, nor did he regard the essentially moral quest for its attainment as an unworthy or futile enterprise. Moreover, the passage suggests—and the full essay makes clear—that he considered interest group competition as an evil to be rendered tolerable, not as a democratic safeguard to be embraced:

> By a faction I understand a number of citizens, whether amounting to a majority or minority of the whole, who are united and actuated by some common impulse of passion, or of interest, *adverse to the rights of other citizens, or to the permanent and aggregate interests of the community.*

THE FEDERALIST No. 10, at 57 (J. Cooke ed. 1961) (emphasis added).

Lowi demonstrates that the moral dimension of Madison's definition is often lost when pluralists invoke Madison as a spiritual forebear. David Truman, he points out, quotes the definitional passage but leaves off the crucial italicized clause, thereby removing from "faction" the pejorative connotation Madison intended and incidentally obscuring Madison's moral concern. T. LOWI, *supra* note 59, at 296 (discussing D. TRUMAN, *supra* at 4).

visionary than a realistic enterprise in those days. The world had scarcely known such a creature. But the Framers persevered. And the power of that vision of self-government which they wrote into the Constitution and the Bill of Rights has earned the respect even of realists. As Meiklejohn put it: "[T]he adoption of the principle of self-government . . . set loose upon us and upon the world at large an idea which is still transforming men's conceptions of what they are and how they may best be governed."[73] "No institution," Charles Black has written, "can be as perfect, in men or work, as its ideal model, [but] the very mark of the truly living institution is that it has an ideal model which is always there nudging its elbow."[74] The 1974 law, in its own modest way, escalated the nudge to a gentle shove.[75] If we are realistic, and not cynical, we will hold fast to such fragments of progress toward the ideal the Framers held out to us.

73. Meiklejohn, *The First Amendment is an Absolute,* 1961 SUP. CT. REV. 245, 264.

74. C. BLACK, THE PEOPLE AND THE COURT 50 (1960).

75. The court of appeals opinion in the *Buckley* case came to a close on a similar note:

> [T]hese latest efforts on the part of our government to cleanse its democratic processes should at least be given a chance to prove themselves. Certainly they should not be rejected because they might have some incidental, not clearly defined, effect on First Amendment freedoms. To do so might be Aesopian in the sense of the dog losing his bone going after its deceptively larger reflection in the water.

519 F.2d at 897-98.

4

Money and the Pollution of Politics: Is the First Amendment an Obstacle to Political Equality?

In this article Judge Wright carries the argument of Chapter 3 a giant step further. He criticizes the Supreme Court in the strongest terms, calling its decisions in Buckley v. Valeo *(1976) and* First National Bank of Boston v. Bellotti *(1978) "tragically misguided." To Wright, the power of concentrated wealth, now constitutionalized by the Supreme Court in those two first amendment decisions, badly distorts political campaigns and referenda. This means that the "voices of individual citizens are being drowned out in election campaigns." The net result, Wright maintains, is that the constitutional principle of one person, one vote is fast becoming a "hollow mockery."*

This chapter, thus, is Judge Wright's strongest condemnation of a trend in Supreme Court decision making that he has published to date. It is a reflection of his deep belief in the democratic process and particularly in the principle of equality. He knows quite well that those with money have disproportionate power in the electoral process, and he believes that Congressional attempts to dilute that power should be sustained under the Constitution. The impact of concentrated wealth in politics threatens the democratic process itself and "the very essence of political equality." The irony is that, as Wright says, the American democratic system is being undermined in the name of the liberties protected by the first amendment. He catches the spirit of the Constitution in these stirring words: "Our democracy has moved a long way from the town hall, one man, one vote conception of the Framers. Politics has become a growth industry and a way of life for millions of Americans. The corrosive influence of money blights our democratic processes. We have not been sufficiently vigilant; we have failed to remind ourselves, as we moved from town halls to today's quadrennial Romanesque political extravagances, that politics is neither an end in itself nor a means of subverting the will of the people."

That is the language of a committed democrat (with a small "d"), a man who is the product of and whose personal philosophy largely reflects the populism of the Progressive Age. It is illustrative, furthermore, of Judge Wright's deep faith in the essential goodness of the people and in their capacity to make wise political decisions once the channels of political communication are cleansed and kept open. Hence his dismay, as shown in this article, at what he considers to be the Supreme Court myopic refusal to perceive the obvious.

In the name of the very first amendment in our Bill of Rights, the present Supreme Court has put serious obstacles in the path of our society's advancement toward political equality through law. In two vitally important and, in my judgment, tragically misguided first amendment decisions, *Buckley v. Valeo*[1] and *First National Bank of Boston v. Bellotti*,[2] the Court has given protection to the polluting effect of money in election campaigns. As a result, our political system may not use some of its most powerful defenses against electoral inequalities. Concentrated wealth, often channeled through political action committees, threatens to distort political campaigns and referenda. The voices of individual citizens are being drowned out in election campaigns—the forum for the political deliberations of our people. If the ideal of equality is trampled there, the principle of "one person, one vote," the cornerstone of our democracy, becomes a hollow mockery.

Buckley and *Bellotti* create an artificial opposition between liberty and equality. The first amendment tradition of leading cases and scholarly writings shows that the ideals of political equality and individual participation are essential to a proper understanding of the first amendment. Campaign spending reform is imperative to serve the purposes of freedom of expression. Within the confines of *Buckley* and *Bellotti*, only limited reforms are permissible. More effective measures will be possible only if the Court reconsiders these unfortunate precedents.

I. Money and the Pollution of Politics

The corrosive effect of money on the political process is not new to this country or to the modern era,[3] but the problem of money in politics has taken

---

1. 424 U.S. 1 (1976).
2. 435 U.S. 765 (1978).
3. See L. Berg, H. Hahn & J. Schmidhauser, Corruption in the American Political System 14–21 (1976) (background of corruption in America); Leventhal, Courts and Political Thickets, 77 Colum. L. Rev. 345, 362–65 (1977) (history of corrupt practices legislation).

on a new urgency in the American politics of the 1980's. The development of communications technology and campaign techniques has made the political impact of money even more potent and the political consequences of meager financial resources even more devastating. Financial inequalities pose a pervasive and growing threat to the principle of "one person, one vote," and undermine the political proposition to which this nation is dedicated—that all men are created equal.

A. *The Legal Framework*

In the early 1970's, the Watergate scandals gave impetus to popular demand for strong measures to purify the political process,[4] culminating in 1974 with the passage of the Federal Election Campaign Act.[5] The legislation adopted contribution limits,[6] comprehensive spending limits,[7] and public financing of presidential campaigns.[8] It created a new federal agency[9] to enforce these laws and to supervise campaign finance reporting and disclo-

---

4. The Federal Election Campaign Act of 1971, Pub. L. No. 92-225, 86 Stat. 3 (1972) (codified as amended at 2 U.S.C. §§ 431-455 (1976 & Supp. IV 1980)) had required comprehensive disclosure of contributions to and expenditures by federal candidates. Id. §§ 301-311, 86 Stat. at 11-19. It also had imposed per-voter limits on media expenditures by candidates. Id. § 104, 86 Stat. at 5-7. These partial reform measures had failed to avert the Watergate abuses.

The Ervin committee was formed to investigate campaign finance practices and to propose reform measures. See Final Report of the Senate Select Committee on Presidential Campaign Activities of the United States Senate, S. Rep. No. 981, 93d Cong., 2d Sess. (1974). Extensive hearings were held in 1972 by three congressional committees. See Federal Election Reform: Hearings Before the Subcomm. on Elections of the House Comm. on House Administration, 93d Cong., 1st Sess. (1973); Federal Election Reform, 1973: Hearings before the Subcomm. on Privileges and Elections of the Senate Comm. on Rules and Administration, 93d Cong., 1st Sess. (1973); Federal Election Campaign Act of 1973: Hearings on S. 372 Before the Subcomm. on Communications of the Senate Comm. on Commerce, 93d Cong., 1st Sess. (1973).

5. Federal Election Campaign Act Amendments of 1974, Pub. L. No. 93-443, 88 Stat. 1263 (1974) (codified as amended at 2 U.S.C. §§ 431-455 (1976 & Supp. IV 1980)). The House committee report on the Act declared:

> The unchecked rise in campaign expenditures, coupled with the absence of limitations on contributions and expenditures, has increased the dependence of candidates on special interest groups and large contributors. Under the present law the impression persists that a candidate can buy an election by simply spending large sums in a campaign.

H.R. Rep. No. 1239, 93d Cong., 2d Sess. 3 (1974).

6. Congress placed limits on the annual amounts that any individual or committee could contribute to any candidate, in order to reduce the opportunity for corruption and undue influence and the appearance of corruption inherent in massive private campaign contributions. 18 U.S.C. §§ 608(b)(1)-(3) (Supp. IV 1974) (current version at 2 U.S.C. §§ 441a(a)(1)-(3) (1976)).

7. The Act limited the overall amount of campaign expenditures by each candidate, with differing ceilings for House, Senate, and presidential candidates. 18 U.S.C. § 608(c) (Supp. IV 1974) (repealed 1976). It also imposed a separate limit on the amount that a candidate could legally spend from personal or family resources. Id. § 608(a) (repealed 1976). To enforce the contribution and expenditure limits, the law placed a ceiling on the amount of independent expenditures that could be made by any person or committee on behalf of or against a specifically identified candidate for federal office. Id. § 608(e) (repealed 1976).

8. Congress adopted a system of partial public financing for primaries and conventions and complete public financing for the general election campaign. Id. §§ 403-408 (current version at 26 U.S.C. §§ 9001-9042 (1976)).

9. 2 U.S.C. § 437c (1976 & Supp. IV 1980) (powers of Federal Election Commission).

sure.[10] It did not, however, establish a system of public funding for House and Senate elections,[11] missing a golden opportunity, not since recaptured, to diminish the influence of money in congressional politics.

Because it did not reach congressional campaign financing, the 1974 Act did not go far enough. But in the 1976 decision of *Buckley v. Valeo*,[12] upholding parts of the 1974 Act but striking down other basic provisions, the Supreme Court decided that the legislation had gone too far. The Court accepted public financing of presidential elections[13] and held that Congress could constitutionally attach conditions—including spending limits—to the acceptance of those funds.[14] It also approved of the reporting and disclosure requirements for all federal candidates and committees,[15] and agreed that ceilings on campaign contributions were justified by the need to prevent corruption and the appearance of corruption.[16] The *Buckley* decision gutted vital portions of the legislation, however. Equating spending with speech,[17] the Court treated the first amendment as a near-absolute in the sphere of political debate.[18] It unequivocally struck down the Act's limits on overall campaign spending by a candidate who does not receive public financing, restrictions on independent expenditures in support of or against a candidate, and ceilings on candidate spending from personal or family funds.[19] The

---

10. The 1971 Act had established extensive reporting and disclosure requirements for candidates and committees, including periodic reports of the sources and amounts of contributions and expenditures. 86 Stat. 3, 11-19 (1972) (current version at 2 U.S.C. § 434 (Supp. IV 1980)).

11. On April 11, 1974, the Senate passed a bill providing for public financing of congressional election campaigns by a vote of 53-32. 120 Cong. Rec. 10,952 (1974); see S. Rep. No. 689, 93d Cong., 2d Sess. 4-15, reprinted in 1974 U.S. Code Cong. & Ad. News 5587, 5590-96 ("it is clear to us that contribution and expenditure limits which would check excessive influence of great wealth cannot be effectively and fairly implemented without a comprehensive system of public campaign financing").

The House, however, defeated a public financing proposal for congressional campaigns by a vote of 228-187. 120 Cong. Rec. 27,495-96 (1974). In conference, the measure was deleted from the Federal Election Campaign Act of 1974. H.R. Rep. No. 1438, 93d Cong., 2d Sess. 109-10, reprinted in 1974 U.S. Code Cong. & Ad. News 5618, 5685-86 (conference report).

12. 424 U.S. 1 (1976).

13. Id. at 85-109. The Court cited Congress's goals of reducing the deleterious influence of large contributions, facilitating communication by candidates with the electorate, and freeing candidates from the rigors of fundraising. Id. at 95-96. Six of the eight participating Justices fully joined in this holding. Justices Burger and Rehnquist dissented from this holding in whole or in part. Id. at 235 (Burger, C.J., concurring and dissenting in part), 290 (Rehnquist, J., concurring and dissenting in part).

14. Id. at 108-09.

15. Id. at 60-84.

16. Id. at 23-38. Six Justices agreed; Justices Burger and Blackmun dissented. Id. at 235 (Burger, C.J., concurring and dissenting in part), 290 (Blackmun, J., concurring and dissenting in part).

17. In a previous article, I examined the flaws in the Court's conclusion that money is speech. See Wright, Politics and the Constitution: Is Money Speech?, 85 Yale L.J. 1001 (1976).

18. My late colleague Harold Leventhal has pointed out the striking difference in approach between the Court's "pragmatic tone, experimental outlook, and fact-and-record oriented discussion" in the sections upholding Federal Election Campaign Act provisions and the absolutist perspective of the Court's discussion of the unconstitutionality of expenditure limits. Leventhal, supra note 3, at 358; see id. at 373 ("This sweeping pronouncement begs the question by a pejorative statement of the equality principle.").

19. 424 U.S. at 39-59.

Court in *Buckley* insisted that "the concept that government may restrict the speech [i.e., spending] of some elements of our society in order to enhance the relative voices of others is wholly foreign to the First Amendment."[20]

Justice White, who had practical experience in nationwide campaigning in 1960 as coordinator of John Kennedy's preconvention campaign in Colorado and then as head of National Citizens for Kennedy, was the sole member of the Court to disagree with the Court's holding that expenditure limits violate the first amendment.[21] He rejected the Court's contention that money is speech. Writing with an apparent touch of sarcasm, he observed, "[A]s it should be unnecessary to point out, money is not always equivalent to or used for speech, even in the context of political campaigns."[22] In his view, expenditure ceilings reinforced the contribution limits and helped "eradicate the hazard of corruption."[23] He took judicial notice that

> [t]here are many illegal ways of spending money to influence elections. One would be blind to history to deny that unlimited money tempts people to spend it on *whatever* money can buy to influence an election. On the assumption that financing illegal activities is low on the campaign organization's priority list, the expenditure limits could play a substantial role in preventing unethical practices. There just would not be enough of "that kind of money" to go around.[24]

Like the congressmen and senators—presumably more knowledgeable than most about corruption in politics—who passed the 1974 Act, and unlike the other Justices, Justice White recognized and understood the realities of political campaigns.

Two years after *Buckley*, the Court again repudiated the goal of political equality in *First National Bank of Boston v. Bellotti*.[25] Trying to prevent one-sided corporate messages from swamping referendum campaigns, Massachusetts had enacted a statute prohibiting corporate expenditures on statewide referendum issues not directly related to a corporation's business interests. The Supreme Court, however, struck down the statute, relying on *Buckley*'s facile equation of spending and speech, and insisting that there was no possibility of corruption in a referendum campaign.[26] The Court thereby effectively declared open season for the influence of concentrated wealth upon initiative and referendum campaigns.[27]

---

20. Id. at 48–49. This passage has been quoted by the Court in several subsequent cases. See infra note 138.

21. Id. at 257–66. Justice White would have accepted Congress's judgment that limitations on independent expenditures and overall candidate spending are necessary to "counter the corrosive effects of money in federal election campaigns," observing that Congress "undeniably included many seasoned professionals who have been deeply involved in elective processes and who have viewed them at close range over many years." Id. at 260–61.

22. Id. at 263.

23. Id. at 264.

24. Id. at 265.

25. 435 U.S. 765 (1978).

26. Id. at 784–92.

27. This term the Court reversed a decision by the Supreme Court of California that had upheld a Berkeley city ordinance forbidding more than $ 250 in contributions by any individual to

In my view, these two decisions—though they quote the landmarks of our first amendment heritage—enunciated principles that are, to borrow the words of the *Buckley* Court, "wholly foreign to the First Amendment."[28] The two decisions have also had a direct, significant, and pernicious impact on political campaigning in America.[29]

The federal campaign reform provisions that survived *Buckley v. Valeo* have worked well. The disclosure and reporting requirements allow citizens and the press to discover the sources of a candidate's financial backing.[30] Public financing of presidential campaigns has relieved candidates of much of the draining, demeaning, and obligation-creating task of begging for funds from large contributors. At the same time, the limits on spending by candidates who accept financing are sufficiently high to allow ample discussion of the issues.[31]

A similar program for congressional campaigns would also pass judicial muster, but so far, despite strenous efforts by reformers, Congress has been unwilling to extend public financing to House and Senate campaigns.[32] Money continues to infect House and Senate races, campaigns for state and local offices, and referendum and initiative voting. In these political contests,

---

a committee formed to support or oppose a ballot measure. Citizens Against Rent Control v. City of Berkeley, 102 S. Ct. 434 (1981), rev'g 27 Cal. 3d 819, 614 P.2d 742, 167 Cal. Rptr. 84 (1980). The decision by the United States Supreme Court relied on *Bellotti*'s premise that the problem of corruption cannot possibly arise in a popular vote on a public issue, and on *Buckley*'s insistence that government may not restrict the speech of some elements of our society in order to enhance the relative voices of others.

28. 424 U.S. at 48–49. See infra text accompanying notes 138–98 for a discussion of these cases from the perspective of first amendment theory and precedent.

29. That impact was recently reinforced in Common Cause v. Schmitt, 102 S. Ct. 1266 (1982). The Supreme Court, by a four-four vote, let stand a three-judge district court decision holding that the first amendment prohibits limits on independent expenditures for the benefit of any presidential candidate, even if he accepts federal funding. The 1974 Act still precludes a general election candidate who receives federal funding from accepting private contributions. 26 U.S.C. § 9003(b) (1976). But by allowing candidates to benefit from unlimited "independent" spending, the district court's decision, affirmed by the Supreme Court, thwarts Congress's attempt to assure major party presidential candidates equal financial resources in the general election. See Claude & Kirchhoff, The "Free Market" of Ideas, Independent Expenditures, and Influence, 57 N.D. L. Rev. 337, 364–65 (1981) (multimillion dollar war chests raised and spent by independent committees subvert intent of Congress and have potential for creating implicit obligations).

30. Arterton, The Federal Election Commission, *in* Campaign Finance Study Group, Institute of Politics, John F. Kennedy School of Government, Harvard University, An Analysis of the Impact of the Federal Election Campaign Act, 1972–78, at 1–24 to 1–25, 6–5 to 6–8 (1979) [hereinafter cited as Harvard Campaign Finance Study].

31. F. Wertheimer & R. Huwa, Campaign Finance Reforms: Past Accomplishments, Future Challenges 5 (unpublished paper presented at Colloquium on Election Law in the 80's, sponsored by New York University Review of Law and Social Policy, New York, Nov. 15, 1980).

32. In 1977 proposed legislation to establish a voluntary system of matching federal grants to House and Senate candidates was blocked by a filibuster in the Senate and by opposition in the House Administration Committee. In 1978, despite two attempts to attach the measure to related election law legislation, supporters of public financing of congressional campaigns were unable to obtain consideration of the bill on the floor of the House. Again in 1979, the legislation was blocked in the House when a bill covering House elections was rejected by the House Administration Committee by a vote of 8–17. See 5 Congressional Quarterly, Congress and the Nation, 1977–1980, at 943–47 (1981).

democracy is often shadowed by lopsided inequalities in campaign resources. The predominance of money comes at the expense of the ideals of liberty and equality that underlie our political system.

B. *Political Action Committees*

Political Action Committees (PAC's), perhaps the fastest-growing phenomenon in modern American politics, epitomize the contemporary threat to electoral integrity. The stark reality of PAC's is that they bring the power of concentrated wealth to bear on office-holders and candidates—national, state, and local—on behalf of special interests. Although only a small fraction of these groups promote particular ideologies or advocate single issues,[33] PAC's generally represent the interests of organizations, such as corporations, labor unions, and trade associations, that are forbidden by law to contribute or spend directly in federal campaigns.[34]

In recent years, PAC's—especially those connected with corporations and trade associations—have grown explosively in numbers and influence. Provisions in the 1974 Act facilitated their formation and operation.[35] In 1974 there were 89 corporate PAC's; now there are 1,327.[36] Between 1976

---

33. Only 11.2% of the PAC's that reported making contributions to federal candidates in the 1980 elections were unconnected with another organization; they contributed only 8.4% of the total dollar amount. Federal Election Commission press release (August 4, 1981).

34. Since 1907, federal law has prohibited the use of corporate treasury money in federal election campaigns. Act of January 26, 1907, ch. 420, 34 Stat. 864 (current version at 2 U.S.C. § 441b (1976 & Supp. IV 1980)). The same prohibition has applied to labor unions continuously since 1947. Labor Management Relations Act, ch. 120, tit. III, 61 Stat. 159 (1947) (current version at 2 U.S.C. § 441b (1976 & Supp. IV 1980)). The law did not prevent unions or corporations from persuading their members or stockholders to contribute to separate political funds segregated from the treasury. Labor unions therefore established an elaborate network of separate funds. See Pipefitters Local Union No. 562 v. United States, 407 U.S. 385, 402–09 (1972) (discussing history of the ban on union contributions and expenditures and establishment of CIO Political Action Committee).

35. In the past, corporations were less active than unions in operating separate political funds, but one major obstacle—a ban on political activity by government contractors—was repealed in 1974. 2 U.S.C. § 441c(b) (1976) (authorizing government contractors to establish separate segregated funds), repealing Pub. L. No. 76-753, § 5(a), 54 Stat. 772 (1940); see 5 Congressional Quarterly, supra note 32, at 948. The 1974 legislation also clarified the limits on solicitation by corporate PAC's. See Mayton, Politics, Money, Coercion, and the Problem with Corporate PACs, 29 Emory L.J. 375 (1980). At the same time, the limits placed on individual and party contributions by the 1974 legislation generated exploration for new sources of campaign funds. Bolton, Constitutional Limitations on Restricting Corporate and Union Political Speech, 22 Ariz. L. Rev. 373, 405–06 (1980); Epstein, The PAC Phenomenon: An Overview, 22 Ariz. L. Rev. 355, 360 (1980). The PAC boom had begun.

Corporate and trade association PAC's now surpass labor PAC's in financial activity by a large margin. In the 1979–80 election cycle, labor union PAC's spent $26.4 million, including $14.1 million in direct contributions to candidates. Corporate PAC's spent $31.8 million, including $21.7 million to candidates, while trade, membership, and health organizations spent an additional $33.6 million, including $17.2 million in candidate contributions. Federal Election Commission press release (August 4, 1981). Experts estimate that approximately half of the PAC's in the latter category are business-related. See Wertheimer, The PAC Phenomenon in American Politics, 22 Ariz. L. Rev. 603, 606 n.19 (1980).

36. Federal Election Commission press release (January 17, 1982); Washington Post, Jan. 19, 1982, at A7, col. 1. While corporate PAC's have grown rapidly in number, labor union PAC's have remained relatively stable. In 1975 there were 226 labor union PAC's. Brief for Plaintiffs at

and 1980 PAC's more than doubled the amounts of money they poured into House and Senate campaigns—$22.6 million in 1976, $35.2 million in 1978, and $55.3 million in 1980.[37] And PAC's are taking on growing importance in the strategies of candidates and their fundraisers.[38] They are rapidly becoming the dominant force among categories of contributors. The PAC component of House candidates' campaign funds has risen steadily from 17% in 1974 to 26.4% in 1980.[39] And PAC's have far outdistanced the federal campaign funding contributions of all national, state, and local political parties combined.[40]

While the overall figures are impressive, the patterns of PAC spending make them an even more formidable influence in congressional politics. PAC's concentrate their giving upon strategic categories of candidates—those who are more likely to win and to have useful influence in Congress. PAC's rarely contribute to candidates who lose in the primary,[41] and they donate much more heavily to incumbents than to challengers.[42] In addition, some

---

14, International Ass'n of Machinists & Aerospace Workers v. FEC, No. 81-1664 (D.C. Cir. April 6, 1982). By December 1981 the number had grown to only 318. Political Finance/Lobby Reporter, Jan. 20, 1982, at 11. Total union PAC funds grew from $18.5 million in 1976 to $26 million in 1979-80, slower than the increase in the cost of living. Brief for Plaintiffs, supra, at 14.

Despite the recent growth in the number of corporate PAC's, the potential for future growth is immense. A significant number of leading corporations have not yet established their own PAC's. Adamany, PAC's and the Democratic Financing of Politics, 22 Ariz. L. Rev. 569, 589 (1980) (in 1978 only 40% of firms in top 500 had PAC's); Wertheimer, supra note 35, at 607 (only 17% of firms with $100 million or more in assets had formed PAC's by May 1978).

37. Epstein, supra note 35, at 356; Federal Election Commission press release (August 10, 1981).

38. The number of House candidates receiving more than $50,000 in PAC money more than tripled from 57 in 1976 to 176 in 1978. Those who received more than $100,000 increased from 3 in 1976 to 21 in 1978. Kenski, Running With and From the PAC, 22 Ariz. L. Rev. 627, 640 n. 71 (1980). In the 1974 campaign, 78 members of the House received 40% or more of their total contributions from PAC's; in 1978 the number was 136. Wertheimer, supra note 35, at 607.

39. Kenski, supra note 38, at 641-42; Federal Election Commission press release (August 10, 1981).

In Senate campaigns in 1976, PAC's gave 15% of the funds received by candidates—winners and losers, incumbents and challengers together. In 1978 the figure was 13% and in 1980 it was 16%. Kenski, supra note 38, at 641; Federal Election Commission press release, supra.

40. In the 1977-78 election cycle, the two major parties directly contributed a total of $6.4 million to federal candidates and spent an additional $4.8 million on their behalf. In contrast, during the same election cycle, PAC's gave $35.2 million to federal candidates. Epstein, supra note 35, at 361. A significant shift took place during the 1970's. In 1972, political parties supplied 17.3% of the funds obtained by House candidates, while nonparty committees provided 14.0%. In 1978 parties gave only 4.5% of the funds, nonparty committees 25.3%. Jacobson, The Pattern of Campaign Contributions to Candidates for the U.S. House of Representatives, 1972-1978, *in* Harvard Campaign Finance Study, supra note 30, at 2-2 to 2-3.

Some commentators assert that PAC's have been a major factor in the decline of parties. See, e.g., Epstein, supra note 35, at 360-61; Wertheimer, supra note 35, at 616. Others believe that PAC's have simply benefited from trends that have at the same time reduced party influence on elections. See, e.g., Adamany, supra note 36, at 593-94; Sorauf, Political Parties and Political Action Committees: Two Life Cycles, 22 Ariz. L. Rev. 445, 454 (1980).

41. In the 1980 election campaign, 93.4% of total PAC contributions went to candidates who contested the general election—$51.7 million out of $55.3 million. Federal Election Commission press release (August 10, 1981).

42. In 1980 PAC's gave $33.8 million to incumbents, many of them holding safe seats, and only $14.3 million to challengers. Id. In 1978 the largest donor, the American Medical Associa-

PAC's, especially those with ideological or single-issue orientations, spend large sums of money on highly effective campaigns against "hit listed" candidates. Collectively, PAC's devoted more than $14 million in 1980 to independent campaign activities for or against particular candidates.[43] Because *Buckley v. Valeo* constitutionally invalidated ceilings on "independent" expenditures,[44] this type of spending may theoretically be unlimited.

When wealth of this magnitude is injected into the political bloodstream,[45] the legislative process itself is affected. PAC contributions are given with a legislative purpose and it is a telling fact that they are most numerous in the more highly regulated industries, such as oil, transportation, utilities, drugs, health care, and government contracting.[46] High-level corporate employees are solicited to give to the company's PAC precisely because it will advance the business interests of the firm.[47] One PAC formed by a major corporation explained to its employees, "Our aim is to gain for [our] managers the same rapt attention from their Congressmen and Senators which labor leaders now command."[48] Another PAC reported progress in achieving the corporation's goals: "We *have* strengthened our relationships with our 'constituent' Senators and Congressmen . . . . One or more of us on the PAC Steering Committee has developed a personal relationship with each incumbent to whom we give campaign contributions."[49]

The political generosity of the PAC's is directed to legislators who are in a position to help, especially members of committees with jurisdiction over legislation affecting the sponsors. For example, from the beginning of 1975 through mid-1978, dairy PAC's gave $380,000 to members of the House Agriculture Committee, and labor groups donated almost $600,000 to mem-

---

tion, gave $823,542 to House incumbents, compared to $301,900 to challengers. Common Cause press release (December 18, 1979). PAC money represented 32% of the total receipts of incumbents in 1978, Wertheimer, supra note 35, at 611, and 33.8% in 1980, Federal Election Commission press release (August 10, 1981).

43. Federal Election Commission Record, March 1982, at 7. This figure represented approximately 10.5% of total PAC spending. Id. For discussions of independent expenditures in United States Senate campaigns, see N.Y. Times, Nov. 30, 1980, § 1, at 39, col. 1; Washington Post, Nov. 12, 1980, at A10, col. 1.

The Supreme Court, by a four-four vote, recently affirmed a three-judge district court's decision that Congress may not limit the amount of independent expenditures that may be made by persons or committees to support or oppose presidential candidates in the general election. See supra note 29.

44. 424 U.S. at 39–51.

45. PAC's are also a growing force in state politics. See Adamany, supra note 36, at 588; Epstein, supra note 35, at 362–63.

46. Budde, The Practical Role of Corporate PAC's in the Political Process, 22 Ariz. L. Rev. 555, 560 (1980). Coal, oil, and gas interests had 12 registered PAC's in 1974 and 110 in 1978. Utilities had no PAC's in 1974 and 64 in 1978. Banking interests had 36 PAC's in 1974 and 161 in 1978. Wertheimer, supra note 35, at 606; see G. Adams, The Iron Triangle 110–24 (1981) (activities of PAC's formed by defense contractors).

47. See Findings of Fact and Constitutional Questions for Certification Under 2 U.S.C. § 437(h), findings 4–27, at 8–16, International Ass'n of Machinists & Aerospace Workers v. FEC, No. 80-0354 (D.D.C. filed June 3, 1981).

48. Id., finding 11, at 11.

49. Id., finding 19, at 14.

bers of the House Education and Labor Committee.[50] In 1978 PAC's provided 56% of the campaign money spent by 22 House committee chairmen,[51] compared with 25% for House candidates as a whole.[52] The chairman of the House Ways and Means Committee, the committee in which all tax legislation begins, received $157,425 from corporate PAC's to finance his 1980 re-election campaign. He won with 84% of the vote.[53]

Carefully targeted PAC giving has two parallel effects on Congress. First, PAC money, like money from any source, allows a candidate to spend more on his campaign and statistically enhances his chances of winning.[54] Second, once a candidate has been elected, he knows that if he wants to be re-elected it is important to give attention and deference to the views of those who helped him financially.[55] One chairman of a large corporation has said that dialogue with politicians "is a fine thing, but with a little money they hear you

---

50. Wertheimer, supra note 35, at 608. In addition, during that period, health groups contributed over $200,000 to members of the House Commerce Committee, which handles health matters. In 1977 and 1978 alone, banking PAC's gave nearly $225,000 to the members of the House Committee on Banking, Housing, and Urban Affairs. Id. at 608. During the 1980 election cycle, members of the House Ways and Means Committee received $1.73 million from corporate PAC's, including large sums from the steel, auto, airline, and railroad industries, which were seeking special tax breaks. Public Citizen, Congress Watch, Supply-Side Economics: Campaign Contributions to the House Ways and Means Committee, 1979–80, at 6–10 (July 1981); see also Common Cause, Dirty Money . . . Dirty Air? (May 1981) (study of PAC contributions to congressional committees reviewing the Clean Air Act); G. Adams, supra note 46, at 116–18 (patterns of giving by defense contractor PAC's).

51. Wertheimer, supra note 35, at 608. Senate Finance Committee Chairman Russell Long received $518,000 in PAC money, including $409,000 from corporate and business-related trade association PAC's; Robert Dole, ranking Republican on the same committee, received $328,055 from PAC's, including $255,000 from business or business-related PAC's. PAC's in these categories gave $170,000 to Senator Strom Thurmond, ranking Republican on the Senate Judiciary Committee, and $192,000 to Senator Jake Garn, then ranking Republican on the Senate Banking Committee. Common Cause Guide to Money, Power and Politics in the 97th Congress (1981).

52. Kenski, supra note 38, at 641-42.

53. Public Citizen, supra note 50, at 4. Sometimes the legislative purpose of campaign contributions is particularly transparent. In the first six months of 1981, one House election was just over and the next was a full cycle away, but Congress was considering legislation to lower corporate income taxes. Corporate PAC's poured more than $280,000 into the campaign coffers of 24 of the 35 members of the House Ways and Means Committee, most of whom represent safe districts. Five of the six largest recipients had had essentially no primary opposition and had received over two-thirds of the vote in the general election. Public Citizen, Congress Watch, Dealing from a PAC'd Deck: Corporate Campaign Contributions to the House Ways and Means Committee During the First Half of 1981 (Oct. 1981).

54. By definition, only 50% of major party general election candidates win in contested elections. But almost 80% of the 176 candidates who received at least $50,000 in PAC contributions in the 1978 campaign were winners. Although only 5% of all challengers won nationally, 52% of those who received more than $50,000 in PAC money won the election. Kenski, supra note 38, at 646–48.

55. See generally G. Adams, supra note 46, at 112; Chevigny, Review Essay: The Paradox of Campaign Finance, 56 N.Y.U. L. Rev. 206, 214 (1981). The Washington Post reported that Representative Phil Gramm, who received $6,200 in contributions from the used car dealers' PAC in 1980, addressed their 1981 annual convention and told them, "Your political action committee was a substantial contributor to my campaign. I can say that without your political action contribution, I would have lost. And without your contribution, I would not have been able to come up with the Gramm-Latta budget." Washington Post, Nov. 22, 1981, at C2, col. 3. In fact, Gramm was engaging in hyperbole; he won the 1980 election by a margin of 70% to 30%. 38 Cong. Q. Weekly Reports 3344 (1980).

better."[56] PAC defenders and critics disagree on which effect is more important for PAC contributors and recipients. PAC champions insist that they simply reward their friends and withhold favors from their adversaries.[57] PAC critics charge that lavish contributions to members of key committees are not rewards for past support but down payments for future influence.[58] It is not important to my analysis to choose between these conflicting positions. In one case PAC's exercise a form of "multiple voting,"[59] and in the other they engage in a form of legalized bribery.

Whatever the cause and effect relationship, studies of issue after issue demonstrate that a much higher percentage of legislators who voted with a PAC's position received money from that PAC in the previous campaign than those who voted the other way, and among the beneficiaries of PAC money, those supporting the PAC position had received a substantially higher average contribution. Whether the issue on the floor is the windfall profits tax on oil companies,[60] hospital cost containment,[61] efforts to create a superfund for

---

56. Quoted in Ulman, Companies Organize Employees and Holders into a Political Force, Wall St. J., Aug. 15, 1978, at 1, col. 6.

57. See Budde, supra note 46, at 558; Malbin, Of Mountains and Molehills: PAC's, Campaigns, and Public Policy, *in* Parties, Interest Groups, and Campaign Finance Laws 152, 176 (M. Malbin ed. 1980).

58. See, e.g., Wertheimer, supra note 35, at 614–15. PAC critics assert that the voting patterns of freshmen congressmen often conform with the positions of the PAC's that helped to finance their campaigns, and contend that the PAC money could not possibly have served as a reward for past support. In 1979, the National Association of Realtors (NAR) strongly supported a proposal to eliminate HUD enforcement powers against fraudulent real estate developers. In the previous campaign, the NAR had contributed to 51 of the 71 House freshmen; 43 of those 51 sided with the realtors. Of the 20 who opposed the NAR proposal, 13 had received no NAR contributions. Id. at 615.

In 1979 the AMA lobbied strongly against President Carter's hospital cost containment bill, which was defeated. Thirty-seven out of 49 freshmen who received AMA contributions in the 1978 campaign voted with the AMA; they had received average contributions of $9,454. Those who received AMA money but voted against the AMA had received an average of less than half that figure, $4,717 per member. Thirteen of the 25 freshmen who opposed the AMA had received no AMA PAC contributions. AMA Campaign Contributions Helped Kill Hospital Cost Containment Bill, According to Common Cause Study, Common Cause press release (December 18, 1979).

59. See L. Berg, H. Hahn & J. Schmidhauser, supra note 3, at 43–46 (discussing concept of "weighted voting," which recognizes that some persons not only cast their own ballots but exercise a multiplier effect by contributing money to influence the votes of others); Adamany, supra note 36, at 571 ("Money's extreme potential for multiple voting points to an important issue of political finance policy in a democracy: preventing gross inequalities in the meaning of the vote." (footnotes omitted)); id. at 570–71 (noting that ability and inclination to give large sums to political candidates "has greater potential than any other form of political activity for differential participation by presumably equal citizens"); cf. Freund, Commentary, *in* A. Rosenthal, Federal Regulation of Campaign Finance: Some Constitutional Questions 74 (Citizens' Research Foundation Study No. 18, 1971) (large contributors "are operating vicariously through the power of their purse, rather than through the power of their ideas, and . . . I would scale that relatively lower in the hierarchy of First Amendment values").

60. Nader Study Links Oil Contributions to Pro-Oil House Vote, Public Citizen, Congress Watch press release (July 23, 1979) (95% of House members who received more than $2,500 from oil industry PAC's voted to reduce windfall profits tax; three-quarters of the 267 House members who received oil PAC money voted for the measure; 83% of the 236 Congressmen who supported the measure, and only 39% of its opponents, had received oil PAC contributions).

61. AMA Campaign Contributions Helped Kill Hospital Cost Containment Bill, According to Common Cause Study, supra note 58 (202 of 234 House members who voted against Carter

victims of toxic chemicals,[62] or any other legislation that affects powerful, organized interests,[63] PAC money augments interest-group lobbying.

A graphic example of the manner in which interest groups seek political return on their PAC contributions is provided by the lobbying efforts of used car dealers. Their National Automobile Dealers Association was the fourth largest PAC contributor in the country in the 1980 elections, giving slightly more than $1 million to congressional candidates. Used car dealers successfully lobbied for a congressional veto of proposed FTC regulations requiring them to disclose known defects in used cars they offer for sale.[64] At the Association's convention this past fall in Washington D.C., the Association's government relations chairman gave the delegates a pep talk, urging them to go see their Congressman and adding that PAC contributions had opened the door. By the end of the convention, more than ninety House members and more than twenty senators had signed on as co-sponsors of the veto resolution. In another few weeks, thirty-three more representatives and one more senator had joined. About 80% of the legislators on the bandwagon had received PAC contributions in 1980.[65]

Not only do PAC's buy legislative clout by investing in congressional candidates, they also squeeze out the individual voice in congressional politics. PAC's tend to be bureaucratically organized and centralized, often at the national level. The voice of a PAC is not that of its small givers whose participation is extolled by PAC publicists,[66] but that of its leadership, who decide where to bestow the money.[67] National PAC's compete with local constituents for the attention of congressmen,[68] and as the PAC share of

---

administration's hospital cost containment legislation received funds from AMA PAC's; bill's opponents received average AMA PAC contributions four times as great as bill's supporters).

62. Nader Group Links Chemical Contributions to Pro-Industry Efforts, Public Citizen, Congress Watch press release (August 25, 1980) (among top recipients of chemical industry PAC money were several Senators and Representatives leading opposition to superfund bill).

63. Public Citizen, supra note 50, at 6–10. In a vote on a refundable investment credit for steel, auto, airline, and railroad companies in June 1981, those who voted yes had received an average of $12,420 from corporation and labor PAC's in the affected industries; those who voted present or did not vote received an average of $8,296; and those who voted no received only $3,585. Id. at 10.

64. The FTC regulations were submitted to Congress for review on September 9, 1981. Veto resolutions were introduced in both the House (H. Con. Res. 178) and the Senate (S. Con. Res. 33). The Senate committee held a hearing on October 30; the House committee held a hearing on December 8. On December 16, 1981, the House committee favorably reported the veto resolution to the floor. Congress adjourned, however, before the completion of action on the proposed veto. Under the terms of the FTC Improvements Act of 1980, the agency was required to resubmit the rule for review at the beginning of the 1982 session. See 15 U.S.C. § 57a-1(a)(2) (Supp. IV 1980). On May 18, 1982, the Senate voted 69–27 to disapprove the FTC regulation. 128 Cong. Rec. S5380–5402 (daily ed. May 18, 1982). On May 26, 1982, the House voted by a margin of 286 to 133 to veto the rule. 128 Cong. Rec. H2856–2883 (daily ed. May 26, 1982).

65. Can the Used Car Lobby Sell Congress?, Washington Post, Nov. 22, 1981, at C2, col. 3.

66. See, e.g., Budde, supra note 46, at 556–57; Rhodes, In Response to Obey-Railsback, 22 Ariz. L. Rev. 670, 670–71 (1980).

67. Mayton, supra note 35, at 391.

68. Adamany, supra note 36, at 596; Campaign Finance Study Group, Summary of Findings and Major Recommendations, *in* Harvard Campaign Finance Study, supra note 30, at 1–8; Kenski, supra note 38, at 639; Mayton, supra note 35, at 386–87. As the Harvard study warned, "Candidates now rely more heavily on money from outside their districts or states. As Washing-

candidate funding increases, local voices and constituent concerns are bound to carry less weight.

C. *Spiraling Campaign Costs and Monied Influence*

PAC's have become increasingly influential in congressional campaigns and legislative lobbying because of the dramatic escalation of campaign expenses.[69] The cost of goods and services used in campaigns has been rising faster than the consumer price index.[70] In 1972 the total cost of House and Senate campaigns nationwide was $98 million;[71] in 1980 it was $242 million.[72] Media time and production costs, which often comprise 30 to 40% of the amounts spent by candidates,[73] are becoming more and more expensive. For example, a thirty-second evening prime time spot on a Portland, Oregon television station cost $55 in 1974; today it costs $3,000. In the same period, the price of thirty prime time seconds on TV in San Diego has jumped from $509 to $3,000.[74] Direct mailing, too, is expensive. The cost of postage continues to escalate, and the direct mail consultants charge hefty fees for their computerized mailing lists and sophisticated techniques.[75]

---

ton D.C. has become the best place to raise campaign funds, a concomitant concern is the increasing detachment of candidates from their constituencies." Campaign Finance Study Group, supra, at 1-8.

Not all observers agree that PAC's are overly influential. See Elliott, Political Action Committees—Precincts of the '80's, 22 Ariz. L. Rev. 539, 549-50 (1980) (written by former executive director of AMA PAC) ("Those who would argue that PAC's are dominating or taking over the political process are overstating both the role and the impact of PAC's since only 17.5% of all funds spent by federal candidates in 1978 came from PAC's."); Epstein, supra note 35, at 371–72 ("Whenever PAC contributions, as a percentage of total contributions to candidates, exceed the current level of approximately twenty-five percent, the time will have come for Congress to consider limiting PAC activities.").

69. See Adamany, supra note 36, at 570 ("The rapid shift from traditional political methods to high-technology campaigning makes money more important precisely because it is readily converted into polling, computerized appeals, professional staff, and media messages.").

70. See Brief for Appellees Center for Public Financing of Elections, Common Cause, League of Women Voters, et al. at 67–69, Buckley v. Valeo, 424 U.S. 1 (1976) (from 1952 to 1972, consumer price index rose 57.6%; federal campaign spending increased almost 300%); Brief of Senators Hugh Scott and Edward M. Kennedy, Amici Curiae, at 35 n.14, Buckley v. Valeo, 424 U.S. 1 (1976) (separate charts for congressional and presidential campaign expenditures); F. Wertheimer & R. Huwa, supra note 31, at 18.

71. F. Wertheimer & R. Huwa, Has the Tree Really Fallen? The Role of Television in American Politics 27 (unpublished paper prepared for presentation at annual meeting of Association for Public Policy Analysis and Management, Boston, Mass., Oct. 24, 1980).

72. Federal Election Commission press release (August 10, 1981).

73. D. Graber, Mass Media and American Politics 161 (1980). Time Magazine reported an even higher estimate, 60 to 70% of campaign funds. Time, Nov. 20, 1978, at 35. A study of 86 House campaigns in 1978 found that "the single most expensive activity on the average . . . was broadcasting." F. Wertheimer & R. Huwa, supra note 71, at 26–27.

74. F. Wertheimer & R. Huwa, supra note 71, at 27. From 1974 to 1980, the price of 30 prime time seconds on TV in Baltimore increased from $1,100 to $3,000; from 1978 to 1980, the cost of five minutes of TV time in rural Wisconsin escalated from $250 to $950. One political consultant in Washington, D.C. estimated that spot advertising costs generally increased 40% from 1979 to late 1980. Id.

75. L. Sabato, The Rise of Political Consultants: New Ways of Winning Elections 228–30, 250–53 (1981) (costs of direct mailing).

The fixation of American politicians upon expensive, media-dominated, highly professional campaigns has made the political process much more vulnerable to the corrosive influence of money. That is the root of my concern. I am not calling for reform on the ground that the new campaign techniques in themselves are prone to confuse or mislead American voters. I do not believe in content regulation or censorship, and all things being equal, I have faith in the common sense of the American electorate.[76] But I am worried by the side effects of the new style of campaigning.

One side effect is that political candidates, caught in a spiraling spending race, turn more readily to PAC's, which can mobilize money and may legally give five times as much as individuals to favored candidates.[77] Another side effect is that able, dedicated individuals, whose ideas and personal qualifications might attract many voters, are deterred from even entering the race for political office because of the immense sums of money required to run a media-based campaign. Unless the potential candidate is personally wealthy or is willing to become beholden to special interests and wealthy donors, he or she may consider the effort hopeless.[78] Such people are the silent casualties of the political process; we do not hear about them because they are defeated before they start. The nation is often the loser.

The growing technological sophistication and rising costs of election campaigns are also closely related to massive inequalities in campaign spending. For a candidate or an issue position with ample supplies of money, the sky is the limit; there are always more ways to spend money if it is available. The result is sometimes grossly unequal spending totals in both candidate and referendum campaigns. Lopsided media spending, in turn, may, in the words

---

76. See Business Executives' Move for Vietnam Peace v. FCC, 450 F.2d 642, 658 (D.C. Cir. 1971) (Wright, J.), rev'd sub nom. CBS v. Democratic Nat'l Comm., 412 U.S. 94 (1973). In the court of appeals decision, I rejected the contention that "spot" editorial advertisements are unworthy of protection because they may be cursory and uninformative. "We must . . . be very, very slow to judge any sort of speech on public issues worthless. The marketplace of ideas protected by the First Amendment, after all, is not governed by the tastes and intellectual standards of the universities or the broadcast newsroom—or even of judicial chambers." 450 F.2d at 658.

77. See F. Wertheimer & R. Huwa, supra note 71, at 28. PAC's may legally give $5000 to a candidate in a primary or general election campaign; an individual is limited to a $1000 contribution. 2 U.S.C. § 441a(a)(1)(A) (1976).

78. See L. Berg, H. Hahn & J. Schmidhauser, supra note 3, at 80; D. Graber, supra note 73, at 161-62; Leventhal, supra note 3, at 375; Nicholson, Campaign Financing and Equal Protection, 26 Stan. L. Rev. 815, 816 (1974). The specter of heavy personal campaign debts may also serve as a deterrent to candidacy. One former congressional candidate has vividly described the pressures placed on him during the campaign to incur personal liability in order to provide funds for his campaign, because the candidate is the only "contributor" not limited by statute. Firmage & Christensen, Speech and Campaign Reform: Congress, the Courts and Community, 14 Ga. L. Rev. 195, 210–12 (1980). On the average, the proportion of campaign receipts coming from a candidate's own funds increased from 5.6% in 1974 to 8.9% in 1976 and 9.2% in 1978. The average personal contribution of a House candidate rose from $3,500 in 1974 to $10,200 in 1978. F. Wertheimer & R. Huwa, supra note 31, at 10.

On the other hand, wealthy candidates have figured prominently in recent campaigns. See Firmage & Christensen, supra, at 210; Leventhal, supra note 3, at 382–83. In 1976 nine House candidates spent more than $100,000 of their own funds in their campaigns, and three Senate candidates each spent more than $500,000. F. Wertheimer & R. Huwa, supra note 31, at 10.

of Dean Rosenthal, "overwhelmingly and effectively blo[t] out the messages of [a candidate's] opponents."[79]

The Federal Election Commission's spending data for House and Senate races in 1978 graphically show the extent of inequalities in spending and their correlation with winning and losing.[80] There were 307 contested House races. The winner outspent the loser in 78.8% of those races. Where the spending margin was more than two to one, as it was in 159 races, the bigger spender won 93% of the time. Where one side outspent the other by more than five to one, as occurred in 58 House campaigns, the bigger spender won 100% of the time. The same story is repeated on the Senate side, where the bigger spender won in 31 out of 35 races—88.6%—in 1978.[81] In open-seat Senate races, which eliminated the incumbency advantage, the winner outspent the loser 13 out of 14 times—92.8% of the campaigns. The correlation between success and money is not a statistical artifact. It is a product of the expensive goods and services—television and radio time, media consultants, sophisticated polls, computerized direct mailing operations, political strategists—that money can buy.[82]

D. *Referenda and Initiatives*

The unholy alliance of big spending, special interests, and election victory is found, perhaps in its most dramatic form, in referendum contests. Referenda and initiatives are vehicles of direct popular democracy in twenty-two states and the District of Columbia.[83] Created by the progressive reform movement in the early part of this century, these processes allow the voters to express their views on major public issues directly rather than through elected representatives. They were designed to lessen the influence of special interests and corrupt maneuvering upon major public decisions.[84] Ironically, the advent of media campaigning has made it possible for concentrated wealth to have a powerful impact on referendum campaigns as well. Drastically unequal spending for the tools of persuasion shapes and limits the people's awareness

---

79. A. Rosenthal, supra note 59, at 40.

80. Tabulations are based on Federal Election Commission, FEC Reports on Financial Activity 1977–1978, Interim Report No. 5, U.S. Senate and House Campaigns 121–340 (June 1979) (charts of financial activity in individual Senate and House campaigns arranged by state).

81. In the bulk of the Senate races, the spending was not even close. In 23 of the 35 races, the winner outspent the loser by 50% or more; in 15 of the 35 races, the margin was 2:1 or more. In dollar terms, the winner outspent the loser by more than $100,000 in 26 races, by more than $200,000 in 23 races, and by more than $500,000 in 11 races.

82. L. Sabato, supra note 75, at 49–53 (fees, expenses, and commissions charged by political consultants); id. at 79–81 (costs of in-person polls and telephone polls); id. at 179–82 (costs of media advertising); id. at 250–53 (direct mailing expenses and fees).

83. Statement of Professor Larry L. Berg, *in* Voter Initiative Constitutional Amendment, Hearings Before the Subcomm. on the Constitution of the Senate Comm. on the Judiciary on S.J. Res. 67, 95th Cong., 1st Sess. 50, 51 (1977) [hereinafter cited as Voter Initiative Constitutional Amendment].

84. See Shockley, The Initiative, Democracy, and Money: The Case of Colorado, 1976, *in* Voter Initiative Constitutional Amendment, supra note 83, at 172. See generally Voter Initiative Constitutional Amendment, supra note 83.

of the issues. And the Supreme Court's decision in *Bellotti* appears to leave the political system powerless to defend itself.[85]

A number of studies show that, in state after state, in election after election, massive spending and sophisticated media campaigns by special interest groups have swamped referenda that were initially favored by a majority of the voters.[86] One study of referendum and initiative campaigns across the country in 1978 found that the side spending the most won in eleven of fifteen contested campaigns. The side with corporate support outspent its opponents in twelve cases—in eight of these by margins of ten to one or more— and won in two-thirds of these contests. When the corporate side was outspent, it lost every time.[87]

The antismoking initiative on the California ballot in 1978 gives one vivid example of the lopsidedness introduced into the political process by unlimited spending.[88] The initiative proposed to prohibit smoking in enclosed public places, places of employment, and educational and health facilities. At the beginning of September, two months before the election, polls showed 58% of the voters in favor of the measure and only 38% opposed. Then tobacco interests spent $6.4 million in the opposition campaign, almost ten times as much as the proponents of the measure. Philip Morris, Inc. contributed $1.7 million; the R. J. Reynolds Tobacco Company gave $1.7 million. Two other tobacco companies gave $882,000 and $638,000 respectively. The combined expenditures of these four companies alone exceeded the cost of the entire general election campaign for the governorship of California. Buying extensive television spot coverage under the label "Californians for Common Sense," the tobacco industry carried the day. Support for the initiative gradually eroded in the polls, and on election day the vote was 45% for and 55% against.

A similar experience occurred in Colorado in a 1976 referendum ballot on container deposits.[89] Again, the polls showed that in late September the

---

85. Before 1978, 18 states and a number of municipalities had laws that limited or prohibited corporate contributions or expenditures in ballot question campaigns. S. Lydenberg, Bankrolling Ballots: The Role of Business in Financing State Ballot Question Campaigns 13 (1979). However, taken together, Buckley v. Valeo, 424 U.S. 1 (1976), and First Nat'l Bank v. Bellotti, 435 U.S. 765 (1978), protect the right of any person, group, or corporation to make unlimited direct expenditures for or against a ballot proposition. The Supreme Court recently struck down a municipal ordinance limiting contributions by any person to committees favoring or opposing referenda or initiatives. Citizens Against Rent Control v. City of Berkeley, 102 S. Ct. 434, 443 (1981); see supra note 27.

86. S. Lydenberg, supra note 85; Mastro, Costlow & Sanchez, Taking the Initiative: Corporate Control of the Referendum Process Through Media Spending and What to Do About It, 32 Fed. Com. L.J. 315 (1980); Shockley, supra note 84, at 177–80; Brief in Support of Appellees by Amicus Curiae City and County of San Francisco at 21–25, Citizens Against Rent Control v. City of Berkeley, 102 S. Ct. 434 (1981) [hereinafter cited as San Francisco Amicus Brief].

87. S. Lydenberg, supra note 85, at 22–23 (ratios of spending in these 12 cases were 197:1, 96:1, 48:1, 26:1, 25:1, 24:1, 13:1, 10:1, 4.5:1, 4:1, 1.7:1, and unknown). The same author studied 19 ballot issue campaigns in the 1980 election; the side with corporate backing outspent opponents by better than two to one in 15 campaigns and won in 12 of them. See Citizens Against Rent Control v. City of Berkeley, 102 S. Ct. 434, 443 n.4 (1981) (White, J., dissenting).

88. S. Lydenberg, supra note 85, at 30–34.

89. Mastro, Costlow & Sanchez, supra note 86, at 320–27, 330–33, 360–69.

public was strongly in favor of the measure—57% in favor and 27% against. Again, opponents—from the soft drink industry, can manufacturing, iron, steel, and other directly affected interests—poured large amounts of money into the campaign. The opposition war chest totaled $587,000,[90] with more than half a dozen single contributors each outspending the entire campaign in favor of the measure. The industry message dominated television, radio, and newspaper advertising.[91] In prime time, opposition television spots outnumbered favorable spots by 72 to 12, and in non-prime time by 113 to 28. Perhaps it comes as little surprise that there was a significant shift in voter opinion during October and that the initiative was defeated by a vote of nearly two to one, virtually reversing the initial polling results.[92]

Not only are the two sides in referendum contests often devastatingly unequal in the amounts of money they spend, but their sources of money are also dramatically different. Large corporate and trade association contributions made up the bulk of the funds against the two ballot measures I have described, and the same was true in other initiative campaigns that have threatened special interests. In contrast, proponents have relied very heavily on small contributions.[93] To give just one more example, in 1978 the citizens of Long Beach, California voted on a referendum to reject a proposed lease between the city and Standard Oil for construction of an oil storage terminal. Community opponents of the lease raised $17,721, all of it in contributions under $1,000. Standard Oil and related companies pumped in $864,568; the smallest contribution was over $16,000.[94]

The big-spending media campaigns do not always win,[95] but they win much more often than they lose, distorting the expressed will of the people by

---

90. Corporate donations of $500 or more accounted for 91% of the opposition's campaign fund. Id. at 321.

91. Opponents spent $69,415 on television advertising; under the Fairness Doctrine supporters obtained free time valued at $13,850. On radio, container deposit opponents spent $35,076; proponents had $1,688 worth of free radio time. In the local newspapers, opponents outspent supporters by more than three to one. Id. at 325–26.

92. The authors found the same phenomena—heavy media spending by the corporate side, an overwhelming imbalance in finances and publicity, and defeat of a grassroots initiative despite strong support in early polls—in two other 1976 Colorado ballot initiatives, one on nuclear safety and one on reform of public utilities regulation. Id. at 320–27, 330–33, 360–69; see Shockley, supra note 84, at 177–89 (case studies of 1976 Colorado initiatives on nuclear safety, bottle deposits, and tax reform, arriving at substantially similar conclusions and discussing shifts in public opinion over the course of each campaign).

93. S. Lydenberg, supra note 85, at 26–27 (1978 Alaska bottle bill initiative); id. at 33–34 (1978 California antismoking initiative); id. at 37 (1978 Long Beach, California initiative against oil storage terminal); id. at 39–40 (1978 Nebraska bottle deposit initiative); id. at 47–48 (1978 Oregon people's utility district initiative); id. at 54–56 (1978 Montana anti-nuclear initiative); id. at 59 (1978 Oregon utilities rates initiative); Mastro, Costlow & Sanchez, supra note 86, at 321–23 (1976 Colorado initiatives on nuclear safety, container deposits, and public utilities regulation reform); San Francisco Amicus Brief, supra note 86, at 22–24 (1980 California initiatives on smoking limitations, oil profits tax, and repeal of rent control ordinances).

94. S. Lydenberg, supra note 85, at 37, cited in part in Citizens Against Rent Control v. City of Berkeley, 102 S. Ct. 434, 443 (1981) (White, J., dissenting).

95. Studies in California have found that massive spending is more likely to defeat a referendum opposed by special interests than to pass a measure which they favor. See Statement of Professor Larry L. Berg, supra note 83, at 54; Appellee's Brief at 11, Citizens Against Rent

the sheer inequality of financial resources and the avalanche of campaign messages. Regardless of their message, they simply drown out their opponents when they have the wherewithal to outspend them by margins of up to fifty to one.[96] In America money controls access to the communications media. In some other presumably civilized countries, those interests monopolizing access to the means of communication have used the big lie, the half truth, and the sly innuendo, amplified and repeated over and over again, to pervert the minds of the people. We, in this country, should be too sophisticated to succumb to such crass approaches, but the election returns that I have discussed seem to indicate that our political hucksters must be pretty sophisticated people too.

As individuals are squeezed out, as the behemoths of concentrated wealth dwarf the individual and bid fair to dominate the political field, the very purpose of direct democracy is defeated, and voters are bound to become disillusioned and apathetic.[97] This picture might not trouble a convinced pluralist who sees democratic government as nothing more than the result of the pull and tug of aggregated interests in a field of political vectors and partisan forces of greater or lesser intensity.[98] But I believe in the role of equal individuals in the process of American self-government, and I am convinced that this role cannot be snuffed out without at the same time destroying the integrity of our electoral process and the essence of our political faith.

II. The Ideal of Political Equality

Political equality is the cornerstone of American democracy. Today's electoral processes, tainted by huge inequalities in funds and special access for

---

Control v. City of Berkeley, 102 S. Ct. 434 (1981) (quotes systematic study of California statewide ballot measures between 1968 and 1980 which concludes that "one-sided spending is ineffective when it supports the proposition but is dominant when it opposes the measure"); Brief of Amicus Curiae New England Legal Foundation in Support of Appellants, Citizens Against Rent Control v. City of Berkeley, 102 S. Ct. 434 (1981).

Money is not the only factor determining the results of a referendum campaign. Initial public attitudes, the strength or weakness of the specific measure, events during the campaign, endorsements or opposition by prominent political figures, and other factors play an important part. However, the greater the lopsidedness in spending, the greater the impact that money differentials will have on the outcome of an election.

96. See supra note 87. One media specialist who worked for two initiative campaigns during the 1976 Colorado elections stated, "I'm afraid money can buy an election. But it's not money alone. It's money cleverly spent." Shockley, supra note 84, at 178.

97. After three initially popular initiatives were opposed by high-spending media campaigns and defeated at the polls in Colorado in 1976, the Colorado Daily editorialized:

> What was lost on Tuesday was more than . . . good amendments. The big money boys have undoubtedly put a chill on the efforts of citizen groups to put issues on the ballot. Obtaining the needed signatures for an initiative is hard work, and nobody wants to waste his or her time if all is to be stomped under the bankrolls of those with power.

Shockley, supra note 84, at 188; see L. Berg, H. Hahn & J. Schmidhauser, supra note 3, at 49–51 (discussion of voter alienation). Political apathy by the populace runs counter to the purposes and ideals of the democratic system. As Justice Brandeis wrote in Whitney v. California, 274 U.S. 357, 375 (1927) (Brandeis, J., concurring), "the greatest menace to freedom is an inert people."

98. See Wright, supra note 17, at 1013–21 (criticizing pluralists' vision of politics).

special interests, fall far short of that ideal and are moving further away every year. But rather than give up faith and drift with the tide, we must reexamine and renew our commitment to realizing America's fundamental political ideals.

The concepts of political equality and self-government stand or fall together. If persons are equal, then none has an inherent right to dominate or impose his will on others. Government can be legitimate only if it is based on the informed consent of all citizens.[99] Rational self-interest dictates, therefore, that each assure his or her own liberty by agreeing to equal liberties for all, including the right to equal political participation.[100] In explaining the essence of the social contract, Rousseau declared that "each giving himself to all, gives himself to nobody; and as there is not one associate over whom we do not acquire the same rights which we concede to him over ourselves, we gain the equivalent of all that we lose, and more power to preserve what we have."[101] These principles of mutual tolerance, respect, and equality are enshrined as well in our own Declaration of Independence.[102]

Throughout American history the ideal of political equality has found eloquent expression, and gradual steps have been taken toward its realization. Nearly two hundred years after the framing of the Constitution, James Madison's words in *Federalist No. 57* challenge us to fulfill their promise:

> Who are to be the electors of the Federal Representatives? Not the rich, more than the poor; not the learned, more than the ignorant; not the haughty heirs of distinguished names, more than the humble sons of obscurity and unpropitious fortune. The electors are to be the great body of the people of the United States. . . .
>
> Who are to be the objects of popular choice? Every citizen whose merit may recommend him to the esteem and confidence of his country. No qualification of wealth, of birth, of religious faith, or of civil profession is permitted to fetter the judgment or disappoint the inclination of the people.[103]

---

99. See 2 J. Locke, Two Treatises of Government ii, 4; viii, 95, reprinted in Readings on Political Philosophy 530, 551 (F.W. Coker ed. 1938) [hereinafter cited as Readings].

100. J. Rawls, A Theory of Justice 11–19, 205–07, 221–28 (1971); see also Scanlon, A Theory of Freedom of Expression, 1 Phil. & Pub. Aff. 204, 214 (1972) (For a government to be legitimate, citizens must be able to recognize its authority "while still regarding themselves as equal, autonomous, rational agents.").

101. J. Rousseau, The Social Contract, 1, vi, reprinted in Readings, supra note 99, at 639; see id. at 2, iv, reprinted in Readings, supra note 99, at 646–47 ("[t]he social compact establishes among the citizens such an equality that they all pledge themselves under the same conditions and ought all to enjoy the same rights.").

102. In the words of Alexander Meiklejohn, "[i]f the Declaration of Independence means what it says, if we mean what it says, then no man is called upon to obey a law unless he himself, equally with his fellows, has shared in making it." A. Meiklejohn, Free Speech and Its Relation to Self-Government 10–11 (1948). The people are both the governors and the governed. Under the Constitution, we are agreed that, in Meiklejohn's words, "as free men, politically equal, we alone will make the laws and that, as loyal citizens, equal before the laws, we will obey them." Id. at 105; see id. at 3–11, 22–23.

Meiklejohn subsequently wrote that "the adoption of the principle of self-government by 'The People' of this nation set loose upon us and upon the world at large an idea which is still transforming men's conceptions of what they are and how they may best be governed." Meiklejohn, The First Amendment is an Absolute, 1961 Sup. Ct. Rev. 245, 264.

103. Federalist No. 57, at 305 (J. Madison) (J. Cooke, ed. 1961).

In the 1830's Alexis de Tocqueville captured the spirit of Jacksonian democracy when he traveled through America. "[T]he principle of the sovereignty of the people hovers over the whole political system of the Anglo-Americans," Tocqueville wrote. "[E]ach individual forms an equal part of that sovereignty and shares equally the government of the state."[104] With great interest, Tocqueville described the civic spirit, energy, and individual self-respect that pervaded American life, which he attributed to the widespread exercise of political rights and responsibilities in a spirit of equality.[105] He also engaged in more theoretical speculations about the philosophical nature of equality, and like Rousseau, postulated a point at which freedom and equality would meet and blend:

> Let us suppose that all the citizens take a part in the government and that each of them has an equal right to do so. Then, no man is different from his fellows, and nobody can wield tyrannical power; men will be perfectly free because they are entirely equal, and they will be perfectly equal because they are entirely free. Democratic peoples are tending toward that ideal. That is the completest possible form for liberty on this earth.[106]

Complete equality and complete freedom were not found in America in Madison's time,[107] or in Tocqueville's. But the Jacksonian period did see major expansions of the suffrage—elimination of property qualifications for voting in state after state.[108] At the federal level, several constitutional amendments have since extended the vote to new categories of citizens.[109]

The Supreme Court, in the twentieth century, has played a major role in eliminating artificial barriers to equal electoral participation: the white primary,[110] the poll tax,[111] and voter qualifications based on property.[112] Most

---

104. A. de Tocqueville, Democracy in America 59 (J.P. Mayer & M. Lerner eds., G. Lawrence trans. 1966); see id. at 474.

105. Id. at 217–25.

106. Id. at 473.

107. Tuttle, Equality and the Vote, 41 N.Y.U. L. Rev. 245, 246 (1966).

108. See Kirby, The Right to Vote, *in* The Rights of Americans: What They Are—What They Should Be 175, 179–80 (N. Dorsen ed. 1970). Describing the Massachusetts debate in which universal male suffrage was adopted, one historian observed, "The most impressive thing about this entire movement toward broader suffrage is that men came to be filled with a fixed determination that as this country was a democracy all men should have a hand in running it . . . ." Id. at 180 (quoting K. Porter, A History of Suffrage in the United States 70–72 (1969)).

109. U.S. Const. amend. XIX (admitting women to suffrage); amend. XXIII (enfranchising citizens of District of Columbia in presidential elections); amend. XXIV (abolition of poll tax as precondition for voting); amend. XXVI (admitting 18-to-21-year-olds to vote); see also amend. XVII (direct popular election of senators).

110. Terry v. Adams, 345 U.S. 461 (1953); Smith v. Allwright, 321 U.S. 649 (1944).

111. Harper v. Virginia Bd. of Elections, 383 U.S. 663 (1966). The Court declared unequivocally, "Wealth, like race, creed, or color, is not germane to one's ability to participate intelligently in the electoral process." Id. at 668.

112. Hill v. Stone, 421 U.S. 289 (1975); City of Phoenix v. Kolodziejski, 399 U.S. 204 (1970); Cipriano v. City of Houma, 395 U.S. 701 (1969); Kramer v. Union Free School Dist. No. 15, 395 U.S. 621 (1969). But see Salyer Land Co. v. Tulare Lake Basin Water Storage Dist., 410 U.S. 719 (1973). The Court has also struck down unreasonably long residency requirements for voting. Dunn v. Blumstein, 405 U.S. 330 (1972).

importantly, in the one person, one vote cases the Court emphasized in the strongest and most eloquent manner the centrality of equal voting rights in the American democratic system.[113] In *Reynolds v. Sims*[114] Chief Justice Warren wrote, "[R]epresentative government is in essence self-government through the medium of elected representatives of the people, and each and every citizen has an inalienable right to full and effective participation in the political processes of his State's legislative bodies."[115]

In the reapportionment cases, the Court moved toward a functional view of equal political participation. Previous cases had established the right to cast a primary or general election ballot and to have the vote counted.[116] In *Wesberry v. Sanders*[117] and *Reynolds v. Sims*[118] the Court added another building block—the vote that is cast and counted must have a proportionately equal opportunity to influence the outcome of the election. Chief Justice Warren recognized that "the right of suffrage can be denied by a debasement or dilution of the weight of a citizen's vote just as effectively as by wholly prohibiting the free exercise of the franchise."[119]

In *Bullock v. Carter*,[120] the Court took a different step toward a functional view of equality. The Texas system of requiring candidates to pay high filing fees was unconstitutional, the Court held, because it tended to exclude potential candidates who lacked both personal wealth and affluent backers, "no matter how qualified they might be, and no matter how broad or enthusiastic their popular support."[121] Not only did the system deny some voters—especially the less affluent—the opportunity to vote for a candidate of their choosing;[122] it also gave the wealthy the power to place names on the bal-

---

113. Hadley v. Junior College Dist., 397 U.S. 50 (1970) (apportionment for school district trustees election); Avery v. Midland County, 390 U.S. 474 (1968) (county legislature); Reynolds v. Sims, 377 U.S. 533 (1964) (state legislative apportionment); Wesberry v. Sanders, 376 U.S. 1 (1964) (apportionment for congressional seats).

114. 377 U.S. 533 (1964).

115. Id. at 565. The Chief Justice also declared, "No right is more precious in a free country than that of having a voice in the election of those who make the laws under which, as good citizens, we must live." Id. at 560 (quoting Wesberry v. Sanders, 376 U.S. 1, 17 (1964)).

116. United States v. Saylor, 322 U.S. 385 (1944) (right to vote protected against ballot-box stuffing); United States v. Classic, 313 U.S. 299 (1941) (right to have vote counted as cast in primary election); Guinn v. United States, 238 U.S. 347 (1915) (right to cast general election ballot); United States v. Mosley, 238 U.S. 383, 386 (1915) (right to have vote counted in general election); Ex parte Yarbrough, 110 U.S. 651 (1884) (same); see Bixby, The Roosevelt Court, Democratic Ideology, and Minority Rights: Another Look at *United States v. Classic*, 90 Yale L.J. 741, 786–812 (1981).

117. 376 U.S. 1, 14–17 (1964).

118. 377 U.S. 533 (1964); see Auerbach, The Reapportionment Cases: One Person, One Vote—One Vote, One Value, 1964 Sup. Ct. Rev. 1.

119. 377 U.S. at 555 (footnote omitted). Nearly three centuries earlier, John Locke had recognized that malapportionment and rotten boroughs were inconsistent with his theory of the social contract. See J. Locke, supra note 99, xiii, 158, reprinted in Readings, at 572–73.

120. 405 U.S. 134 (1972).

121. Id. at 143.

122. "[T]he rights of voters and the rights of candidates," the Court wrote, "do not lend themselves to neat separation; laws that affect candidates always have at least some theoretical, correlative effect on voters." Id.

lot.[123] In other ballot-access cases the Court protected the right of voters to vote effectively by invalidating state requirements that discriminated unjustifiably against minor party and independent candidates.[124]

When barriers to equality are imposed not by state action, but by circumstances or economic resources or private persons, the equal protection clause might no longer provide protection.[125] Nevertheless, the bounds imposed by the state action requirement do not limit the fundamental ideal of political equality that underpins our democratic system of government. That ideal must inspire all of us as citizens. In the words of Dean Rosenthal,

> The goal of enriching the electoral system, through broadening the base of citizen influence and reducing inequities in the opportunities of candidates and their supporters to persuade the electorate, is a worthy one; it is not only consistent with but indispensable to the attainment of the most fundamental purposes of the Constitution.[126]

Political inequalities stemming from disparities in wealth have historically made Americans uneasy. As my late colleague Harold Leventhal observed, many Americans have long perceived a need for a "larger purpose of democratic government, the need of a self-governing people to trammel the exploding capabilities of what were called the vested interests."[127] He referred to, among others, Theodore Roosevelt, who in 1910 theorized that "if our political institutions were perfect, they would absolutely prevent the political domination of money in any part of our affairs." Recognizing, however, the reality of American politics in his time, Roosevelt called for a corrupt practices act "to prevent the advantage of the man willing recklessly and unscrupulously to spend money over his more honest competitor."[128]

Political philosopher John Rawls has recognized that the dominance of wealth in the political process is inconsistent with both the philosophical meaning and the practical exercise of political equality. Rawls maintained that

---

123. Id. at 143–44. Subsequently, in Lubin v. Panish, 415 U.S. 709 (1974), the Court struck down another filing-fee requirement, stressing that "voters can assert their preferences only through candidates or parties or both and it is this broad interest that must be weighed in the balance." Id. at 716. Chief Justice Burger wrote, "[O]ur tradition has been one of hospitality toward all candidates without regard to their economic status." Id. at 717–18. The Court has also invalidated a requirement that candidates be property owners. Turner v. Fouche, 396 U.S. 346, 363–64 (1970).

124. Storer v. Brown, 415 U.S. 724, 738–40 (1974); Williams v. Rhodes, 393 U.S. 23 (1968). But see American Party of Texas v. White, 415 U.S. 767 (1974); Jenness v. Fortson, 403 U.S. 431 (1971).

125. See Buckley v. Valeo, 424 U.S. 1, 49 n.55 (1976). But see Pekelis, Private Governments and the Federal Constitution, *in* Law and Social Action 91, 113–14 (1970) (proposing new view of state action based on sociological test of "actual influence"; illegitimate economic pressures may be unconstitutional if they "do control in fact the political processes of a given society"); Nicholson, supra note 78, at 830 (suggesting "state action" as basis for requiring campaign finance restrictions under equal protection clause).

126. Rosenthal, Campaign Financing and the Constitution, 9 Harv. J. Legis. 359, 360 (1972).

127. Leventhal, supra note 3, at 370.

128. Quoted in id. at 363.

the "worth of liberty" was not the same for everyone, because of "the inability to take advantage of one's rights and opportunities as a result of poverty and ignorance, and a lack of means generally."[129] He added:

> The liberties protected by the principle of participation lose much of their value whenever those who have greater private means are permitted to use their advantages to control the course of public debate. For eventually these inequalities will enable those better situated to exercise a larger influence over the development of legislation.[130]

More recently Chief Justice Burger seized upon this theme to justify allowing the television networks to close their airwaves to paid political announcements.[131] Although I do not agree with the conclusion in that case,[132] the Court's discussion of the potential impact of wealth upon politics is worth noting. The public interest in providing access to the marketplace of ideas and experiences, the Chief Justice wrote, "would scarcely be served" by compelling broadcasters to accept paid political ads, because this system would be "so heavily weighted in favor of the financially affluent, or those with access to wealth." Even under a first-come, first-served system, the Chief Justice continued, "the views of the affluent could well prevail over those of the others, since they would have it within their power to purchase time more frequently,"[133] and they might monopolize the available time. Requiring broadcasters, under the Fairness Doctrine, to provide free time for opposing views would not redress the imbalance, because "the affluent could still determine in large part the issues to be discussed."[134] The right of access, the Chief Justice concluded, "would have little meaning to those who could not afford to purchase time in the first instance."[135] The unstated but inescapable

---

129. J. Rawls, supra note 100, at 204. This distinction between rights and the power to secure these rights is also made by philosopher Bernard Williams. He writes:

> It may be said that in a certain society, men have equal rights to a fair trial, to seek redress from the law for wrongs committed against them, etc. But if a fair trial or redress from the law can be secured in that society only by moneyed and educated persons, to insist that everyone *has* this right, though only these particular persons can *secure* it, rings hollow to the point of cynicism: we are concerned not with the abstract existence of rights, but with the extent to which those rights govern what actually happens.

Williams, The Idea of Equality, *in* Philosophy, Politics and Society, ser. II, at 110–31 (1962), reprinted in Justice and Equality 116, 128–29 (H. Bedau ed. 1971) (emphasis in original).

130. J. Rawls, supra note 100, at 225. Rawls therefore suggests public funding of campaigns, "for when parties and elections are financed not by public funds but by private contributions, the political forum is so constrained by the wishes of the dominant interests that the basic measures needed to establish just constitutional rule are seldom properly presented." Id. at 226.

These insights should carry over into constitutional analysis. As Dean Rosenthal has written, "[I]f the Constitution requires that each man's vote count equally, may not that fact be deemed pertinent in consideration of the validity of measures intended to reduce inequalities in men's opportunities to affect the vote?" Rosenthal, supra note 126, at 377.

131. CBS v. Democratic Nat'l Comm., 412 U.S. 94, 123 (1973).

132. See Business Executives' Move for Vietnam Peace v. FCC, 450 F.2d 642 (D.C. Cir. 1971), rev'd sub nom. CBS v. Democratic Nat'l Comm., 412 U.S. 94 (1973).

133. 412 U.S. at 123.

134. Id.

135. Id.

premise of this discussion is that the political arena is less healthy, and less likely to serve the public interest and democratic ideals, if the agenda and the discussion are dominated by those with ample financial resources. Apparently the Chief Justice and the Court did not have these concerns in mind when *Buckley* and *Bellotti* were under consideration.

The broader purposes of our political system are ill-served by allowing the power of money to drown out the voices of the relatively moneyless, or by allowing too many contests to turn on the differences in the amounts of money that candidates have to spend. We cannot rest content with our past achievements, proud as they are, in advancing toward legal equality in the political process. The trenchant social critic Anatole France wrote, in the late nineteenth century, "The law, in its majestic equality, forbids the rich as well as the poor to sleep under bridges, to beg in the streets, and to steal bread."[136] A latter-day Anatole France might well write, after observing American election campaigns, "The law, in its majestic equality, allows the poor as well as the rich to form political action committees, to purchase the most sophisticated polling, media, and direct mail techniques, and to drown out each other's voices by overwhelming expenditures in political campaigns." And the law, in its majestic equality, has imported the decision criteria of the commercial marketplace into the sanctum of political decisionmaking.[137] When money becomes more important than people, when media mastery weighs more heavily than appeals to judgment, when opportunities to communicate with voters are extremely unequal, the result is a cynical distortion of the electoral process. The people's choices are not based on their informed preferences among ideas and candidates, and government of the people, by the people, and for the people becomes an empty shibboleth.

III. Is the First Amendment the Obstacle to Political Equality the Supreme Court Says It Is?

As I have indicated, Congress, in the aftermath of Watergate, tried to turn the tide of moneyed influence and to enhance political equality by statutory restrictions on campaign spending. In significant part, these efforts were repudiated by the Supreme Court in *Buckley* and *Bellotti*, under the guise of first amendment protection for political speech.[138] Paradoxically, by

136. A. France, The Red Lily 91 (W. Stephens trans. 1894). This passage was quoted by Justice Frankfurter in Griffin v. Illinois, 351 U.S. 12, 23 (1956) (Frankfurter, J., concurring), and by Justice Brennan in Maher v. Roe, 432 U.S. 464, 483 (1977) (Brennan, J., dissenting).

137. See L. Berg, H. Hahn & J. Schmidhauser, supra note 3, at 41–46 (explaining differences between principles underlying economic market and one-person, one-vote in the political arena). Financial participation in politics is far more expandable than other political activities and hence creates much greater potential for unequal influence. Adamany, supra note 36, at 570–71; see also Note, The Corporation and the Constitution: Economic Due Process and Corporate Speech, 90 Yale L.J. 1833, 1855 (1981) (criticizing *Bellotti* decision because it "allows access to political audiences to be allocated in ways that more closely reflect the dominance of corporate wealth in the economy").

138. The Court asserted that "the concept that government may restrict the speech [i.e., spending] of some elements of our society in order to enhance the relative voices of others is

equating political spending with political speech and according both the same constitutional protection, the Court placed the first amendment squarely in opposition to the democratic ideal of political equality. This perverse result derives from a narrow view of freedom of expression, divorced from the broader ideals of our political system.

In *Buckley* and *Bellotti* the Court donned the mantle of the first amendment heritage. The Court's opinions in those two cases cited earlier decisions touching on virtually all of the major areas of sustained first amendment controversy in this century—political libel, seditious speech, freedom of the press, comtempt of court, labor picketing, obscenity, commercial speech, civil rights activity, and the right to petition.[139] From Justice Holmes's dissent in *Abrams v. United States* and Justice Brandeis's concurrence in *Whitney v. California* to the opinions for the Court in *Thornhill v. Alabama*, *NAACP v. Alabama*, and *New York Times Co. v. Sullivan*, the authorities relied on in the two recent election law cases are virtually an honor roll of great first amendment cases.

Bellotti also cited an article by one of the leading theoreticians of the first amendment, Alexander Meiklejohn's "The First Amendment is an Absolute."[140] Facile absolutism indeed marks the tone of the Court's discussion of expenditure limits in both *Buckley* and *Bellotti*.[141] In an earlier discussion I

---

wholly foreign to the First Amendment." Buckley v. Valeo, 424 U.S. 1, 48–49 (1976); First Nat'l Bank of Boston v. Bellotti, 435 U.S. 765, 790–91 (1978); Citizens Against Rent Control v. City of Berkeley, 102 S. Ct. 434, 437 (1981).

139. Virginia State Bd. of Pharmacy v. Virginia Citizens Consumer Council, 425 U.S. 748 (1976) (commercial speech) (cited in *Bellotti*, 435 U.S. at 783, 784 n.20); Miami Herald Pub. Co. v. Tornillo, 418 U.S. 241, 250 (1974) (freedom of the press) (cited in *Buckley*, 424 U.S. at 50–51, and in *Bellotti*, 435 U.S. at 791 n.30); Mills v. Alabama, 384 U.S. 214, 218, 220 (1966) (freedom of the press) (cited in *Buckley*, 424 U.S. at 45, 50, and in *Bellotti*, 435 U.S. at 776–77, 781); New York Times Co. v. Sullivan, 376 U.S. 254 (1964) (political libel) (cited in *Buckley*, 424 U.S. at 48, 49, and in *Bellotti*, 435 U.S. at 783, 785 n.21, 786 n.23); NAACP v. Button, 371 U.S. 415 (1963) (civil rights activity) (cited in *Buckley*, 424 U.S. at 22–23, 41, 48); Wood v. Georgia, 370 U.S. 375, 388 (1962) (contempt of court) (cited in *Bellotti*, 435 U.S. at 790, 792); Eastern R. Presidents Conf. v. Noerr Motor Freight, Inc., 365 U.S. 127 (1961) (right to petition) (cited in *Buckley*, 424 U.S. at 49); Kingsley Int'l Pictures Corp. v. Regents, 360 U.S. 684 (1959) (obscenity; prior restraint) (cited in *Bellotti*, 435 U.S. at 790); NAACP v. Alabama ex rel. Patterson, 357 U.S. 449 (1958) (civil rights activity) (cited in *Buckley*, 424 U.S. at 22, and in *Bellotti*, 435 U.S. at 780, 786); Roth v. United States, 354 U.S. 476 (1957) (obscenity) (cited in *Buckley*, 424 U.S. at 49); Associated Press v. United States, 326 U.S. 1, 20 (1945) (freedom of the press) (cited in *Buckley*, 424 U.S. at 49, and in *Bellotti*, 435 U.S. 777 n.12); Bridges v. California, 314 U.S. 252, 270 (1941) (contempt of court) (cited in *Buckley*, 424 U.S. at 48); Thornhill v. Alabama, 310 U.S. 88 (1940) (labor picketing) (cited in *Bellotti*, 435 U.S. at 776, 791 n.31); Whitney v. California, 274 U.S. 357, 377 (1927) (Brandeis, J., concurring) (seditious speech) (cited in *Buckley*, 424 U.S. at 53, and in *Bellotti*, 435 U.S. at 791–92 n.31); Abrams v. United States, 250 U.S. 616, 634 (1919) (Holmes, J., dissenting) (seditious speech) (cited in *Bellotti*, 435 U.S. at 791–92 n.31).

140. Meiklejohn, supra note 102, cited in *Bellotti*, 435 U.S. at 791 n.31. The Court referred to Meiklejohn in support of the proposition that "[g]overnment is forbidden to assume the task of ultimate judgment, lest the people lose their ability to govern themselves." Id. The *Bellotti* opinion also cited Meiklejohn's book, Free Speech And Its Relation to Self-Government (1948), and a book by Thomas Emerson, Toward a General Theory of the First Amendment (1966). 435 U.S. at 777 n.11.

141. See Leventhal, supra note 3, at 358–59, 373; Nicholson, Buckley v. Valeo: The Constitutionality of the Federal Election Campaign Act Amendments of 1974, 1977 Wisc. L. Rev. 323,

examined the fallacies in the reasoning in *Buckley* that led the Court to conclude that Congress may not constitutionally attempt to equalize speech opportunities by placing a ceiling on expenditures by candidates and committees.[142] Here I will attempt a broader task—showing that the Court in *Buckley* and *Bellotti* misappropriated the talismans of our first amendment past. By ritual incantation of the notion of absolute protection, by applying it to the quantity as well as the content of political expression, and by making the unexamined and unprecedented assertion that money is speech, the Court elevated dry formalism over substantive constitutional reasoning. Political discussion is indeed at the core of the first amendment's guarantees,[143] but the very centrality of political speech calls for a thorough rather than a conclusory analysis.

In order to understand the missteps taken by the Supreme Court, we must return to the first amendment heritage—the principles developed during this century to protect first amendment liberties.[144] The landmark cases invoked by the Court in *Buckley* and *Bellotti* quite properly carried the message that particular opinions and beliefs may not be suppressed by the government even if their content is unpopular with the majority,[145] threatening to dominant economic or social groups,[146] or critical of the structure or personnel of government.[147] It is not enough, however, to look at selected references from these cases. To appreciate their contribution to the development of first

---

372; Comment, Cases That Shock the Conscience: Reflections on Criticism of the Burger Court, 15 Harv. C.R.-C.L. L. Rev. 713, 736–37 (1980) (criticizing *Buckley* and *Bellotti* for "detach[ing] the auxiliary rules from their original purpose on the basis of the right's all-encompassing, indiscriminate character").

142. Wright, supra note 17; see Leventhal, supra note 3, at 358–67, 369 (discussing weaknesses in Court's analysis in *Buckley* opinion). Judge Leventhal observed pointedly, "[W]hat is missing from the Supreme Court's opinion is any sense of the history of campaign reform legislation, of the grievous abuses that prompted it, the frustration that accompanied it, the evasion and political pressures that have undermined all less-than-comprehensive measures of reform." Id. at 362.

143. First Nat'l Bank of Boston v. Bellotti, 435 U.S. 765, 776 (1978) ("the heart of the First Amendment's protection"); Buckley v. Valeo, 424 U.S. 1, 14 (1976) ("area of the most fundamental First Amendment activities"); Monitor Patriot Co. v. Roy, 401 U.S. 265, 272 (1971) ("it can hardly be doubted that the constitutional guarantee has its fullest and most urgent application precisely to the conduct of campaigns for political office").

144. The Court has never developed a comprehensive theory of the meaning of the first amendment; it has used a hodge-podge of different doctrines at various times and in various contexts. See N. Dorsen, P. Bender & B. Neuborne, 1 Emerson, Haber, & Dorsen's Political and Civil Rights in the United States 57–59 (4th ed. 1976); T. Emerson, The System of Freedom of Expression 15–16 (1970); Bork, Neutral Principles and Some First Amendment Problems, 47 Ind. L.J. 1, 20 (1971); Van Alstyne, A Graphic Review of the Free Speech Clause, 70 Calif. L. Rev. 107 (1982). But some principles have stood the test of time.

145. See, e.g., New York Times Co. v. Sullivan, 376 U.S. 254 (1964) (Alabama libel judgment against newspaper for publication of civil rights group advertisement).

146. See, e.g., Kingsley Int'l Pictures Corp. v. Regents, 360 U.S. 684 (1959) (censorship based on film's presentation of adultery in a favorable light); Thornhill v. Alabama, 310 U.S. 88 (1940) (ban on labor picketing).

147. See, e.g., Wood v. Georgia, 370 U.S. 375 (1962) (contempt conviction of sheriff who had criticized county judge); Grosjean v. American Press Co., 297 U.S. 233 (1936) (discriminatory tax imposed by Huey Long regime on selected group of newspapers).

amendment principles, we must examine their historical context and the intellectual influences that they reflect.

Abrams and *Whitney,*[148] landmark opinions by Justices Holmes and Brandeis in the decade after the First World War, grew out of the postwar obsession with subversives and seditious groups. *Abrams* was an appeal from the conviction of a small handful of radicals who had published two pamphlets seeking to arouse workers to international unity and had flung some copies out of a Manhattan window. *Whitney* sought to overturn the conviction of an official of the California branch of the Communist Labor Party under the state's criminal syndicalism statute. Holmes and Brandeis disapproved of both convictions but failed to convince the majority of the Court.[149] Both Justices were significantly influenced by the seminal theoretical writings of Zechariah Chafee, Jr.,[150] who had begun to write about the first amendment because he was deeply troubled by the wholesale trials and convictions of radicals and pacifists under the World War I Espionage Act.[151]

A similar concern with suppression of unpopular messages is found in the context and intellectual roots of *New York Times Co. v. Sullivan.*[152] The newspaper had been subjected to a libel judgment of $500,000 by an Alabama jury for publishing a political advertisement by a civil rights group that contained partially inaccurate statements about the actions of Alabama officials.[153] In fashioning a constitutional libel standard protecting negligently

---

148. Abrams v. United States, 250 U.S. 616 (1919); see id. at 624 (Holmes, J., dissenting). Whitney v. California, 274 U.S. 357 (1927); see id. at 372 (Brandeis, J., concurring).

149. Holmes dissented in *Abrams* and was joined by Brandeis. 250 U.S. at 624. In *Whitney* Brandeis, joined by Holmes, concurred in the Court's opinion upholding the syndicalism conviction, but his approach differed fundamentally from that of the majority. The majority, citing Gitlow v. New York, 268 U.S. 652, 666–68 (1925), held that the state legislature's decision to make criminal any association with a group that advocated violence or terrorism as a means of accomplishing political change was a legitimate exercise of police power to prohibit "utterances inimical to the public welfare, tending to incite to crime, disturb the public peace or endanger the foundations of organized government and threaten its overthrow by unlawful means." 274 U.S. at 371. Brandeis took issue with this approach. Finding the statute to aim "not at . . . criminal syndicalism . . . but at association with those who propose to preach it," id. at 373, Brandeis argued that a legislature could not curtail such speech unless it presented a clear and present danger of an immediate and a serious harm. Id. at 374–77. The mere legislative act of proscribing the speech was insufficient to support a finding of clear and present danger, he contended. Despite arguing for the significantly higher threshold, Brandeis concurred in the Court's judgment because the defendant had failed to raise the absence of clear and present danger as a defense at trial, and Brandeis felt constrained from inquiring into the issue on review of a state court judgment. Id. at 379–80. Nonetheless, the concurrence registered a fundamental disapproval of the majority approach. See Bork, supra note 144, at 23.

150. Rabban, The First Amendment in Its Forgotten Years, 90 Yale L.J. 514, 591–94 (1981).

151. Id. at 586–91; Chafee, Thirty-Five Years with Freedom of Speech, 1 U. Kan. L. Rev. 1, 1-2 (1952). Chafee's basic theoretical insights were set forth in a Harvard Law Review article published in June 1919. Chafee, Freedom of Speech in War Time, 32 Harv. L. Rev. 932 (1919). Chafee repeated his message in several of his subsequent works. See, e.g., Z. Chafee, Freedom of Speech (1920); Z. Chafee, Free Speech in the United States 1-35 (1941).

152. 376 U.S. 254 (1964).

153. The Court found, however, that the evidence did not support a finding that the allegedly libelous statements were made "of and concerning" the particular public official who was plaintiff in the case. Id. at 288–92.

inaccurate criticism of public officials, the Court emphasized our "profound national commitment to the principle that debate on public issues should be uninhibited, robust, and wide open."[154] Underlying this commitment was the conception that the very idea of self-government bestows upon the public the privilege, the right, and the duty of criticizing government and government officials.[155] The "central meaning of the First Amendment," the Court declared, "is to secure 'the widest possible dissemination of information from diverse and antagonistic sources,' " and "to assure unfettered interchange of ideas for the bringing about of political and social changes desired by the people."[156] As Justice Brennan, the author of *New York Times Co. v. Sullivan*, has observed,[157] these ideas reflect the views of Alexander Meiklejohn, who, like Chafee, first forayed into the first amendment arena at a time of governmental suppression of ideas. Meiklejohn's *Free Speech and Its Relation to Self-Government*[158] was published in the shadow of the McCarthy era. The book decried legislative investigations and administrative programs that sought to protect the minds of citizens "from the influence of assertions, of doubts, of questions, of plans, of principles which the government judges to be too 'dangerous' for us to hear."[159]

The terrain of first amendment work on political expression up to the 1970's is thus a landscape dominated by content-regulation questions.[160] The theory of the first amendment expressed in *Abrams* and *Whitney* differs in some important ways from the theory underlying the *Sullivan* case,[161] and Chafee's views are by no means the same as Meiklejohn's,[162] but these very divergences emphasize the context they have in common. That context is the need to defend political expression, no matter how unorthodox its ideas, from the majority's tendency to suppress dissident voices, and from efforts by those in power to muzzle their political opponents.

I favor a reading of the first amendment that is powerful and expansive, one that accords with the view of Justice Hugo Black that the first amendment

---

154. Id. at 270.

155. Id. at 269–75, 282; see Kalven, The New York Times Case: A Note on "The Central Meaning of the First Amendment," 1964 Sup. Ct. Rev. 191, 209.

156. 376 U.S. at 273, 266, 269 (quoting Associated Press v. United States, 326 U.S. 1, 20 (1945), and Roth v. United States, 354 U.S. 476, 484 (1957)). These words were the centerpiece of the Court's decision to protect unlimited political spending in *Buckley v. Valeo*—but they originated in judicial protection of a newspaper that had served as a vehicle for criticism of public officials on the inflammatory issue of civil rights. See Kalven, supra note 155, at 192 (noting that the case is a major instance of the important constitutional consequences of the civil rights movement).

157. Brennan, The Supreme Court and the Meiklejohn Interpretation of the First Amendment, 79 Harv. L. Rev. 1, 10, 14–15, 18 (1965); see Kalven, supra note 155, at 209, 221.

158. A. Meiklejohn, supra note 102.

159. Id. at xiii; see id. at x–xi, 46, 93.

160. In Police Department v. Mosley, 408 U.S. 92, 95–96 (1972), the Court stressed, "above all else, the First Amendment means that government has no power to restrict expression because of its message, its ideas, its subject matter, or its content . . . . The essence of this forbidden censorship is content control."

161. See Brennan, supra note 157, at 9–10.

162. See A. Meiklejohn, supra note 102, at 61–70 (criticizing Chafee's first amendment theories).

rightfully takes first place in the Bill of Rights.[163] Like constitutional law generally, first amendment thinking must necessarily adapt to the changing needs and evolving perceptions of society.[164] But while theoretical formulation and emphasis may change, the core notion of the first amendment remains the protection of diverse, antagonistic, and unpopular speech from restriction based on substance. To invoke the first amendment, not to protect diversity, but to prevent society from defending itself against the stifling influence of money in politics is to betray the historical development and philosophical underpinnings of the first amendment.

None of the rationales for strong protection of free expression—truth, autonomy and self-fulfillment, social stability, or self-government—justifies the continuing and unchecked abuses that excessive spending has brought to the electoral process. Chafee's thought, elaborated in a series of articles and books, was based on a single core idea—that freedom of expression is essential to the search for truth.[165] Holmes stated the same view with unmatched eloquence in *Abrams*:

> [W]hen men have realized that time has upset many fighting faiths, they may come to believe even more than they believe the very foundations of their own conduct that the ultimate good desired is better reached by free trade in ideas—that the best test of truth is the power of the thought to get itself accepted in the competition of the market, and that truth is the only ground upon which their wishes safely can be carried out. That at any rate is the theory of our Constitution.[166]

But the truth-producing capacity of the marketplace of ideas is not enhanced if some are allowed to monopolize the marketplace by wielding excessive financial resources. Just as proponents of the free market system generally recognize the need for government policing of the competitive economic process by enforcement of antitrust laws,[167] proponents of freedom of expression must recognize the need for government policing of the competitive electoral process by campaign finance laws.[168]

---

163. See E. Cahn, The Firstness of the First Amendment, *in* Confronting Injustice 86 (1962).

164. See Wright, Professor Bickel, The Scholarly Tradition, and the Supreme Court, 84 Harv. L. Rev. 769, 786 (1971) ("[P]articular fact situations influence the course of the law. If an unanticipated fact situation forces a modification of previously articulated goals and rules, then so be it. But the general thrust of constitutional adjudication should remain firmly grounded in the ideals of the constitutional text."). Cf. Brest, The Misconceived Quest for the Original Understanding, 60 B.U. L. Rev. 204, 228–29 (1980) (constitutional decisionmaking must respond to changes in social needs and values); Reich, Mr. Justice Black and the Living Constitution, 76 Harv. L. Rev. 673, 736 (1963) ("A constitutional provision can maintain its integrity only by moving in the same direction and at the same rate as the rest of society. In constitutions, constancy requires change.").

165. Z. Chafee, Free Speech in the United States, supra note 151, at 31, 137–38; Chafee, Freedom of Speech in War Time, supra note 151, at 956.

166. Abrams v. United States, 250 U.S. 616, 630 (1919) (Holmes, J., dissenting).

167. See, e.g., R. Posner, Antitrust Law: An Economic Perspective 8–18 (1976) (economic inefficiency of monopoly supports effective antitrust policy).

168. See Leventhal, supra note 3, at 373–74. Similarly, structural obstacles to free competition in the marketplace of ideas create the need for government-mandated rights of access to the

The first amendment absolutism of Justice Hugo Black[169] and Thomas Emerson[170] is consistent with financial reform of the electoral process. Emerson stressed the dynamics of freedom of expression, pointing out that intense pressures for conformity exist at all times and in all places and require the utmost vigilance to protect free speech against abridgment.[171] Both Black and Emerson also emphasized the need for self-expression as an element of personal autonomy and self-fulfillment, and warned that suppression of a person's beliefs subjects his mind to the dehumanizing control of others.[172] Campaign finance reforms promote the same values that these thinkers found in the first amendment. Unchecked political expenditures, no less than crass regulation of ideas, may drown opposing beliefs, vitiate the principle of political equality, and place some citizens under the damaging and arbitrary control of others.[173] Limiting the amount that wealthy interests may spend to publicize their views enhances the self-expression of individual citizens who lack wealth, furthering the values of freedom of speech.

The safety-valve function of the first amendment, expounded by Justice Brandeis in *Whitney v. California*,[174] also harmonizes with the goals of cam-

---

broadcast media. As Jerome Barron has contended, the assumption that there is a self-sustaining free market mechanism for ideas stems from "an essentially romantic view of the first amendment." Changes in the communications industry, Barron recognizes, have destroyed the equilibrium in the marketplace of ideas, making laissez-faire irrelevant and requiring active government intervention to assure access to the media by speakers with varying viewpoints. Barron, Access to the Press—A New First Amendment Right, 80 Harv. L. Rev. 1641, 1647-48, 1653-56 (1967).

169. Black, The Bill of Rights, 35 N.Y.U. L. Rev. 865, 881 (1960) ("Our First Amendment was a bold effort . . . to establish a country with no legal restrictions of any kind upon the subjects people could investigate, discuss, and deny."); cf. id. at 880 (other provisions of Bill of Rights buttress first amendment by protecting "the weak and the oppressed from punishment by the strong and the powerful who wanted to stifle the voices of discontent raised in protest against oppression and injustice in public affairs"). Black also relied on a slippery-slope analysis that resembled Emerson's. See Cahn, Justice Black and First Amendment "Absolutes": A Public Interview, 37 N.Y.U. L. Rev. 549, 559 (1962); Reich, supra note 164, at 719-20.

170. T. Emerson, supra note 144, at 10.

171. Emerson wrote, "[I]t is necessary to recognize the powerful forces that impel men towards the elimination of unorthodox expression. Most men have a strong inclination, for rational or irrational reasons, to suppress opposition." T. Emerson, supra note 144, at 9; see id. at 9-11; Emerson, Toward a General Theory of the First Amendment, 72 Yale L.J. 877, 887-93 (1963).

172. See T. Emerson, supra note 144, at 6, 21; Cahn, supra note 169, at 554 (Black's view that, to "preserve a dictatorship, you must be able to stifle thought, imprison the human mind and intellect"); cf. Black, supra note 169, at 880 ("Our own free system to live and progress has to have intelligent citizens, citizens who can not only think and speak and write to influence people, but citizens who are free to do that without fear of governmental censorship or reprisal."). Both men agreed, however, that actions were properly subject to government control. See T. Emerson, supra note 144, at 17; Cahn, supra note 169, at 558.

173. See supra text accompanying notes 99-137.

174. 274 U.S. 357, 375 (1927) (Brandeis, J., concurring); see Rabban, supra note 150, at 592-93 (discussing influences on Brandeis's thought); id. at 578-79 (views of prewar scholars Ernst Freund, Thomas Cooley, and Theodore Schroeder that libertarian standards for speech reduced danger of violence and crime); cf. T. Emerson, supra note 144, at 7 (freedom of expression is a method of achieving a more adaptable and hence more stable community). But see Bork, supra note 144, at 25 (safety-valve function involves solely issues of expediency or prudence, not of constitutional magnitude).

paign finance reform. Brandeis was concerned with the views of the downtrodden and discontented. The Founders knew, he wrote,

> that it is hazardous to discourage thought, hope, and imagination; that fear breeds repression; that repression breeds hate; that hate menaces stable government; that the path of safety lies in the opportunity to discuss freely supposed grievances and proposed remedies; and that the fitting remedy for evil counsels is good ones.[175]

But the argument of stability and order does not support unlimited political expenditures by the wealthy, nor does it immunize the lengthening shadow of PAC's in congressional elections.[176] Indeed, if Brandeis, who fought vigorously against big oppressive organizations and against concentrated wealth, [177] had witnessed the contemporary electoral scene, he might have written that it is hazardous to discourage civic spirit, hope, and participation; that disillusionment breeds alienation; that alienation breeds apathy; that apathy menaces the democratic idea; and finally that the path of safety lies in allowing individuals an opportunity to persuade the public by participating freely and equally in the electoral process.

Although all of the leading first amendment rationales may be comfortably reconciled with campaign spending reforms, the theory of Alexander Meiklejohn more than any other permits—perhaps even demands—restrictions on inequalities of financial resources.[178] Meiklejohn saw self-government as the fundamental principle of the first amendment.[179] Freedom of expression, he wrote, was the indispensable prerequisite for informed, rational decisionmaking; it was therefore essential to a self-governing populace of political equals bound by voluntary compact. In earlier controversies self-government was best served by removing government restrictions on political expression. In today's political forum that ideal is also served by permitting government regulation of the influence of money in politics, so that the wealthiest voices may not dominate the debate by the strength of their dollars rather than their ideas.

Meiklejohn made a perceptive distinction between abridging speech—which is sometimes permissible—and abridging the freedom of speech—which

---

175. 274 U.S. at 375.

176. Cf. Barron, supra note 168, at 1649 ("If freedom of expression cannot be secured because entry into the communication media is not free but is confined as a matter of discretion by a few private hands, the sense of the justice of existing institutions, which freedom of expression is designed to assure, vanishes from some section of our population . . . .").

177. Mason, Louis D. Brandeis, *in* 3 The Justices of the United States Supreme Court 1789-1969, at 2043, 2044-45 (L. Friedman & F. Israel eds. 1969).

178. Several commentators have recognized that a clash of first amendment values is involved in campaign finance cases. See, e.g., Emerson, supra note 171, at 948 ("not the reconciliation of freedom of expression with another kind of interest but the reconciliation of opposing interests within the system of free expression itself"); Freund, supra note 59, at 72; Leventhal, supra note 3, at 372.

179. A. Meiklejohn, supra note 102; cf. Bork, supra note 144, at 23, 26 (political speech is only type of expression protected by the first amendment). I do not agree with Bork's narrow view of the scope of the constitutional protection of freedom of expression, but I agree with him and with Meiklejohn that self-government and free speech are inextricably interrelated.

is almost always forbidden.[180] His analogy was the town meeting, the paradigm of the direct democratic ideal.[181] There, he noted, regulating and abridging communication is necessary for orderly presentation and intelligent deliberation. "It is not a dialectical free-for-all," he reminded his readers. "It is self-government."[182] In Meiklejohn's view, the first amendment protects not the individual's desire for self-fulfillment but the collective thought processes of the community.[183]

It is to prevent mutilation of these communal thought processes that campaign finance reforms are so essential. An election campaign is finite in time and focuses on specific ballot decisions regarding specific alternatives.[184] Expenditure limits and other curbs on campaign finance practices are analogous to rules of order at a town meeting, enforced so that the deliberative process is not distorted. The first amendment does not permit curbs on general discussion of political, economic, or social controversies. But, like the loud mouth and long talker at the town meeting, untrammeled spending during an election campaign does not serve the values of self-government, nor can it lay claim to first amendment protection.

In two categories of cases the Supreme Court has recognized that speech may be abridged without abridging the freedom of speech guaranteed by the first amendment—those that involve time, place, and manner restrictions, and those that involve allocation schemes. Time, place, and manner restrictions limit the untrammeled freedom of would-be speakers in the interests of would-be non-listeners. These restrictions serve interests in peace and quiet unrelated to suppressing communication. Thus, a nondiscriminatory ordinance may prohibit unreasonably loud, raucous operations by sound trucks on the streets of a community. As the Court recognized in *Kovacs v. Cooper*,[185] the Constitution does not require a community to suffer the nuisance of unregulated broadcasts that impose uninvited messages upon a captive audience.[186]

---

180. A. Meiklejohn, supra note 102, at 19. As Meiklejohn noted, "The First Amendment . . . is not the guardian of unregulated talkativeness." Id. at 25; see J. Rawls, supra note 100, at 203; Meiklejohn, supra note 102, at 252, 261.

181. A. Meiklejohn, supra note 102, at 22–27. But see Karst, Equality as a Central Principle in the First Amendment, 43 U. Chi. L. Rev. 20, 39–40 (1975) (criticizing town meeting analogy).

182. A. Meiklejohn, supra note 102, at 23.

183. Id. at 24–26, 65.

184. See T. Emerson, supra note 144, at 639–40 (contrasting limits on election campaigns, which may be permissible because they "are directed to a limited end and deal with a limited situation," and limitations on expression in other contexts, which are forbidden); Chevigny, supra note 55, at 219 ("election campaign is not an unlimited field of debate"; "the fact that a reply is theoretically possible after the election or outside the campaign is of little importance"). In contrast, in the area of general political discussion unrelated to campaigns, Brandeis's prescription holds good: "If there be time to expose through discussion the falsehood and fallacies, to avert the evil by the processes of education, the remedy to be applied is more speech, not enforced silence." Whitney v. California, 274 U.S. 357, 377 (1927) (Brandeis, J., concurring).

185. 336 U.S. 77 (1949).

186. Id.; cf. Freund, supra note 59, at 72 ("We are dealing here not so much with the right of personal expression or even association, but with dollars and decibels. And just as the volume of sound may be limited by law, so the volume of dollars may be limited, without violating the First Amendment.").

In contrast to time, place, and manner restrictions, allocation schemes limit the freedom of would-be speakers in the interest of would-be listeners. These schemes protect the integrity of the system of communications itself. When the forum is limited by physical, technological, or economic factors, the messages of some speakers must be limited if all points of view are to be heard, so that the audience may enjoy a full range of uninhibited debate. Allocation of limited opportunities for speech prevents mutual interference or distortion, and thus enhances the flow of information to listeners. Thus, in the broadcasting industry, in which the number of usable frequencies is technologically limited, the Court has been compelled to recognize the existence of clashing first amendment interests: the claimed exclusive rights of the broadcasting licensees and the rights of others who seek access to the media to express their views. To cushion the clash between the two groups the Court has focused instead on the listeners and has recognized that their first amendment rights are better served by diversity than by monopoly. As Justice White wrote for the Court in *Red Lion Broadcasting Co. v. FCC*,[187] it is "the right of the viewers and listeners, not the right of the broadcasters, which is paramount."[188]

Regulating campaign finance to prevent the polluting effects of financial inequalities involves a hybrid of both categories of permissible limitations on speech—time, place, and manner regulation and allocation schemes. Like time, place, and manner regulations, it serves social interests unrelated to suppressing communication, such as the fundamental interest in preserving political equality, and the more specific goals of removing financial barriers to candidacy, encouraging citizen involvement in the political process, and avoiding the danger that the wealthy can hold elected officials in political captivity.[189] Also, like the allocation of broadcasting licenses and the Fairness Doctrine, campaign finance restrictions protect the system of communications itself in the interest of speakers and voter-listeners. Excessive and unequal spending by one side interferes with the other's communication and, if the inequality is great enough, can effectively and completely drown out the other's message to the voters.[190] Even though the forum for electoral com-

---

187. 395 U.S. 367 (1969).

188. Id. at 390. Justice White added:

> It is the purpose of the First Amendment to preserve an uninhibited marketplace of ideas in which truth will ultimately prevail, rather than to countenance monopolization of that market, whether it be by the Government itself or a private licensee. . . . It is the right of the public to receive suitable access to social, political, esthetic, moral, and other ideas and experiences which is crucial here.

Id. The opinion essentially adopts Meiklejohn's view of the first amendment.

The Court has reaffirmed the general principle stated in *Red Lion* in subsequent cases. See CBS v. FCC, 453 U.S. 367, 395 (1981); CBS v. Democratic Nat'l Comm., 412 U.S. 94, 101-02 (1973).

189. See Brief for Appellees Center for Public Financing of Elections, Common Cause, League of Women Voters of the United States, et al. 65-74, 81-88, Buckley v. Valeo, 424 U.S. 1 (1976); Leventhal, supra note 3, at 361-62, 367-72.

190. Justice White observed in his *Buckley* dissent that "[t]he ceiling on campaign expenditures represents the considered judgment of Congress that elections are to be decided among candidates none of whom has overpowering advantage by reason of a huge campaign war chest." 424 U.S. at 265 (White, J., dissenting).

munications is not limited in the same technical sense that the broadcasting spectrum is, it is limited in time and subject matter, so that the first amendment interests of candidates and voters require safeguards against the potential for distortion and monopoly created by unlimited spending.

The financial structuring of political contests, like the allocation of access to the broadcast media, undeniably produces a tension between competing first amendment values. Those with unlimited resources have a colorable first amendment claim to be free to decide how, where, and when to spend their money to advertise their candidates and political viewpoints. But the first amendment analysis does not end with the identification of a single first amendment interest. In resolving the first amendment conflict, the *Red Lion* principle supplies the appropriate rule of decision. The interests of the listeners in hearing a broad range of ideas are paramount. In *Buckley* and *Bellotti,* however, the Court paid only lip service to the rights of listeners[191] and limited the *Red Lion* principle to the regulation of the media.[192] Its primary solicitude was given to the privileged few who can spend unlimited amounts of money to purchase political effectiveness, rather than to the listeners—the citizens who, by their vote, perform the most important of public duties.[193]

The Court's one-sided reconciliation of competing first amendment values is particularly skewed—if not perverse—in *Bellotti.* In giving strong first amendment protection to corporations, it ignored Justice White's sound reminder that

> [c]orporations are artificial entities created by law for the purpose of furthering certain economic goals. . . . It has long been recognized . . . that the special status of corporations has placed them in a position to control vast amounts of economic power which may, if not regulated, dominate not only the economy but also the very heart of our democracy, the electoral process.[194]

The inevitable result of the growth of corporate political power and influence, and its effective sanction by the Court, was recently analyzed by Archibald Cox.

---

191. In *Buckley*, the Court wrote, "In the free society ordained by our Constitution it is not the government, but the people—individually as citizens and candidates and collectively as associations and political committees—who must retain control over the quantity and range of debate on public issues in a political campaign." 424 U.S. at 57. In *Bellotti*, the Court declared, "[T]he people in our democracy are entrusted with the responsibility for judging and evaluating the relative merits of conflicting arguments." 435 U.S. at 791. The Court was apparently oblivious to the fact that the citizens, acting collectively through their elected representatives, had adopted the challenged legislation in order to protect their rights as listeners. Cf. Leventhal, supra note 3, at 368.

192. *Buckley*, 424 U.S. at 49–50 n.55.

193. See A. Meiklejohn, supra note 102, at 24–25 (comparing first amendment protection of speech by all citizens with speech or debate clause immunity for speech by legislators).

194. 435 U.S. at 809 (White, J., dissenting); see Brudney, Business Corporations and Stockholders' Rights Under the First Amendment, 91 Yale L.J. 235, 237–38, 240–41 (1982) (discussing political influence of corporate wealth and nature of corporate entities); Note, supra note 137, at 1853–60 (arguing that *Bellotti*'s emphasis on formal equality and its protection of corporate power reflect the spirit of pre-1937 economic due process jurisprudence, and contending that corporate speech rights do little if anything to serve genuine speech interests).

> If liberty means the opportunity of the individual man or woman to express himself or herself in a society in which ideas are judged principally by their merit, increasing the relative influence of organizations with large financial resources and shrinking the attention paid to truly individual voices means a net loss of human freedom.[195]

Such an outcome is fundamentally inconsistent with the underlying principles of the first amendment.

To return to the question: Is the first amendment an obstacle to democratic equality? The answer to me is clear. Liberty and equality must complement each other as equally indispensable linchpins of an open, democratic society. As Kenneth Karst has written,[196] and as the foregoing discussion of first amendment theory implies, equality is part of the central meaning of the first amendment and underlies each of its most important purposes.[197]

Indeed, instead of asking the defeatist question, "Is the first amendment an *obstacle* to democratic equality?" We should be asking, "How must we interpret and implement the first amendment in order to *enhance* equality?" In a world of advancing technology, scarce resources, and practical barriers to full freedom of discussion, we must not look at the first amendment solely as a negative prohibition. Although freedom of speech has generally been perceived as a limitation on government, I agree with Professor Emerson that the frontier of the first amendment today is the need for affirmative measures by government to protect, preserve, and enhance freedom of expression.[198]

IV. Remedies

Recognizing that fundamental principles of political equality are inseparable from first amendment values, the American people, the Congress, and the courts must make a concerted and timely effort to cleanse our body politic. Without providing detailed prescriptions, I would like to point to avenues of reform that respond to the grievous problems described earlier in this Article.

---

195. Cox, Foreword: Freedom of Expression in the Burger Court, 94 Harv. L. Rev. 1, 70 (1980).

196. Karst, supra note 181.

197. Id. at 23.

198. T. Emerson, supra note 144, at 627–30. Emerson notes that "[s]earch for the truth is handicapped because much of the argument is never heard or heard only weakly. Political decisions are distorted because the views of some citizens never reach other citizens, and feedback to the government is feeble." Under these circumstances, he urges, "it becomes essential, if the system [of freedom of expression] is to survive, that a search be made for ways to use the law and legal institutions in an affirmative program to restore the system to effective working order." Id. at 628–29.

See Z. Chafee, Free Speech in the United States, supra note 151, at 559–60; A. Meiklejohn, supra note 102, at 16–17, 104 (freedom of speech must not be given merely a negative meaning); Barron, supra note 168, at 1641 (marketplace of ideas is not self-operating); id. at 1654–56 ("Creating opportunities for expression is as important as ensuring the right to express ideas without fear of governmental reprisal.").

First, there is the alarming influence of political action committees sponsored by special interests. PAC's have taken a dominant position in the process of electing senators and congressmen and are increasingly active at the state level. It is vital to reduce their undue influence on candidates and, through candidates, on legislation. Congress should reduce the legal ceiling on the amount that each PAC may give to any candidate, and the amount that any candidate may receive from all PAC's taken together.[199] We should recognize that PAC contributions and expenditures inflict the same evils on the body politic as direct contributions and expenditures by corporations and labor unions, which have been banned by federal law for decades.[200]

Second, there is the growing cost of political campaigns, which tends to foster inequalities in spending, and thus to distort the political debate and to exclude all but the wealthy or the well-financed from running for office. The best and most comprehensive remedy would be public financing of political campaigns for the House and Senate.[201] Public financing may constitutionally be accompanied by limits on spending and contributions.[202] With one stroke public financing legislation could do much to remove the poison of money from the political bloodstream—even within the confines of the narrow constitutional limitations the present Supreme Court imposes on us.

If public financing is not enacted, less comprehensive stopgap measures should be considered. Given the prominent share of media spending in campaign budgets, reducing the cost of access to the media would do much to alleviate the blight of rising campaign costs and the resulting inequalities.

---

199. In the fall of 1979, the House of Representatives passed the Obey-Railsback bill, which would have lowered the permissible PAC contribution to a House candidate during an election cycle from $10,000 to $6,000 and would have created a $70,000 ceiling on the aggregate contributions from all PAC's to a House candidate. A filibuster threat blocked the bill in the Senate. See Alexander, The Obey-Railsback Bill: Its Genesis and Early History, 22 Ariz. L. Rev. 653, 663–65 (1980); Railsback, Congressional Responses to Obey-Railsback, 22 Ariz. L. Rev. 667 (1980); Kenski, supra note 38.

200. See supra note 34. In *Bellotti* the Court was careful to distinguish the prohibition on referendum spending by corporations, which it was invalidating, from the Corrupt Practices Act's ban on corporate spending in candidate campaigns, which it did not reach.

> The overriding concern behind the enactment of statutes such as the Federal Corrupt Practices Act was the problem of corruption of elected representatives through the creation of political debts. . . . The importance of the governmental interest in preventing this occurrence has never been doubted. The case before us presents no comparable problem, and our consideration of a corporation's right to speak on issues of general public interest implies no comparable right in the quite different context of participation in a political campaign for election to public office.

435 U.S. at 788 n.26.

201. See F. Wertheimer & R. Huwa, supra note 31, at 11; Chevigny, supra note 55, at 221–25 (discussing advantages and disadvantages of various public financing schemes).

The Court has held that the public must bear the cost of administering primary elections; the same policies support public funding of campaigns. "Viewing the myriad governmental functions supported from general revenues," the Court stated, "it is difficult to single out any of a higher order than the conduct of elections at all levels to bring forth those persons desired by their fellow citizens to govern." Bullock v. Carter, 405 U.S. 134, 148–49 (1972).

202. *Buckley,* 424 U.S. at 57 n.65 (candidate may voluntarily refuse public funding and therefore avoid subjection to spending limits); Republican Nat'l Comm. v. FEC, 487 F. Supp. 280 (S.D.N.Y.) (three-judge district court), aff'd mem. 445 U.S. 955 (1980) (rejecting first amendment challenge to spending limits upon presidential candidate who accepts public funds).

Government control over the broadcast media is pervasive; reductions in the cost of political campaign advertising would be well within the power of Congress and well within the first amendment.[203] Congress should also consider requiring broadcasters to provide specified amounts of free television and radio time to recognized candidates.[204] The Fairness Doctrine should be preserved and strengthened, so that the networks and licensees bear responsibility for assuring reasonably balanced presentations in candidate and issue campaigns.[205]

All of these measures are probably within the Supreme Court's cramped version of the Constitution. But the Court's warped interpretation of the first amendment proscribes some of society's most powerful defenses against the polluting influence of money. *Buckley* unconditionally condemns limitations on overall candidate spending, spending from personal and family resources, and independent spending activity for or against specified candidates.[206] *Bellotti* gives corporations the right to spend money in political-issue referendum campaigns, even those totally unrelated to corporate business.[207] Yet spending limits are an essential weapon against gross inequalities in campaign communications. Although public funding is a workable remedy for candidate contests, in referendum and initiative campaigns it might well be impracticable as a comprehensive solution. In these political contests, the only way to prevent distorting inequalities in campaign spending may be the imposition of spending limits at a level high enough to assure adequate debate but low enough to permit all views to find clear, unstifled expression. Clinging to its tragic misconception of money as speech, however, the Court condemns the American electorate to distorted political perceptions arising from one-sided political campaigns. I fervently hope that, as the evidence mounts that the political process is in trouble, the Supreme Court will be moved to alter its position.

Conclusion

The Supreme Court, of course, says what the law is. But on a number of occasions in the past when the Court's doctrine has been both wrong and

---

203. See A. Rosenthal, supra note 59, at 62; F. Wertheimer & R. Huwa, supra note 71, at 29-32 (discussing proposed reduction in maximum unit cost for political campaign ads on television).

204. See L. Sabato, supra note 75, at 327 (discussing British system of free television broadcasts on all channels for political parties during election campaigns); F. Wertheimer & R. Huwa, supra note 71, at 22-24 (discussing proposal to require television licensees to supply free time to qualifying candidates). Dean Rosenthal has concluded that such requirements would be constitutional; Congress's power to ensure that licensees used their facilities in the public interest would "undoubtedly be sufficiently broad to sustain the provision." A. Rosenthal, supra note 59, at 62-63; Rosenthal, supra note 126, at 422.

205. See Mastro, Costlow & Sanchez, supra note 86, at 327-49 (Media Access Project's proposals for strengthening Fairness Doctrine in referendum campaigns).

The Fairness Doctrine is currently under attack by some members of the FCC. See Broadcasting, Nov. 2, 1981, at 36. But its repeal would eviscerate the reality, limited as it now is, of "robust, uninhibited, wide-open" debate. See Barron, supra note 168.

206. 424 U.S. at 39-59.

207. 435 U.S. at 765.

harmful, the pressure of sharply-etched needs has made it clear, first to observers and then to the Court itself, that the doctrine must be changed. Such was the case in the late 1930's when the Court began to uphold New Deal legislation,[208] and such was the case in 1954 when the Court overruled *Plessy v. Ferguson*.[209]

The growing impact of concentrated wealth on the political process, and the glaring inequalities in political campaign resources, threaten the very essence of political equality. The warning signs are plain for all to see. Today's threat to democracy is not the impending collapse of the structure of democratic institutions, but their continuing erosion from within. If this erosion is not checked, the principle of one person, one vote could become nothing more than a pious fraud. Ironically, the underpinnings of our democratic system are being menaced by decisions made by the Supreme Court in the name of the liberties of the first amendment.

The words I wrote in 1975 to close our Court of Appeals decision in *Buckley* did not then move the majority of the Supreme Court. Their message, however, has gained new urgency with the accumulated political experience of the intervening years:

> Our democracy has moved a long way from the town hall, one man, one vote conception of the Framers. Politics has become a growth industry and a way of life for millions of Americans. The corrosive influence of money blights our democratic processes. We have not been sufficiently vigilant; we have failed to remind ourselves, as we moved from town halls to today's quadrennial Romanesque political extravagances, that politics is neither an end in itself nor a means for subverting the will of the people.[210]

---

208. See, e.g., Wickard v. Filburn, 317 U.S. 111 (1942) (recognizing broad scope of commerce clause); United States v. Darby, 312 U.S. 100 (1941) (upholding Fair Labor Standards Act); Steward Machine Co. v. Davis, 301 U.S. 548 (1937) (upholding Social Security Act); NLRB v. Jones & Laughlin Steel Corp., 301 U.S. 1 (1937) (upholding National Labor Relations Act).

209. Brown v. Board of Educ., 347 U.S. 483 (1954), overruling Plessy v. Ferguson, 163 U.S. 537 (1896).

210. 519 F.2d 821, 897 (D.C. Cir. 1975), rev'd in part, 424 U.S. 1 (1976).

5

Judicial Review and the Equal Protection Clause

To some, this essay marks a change in Judge Wright's judicial philosophy. He asks this question: "Should judges be meddling less in the running of the country?" He answers by stating that judges should be "more reluctant" to substitute their judgments for those of the officers of other branches of government. But he goes on to say that he remains an "uncompromising activist" in the area of equality for disadvantaged minorities. Certainly, therefore, the essay can be read as an indication that Wright is pulling back from his advanced position of judicial activism.

That, however, is not an entirely accurate appraisal of what he has to say in Chapter 5. His main concern is with the equal protection clause of the Constitution and how it is employed to help victims of discrimination. He does counsel some retreat from judicial activism, particularly in the area of review of the actions of the public administration, but he emphasizes the need for affirmative governmental action to help members of disadvantaged minorities. His main concern, it seems, lies in the way that corporate enterprises can manipulate the administrative process; hence his strong belief, stated in this essay, in allowing more administrative judgments to stand: "The most obvious case for judicial retreat is when courts are reviewing administrative action by government agencies and departments for nonconstitutional error. We tend to forget that, once upon a time, it was not self-evident that judges had any *business overseeing the work of departments or other agencies of government, except when it was charged that constitutional rights had been violated. I am now wondering why that is not the right rule, why courts should do more than keep administrators within constitutional bounds." But he goes on to point out that there is a wide range of statutory review of administrative action.*

This means, in effect, that judges will—even if they follow Judge Wright's advice—still have much to say about the legality and propriety of administrative action. In so doing, they will be carrying out the will of Congress and thus will, according to Wright, serve the democratic principle that basic policy decisions should be made by the legislature.

Is, then, Judge Wright changing his judicial philosophy? The answer must be "no"; he is still promoting judicial activism, albeit in a somewhat different guise.

Francis Biddle, the man in whose honor we are assembled this evening, would, I think, have accepted the concept of equality as I shall attempt to define it. Patrician though he was, he participated wholeheartedly in the revolution attempted by that other patrician, Franklin Roosevelt. He believed in democracy and understood the popular yearning for a New Deal in which the have-nots would, at last, obain a more appropriate share of the Nation's bounty. As one of the first Chairmen of the new National Labor Relations Board, he helped establish the rights of the working people of this country. As Solicitor General he personally argued, and won, the great case of *United States v. Darby,*[1] sustaining the constitutionality of the Fair Labor Standards Act[2] and establishing the proposition that judicial review of majoritarian social and economic regulation ought to be minimal.

Francis Biddle believed in government by the people, not by judges.[3] But he did not condone majoritarian persecution of the weak,

---

[1] 312 U.S. 100 (1941).

[2] 29 U.S.C. §§ 201-19 (1976).

[3] Biddle's view of the limited scope of judicial review in testing social and economic regulation was doubtless influenced by Mr. Justice Holmes, whose "Secretary" he had been during the 1911 Supreme Court term. *See* F. BIDDLE, A CASUAL PAST 261–92 (1961). As Biddle was later to stress, Holmes was in most respects an economic and political conservative who differed from his bretheren on the Supreme Court primarily in his refusal to translate his own opinions into constitutional man-

Reprinted by permission of the *Harvard Civil Rights-Civil Liberties Law Review*, Vol. 15, pp. 1-28 (1980).

the unpopular, the outcast. In 1940, when pre-war hysteria swept the country, he roundly condemned attacks on aliens, and on Jehovah's Witnesses who would not salute the flag.[4] And, together with Attorney General Robert Jackson, he decried as a bill of attainder the congressional proposal to deport the unpopular Harry Bridges.[5] Moreover, face to face with his own Pennsylvania Bar Association, he chided them and the leaders of the American Bar for not protesting the bill.[6]

Nor did Biddle turn a blind eye to racial discrimination—as many did during those early war years. While he was Solicitor General and Attorney General[7] he repeatedly spoke out against race discrimination, using his position as the Nation's chief legal officer to provide important leadership.[8] Although in most things he urged moderation, here, he said, "there is no ground for compromise for those who take their democracy seriously, and who insist that this greatly underprivileged group is given a more equal opportunity to share with the rest of us in the fruits of a democracy that includes us all."[9] I am pleased indeed to participate in these proceedings honoring such a man.

The most insistent question of the present decade for all those connected with the law in this country is whether we went too far in the

---

dates, binding on all legislators and administrators. *See* F. BIDDLE, JUSTICE HOLMES, NATURAL LAW AND THE SUPREME COURT 10–13, 68–69 (1961).

[4] "Leadership and Democracy," Address to the Pennsylvania Bar Association (June 19, 1940)(U.S. Dep't of Justice collection) at 6.

[5] *Id.* at 5–5b.

[6] *Id.* at 5.

[7] Biddle was Solicitor General from January 1940 to September 1941, when he became Attorney General, a position he held until mid-1945. BIOGRAPHICAL DIRECTORY OF THE UNITED STATES EXECUTIVE BRANCH 1774–1977, at 25 (R. Sobel ed. 1977).

[8] During Biddle's time as Solicitor General and Attorney General, the Government began taking a more active role in civil and criminal litigation challenging race discrimination. During these years, the United States participated as a party or as *amicus curiae* in urging the Supreme Court to find in federal statutes some protection for blacks against peonage, Taylor v. Georgia, 315 U.S. 25 (1942), against discrimination on public carriers, Mitchell v. United States, 313 U.S. 82 (1941), and in labor relations, Steele v. Louisville & Nashville R.R. 323 U.S. 192 (1944); Turnstall v. Brotherhood of Locomotive Firemen, 323 U.S. 210 (1944), and against official violence, Screws v. United States, 325 U.S. 91 (1945).

[9] Address at the Commencement Exercises of LaSalle College, Philadelphia (May 26, 1942)(U.S. Dep't of Justice collection) at 5.

1960's in declaring legal rights and fashioning legal remedies; whether we ought to call a halt or, indeed, somehow cut back. In a hundred forms, some rude, some more moderate, that question has been asked since at least the dawning of the 1970's. It encompasses complaints that the Washington bureaucracy stifles our lives, that too many legal restrictions paralyze the police, that too many laws inhibit free choice, that civil claims succeed too often and criminal prosecutions too seldom, and that the law is too complex and too pervasive, sometimes benefitting the very poor and the very rich, but mostly benefitting the lawyers.

The complaint is general. It is part of the mood of the times. It is echoed by congressmen, by Supreme Court Justices, by the President of the United States, even by Harvard Law School professors. I do not propose to hurl myself against this great tide. Even if I could, I would not defend most of the beleaguered land. But, in any case, I am concerned only with the role of courts. How, if at all, should judges respond to the prevailing current?

I put to one side the ordinary business of the courts: adjudicating private disputes between individuals and holding criminal trials. There is doubtless much room for argument whether, in a country as litigious and lawless as ours, it is necessary to undertake some reforms affecting the overwhelming volume, the prohibitive cost, and perhaps the predictable outcome, of such traditional cases. But that is not the subject of this address.

Moreover, in the constitutional area, I shall not address questions of criminal procedure or procedural due process. No doubt judicial intervention in these areas has contributed heavily to the cynical national mood I have described, and no doubt issues such as the exclusionary rule have raised some serious questions about the role of the judiciary with respect to the other branches of government. Those concerns have been fully addressed elsewhere. Although I certainly cannot promise very bright lines, my aim is to suggest, however tentatively, what sorts of tasks are truly "committed to the judiciary" and what are not. I want to concentrate on that vast area of governmental action in the social and economic spheres that we often clumsily hold together under the name "policy." So I am addressing only the role of the courts—primarily the federal courts—insofar as they perform the more ambitious task of reviewing the actions of government at the instance of dissatisfied citizens. To put the question baldly: Should judges be meddling less in the running of the country?

There is no easy answer. The more the Congress by its laws and the Executive by regulations intrude into the lives of the citizenry and the operations of the business community, the more the judicial branch is asked to intervene to safeguard property or liberty. Moreover, the courts themselves are often accused of imposing their own unwanted restrictions on the operation of government. For my part, I believe the judges *should* retrench from their disposition to act as the final arbiters of the public good. We should, I think, be more reluctant than we have been to fault the other agencies of government and, also, more hesitant about filling the void when, in our judgment, the elected branches of government should have acted and failed. But I make one important exception: the area of equal rights for disadvantaged minorities. As to that, I remain an uncompromising "activist." Let me elaborate.

I.

The most obvious case for judicial retreat is when courts are reviewing administrative action by government agencies and departments for nonconstitutional error. We tend to forget that, once upon a time, it was not self-evident that judges had *any* business overseeing the work of departments or other agencies of government, except when it was charged that constitutional rights had been violated. I am now wondering why that is not the right rule, why courts should do more than keep administrators within constitutional bounds.

Some will answer: Because somebody has to police the bureaucrats and Congress has given that job to the courts. It is true, of course, that under the Administrative Procedure Act[10] and other like statutes,[11] federal courts are required to review administrative action for legality, as well as constitutionality.[12] This is entirely appropriate. To confine the unelected bureaucracy within the limits fixed by the people's representatives is not judicial usurpation; it is to *serve* the

[10] 5 U.S.C. §§ 551–59, 701–06 (1976).

[11] *E.g.*, Social Security Act, 42 U.S.C. § 405(g) (1976).

[12] The Administrative Procedure Act, 5 U.S.C. § 706(2)(A) (1976), in relevant part, requires courts to determine whether agency action is "arbitrary, capricious, an abuse of discretion, or otherwise not in accordance with law."

democratic principle that fundamental policy decisions should be made by the popular branch of government.

A.

The claim that close judicial supervision of administrators' discretion is necessary, however, is questionable. Of course, there are today more bureaucrats, with more power, than ever before. But the legislative practice of investing officials with fairly broad discretion to "get on with the job" is hardly new. A century and a half ago the Supreme Court had occasion to say:

> A practical knowledge of the action of any one of the great departments of the government, must convince every person that the head of a department, in the distribution of its duties and responsibilities, is often compelled to exercise his discretion. He is limited in the exercise of his powers by the law; but it does not follow that he must show a statutory provision for every thing he does. No government could be administered on such principles. To attempt to regulate, by law, the minute movements of every part of the complicated machinery of government would evince a most unpardonable ignorance on the subject. Whilst the great outlines of its movements may be marked out, and limitations imposed on the exercise of its powers, there are numberless things which must be done, that can neither be anticipated nor defined, and which are essential to the proper action of the government.[13]

This remains true. The difference is that today the courts are constantly asked to *supervise* administrators acting under such broad delegations. I wonder whether the judges have not responded too enthusiastically to the invitation. Indeed, it is not clear how far it is, or can be made, the duty of the federal courts to review administrative decisions for nonconstitutional error.

Surely, Congress cannot insist that an Article III court should "screen" agency rules, regulations, or decisions before they take

[13] United States v. MacDaniel, 32 U.S. (7 Pet.) 1, 13–14 (1833).

effect, or thereafter, in the absence of a specific "case or controversy."[14] Nor, presumably, does the constitutional principle of separation of powers permit the courts, even at the request or direction of the legislative branch, to exercise a policy veto over the acts of the bureaucracy. Yet, in all but name, that is what often occurs, with congressional acquiescence. I am not at all sanguine about the constitutional propriety of courts reviewing administrative action for "abuse of discretion," except when the "abuse" amounts to arbitrariness or discrimination in violation of the Constitution. As Mr. Justice Frankfurter once wrote, "The Framers . . . did not make the Judiciary the overseer of our government."[15]

B.

As for the appeal to democratic theory as the reason for having courts supervise the agencies and departments of government, I reject it utterly. It is all too true that unelected bureaucrats are often left at large to govern under legislative mandates that embody no clear directive and few restraints. But this is no justification for unelected judges to supply the missing guidelines and test agency action accordingly. To the extent that a bureaucrat—or indeed the President—is acting without statutory authority, or plainly contrary to statute, the action is unconstitutional and, when their jurisdiction is properly invoked, it is the duty of courts to intervene. But judges do not have a roving commission as agents of the Congress to oversee the implementation of legislation by the bureaucracy.

On the contrary, insofar as Congress has permissibly delegated its legislative prerogatives to an administrator, the latter is entitled to the deference due the elected legislator, whose decisions the courts review only for constitutionality. The same principle holds for the agents of the elected President. As I have elsewhere suggested,[16] the time may

---

[14] *See, e.g.*, Buckley v. Valeo, 424 U.S. 1, 11–12 (1976); Aetna Life Ins. Co. v. Haworth, 300 U.S. 227, 239–41 (1937)(Congress may not require judicial opinion in absence of a case or controversy).

[15] Youngstown Sheet & Tube Co. v. Sawyer, 343 U.S. 579, 594 (1952) (Frankfurter, J., concurring).

[16] Wright, *Review: Beyond Discretionary Justice*, 81 YALE L.J. 578, 582–87 (1972).

be ripe to revive the doctrine that condemns excessive delegation of legislative power. Some contemporary legislation may well overstep permissible bounds in purporting to leave the making of laws to others. The courts perhaps may properly entertain that constitutional question. But when the agency is acting under a valid statute and does not itself offend the Constitution, it is not obvious why the judge's task is not at an end.

C.

If the judiciary were to limit its review to constitutional error, it would hardly leave the bureaucracy unchecked. We need only remember that the primary authority which federal courts have over state governmental action is to insist on conformity to the Constitution,[17] and no one complains that the weapon is too weak or the standard too lax. Why is it necessary to review *federal* agency action more stringently? To be sure, in federal cases courts tend to avoid reliance on the Constitution and to fault the agency for acting beyond statutory authority or for reaching its decision by a process inconsistent with the statutory mandate.[18] But, in many cases, the same result would follow even if conformity to the Constitution were the only criterion. Adversely to affect the liberty or property of citizens without being so authorized by law is, after all, to break the first commandment of our constitutional system, which ordains a "government of laws, not men."[19] So, also, whether or not the statute says so, the due process clause imposes restraints on how decisions are made.[20] And, of course, the Constitution itself—independently of the Adminstrative

[17] *See, e.g.*, Martin v. Hunter's Lessee, 14 U.S. (1 Wheat.) 304 (1816) (Supreme Court's interpretation of the Constitution binds state courts); C. BLACK, STRUCTURE AND RELATIONSHIP IN CONSTITUTIONAL LAW 74 (1969)("On the whole, there is nothing in our entire governmental structure which has a more leak-proof claim to legitimacy than the function of the courts in reviewing state acts for federal unconstitutionality.").

[18] *See* Ashwander v. Tennessee Valley Auth., 297 U.S. 288, 347 (1936)(Brandeis, J., concurring)(discussing the basis for judicial preference of nonconstitutional grounds of decision).

[19] 4 J. ADAMS, THE WORKS OF JOHN ADAMS 230 n.1 (C.F. Adams ed. 1851).

[20] *E.g.*, Morrissey v. Brewer, 408 U.S. 471 (1972).

Procedure Act or any other law—forbids governmental action that is obviously arbitrary, capricious, or discriminatory.[21]

Yet, agencies are often faulted for alleged deficiencies that *no one* would label constitutional. Those are precisely the cases about which I have doubts. If judges approached the review of agency action wearing only a "constitutional hat," they would be more restrained. And they would be on firmer ground when they did intervene. It would do no harm if the federal courts were to start from the premise that they could fault administrators only for constitutional error, at least pausing before going beyond that point. I suspect this habit, if generally followed, would help restore the balance between the judiciary and the popularly elected branches of government.

II.

I come, then to the primary mission of the federal judiciary: enforcing the Constitution against whoever, including the President and the Congress, would ignore its commands and its restraints. It *is* a vital task, which distinguishes the courts of the United States from most others in the world. But some of us, I fear, have gotten carried away. There has been a tendency to blow the trumpets more often than is seemly for judges who, since Jefferson's day, do not wear full-bottomed wigs and scarlet robes trimmed in ermine, and who have long since had to abandon the notion that, like ancient oracles, they "hand down" judgments conceived in high heaven.

A.

The essential point is that the courts are not the sole guardians of the Constitution. Like judges, other government officials, state and federal, also take an oath to protect and defend the Constitution.[22] Not only do the other branches of government have an independent duty to observe constitutional limitations, but, sometimes, they must be left to keep their own house in order. There are breaches of the Constitution that are none of the courts' business. Thus, no judge or group of judges presumably can, or should, do anything about such

---

[21] *E.g.*, Joint Anti-Fascist Refugee Comm. v. McGrath, 341 U.S. 123 (1951).

[22] U.S. CONST. art. VI, cls. 2 & 3.

constitutional derelictions as a congressional grant of a title of nobility[23] or a presidential refusal to receive ambassadors.[24] More importantly, I do not suppose the courts are competent to give relief against an irresponsible President who declined to nominate Justices of the Supreme Court even when vacancies prevented the Court from functioning,[25] or against an irresponsible Congress that failed to appropriate monies for the running of the government.[26] Even with respect to the Constitution, judges are not *always* supreme.

So much is, I suppose, agreed on all sides. But the question remains whether the courts are too reluctant to concede their incompetence, whether they should decline jurisdiction more than they do. I have little sympathy with the traditional devices for avoiding decision of awkward issues: lack of a concrete "case or controversy," prematurity, mootness, the "political question" doctrine, official immunity, sovereign immunity, lack of standing, and the rest. Yet such devices, however contrived, may be necessary in a country where every issue of domestic policy—and some of foreign policy—is tendered to judges on the claim of unconstitutionality.

There are no innocents in this matter. It was the State of Alabama, in one instance seconded by Mississippi, that invoked the Supreme Court's original jurisdiction and the Constitution to enjoin the President from assembling troops near Birmingham: to restore order in one case,[27] to halt school desegregation enforcement proceedings in the state in another,[28] and to restrain the collection of federal income taxes while religious organizations remained exempt in still another.[29] It was the Commonwealth of Massachusetts that asked the Court to stop American participation in the Vietnam conflict[30] as violating the declaration of war clause of article I.[31] And it was a

---

[23] *Id.* art. I § 9, cl. 8.

[24] *Id.* art. II, § 3, cl. 3.

[25] *See id.* art. II § 2, cl. 2; 28 U.S.C. § 1 (1976).

[26] *See id.* art. I, § 8.

[27] Alabama v. United States, 373 U.S. 545 (1963).

[28] Alabama v. Finch, 396 U.S. 552 (1970); Mississippi v. Finch, 396 U.S. 553 (1970).

[29] Alabama v. Connally, 404 U.S. 933 (1971).

[30] Massachusetts v. Laird, 400 U.S. 886 (1970).

[31] U.S. CONST. art. I § 8, cl. 11.

group of Western, Midwestern, and Southern States that applied to the Court under the property clause of article IV[32] to prevent execution of the Panama Canal Treaty.[33]

In short, everybody complains about the interference of the federal courts, often labeling it "usurpation," but, when it serves their purpose, the critics are not slow to invoke judicial intervention. If judges are to stop trying to run the country in the name of the Constitution, they can expect little outside help; they must restrain themselves. Nor should they wait. For if a sufficient public backlash against the Court produces involuntary restrictions, these are most likely to strike at that jurisdiction—equal protection under law—which it is essential to maintain undiminished. Preserving the authority of the courts where it counts counsels us to take a step back elsewhere.

Time does not permit a full elaboration of areas where the courts could cut back. Let me begin by simply suggesting that the nation would not come to an end if the judges were to hold themselves incompetent to enforce the provisions of the original Constitution—as opposed to the amendments—except for the prohibitions against suspension of the writ of habeas corpus[34] and the passage of bill of attainder and ex post facto laws[35] and some of the other prohibitions of sections 9 and 10 of Article I,[36] the full faith and credit[37] and privileges and immunities[38] clauses of article IV, and the supremacy clause of article VI.[39] This would not affect the majority of constitutional cases reaching the courts, but it certainly would affect some. Of the remainder, probably most are criminal prosecutions or involve issues of procedural due process—cases which no doubt are proper candidates for judicial intervention. Consequently, I will confine my discussion of where courts could cut back to substantive constitutional claims founded on the first ten and the fourteenth amendments, claims of citizens against government.

---

[32] *Id.* art. IV, § 3, cl. 2.

[33] Idaho v. Vance, 434 U.S. 1031 (1978).

[34] U.S. Const. art. I, § 9 cl. 2.

[35] *Id.* art. I,§ 9, cl. 3.

[36] *Id.* art. I, §§ 9 & 10.

[37] *Id.* art. IV, § 1.

[38] *Id.* art. IV, § 2, cl. 1.

[39] *Id.* art. VI, cl. 2.

B.

Of course, when judges are asked to enforce the Bill of Rights or the privileges and immunities, due process, and equal protection clauses in section 1 of the fourteenth amendment, there is generally no debatable question of justiciability. It *is* the duty of the courts, federal and state, to vindicate individual rights against undue governmental interference, whether or not supported by the majority.[40] After all, the point of these provisions of the Constitution is, in large measure, to qualify democracy whenever popular fervor would trample liberty, deny equality, or expropriate private property. Yet, even here, the courts must be very sure before they override the will of the current majority in the name of the people who adopted the Constitution. Otherwise, as they did with respect to substantive due process,[41] judges might be imposing their own views on the citizenry on the pretext of enforcing the Bill of Rights or the fourteenth amendment.

The danger is real because the necessarily imprecise restraints of the original Bill of Rights and the "majestic generalities"[42] of the fourteenth amendment can be read very expansively, especially by judges, who as "jumped-up lawyers" are adept by training at making almost any proposition seem reasonable, to others and to themselves. Even if we confine the inquiry to the first section of the fourteenth amendment, the possibilities are awesome. We need only remember what was almost done in the name of the privileges and immunities clause by the post-Civil War Supreme Court and what was actually done in the name of the due process clause by the Court that came to an end in 1937.

C.

For example, it is, in the end, very fortunate that John A. Daniel, that former Supreme Court Justice who had resigned a decade earlier to join the Confederacy, did not, despite his special "eloquence"

[40] *See* L. TRIBE, AMERICAN CONSTITUTION LAW 564–67 (1978).

[41] *See* text accompanying notes 46–48 *infra*.

[42] The phrase is from Mr. Justice Jackson's opinion for the Court in Fay v. New York, 332 U.S. 261, 282 (1947).

before the Supreme Court, prevail in the *Slaughterhouse Cases*.[43] It was a near thing: four Members of the Court, including Chief Justice Chase and Justice Bradley, dissented and only the vote of a new Justice appointed before the reargument of the case saved the day.[44]

I say "saved the day" advisedly. Remember that the case was not about civil rights in the usual sense.[45] Remember, too, that the privileges and immunities clause on which it was based is, like the first amendment, absolute; it is not subject to state abridgement by due process of law or otherwise. What almost succeeded was the claim of business competitors that the grant of a slaughterhouse monopoly by the Louisiana legislature abridged their constitutional privilege to ply that trade.

The argument may seem far-fetched today, but, as the dissenting opinions demonstrate, it could be made to seem plausible. Imagine the consequences. The privileges embraced by the clause are guaranteed absolutely. If the right to engage in any trade or profession were a privilege of national citizenship that cannot be "abridged"—presumably by either state or federal governments—the courts would be free to invalidate most economic regulation. Substantive due process would never have been invented.

D.

I turn to the due process clause which, after the *Slaughterhouse Cases*, became the substitute for the privileges and immunities clause as the basis for striking down economic and social legislation. Here, particularly, one has to marvel at the inventiveness of the judicial mind.

---

[43] 83 U.S. (16 Wall.) 36, 44, 57–58, 65 (1873)(laws enacted by Louisiana legislature establishing a slaughterhouse monopoly did not violate fourteenth amendment's privileges and immunities clause).

[44] The new Justice was Ward Hunt, appointed in 1872. For the full story of the *Slaughterhouse Cases* see C. FAIRMAN, VI HISTORY OF THE SUPREME COURT OF THE UNITED STATES, RECONSTRUCTION AND REUNION 1864–88, PART ONE 1320–63 (1971).

[45] Those who dissented in the *Slaughterhouse Cases* were not noted for their dedication to civil rights. Thus, the very next day, three of them joined the rest of the Court in rejecting the claim of Myra Bradwell that, as a citizen, fully qualified, she could not be denied a license to practice law. Bradwell v. Illinois, 83 U.S. (16 Wall.)

The problem, of course, was not whether "liberty of contract" is an aspect of the "liberty" protected by that clause. Presumably, it is. But as even Mr. Justice Sutherland recognized,[46] the due process clause, in both the fifth and fourteenth amendments, only prohibits the deprivation of "life, liberty, or property, *without due process of law,*" and that phrase presumptively means no more than that traditional legal procedures shall be followed or, in the words of the Magna Carta, that the citizen should be secure in his person and property against official action not sanctioned "by the lawful judgment of his peers or by the law of the land." While the provision was obviously intended as a shield against arbitrary acts of the Executive, it is not apparent that it applies when liberty has been restrained, or the value of property diminished, by legislation duly enacted by the people's elected representatives.

Yet, it is familiar history that, for some fifty years, continuing deep into the present century, the Supreme Court overcame the difficulty without the slightest show of self-doubt. "Without due process of law" came to mean: "We do not believe in the soundness of the views which uphold this law," as Mr. Justice Peckham wrote for the court, striking down a ten-hour day statute in *Lochner v. New York.*[47] The litany of the cases is long and well known, and I must suppress the urge to dilate even on the most outrageous of them. Suffice it to say that a modest exposure to some of these cases—from *Lochner,* involving a state statute, to the cases concerning child labor involving acts of Congress[48]—will convince even the most zealous champion of judicial supremacy that federal judges have no writ to promulgate, in the name of the Constitution, an economic charter of liberties.

Happily, that era of the Court's long love affair with substantive due process is past. But there are contemporary lessons. We must, first, remember why it happened. It is no accident that the due process

---

130 (1873). And, of course, ten years later Mr. Justice Bradley was writing for the Court in the Civil Rights Cases, 109 U.S. 3 (1883)(federal laws, based on the fourteenth amendment, held unconstitutional for prohibiting purely private discrimination).

[46] Associated Press v. NLRB, 301 U.S. 103, 135 (1937) (Sutherland, J., dissenting).

[47] 198 U.S. 45, 61 (1905).

[48] Hammer v. Dagenhart, 247 U.S. 251 (1918); Child Labor Tax Case (Bailey v. Drexel Furniture Co.), 259 U.S. 20 (1922).

clause was rediscovered and exploited by one side only in the great industrial age of this country. When, at last, the ordinary citizenry—or, more accurately, the white, male, adult citizenry—had achieved some measure of control over the legislative branch of government, modest laws were enacted to protect otherwise helpless men, women and children from the sweat shops and the worst of the other abuses then current. Hardly seriously threatened, but nevertheless affected in their pocket book, the captains of industry reacted swiftly. Where, by whatever means, they could not secure repeal of the offending statute, they went to their lawyers to challenge the law in court. And this cadre of resourceful company lawyers from the newly formed American Bar Association did their job well.[49] Too often, they succeeded in persuading the courts, especially the Supreme Court, to override the considered decision of the people's representatives for no better reason than disagreement with the economic philosophy underlying the challenged statute.

The Court's rulings were not merely undemocratic, however. Precisely because they were informed by *their* view of right policy, rather than a legal principle, the decisions were primarily in one direction. The liberty of the working man to organize, or to strike or boycott, received no comparable recognition. Nor is that surprising. Once it is conceded that judges are entitled to impose their own views of sound social or economic policy, regardless of the popular will, one expects them to be true to their faith, and reasonably consistent about it. And, in that day at least, most of those who sat on the federal bench were inclined to believe in privilege and property.[50]

Today, to be sure, things are different. But not quite so different as we might be tempted to think. The privileges and immunities and due process clauses are no longer available to strike down economic and social legislation. Yet, the lawyers representing big business and other entrenched interests, exhibiting their customary resourcefulness, have not given up. At the annual convention of the American Bar Association held in Dallas in August 1979, the House of Delegates passed a resolution calling for legislation abolishing the presumption

---

[49] *See generally* J. AUERBACH, UNEQUAL JUSTICE: LAWYERS AND SOCIAL CHANGE IN MODERN AMERICA 62–65 *passim* (1976).

[50] *See generally* R. MCCLOSKEY, THE AMERICAN SUPREME COURT 136–79 (1960).

of legality of government agency and departmental action and requiring de novo review of such action in federal courts.[51]

Even one less cynical than I can see what these lawyers and their clients for whom they speak are up to. Having lost the fight for substantive due process in the economic area with respect to legislation, they are now trying to enlarge the role of federal judges in the administrative process which, in today's world, by legislative delegation implements and interprets economic legislation passed by the elected representatives of the people. Thus, since their fifty years of success in attacking economic legislation itself has come to an end,[52] now they will train their legal guns on its administrative implementation. After all, if the implementation can be frustrated, even by delay, that is almost as satisfying to their clients as having the legislation itself declared unconstitutional.

While opposition to economic legislation at the administrative level is like trench warfare compared to attacking its constitutionality in court, in the long run it can be very effective, particularly because of the potential for delay. Indeed, most lawyers opposing implementation of legislation at the administrative level, if put on their Boy Scout honor, will agree that delay, often with interlocutory intervention into the administrative proceedings by a federal court, is the most effective weapon against implementation. Delay in administrative proceedings has been a scandal for many years, condemned by Congress and even the courts who contribute to it, but it continues unabated. All concerned know that if implementation can be delayed long enough, with campaign contributions in the right places new elections might bring a change in personnel and policy which might make further proceedings

---

[51] *See* 65 A.B.A.J. 1286 (1979). Legislation introduced by Sen. Dale Bumpers to remove the presumption of validity from agency rules and regulations has passed the Senate. Bumpers Amendment to Federal Courts Improvement Act of 1979, S. 1477, 96th Cong., 1st Sess. (1979). 125 CONG. REC. S12145–66, 12171–72 (daily ed. Sept. 7, 1979)(text, debate, and passage of Bumpers Amendment); 125 CONG. REC. S15437 (daily ed. Oct. 30, 1979)(Senate passage of S. 1477); 125 CONG. REC. H10245 (daily ed. Nov. 2, 1979)(referral of S. 1477 to House Committee on the Judiciary).

[52] *See* West Coast Hotel Co. v. Parrish, 300 U.S. 379 (1937) (upholding a state minimum wage law); NLRB v. Jones & Laughlin Steel Corp., 301 U.S. 1 (1937)(upholding the National Labor Relations Act); Lincoln Federal Labor Union v. Northwestern Iron & Metal Co., 335 U.S. 525, 535–37 (1949) (repudiating the "*Allgeyer-Lochner-Adair-Coppage* constitutional doctrine").

unnecessary. Thus if the industry leaders and their lawyers succeed in heavily involving federal judges in the administrative process, both during and after it eventually comes to an end with a final order, time will always be on their side and the opportunities for frustrating implementation of the legislative mandate will be virtually endless.

In sum, the era of substantive due process has taught us how far the law and the courts can be manipulated by resourceful advocates representing those who have the most to lose from any change toward an egalitarian society, and it cautions us to be vigilant lest the same end be reached by other means. But there is another lesson to be learned. It is that the due process clause is a very dangerous weapon in *any* hands, if it is read as authorizing judges to make policy.

Mr. Justice Black never tired of giving us that warning, even when the due process clause was invoked to strike down archaic birth-control laws.[53] For Justice Black, it was impermissible to give substantive content to the due process clause, except as it "incorporated" the specific guarantees of the Bill of Rights, notably the first amendment. That is the safe stance. Yet, it is difficult to fault the Court for straying from that strict rule when confronted with laws that seriously inhibit vital personal liberties that are not expressly mentioned in the first eight amendments.[54] It is well, however, to guard against recreating the *Lochner* monster in new guise. Judges with persuasions opposite to those prevailing in the judiciary of 1905 should be no freer to impose their notions of good policy on the citizenry. Fortunately, I believe the Court is too aware of the discredit attending the earlier experience in substantive due process to repeat the error.[55] Justice Black's view remains a valuable warning to contemporary judges.

As of now, with only very limited exceptions, the privileges and immunities clause and the due process clause are not being construed to create new substantive rights. I leave procedural due process to one side, and turn to the equal protection clause. This is where I stop blowing "Retreat," because in my view giving life and breath to the equal protection clause is the noblest mission of the federal judiciary.

---

[53] Griswold v. Connecticut, 381 U.S. 479, 507–27 (1965) (Black, J., dissenting).

[54] *E.g.*, Roe v. Wade, 410 U.S. 113, 153 (1973)(state criminal abortion laws held to violate constitutional right to privacy).

[55] *See, e.g., id.* at 117.

III.

Thus far, I have been gradually conceding away as unessential, or mischievous, or even dangerous, certain areas of the jurisdiction of the federal courts. That was not mere tactics. The exercise does serve to demonstrate that a plea for retaining, and in some respects increasing, the equal protection jurisdiction is not necessarily unchecked judicial activism. There are, in my view, special reasons why judicial intervention on behalf of the principle of equality is more legitimate than in other areas. That perception is not new. Charles Black,[56] Laurence Tribe,[57] John Ely,[58] Ronald Dworkin,[59] and Kenneth Karst,[60] among others, have suggested the theme. But let me embroider in my own way.

A.

The potential sweep of the equal protection clause[61] is now known to be much greater than was imagined by the framers of the fourteenth amendment—who conceived the privileges and immunities clause as the prime weapon against oppressive or discriminatory state action. Yet, however expansively read, the equal protection clause has only a limited utility as a tool for imposing judicial views on the legislative process, state or federal. That is, of course, because it speaks in relative, not absolute, terms. Unlike the privileges and

---

[56] *E.g.*, Black, *The Lawfulness of the Segregation Decisions*, 69 YALE L.J. 421 (1960); Black, *The Supreme Court, 1966 Term–Foreword: State Action, Equal Protection, and California's Proposition 14*, 81 HARV. L. REV. 69 (1967).

[57] *E.g.*, L. TRIBE, *supra* note 40, at 991–1136.

[58] *E.g.*, Ely, *Legislative and Administrative Motivation in Constitutional Law*, 79 YALE L.J. 1205, 1228–30 (1970).

[59] *E.g.*, R. DWORKIN, TAKING RIGHTS SERIOUSLY 223–39 (1977).

[60] *E.g.*, Karst, *The Supreme Court, 1976 Term–Foreword: Equal Protection Under the Fourteenth Amendment*, 91 HARV. L. REV. 1 (1977).

[61] Although I mention only the equal protection clause of the fourteenth amendment, I assume that the same rule of equal treatment is binding on federal officials—including the Congress and the President—by virtue of the "equal protection component" of the due process clause of the fifth amendment. I am content to follow the Supreme Court in saying "it would be unthinkable that the same Constitution would impose a lesser duty on the Federal Government." Bolling v. Sharpe, 347 U.S. 497, 500 (1954).

immunities clause and the due process clause, the equal protection clause cannot be invoked to require either the national government or the states to create wholly new rights in their residents. It merely commands that governmental benefits and immunities shall be available to all, if granted to any. The equal protection clause is therefore the least dangerous of the constitutional precepts embodied in the fourteenth amendment.[62]

B.

At the same time, the ideal of equal treatment at the hands of government is the most difficult to maintain; it does indeed require constant vigilance. The wholesale suppression of fundamental liberties, affecting the entire citizenry, is unlikely to occur, or to be long tolerated, courts or no courts. But officially sanctioned discrimination against particular groups in our society is all too familiar in the history of this Nation. And experience shows us that political remedies are seldom afforded, at least until after the courts have given the lead. Here, then, is an essential role for judges.

The school desegregation cases[63] and the reapportionment decisions[64] are sufficient illustration. However revolutionary, these cases, in my judgment, represent peculiarly appropriate business for a constitutional court. That was not always conceded. Indeed, it has been, and is still being argued in some quarters that voting arrangements are wholly "political" and thus beyond the sphere of the judicial branch.[65] So said Mr. Justice Holmes in an early case, rejecting a

---

[62] *See* Gunther, *The Supreme Court, 1971 Term–Foreword: In Search of Evolving Doctrine on a Changing Court: A Model for a Newer Equal Protection*, 86 HARV. L. REV. 1, 41–43 (1972).

[63] *E.g.*, Brown v. Board of Educ., 347 U.S. 483 (1954); Bolling v. Sharpe, 347 U.S. 497 (1954).

[64] *E.g.*, Baker v. Carr, 369 U.S. 186 (1962)(courts may determine constitutionality of state apportionment statutes); Reynolds v. Sims, 377 U.S. 533 (1964)(equal protection clause requires seats in both houses of bicameral state legislatures to be apportioned on population basis).

[65] *See, e.g.*, Baker v. Carr, 369 U.S. 186, 300–01 (Frankfurter, J., dissenting); Gordon & Woodward, *Congressional Reapportionment: The Pandora's Box of Judicial Intervention in Politics and How to Put the Lid Back On*, 6 MEM. ST. U. L. REV. 403 (1976). *See also* A. BICKEL, THE SUPREME COURT AND THE IDEA OF PROGRESS (1970).

black man's claim to vote in Alabama in 1903.[66] But, as the same Justice Holmes wrote twenty years later in condemning the white primary in Texas, the "political question" challenge to the Court's jurisdiction is "little more than a play upon words."[67] The truth is that safeguarding the right to vote against discrimination is emphatically the province of the judiciary.

The reasons are obvious. Courts defer to legislatures, state and federal, primarily because they are elected and their acts are assumed to represent the will of the people. That, however, presupposes that everyone has an equal vote: if one part of the citizenry is wholly excluded from the franchise, or its voice is significantly diluted, the basis for judicial deference is eroded. Nor do incumbent legislators have the incentive to correct the situation, and the victims of voting discrimination have no clear political remedy. In short, judicial intervention here is necessary.

C.

What is more, the principle of equality before the law is peculiarly appropriate for judicial implementation. Courts are, almost by definition, committed to the idea of equal treatment. In this country all federal judges, from the beginning, have been required by law to swear "to administer justice without respect to persons, and do equal right to the poor and to the rich."[68] And the motto "equal justice under law" was chiseled into the facade of the present Supreme Court building in 1935, well before Roosevelt had changed the complexion of the Court. To decide whether official action accords equal treatment is a task especially congenial to the judicial temperament. And, because it comes naturally and involves few basic policy choices, judges tend to perform the function well.

D.

Perhaps the most important thing equal protection can teach us about the question of judicial activism versus judicial restraint is the

---

[66] Giles v. Harris, 189 U.S. 475, 488 (1903).

[67] Nixon v. Herndon, 275 U.S. 536, 540 (1927).

[68] Judiciary Act of 1789, § 8, 1 Stat. 73, 76 (codified at 28 U.S.C. § 453 (1976)).

fallacy of casting the question as a categorical one. Not rigid postures on activism or deference, but the demands of justice in discrete areas of the law, along with a larger sense of the range of questions the Constitution commits to the judiciary, should help judges determine their proper role. Judicial activism and judicial restraint role models cannot provide answers in particular cases. Indeed, in affirmative action cases, the prototypical judicial restraint judge and the prototypical activist might change roles, the former invalidating the legislation and the latter upholding it.

With this in mind, I want to consider affirmative action and a second vital issue in equal protection—disproportionate impact—to illustrate my sense of the proper role of judicial "activism." I believe federal judges should be "activist" in these matters, but "activist" in a special sense: not the sense of intervening as a matter of temper in legislative judgments, but rather of "actively" examining the social and economic effects of legislation to ensure harmony with the goals of the equal protection clause. And I want to inveigh against what I consider a special form of "restraint" in this area—the form that treats the clause as a rarefied, color-blind "neutral principle,"[69] sometimes deferring to, sometimes overriding legislatures, but often ignoring the real point of equal protection. There is, as I have indicated, a danger of inching back to something akin to *Lochner* in this approach, but in a civilized society, to protect individual core privacy rights, for example, it is a danger we might wish to accept.

IV.

Ever since the beginning, our judicial system has fought to overcome what must be conceded to be the natural order of things in which the rich and the powerful have easier access to the courts and tend to fare better there than the ordinary citizen, and very much better than the poor and the outcast. King John was made to promise that he would no longer "sell . . . refuse or delay . . . justice."[70] I need hardly say that the promise was not kept and that, even today, both in England and in this country, the rich continue to have easier access to courts

---

[69] *See* Wechsler, *Toward Neutral Principles of Constitutional Law*, 73 HARV L. REV. 1 (1959).

[70] MAGNA CARTA, ch. 40.

and to fare better in many cases, if only because they can buy themselves the best lawyers. We have come a long way from the day when Lord Chancellor Bacon exacted bribes to hear a case and defended the practice by insisting the money never influenced his judgment—thereby admitting fraud but denying corruption.[71] But, ironically, the long struggle to eliminate corruption and partiality has developed habits of mind in judges, and expectations about them in the public, that inhibit a creative implementation of the equal protection clause, and ultimately threaten to pervert it.

A.

Consider that cherished symbol of Justice, the blind-folded lady holding the scales. The notion is that the blindfold prevents her from knowing whether the parties to be judged wear rags or furs, whether they are black or white. That is all very well in a tort suit or a criminal prosecution.[72] But it will hardly do when the issue is whether governmental action discriminates against the complainant's class. Obviously, the judges must remove the blinders long enough to notice whether the plaintiff is indeed a member of the group he alleges is the object of discrimination. There is, however, a reluctance to go further. It goes against the grain to base a distinction on whether the victim is white or black. To the traditional judge, it is far easier to speak of impermissible "racial discrimination" than to stress that the adversely affected race is in a disadvantaged minority status.

This would matter little if neutrality were merely a question of language—as it seemed to be with the Warren Court. But, today, the Supreme Court tends to take its "neutral principles" seriously—as in *Bakke*.[73] In my view, the approach is fundamentally wrong. Equal justice does not mean that what is good for the goose is good for the gander.

---

[71] W. & A. DURANT, THE STORY OF CIVILIZATION: THE AGE OF REASON BEGINS 171 (1961).

[72] See the opinion of Mr. Justice Wilson, concurring, in the short-lived decision of Chisholm v. Georgia, 2 U.S. (2 Dall.) 419, 466 (1793). Concluding that a state was no less subject to the jurisdiction of the Supreme Court than other defendants, Wilson wrote that, in respect of the parties before the Court, Justice "is, as she is painted, blind."

[73] Regents of the Univ. of Cal. v. Bakke, 438 U.S. 265 (1978).

The basic fatuousness of the goose-gander approach is captured in that oft-quoted cynicism of Anatole France: "The majestic [e]quality of the law . . . prohibits the wealthy as well as the poor from sleeping under the bridges."[74] A sufficient example is the Supreme Court's ruling in *Griffin v. Illinois*,[75] condemning the charge for a criminal trial transcript as applied to those who cannot afford the price. Of course, the rule assessing everyone a like fee for the transcript was fair on its face and served at least two perfectly legitimate functions: helping to defray the cost of appellate proceedings and discouraging frivolous appeals. But it worked unequally, effectively depriving the poor of the right of appeal which others enjoy. Nor does the new rule compelled by the Court's decision offend the equal protection clause, even though it requires some to pay for transcripts while others get them free. This discrimination *serves* the ends of the equal protection clause.

All I am illustrating is that, in applying the equal protection clause, judges must notice whose ox is gored by the challenged action. So it is with laws that distinguish on the basis of race or ethnic origin. Our courts are fond of repeating that all racial classifications are "immediately suspect."[76] Of course they are. But that is because, usually, such classifications have been made by the dominant white Anglo-Saxon majority—to the disadvantage of a politically impotent racial or ethnic minority—whether it be Orientals in California,[77] or blacks in the South,[78] or Puerto Ricans in New York.[79] There is, however, no general constitutional prohibition on racial or ethnic legislation. In the context and at the time of *Plessy v. Ferguson*,[80] it was useful for Justice Harlan to throw out the slogan that "our Constitution is colorblind,"[81] but he surely knew that the equal protection clause meant more than this.

To be sure, in an ideal world race and ethnic origin would be

---

[74] A. FRANCE, THE RED LILY 87 (1905).

[75] 351 U.S. 12 (1956).

[76] *E.g.*, Korematsu v. United States, 323 U.S. 214, 216 (1944).

[77] *E.g.*, *id.;* Yick Wo v. Hopkins, 118 U.S. 356 (1886).

[78] *E.g.*, Strauder v. West Virginia, 100 U.S. (10 Otto) 303 (1880); Loving v. Virginia, 388 U.S. 1 (1967).

[79] *E.g.*, Katzenbach v. Morgan, 384 U.S. 641 (1966).

[80] 163 U.S. 537 (1896).

[81] *Id.* at 559 (Harlan, J., dissenting).

irrelevancies. But we cannot overcome our history of enslaving black men, women and children so quickly. In 1866, in the first Civil Rights Act, Congress defined equality in the exercise of enumerated rights as measured by those "enjoyed by white citizens."[82] Although the statute's language was deliberately general, and its benefit was ultimately held by the Court to run to whites,[83] this was effectively race legislation, designed to raise the former slave to equality of civil rights. Four years after the passage of the first Civil Rights Act, a like provision for political rights was added to the Constitution by the fifteenth amendment, which expressly condemns discrimination "on account of race [or] color."[84] A century later, it was found necessary to do more to achieve a measure of equality. Thus, the Voting Rights Act of 1965 provides special substantive and procedural rules for the benefit of voters and candidates where "non-white" registration is abnormally low.[85] In other fields, special minority "quota" or "affirmative action" programs were instituted in an attempt to redress the balance.[86]

For my part, I see nothing "suspect" about such affirmative efforts to equalize opportunities. Particular schemes may be vulnerable to objection, but the principle is sound. So long as past discrimination continues to disadvantage the members of the victimized class, it will be right—and constitutional—to attempt to compensate for those adverse effects. The day will come when blacks and other victims of American history have so far achieved their rightful place in our society that they need no longer be "the special favorites of the laws." But that was hardly the fact in 1883 when Justice Bradley wrote those words in the *Civil Rights Cases*,[87] and, partly thanks to him, it is still premature to think that day has arrived a century later. As Professor Laurence Tribe recently wrote: "So long as poverty and race remain so closely linked, the reminder that a nation cannot permanently endure half slave and half free will echo with a haunting relevance."[88] Things

---

[82] Act of April 9, 1866, § 1, 14 Stat. 27 (codified at 42 U.S.C. § 1981 (1976)).

[83] McDonald v. Santa Fe Trail Transp. Co., 427 U.S. 273 (1976).

[84] U.S. CONST. amend. XV, § 1.

[85] 42 U.S.C. § 1973d (1976).

[86] *E.g.*, Office of Fed. Contract Compliance Programs, Affirmative Action Programs, 41 C.F.R. § 60–2 (1979).

[87] 109 U.S. 3, 25 (1883).

[88] L. TRIBE, *supra* note 40, at 1136.

being what they are, I believe hiring quotas for disadvantaged minorities no more offend the equal protection clause than does the progressive income tax, or the Food Stamp program which excludes most of us, or special medical aid and other benefits for American Indians.

My concern is that today a majority of the Supreme Court may not agree. When redressing the balance prejudices an identifiable member of the dominant race, the Court, I fear, may feel compelled to condemn the effort. And if that becomes the rule, the larger quest for equality is in peril.

B.

Unfortunately, my concern with the direction of the Supreme Court goes further. The Court has announced that the equal protection clause only reaches *purposeful* discrimination, whoever the victim, whatever the activity involved.[89] One sensitive to the curse, the cruelty, and the sequelae of slavery in this country is tempted to smile and say "They don't really mean it." Perhaps so. Perhaps if the Court labels "suspect" the most offensive discriminations, expands the notion of "fundamental" rights, and indulges in the presumption of discriminatory purpose absent a "compelling" justification, it will not matter. But, like one of our recent Presidents, I am fearful, first, that "it won't work" and, second, "it is wrong."[90]

We need only recall again *Griffin v. Illinois* and its progeny. There was, I suppose, nothing intentionally discriminatory about charging everyone a fee for a trial transcript, or failing to provide a free lawyer to those who could not afford to pay one,[91] or uniformly imposing "jail time" in default of payment of a fine.[92] Of course, the discriminatory effect of such rules was always obvious, but they were not fashioned with a view to penalize the poor. Nor, in many cases, was the malapportionment of legislative bodies the product of a deliberate scheme to dilute the voice of some voters. Sometimes, the imbal-

---

[89] Arlington Heights v. Metropolitan Hous. Dev. Corp., 429 U.S. 252 (1977); Washington v. Davis, 426 U.S. 229 (1976).

[90] THE WHITE HOUSE TRANSCRIPTS 155 (New York Times ed. 1974).

[91] *E.g.*, Douglas v. California, 372 U.S. 353 (1963).

[92] *E.g.*, Tate v. Short, 401 U.S. 395 (1971); Williams v. Illinois, 399 U.S. 235 (1970).

ance "just grew" like Topsy, and the failure to reapportion was more lethargy than evil purpose. And yet, as the Court has held, that is no excuse to perpetuate gross inequality in the exercise of the franchise.[93]

Are these exceptions that prove the rule? I think not. To be sure, much of the legislation that touched Orientals in the Far West or blacks in the Deep South was purposefully discriminatory. But not all. The San Francisco ordinance prohibiting the wearing of queues by prisoners may well have been a misguided health measure.[94] I am confident that the practice of criminal judges in my native city of New Orleans to select grand jurors from persons "known" to them was perfectly innocent.[95] So was, I assume, the minimum height requirement for policemen ordained by the County of Los Angeles, albeit it effectively excluded almost all applicants of Mexican origin.[96] And there probably were southern colleges that, without racially discriminatory motives, had adopted rules like those of the University of Mississippi requiring every applicant for admission to be recommended by two alumni.[97] But innocent intent did not save these regulations, nor should it have.

A reading of the equal protection clause as reaching only purposeful discrimination is full of dangers. I do not suppose the Court will return to the pretenses indulged at the turn of the last century when Louisiana's "Jim Crow" law in *Plessy v. Ferguson* was said to be discriminatory only in the mind of the black race which "chooses to put that construction on it."[98] But what if a misguided state university board decides to limit entry of blacks "for their own benefit," on the reasoning that there will be no jobs for a greater number of black graduates and that raising exaggerated expectations for them is cruel?

---

[93] *See, e.g.*, Reynolds v. Sims, 377 U.S. 533, 584 (1964).

[94] *But see* Ho Ah Kow v. Nunan, 12 F. Cas. 252 (C.C.D. Cal. 1899) (No. 6,546). The court held the ordinance was adopted "merely to aggravate the severity of [a prisoner's] confinement." *Id.* at 254.

[95] *See* Eubanks v. Louisiana, 356 U.S. 584, 586 (1958)(holding that any jury selection plan that operates to exclude members of a racial group is invalid).

[96] *See* Davis v. County of Los Angeles, 566 F.2d 1334, 1337 (9th Cir. 1977), *vacated as moot,* 440 U.S. 625 (1979).

[97] In the case of Mississippi, the adoption of the rule *was* suspect. *See* Meredith v. Fair, 298 F.2d 696, 701–02, 305 F.2d 343, 352–53 (5th Cir.), *cert. denied,* 371 U.S. 828 (1962).

[98] 163 U.S. at 551.

Does such a genuinely benign motive save the rule? Or suppose a police department removes its officers from the black ghetto on the simple ground that the black community prefers to "sort out" its own affairs: is a ghetto resident who complains to be rebuffed because the practice is well intentioned?

The truth is that benevolence or malignity has little or nothing to do with equal protection. We are so in the habit of using the expression "*guilty* of discrimination" that we tend to forget the underlying principle. True, when we enforce the *criminal* laws that carry out the equal protection clause against a person acting under color of state law, we must prove that the defendant intended to bring about the discriminatory effects or knew that they would occur.[99] But even then, we need not show that the *framers* of the state law under which the defendant illegally acted intended that the law work discrimination.

In any event, the command of the equal protection clause is enforced, under the fourteenth as well as the fifth amendment, primarily by civil injunction and, here, it is not necessary that the defendant have any evil purpose or, indeed, even be aware of the harm he inflicts. What matters is whether the act complained of can be seen adversely to prejudice a discrete group in the enjoyment of important rights without sufficient legitimate justification. A purpose to discriminate against the victims may abbreviate the case, since such an objective is not "legitimate." But, most of the time, the critical focus should be on the effect of the act complained of, not the motive of the actor.

Of course, there remain difficult questions about what kind of adverse effect amounts to a violation of equal protection. Must the injury be the direct consequence of the act complained of? How serious must be the harm? I cannot parse all those complexities now. But I will say this: In my judgment, it ought to be no defense to a claim that a facially neutral state rule deprives the poor of a basic right to urge that the state is not responsible for their poverty. That was the argument advanced by the dissenters in *Griffin v. Illinois*,[100] and it was rejected by Chief Justice Warren, Mr. Justice Black, Mr. Justice Frankfurter, Mr. Justice Douglas, and Mr. Justice Clark. I stand with them.

---

[99] *See* United States v. Classic, 313 U.S. 299, 323 (1941).

[100] 351 U.S. at 28–29, 34 (Burton, Minton, Reed, and Harlan, JJ., dissenting).

C.

This brings me back to my principal theme: that it is *not* embarrassing, or unjudicial, to notice whose ox is gored when assessing legislation or other official action under the equal protection clause. On the contrary, to accurately judge effects, we must know who is the victim and to what class he belongs. The obvious fact is that the same conduct will have very different consequences depending on which group is adversely affected.

The key here is that the equal protection clause is primarily concerned with classes or groups, not individuals. As I am confident Mr. Justice Frankfurter must have written somewhere, a case invoking the equal protection clause, if it is to succeed, must allege something more than a tort, personal to the plaintiff. Once that is appreciated, it is plain that the relative position of the affected group often will determine the degree, and the kind, of injury that results from the particular action. I need not catalog all the variables; suffice it to note that political impotency, numerical minority, low economic status, "outcast" social standing, public unpopularity, a sense of insecurity, and lack of self-confidence are among them. One does not have to be a sociologist or a psychologist to know that, in the American setting, excluding black children from white schools carries implications, inflicts deep scars, and prejudices the future of the victims, whereas no comparable consequences result when the reverse occurs. I simply do not understand those who say that judges are not supposed to take this difference into account in administering the equal protection clause. Nor do I appreciate why the difference should be relevant only if the government whose action is challenged is itself responsible for the disparity. The law of California did not put the queue on the Chinese, but that could not vindicate the law discriminating against all who wore them.

No one today would endorse the idea put forward in the *Slaughterhouse Cases* that the equal protection clause is concerned *only* with discrimination against the black race.[101] Yet, we must not go to the opposite extreme and invalidate a legal classification on the sole ground that it adversely affects the dominant white majority. Of course, I would not confine the reach of the clause to action which has

[101] 83 U.S. (16 Wall.) at 81.

the effect—intended or not—of stigmatizing a group. That is, however, a core area which plainly requires us to look closely at the particular situation of the victimized group to determine the effect *on them* of the action complained of. To do otherwise is to blink reality.

Perhaps Anatole France's bridge law could pass constitutional muster as a safety measure. Perhaps a somewhat similar law would not, such as an apparently pervasive law that would merely raise a smile or cause a frown as addressed to most groups but whose actual victims are more vulnerable and suffer serious injury from its enforcement. We are not born equal. And, even if we were, we would not long remain so. Judges cannot make us equal. But they can assure that those who wield official power will not deliberately exploit or inadvertently exaggerate those inequalities. For some, only the judicial branch offers a shield. Let us not deny them our help in the service of a blind goddess who cannot see their special plight. As my mentor and friend, Mr. Justice Black, wrote some forty years ago in *Chambers v. Florida:*

> Under our constitutional system, courts stand against any winds that blow as havens of refuge for those who might otherwise suffer because they are helpless, weak, outnumbered, or because they are non-conforming victims of prejudice and public excitement. . . . No higher duty, no more solemn responsibility, rests upon this Court, than that of translating into living law and maintaining this constitutional shield deliberately planned and inscribed for the benefit of every human being subject to our Constitution—of whatever race, creed or persuasion.[102]

[102] 309 U.S. 227, 241 (1940).

6

Public School Desegregation: Legal Remedies for De Facto Segregation

Racial discrimination is one of the great injustices of America. Slavery was protected in the original Constitution, as written in 1787; and it took a sanguinary civil war to blot it out in the formal law of the Constitution. During the 1950s, Judge Wright was at the forefront of implementation of the Supreme Court's landmark decision in Brown v. Board of Education *(1954), which declared racial discrimination unconstitutional under the equal protection clause of the Fourteenth Amendment. As a district judge in New Orleans, Skelly Wright took on and defeated not only the city of New Orleans but the state of Louisiana in his ultimately successful effort to apply the* Brown *principle in New Orleans. The issue then was de jure segregation—that required by law. By the 1960s that issue had by and large been settled, and the problem turned to de facto segregation—that brought about by housing patterns.*

Would the Constitution reach that type of racial discrimination also? The answer that Judge Wright gave in this essay—the first Madison Lecture at New York University not given by a Supreme Court Justice—was clear: Yes, de facto segregation was proscribed by the fourteenth amendment. The essay is the first important statement on the question by anyone. It took considerable courage for Wright thus to speak; but that is characteristic of him.

It is also important to note that the essay became controversial when Judge Wright was called upon to rule on Washington, D.C.,'s schools that were separated not by law but by long-established housing patterns and custom. The case, Hobson v. Hansen *(1967), is one of the most controversial that he ever rendered.*

Judge Wright's concern for the plight of black Americans is well summarized in this passage from the essay: "The American Negro is a totally American responsibility. Three hundred years ago he was brought to this country by our forefathers and sold into slavery. One hundred years ago we fought a war that would set him free. For these last one hundred years we have lived and professed the hypocrisy that he was free. The time has now come when we must face up to that responsibility. Let us erase this blemish—let us remove this injustice—from the face of America. Let us make *the Negro free." The courts, Judge Wright tells us, have the power and the responsibility to fulfill that need.*

ONE hundred years ago this country abolished slavery and decreed by solemn constitutional amendment that "all persons born or naturalized in the United States, and subject to the jurisdiction thereof, are citizens of the United States and of the State wherein they reside."[1] Thus, at last, our Negro citizens were included in the truths we hold self-evident, "that all men are created equal, that they are endowed by their Creator with certain unalienable Rights, that among these are Life, Liberty and the pursuit of Happiness."[2]

One hundred years have passed and the promise of equality remains, in large part, unfulfilled. It seems that in these 100 years we have succeeded in changing a system of slavery into a caste system based on race which may, in some respects, be more difficult to uproot than slavery itself.

Before considering the problem of racial discrimination as it confronts this country today, it may be useful briefly to recall how the great hopes and aspirations of 100 years ago were curdled in the aftermath of the Civil War. And it will be particularly interesting to note that the instrument of destruction then—the United States Supreme Court—is now the architect of the new dream of equality and freedom.

I

Immediately following the close of the Civil War, Congress set about the task of insuring, insofar as possible by law, that the rights of the new citizens would be respected. First it considered for enactment a series of civil rights laws. Then, when it became concerned that the Supreme Court might declare them unconstitutional, it proceeded to initiate constitutional amendments which embedded Negro rights in our basic law. The im-

---

1. U.S. Const., amend. XIV, § 1.
2. U.S. Declaration of Independence.

Reprinted by permission of the *New York University Law Review*, Vol. 40, pp. 285-309 (1965).

plementation of these amendments followed quickly in the form of the Civil Rights Acts.[3]

The congressional concern about the post-Civil War Supreme Court was not unwarranted. Nor did the thirteenth, fourteenth and fifteenth amendments succeed in protecting the civil rights legislation from the destructive arm of the Court. In a series of decisions, by a restrictive reading of these amendments, particularly the fourteenth, the Supreme Court made a shambles of the Civil Rights Acts. Statutes protecting the voting rights of Negroes,[4] outlawing the Ku Klux Klan,[5] insuring Negro access to public accommodations,[6] and others, were all declared unconstitutional.

Hardly more than a decade after the close of the Civil War the moral fervor which had supported the recognition of Negro rights was ebbing fast. Discouraged by the action of the Supreme Court, and with this country undergoing an industrial revolution, the great mass of the people turned their attention to more mundane matters. The climate of the times was such that in 1877, after his opponent, Samuel J. Tilden, had won the election for the presidency by over a quarter of a million votes, the followers of Rutherford B. Hayes were able to make a cynical political deal with the Tilden electors in five Southern states under which their votes were cast for Hayes, making him President, in return for which the Hayes forces agreed to, and did, end the protection which the federal government, since the Civil War, had afforded the Negro in the South.[7]

Not long after Hayes assumed the Presidency, segregation laws cautiously began to make their appearances in the states of the old Confederacy. As a substitute for slavery, the Negro would now be isolated from the mainstream of public life by criminal statutes. Initially, not even the proponents of these laws had confidence in their constitutionality. Enforcement was tentative and usually withdrawn when challenged. Finally, in 1896, a test of the Louisiana statute[8] which made it a crime for a Negro to invade the public accommodation on a train reserved for whites reached the Supreme Court.

Eight Justices of the Supreme Court in that case, *Plessy v.*

3. See generally Fairman, Does the Fourteenth Amendment Incorporate the Bill of Rights?, 2 Stan. L. Rev. 5 (1949); Gressman, The Unhappy History of Civil Rights Legislation, 50 Mich. L. Rev. 1323-26 (1952).

4. United States v. Cruikshank, 92 U.S. 542 (1875); United States v. Reese, 92 U.S. 214 (1875).

5. United States v. Harris, 106 U.S. 629 (1882).

6. Civil Rights Cases, 109 U.S. 3 (1883).

7. Woodward, Reunion and Reaction (2d ed. 1956).

8. La. Acts 1890, No. 111.

Ferguson,[9] were able to hold that racial segregation, compelled by law, was legal. One lone member of the Court, however, the first Mr. Justice Harlan, delivered the most powerful dissent in the annals of jurisprudence. It read in part:

> The white race deems itself to be the dominant race in this country. And so it is, in prestige, in achievements, in education, in wealth and in power. So, I doubt not, it will continue to be for all time, if it remains true to its great heritage and holds fast to the principles of constitutional liberty. But in view of the Constitution, in the eye of the law, there is in this country no superior, dominant, ruling class of citizens. There is no caste here. Our Constitution is color-blind, and neither knows nor tolerates classes among citizens. In respect of civil rights, all citizens are equal before the law. The humblest is the peer of the most powerful. The law regards man as man, and takes no account of his surroundings or of his color when his civil rights as guaranteed by the supreme law of the land are involved. It is, therefore, to be regretted that this high tribunal, the final expositor of the fundamental law of the land, has reached the conclusion that it is competent for a State to regulate the enjoyment by citizens of their civil rights solely upon the basis of race.
>
> In my opinion, the judgment this day rendered will, in time, prove to be quite as pernicious as the decision made by this tribunal in the *Dred Scott case*. . . .
>
> If evils will result from the commingling of the two races upon public highways established for the benefit of all, they will be infinitely less than those that will surely come from state legislation regulating the enjoyment of civil rights upon the basis of race. We boast of the freedom enjoyed by our people above all other peoples. But it is difficult to reconcile that boast with a state of the law which, practically, puts the brand of servitude and degradation upon a large class of our fellow-citizens, our equals before the law. The thin disguise of "equal" accommodations for passengers in railroad coaches will not mislead any one, nor atone for the wrong this day done.[10]

Racial segregation, having received the benediction of the Supreme Court, spread like a prairie fire through the Southland. Literally hundreds of statutes were passed requiring segregation from the cradle into the grave[11]—all under pain of imprisonment for violations. The segregation laws were such a success that the legislatures in the Southern states soon turned their attention to disenfranchising the Negro. By the use of grandfather clauses and understanding tests in registration statutes, the registration

---

9. 163 U.S. 537 (1896).

10. Id. at 559, 562.

11. For the citations of many of these statutes, see Supplemental Brief for the United States as Amicus Curiae, pp. 50-63, Bouie v. Columbia, 378 U.S. 347 (1964); Bell v. Maryland, 378 U.S. 226 (1964); Robinson v. Florida, 378 U.S. 153 (1964); Barr v. Columbia, 378 U.S. 146 (1964); Griffin v. Maryland, 378 U.S. 130 (1964).

rolls in practically all of the states of the Confederacy were purged of Negro voters. In Louisiana, for example, over 99 per cent of the Negro voters lost their right to vote. Over 130,000 Negroes in Louisiana alone, one-half of the total registration, were scratched from the voting rolls.[12] Thus, while compelling segregation by law, appropriate steps were taken to insure that the law was not changed.

For almost fifty years from the turn of the century, public apathy toward the plight of the Negro continued. During this time the Negro remained in a state of limbo—half slave and half free. And during this time the politically defenseless and segregated Negro was subjected to 1,780 known lynchings.[13]

After World War II, during which he fought side by side with his white brothers-in-arms, public attention again began to be focused on the plight of the Negro. Guilt feelings were becoming more difficult to suppress. The Supreme Court, now leading the fight for recognition of the Negro's right to full citizenship, began an assault on the wall of segregation. In a series of decisions the Court gradually made it clear that the separate but equal doctrine of *Plessy v. Ferguson* set an unacceptable standard for determining equal protection under the law. And, finally, in the historic *Brown v. Board of Education* opinion, the Chief Justice, speaking for a unanimous Court, held that "separate educational facilities are inherently unequal."[14]

Once "separate but equal" was outlawed as a constitutional test in the field of educational facilities, the Court had no difficulty in applying the new principle to other areas in which segregation compelled by law had resulted in a caste system adversely affecting the Negro. State statutes requiring racial segregation in transportation facilities,[15] parks,[16] playgrounds,[17] hospitals,[18] and other public places[19] have all been declared unconstitutional, so that now the last vestiges of the iniquitous separate but equal doctrine have been expunged from the law.

---

12. Woodward, The Strange Career of Jim Crow 68 (1955).

13. Hearings on H.R. 41, H.R. 57, H.R. 77, H.R. 223, H.R. 228, H.R. 278, and H.R. 800 Before Subcommittee No. 4 of the House Committee on the Judiciary, 80th Cong., 2d Sess. 39 (1948).

14. 347 U.S. 483, 495 (1954).

15. Gayle v. Browder, 352 U.S. 903 (per curiam), affirming 142 F. Supp. 707 (M.D. Ala. 1956).

16. New Orleans City Park Improvement Ass'n v. Detiege, 358 U.S. 54, affirming 252 F.2d 122 (5th Cir. 1958).

17. Watson v. Memphis, 373 U.S. 526 (1963).

18. Simkins v. Moses H. Cone Memorial Hosp., 323 F.2d 959 (4th Cir. 1963), cert. denied, 376 U.S. 938 (1964).

19. See Holmes v. City of Atlanta, 350 U.S. 879 (1955) (per curiam); Mayor and City Council v. Dawson, 350 U.S. 877 (1955) (per curiam).

But as we have learned from our experience under the post-Civil War constitutional amendments, it is one thing solemnly to declare the legal rights of Negroes; it is quite another to make recognition of those rights a reality. Ten years have passed since the Supreme Court's historic pronouncement in *Brown v. Board of Education* and, while the border states generally have sought to comply, in most of the states of the old Confederacy compliance, if any, has been, at best, grudging. The simple truth is that, in most of these states, integration of the public schools ten years after *Brown* is less than one per cent effective.

The 1964 Staff Report on Public Education submitted to the United States Commission on Civil Rights discloses that in seven states of the former Confederacy 499 of every 500 Negro pupils attend 100 per cent Negro schools.[20] Less than one Negro pupil in 500 attend desegregated schools, and then only on a token basis. Based on the progress in desegregation made the first ten years after the Supreme Court handed down its decision in *Brown v. Board of Education*, many more years may be required before the segregated Negro school is eliminated from the deep South.

Progress in desegregation can be accelerated, however, if courts refuse to countenance gerrymandering as a substitute for segregation compelled by law. It is becoming increasingly clear that as Southern school boards change from a dual, that is, separate Negro and white, operation to a single school system, segregation in the schools can remain virtually as before. By careful drawing of neighborhood school boundary lines, the formerly all-white school remains all white, or almost so, and the formerly all-Negro school remains, for all intents and purposes, all Negro. The fact that the segregation is no longer, in terms, compelled by law does not eliminate the discrimination or remedy the inequality. Thus the interdiction of all state statutes compelling racial segregation in public schools is but a short first step on the road to desegregation.

Desegregation in the South may also be accelerated by energetic and effective use of the powers granted the Attorney General under the Civil Rights Act of 1964. Under section 407[21] of that act the Attorney General may initiate suits in behalf of individuals and ask the district courts to end racial segregation in the public schools, at least where the segregation results from the deliberate act of state officials pursuant to state statute or

20. United States Commission on Civil Rights, 1964 Staff Report on Public Education 290-91.

21. 78 Stat. 248, 42 U.S.C.A. § 2000(c)-6 (1964).

discriminatory purpose of their own. It is by no means certain, however, that the Attorney General will be any more successful than the NAACP in achieving actual rather than token desegregation. The difficulties inherent in achieving true desegregation are so great, as ten years of experience testify, and the defenses available to school boards resisting every step of the way so many, that only an alert and conscientious continuous effort on the part of both the executive and judicial branches of our government, plus a compelling desire on the part of Negroes generally, can make Section 407 of the 1964 Civil Rights Act an effective instrument in bringing reality to desegregation in the public schools in the deep South.

II

The obstacles to further integration forecast for the South, once the illegality of de jure segregation is accepted, are already being encountered in other parts of the country. De facto racial segregation infects the public school systems in most urban areas of the North and West. This de facto segregation has its genesis in a combination of conditions, the combination varying from city to city, sometimes from neighborhood to neighborhood in the same city. Historical gerrymandering is a common cause of de facto segregation; restrictive covenants in land titles segregating neighborhoods is another common cause. But more and more it is becoming apparent that perhaps the primary cause of de facto segregation in urban schools is the socio-economic condition of the Negro. The inability of many Negroes, because of overt and covert job discrimination, to find proper employment drives them and their families into the segregated slums which disgrace many of our metropolitan areas.

To understand the magnitude of the problem of de facto segregation, it may be useful to cite some statistics. Of Chicago's 443 elementary schools, only 40 are integrated; 280 are white schools with student bodies less than 10 per cent Negro; and 123 are Negro schools with student bodies less than 10 per cent white.[22] Thus, using the 10 per cent mixing factor, only 9 per cent of Chicago's elementary schools are integrated. If the 10 per cent mixing factor were reduced to 1 per cent, 77 per cent of the elementary schools in Chicago would still be classified as segregated. There is, of course, no compulsory segregation in the Chicago schools. Segregation results from adherence to the neighborhood school assignment policy. But historical gerrymandering

22. Advisory Panel on Integration of the Public Schools, Report to the Board of Education of the City of Chicago 56 (1964).

has played a significant part in the problem presented by de facto segregation in Chicago today.

Still using the 10 per cent mixing factor, only 29.9 per cent of the public elementary schools in the nation's capital are integrated.[23] Of Washington's 129 public elementary schools, 87 are Negro, 15 are white, and 27 are integrated. Using the same factor, of New York's 578 public elementary schools 263 (45.5%) are integrated, 118 (20.4%) are white, and 197 (34.5%) are Negro. In Oakland, California, 29 (45.4%) of the 64 public elementary schools are integrated, 23 (35.9%) are white, and 12 (18.7%) are Negro.

These statistics, and more like them from other cities, indicate that racial segregation in public schools in the North and West, except as to cause, is not unlike that in the South. Presumably the effect is the same. As to that effect the Supreme Court said in *Brown*:

> We come then to the question presented: Does segregation of children in public schools solely on the basis of race, even though the physical facilities and other "tangible" factors may be equal, deprive the children of the minority group of equal educational opportunities? We believe that it does. . . .
>
> To separate them from others of similar age and qualifications solely because of their race generates a feeling of inferiority as to their status in the community that may affect their hearts and minds in a way unlikely ever to be undone. . . .
>
> We conclude that in the field of public education the doctrine of "separate but equal" has no place. Separate educational facilities are inherently unequal.[24]

Various state officials and agencies in the North and West have affirmed the Supreme Court's finding of the damage suffered by the segregated Negro child. In its Report to the Chicago Board of Education, the Advisory Panel on Integration of the Public Schools, March 31, 1964, stated:

> The personality characteristics of the child who has suffered from discrimination, the self-hatred, the deep sense of frustration, the unexpected aggression, and the consequent difficulty in relating to others might be expected to have a major effect on his academic achievement.[25]

The Policy Statement on Integration adopted by the Board of Education of New York City, December 1964, finds segregated schools also damage white children:

---

23. The statistics on the Washington, New York and Oakland public schools are from United States Commission on Civil Rights, 1963 Staff Report on Public Education 144-45.

24. Brown v. Board of Educ., 347 U.S. 483, 493-95 (1954).

25. Advisory Panel on Integration of the Public Schools, supra note 22, at 46.

> The Supreme Court of the United States reminds us that modern psychological knowledge indicates clearly that segregated, racially homogeneous schools damage the personality of minority group children. These schools decrease their motivation and thus impair their ability to learn. White children are also damaged. Public education in a racially homogeneous setting is socially unrealistic and blocks the attainment of the goals of democratic education, whether this segregation occurs by law or by fact.

And Attorney General Mosk of California, in an opinion dated August 15, 1963, to the President of the California State Board of Education, advised:

> The United States Supreme Court in *Brown v. Board of Education* and the Supreme Court of California in *Jackson v. Pasadena City School District* took judicial notice that school segregation results in the emotional crippling of students of minority races. Whether segregation is the result of state policy or merely reflective of neighborhood condition makes little difference to its victims.

Thus it is clear from the Supreme Court in *Brown*, from the various state authorities that have considered the problem, and from the historical background of slavery and the continuing discrimination against the Negro citizen that a segregated Negro school, whether in the North or in the South, is inherently unequal to its white counterpart. In addition to the damage done by segregated education to the minds and hearts and ability to learn of Negro children, to segregate them in public schools, for whatever reason, is to brand them as inferior—in their own minds and in the public mind. The unfortunate fact is that in contemporary America race and color are

> associated with status distinctions among groups of human beings. The public schools reflect this larger social fact in that the proportion of Negroes and whites in a given school is often associated with the status of the school. The educational quality and performance to be expected from that school are frequently expressed in terms of the racial complexion and general status assigned to the school. It is well recognized that in most cases a school enrolling a large proportion of Negro students is viewed as a lower status school.[26]

Experience with segregated Negro schools, in the North as well as the South, confirms the public impression that Negro schools, in addition to being per se inferior, are usually demonstrably inferior in fact. Surveys of school systems throughout the country demonstrate time and again that the Negro school, as compared with its white counterpart, is overcrowded and un-

26. Statement Proposed by the New York State Education Commissioner's Advisory Committee on Human Relations and Community Tensions, June 17, 1963.

derstaffed—usually with inferior teachers. The experienced teachers with a choice of assignment avoid the Negro school. The Negro school buildings themselves are often run down and ill kept. The amount spent to educate the Negro child is, in many cases, substantially less than that spent on the white.

In addition to these overt differences, Negro children in Negro schools suffer from lack of exposure to the middle class culture found in white but not in Negro schools. Shunted off in the slum school, the Negro child is denied the stimulation of competition and association with children of other races and cultures. In sum, whenever a substantial number of Negro children attend public schools in a given area, it appears that the Negro children usually find themselves in schools populated primarily by other Negro children and that these Negro schools somehow usually seem to receive less attention from the school board in terms of money, teachers, books and building care.

Thus in most of the school cases arising from the metropolitan areas, it should not be necessary to reach the issue of whether adventitious de facto segregation, without more, is unconstitutional. In the New Rochelle case,[27] for example, an historical gerrymandering pattern resulting in a primarily Negro school was found offensive to the equal protection clause. The school board, of course, defended on the ground that the school in question was a neighborhood school and that there was no intention in fixing the boundaries to limit its attendance to Negroes. The court was unimpressed with the board's professions of innocent intent—with the result that now Negro children in New Rochelle are distributed throughout the school system and a healthy educational situation obtains in that suburban area.

The Negro plaintiffs, however, were not so fortunate in their efforts to desegregate Gary, Indiana, and Kansas City, Kansas. In those cities, in spite of admitted substantial segregation of Negro children and strong proof of historical gerrymandering, inferior Negro school facilities and inferior Negro faculties in the Negro schools, the district courts in those cases[28] were unable to find either inequality or intentional racial segregation. The courts seemed to be satisfied with the neighborhood school concept of school districting, in spite of the fact that the school boards knew when they drew the boundaries for the Negro schools that those

27. Taylor v. Board of Educ., 294 F.2d 36 (2d Cir.), cert. denied, 368 U.S. 940 (1961).

28. See Downs v. Board of Educ., 336 F.2d 988 (10th Cir. 1964) (affirming unreported opinion of district court), cert. denied, 33 U.S.L. Week 3284 (U.S. Mar. 2, 1965); Bell v. School City, 213 F. Supp. 819 (N.D. Ind.), aff'd, 324 F.2d 209 (7th Cir. 1963).

schools would be racially segregated. And there is no suggestion in either the Gary or the Kansas City cases that the courts ever heard of the Princeton Plan for eliminating de facto segregation which has worked satisfactorily in that and similar cities for almost a decade, or of selecting school sites on the dividing line between the white and Negro residential areas so that the schools may serve both races, or even of open enrollment, used initially as a corrective in New Rochelle, which would have allowed children in a segregated school district to attend a public school of their choice outside that district.

It seems that the courts in the Gary and Kansas City cases were more than willing to allow this entire matter to be handled by the school boards, relying on the boards' judgment and good faith in spite of a long history of segregated schools in the cities concerned. The courts in these cases seem to have applied the principle that, as long as there was a rational relationship between what the school board did and a legal end to be achieved, the courts' inquiry was concluded. The courts rejected the suggestion that the end intended was racial segregation, and held that the boards' actions perpetuating racial segregation were reasonable under the circumstances.

It is true, of course, that the Supreme Court in the recent past, in the field of private business and economics, has not looked behind an action of a state agency as long as the purpose of the agency in instituting the action was a legal one and the action was rationally related to that purpose.[29] But, as we shall see, the rational-relationship doctrine has no application to cases involving racial discrimination and public education. Even if it did, it would be highly questionable whether permitting segregated Negro schools is rationally related to the education of those children who must attend them.[30]

As I read these de facto segregation cases from the North and West, I must confess to a little amusement. After watching, from close range, some of my judicial brethren in the South twisting and turning and reaching for a result in race cases that will not upset the status quo or the local power structure, it seems that now I may be treated to what appear to be similar performances by my brethren in other parts of the country.

Although the Gary and Kansas City cases both concluded that the federal courts were powerless with respect to relieving

29. See Ferguson v. Skrupa, 372 U.S. 726, 731-32 (1963); Williamson v. Lee Optical Co., 348 U.S. 483, 491 (1955).

30. "Segregation in public education is not reasonably related to any proper governmental objective . . . ." Bolling v. Sharpe, 347 U.S. 497, 500 (1954).

de facto segregation, the issue is far from closed. The final word on this subject will, of course, be spoken by the Supreme Court. It is inconceivable that the Supreme Court will long sit idly by watching Negro children crowded into inferior slum schools while the whites flee to the suburbs to place their children in vastly superior predominantly white schools.

Before the Supreme Court acts, some other federal courts[31] no doubt will take a harder look at de facto segregation and will be less inclined to accept the suggestion that the state and its agencies are not, in some degree at least, responsible for it and helpless to correct it. Until now the cases have focused on the responsibility of the school boards administering the segregated schools, and it is clear that these agencies, through historical gerrymandering and other devious means, have contributed to racial imbalance in the schools. But state action contributing to segregated schools is not limited to school boards. And the fourteenth amendment speaks to the state itself.[32] As Mr. Justice Brandeis reminds us, " 'It is a question of the power of the State as a whole;' . . . the powers of the several state officials must be treated as if merged in a single officer."[33]

Where state policy expressed by its several agencies lends itself to, and leads toward, segregated schools, the responsibility of the state is plain. For example, where state policy with reference to housing, or state encouragement of private racial covenants in housing, lead to residential segregation and the school board uses the neighborhood plan in making pupil assignments, the school segregation that results is clearly the responsibility of the state. Certainly the state will not be allowed to do in two steps what it may not do in one. By taking a broader look at state policy and all contributing state agencies, federal courts may be more successful in finding state complicity in segregation. Thus, in most cases, where a forthright effort is made by the courts to determine the cause of racial imbalance, it will be unnecessary to reach the question as to what a state may do, or must do, to relieve purely adventitious segregation. In this connection, however, it should be emphasized again that as long as

31. Barksdale v. Springfield School Comm., 237 F. Supp. 543 (D. Mass. 1965); Blocker v. Board of Educ., 226 F. Supp. 208 (E.D.N.Y. 1964); Branche v. Board of Educ., 204 F. Supp. 150 (E.D.N.Y. 1962), indicate that the rationale of the Gary and Kansas City cases is not acceptable in the Eastern District of New York or in the District of Massachusetts. See also Jackson v. Pasadena City School Dist., 59 Cal. 2d 876, 382 P.2d 878, 31 Cal. Rptr. 606 (1963).

32. Griffin v. School Bd., 377 U.S. 218 (1964); Hall v. St. Helena Parish School Bd., 197 F. Supp. 649 (E.D. La. 1961) (per curiam), aff'd, 287 F.2d 376 (5th Cir.), aff'd, 368 U.S. 515 (1962) (per curiam).

33. Iowa-Des Moines Bank v. Bennett, 284 U.S. 239, 244-45 (1931).

the federal judges hearing segregation cases, in the North or the South, are satisfied with the status quo, it will be more difficult for them to find that racial imbalance in the public schools is not the result of neutral causes.

Where a forthright effort is made to determine the cause of racial imbalance, the probability of finding state action in segregated Negro schools, in some degree at least, is increased immeasurably. Discrimination in job opportunities, housing and other necessities drives Negroes into the segregated slums, and application of the neighborhood school policy seals their children in the slum school which these children are compelled by law to attend. Theoretically, the state's compulsory attendance laws may be satisfied by admission to an accredited private school. Some white children, of course, do attend private schools. But to the Negro child the compulsory attendance law often means only one thing: he must attend the segregated slum school in his neighborhood. This fact alone, the legal compulsion to attend the segregated school, should be sufficient state action to bring all de facto segregation within the rule of *Brown*.

State action is also obvious in the use of school boundaries which inevitably result in a segregated Negro school. When school authorities consciously use school district lines, knowing the result will be a segregated Negro school, the action and the intention of the state are clear.[34] Again the compulsory attendance law, superimposed on the school boundary, provides segregation compelled by law within the rule of *Brown*.

The argument is made, of course, that, irrespective of the resulting segregation, the action of the school board is rationally related to the purpose of education and, therefore, courts must ignore the segregation. But, as already indicated,[35] rational-relationship is not the test of the legality of state action where that action results in racial segregation. While, "[n]ormally, the widest discretion is allowed the legislative judgment in determining whether to attack some rather than all of the manifestations of the evil aimed at; and normally that judgment is given the benefit of every conceivable circumstance which might suffice to characterize the classification as reasonable rather than arbitrary and invidious,"[36] state action resulting in racial segregation, even though "pursuant to a valid state interest, bears a heavy burden of justification, . . . and will be upheld only if it is

34. Taylor v. Board of Educ., 294 F.2d 36 (2d Cir.), cert. denied, 368 U.S. 940 (1961). Compare Gomillion v. Lightfoot, 364 U.S. 339 (1960)

35. See note 30 supra and accompanying text.

36. McLaughlin v. Florida, 379 U.S. 184, 191 (1964).

necessary, and not merely rationally related to, the accomplishment of a permissible state policy."[37]

In short, where racial segregation results from state action, the officials responsible therefor must show, not that their action was only rationally related to a legitimate state purpose, but that there is no way reasonably to accomplish that purpose absent racial segregation. Otherwise intent to segregate will be inferred. And whatever arguments there may be in favor of a neighborhood school policy, no one would seriously suggest that there is no other rational basis for assigning children to schools.

III

Assuming that in some instances school segregation may be purely adventitious, the question has arisen as to whether a state may voluntarily undertake to relieve the racial imbalance. In my judgment, states may not only take the necessary steps to relieve adventitious segregation, but, in so doing, may consider race. When racial imbalance infects a public school system, there is simply no way to alleviate it without consideration of race. But those who really, but covertly, want to maintain the segregated status quo cry: "The Constitution is color-blind." Securely they wrap themselves in the famous words of Mr. Justice Harlan I, and point to the language in *Brown*[38] indicating that classification on the basis of race violates the equal protection clause.

Like most aphorisms, Mr. Justice Harlan's felicitous phrase cannot be taken literally. Certainly the great Justice would be alarmed if he were aware of the use to which it is presently being put. The Constitution not only recognizes Negroes as such, but makes specific provision for their protection in the thirteenth, fourteenth and fifteenth amendments. And the language in *Brown* relates to invidious recognition of race for purposes of discrimination. There is nothing whatever in *Brown* which suggests that recognition of race to relieve an inequality violates the fourteenth amendment. Indeed, as *Brown* fully recognizes, to relieve an inequality with respect to the Negro was, and is, precisely the purpose of the fourteenth amendment.

The suggestion that the state must remain neutral with respect to race was rejected in the Japanese relocation cases[39] in which, for national defense purposes, the placing of a burden on a race was approved. It is strange indeed that this suggestion should be advanced again to prevent the state from relieving a

37. Id. at 196.

38. Brown v. Board of Educ., 347 U.S. 483, 495 (1954).

39. Korematsu v. United States, 323 U.S. 214 (1944); Hirabayashi v. United States, 320 U.S. 81 (1943).

racial inequality. Certainly there is no constitutional right to have an inequality perpetuated.

Voluntary action by school authorities seeking to reduce racial imbalance is easily supported once the "the Constitution is color-blind" argument is analyzed and answered. In fact, it is difficult to understand how a court could actually hold that a state may not act to relieve the inequality caused by de facto segregation; yet several courts have done precisely that.[40] There must be something beguiling about the "color-blind" cliché, particularly to those whose sense of social and racial justice leaves something to be desired. "The Constitution is color-blind" is being used by some today the same way the Court in *Plessy v. Ferguson* used the deceptively simple "separate but equal" slogan. Bitter experience has shown, however, that "separate" is never "equal" and that the Constitution, while in some respects color-blind, is not insensitive to inequality.

Several states, principally New York, New Jersey and California, have undertaken to reduce the racial imbalance in their schools.[41] This effort, of course, has met with stubborn resistance from those enjoying the present inequality. Parents of children attending the pure white, or nearly so, schools have brought law suits in New York to prevent correction of racial imbalance. After some initial success at the trial level, the New York Court of Appeals has upheld the right of the Board of Education to act affirmatively to correct racial imbalance.[42] Thus, as far as New York is concerned, absent arbitrary action, school authorities have a free hand in eliminating the inequality of racial segregation in the public schools.

IV

Whether a state can be, and should be, compelled by law to correct purely adventitious de facto segregation in its public schools admittedly present serious problems—both legal and practical. This question also involves the emotional area of state's rights. How far should the courts go in requiring the

40. See, e.g., Strippoli v. Bickal, 42 Misc. 2d 475, 248 N.Y.S.2d 588 (Sup. Ct.), reversed, 21 App. Div. 2d 365, 250 N.Y.S.2d 365 (4th Dep't 1964); Application of Vetere, 41 Misc. 2d 200, 245 N.Y.S.2d 682 (Sup. Ct. 1963), modified, 21 App. Div. 2d 561, 251 N.Y.S.2d 480 (3d Dep't 1964); Balaban v. Rubin, 40 Misc. 2d 249, 242 N.Y.S.2d 973 (Sup. Ct. 1963), rev'd, 20 App. Div. 2d 438, 248 N.Y.S. 2d 574 (2d Dept.), aff'd, 14 N.Y.2d 193, 199 N.E.2d 375, 250 N.Y.S.2d, cert. denied, 379 U.S. 881 (1964).

41. The New York and California State Boards of Education require local school authorities to establish attendance areas for schools which, insofar as practicable, will avoid racial segregation. The Commissioner of Education of the State of New Jersey has taken a similar position.

42. Balaban v. Rubin, 14 N.Y.2d 193, 199 N.E.2d 375, 250 N.Y.S.2d 281, cert. denied, 379 U.S. 881 (1964).

states affirmatively to afford equal opportunity to equal education? Is the enforcement of this right sufficiently important to risk further assaults on the federal courts in general and the Supreme Court in particular? If the Supreme Court does not undertake this burden, at least initially, by recognizing the constitutional right to equal educational opportunity, can we confidently assume that the Congress or the states will protect the Negro in the realization of this right? Perhaps some background on the importance of public education in this country may be helpful in answering these questions.

The importance of generalized education, at least at the elementary and high school level, is no new dogma. It is as old as the theory of popular government. On these shores, it has always been one of the principal articles of the democratic faith. In 1787, in the Northwest Ordinance, the Continental Congress declared: "[S]chools and the means of education shall forever be encouraged."[43] Jefferson termed general education the only "sure foundation . . . for the preservation of freedom,"[44] "without which no republic can maintain itself in strength."[45] Today, all the more, it remains "the very foundation of good citizenship."[46] But, because our society has grown increasingly complex, education is now also an economic necessity. "In these days, it is doubtful that any child may reasonably be expected to succeed in life if he is denied the opportunity of an education."[47] Thus, adequate schooling is no longer a privilege that can be made available to the few; it is the indispensable equipment of all men.

The critical role of education in our contemporary society gives meaning to the associated constitutional rights. But the full importance of the state's obligation to provide equal education cannot be appreciated without noticing the long and consistent history of general education as a governmental function.

Washington,[48] Jefferson,[49] Madison,[50] and John Adams[51]

---

43. Ordinance of 1787, § 14, art. 3.

44. Letter from Thomas Jefferson to Whyte, Aug. 13, 1786, in 5 Writings of Thomas Jefferson 396 (Berg ed. 1907).

45. Letter from Thomas Jefferson to John Tyler, May 26, 1810, in 12 Writings of Thomas Jefferson 393 (Berg ed. 1907).

46. Brown v. Board of Educ. 347 U.S. 483, 493 (1954).

47. Ibid.

48. See, e.g., Letter from George Washington to Samuel Chase, Jan. 5, 1785, in 28 Writings of George Washington 27 (Bicentennial ed. 1938).

49. For Jefferson's own summary of his proposed "Bill for the More General Diffusion of Knowledge," see his Notes on the State of Virginia 146-49 (Peden ed. 1955).

50. Letter from James Madison to Thomas W. Gilmer, Sept. 6, 1830, in The Complete Madison 314-15 (Padover ed. 1953).

51. See Adams, Dissertation on the Canon and the Feudal Law (1765), in 3 Works of John Adams 455-56 (Charles Francis Adams ed. 1851).

all advocated governmental responsibility in the diffusion of knowledge through common schools. With such leadership, the public school movement soon took root, so that, by 1850, almost every state in the Union had at least made a start toward a comprehensive system of education.[52] There was then no retreat from the view that education is a state function. On the contrary, except for the temporary disruption resulting from the Civil War, the next century is a chronology of progress, studded with important reaffirmations of the doctrine. Very soon most of the states solemnly proclaimed a right to public education in their constitutions. Significantly, the 39th Congress, which drafted the fourteenth amendment, put down public education as one of the fundamental tenets of republicanism,[53] and their immediate successors imposed it as a pre-condition to readmission of the states still considered in rebellion and to the admission of new states.[54] The full development came with the adoption of compulsory school attendance laws which necessarily imply free public education.

The courts, also, have long characterized education as a function of the state. As early as 1874, Judge Cooley, whose *Constitutional Limitations* had appeared in the year of the ratification of the fourteenth amendment, expressed "no little surprise" that anyone should question the propriety of the state's furnishing "a liberal education to the youth of the state in schools brought within the reach of all classes."[55] He "supposed it had always been understood . . . that education, not merely in the rudiments, but in an enlarged sense, was regarded as an important practical advantage to be supplied at their option to rich and poor alike, and not as something pertaining merely to the culture and accomplishment . . . of those whose accumulated wealth enabled them to pay for it."[56] In 1907, the Supreme Court, speaking through Mr. Justice Holmes, recognized that education is properly considered "one of the first objects of public care."[57] And in 1947, Mr. Justice Black, also for the Supreme Court, wrote: "It is much too late to argue that legislation intended to facilitate the opportunity of children to get a secular education serves no public purpose."[58] Now even college training has become a public con-

52. See Brown v. Board of Educ., 347 U.S. 483, 489 n.4 (1954) and authorities cited therein.

53. See, e.g., Act of July 16, 1866, ch. 200, 14 Stat. 173, 176 (1866); Act of March 2, 1867, ch. 157, 14 Stat. 434 (1867).

54. McCollum v. Board of Educ., 333 U.S. 203, 220-21 & n.9 (1948) (opinion of Mr. Justice Frankfurter).

55. Stuart v. School Dist. No. 1, 30 Mich. 69, 75 (1874).

56. Ibid.

57. Interstate Consol. St. Ry. v. Massachusetts, 207 U.S. 79, 87 (1907).

58. Everson v. Board of Educ., 330 U.S. 1, 7 (1947).

cern. As Mr. Justice Frankfurter put it, "The need for higher education and the duty of the state to provide it as part of a public educational system, are part of the democratic faith of most of our states."[59] The full impact of this development was summed up in *Brown v. Board of Education*: "Today, education is perhaps the most important function of state and local governments."[60]

From the fact that public education is the states' most important function, it does not necessarily follow that segregated public education, whatever the cause, is illegal. But the importance of public education in a democratic society imperatively requires affirmative action on the part of the state to assure each child his fair share, and a child in a segregated Negro school does not receive his fair share. Public education, once offered by the state, "must be made available to all on equal terms."[61] And segregated education, being "inherently unequal," is therefore unconstitutional.[62]

A racially segregated Negro school is an inferior school. It is "inherently unequal."[63] No honest person would even suggest, for example, that the segregated slum school provides educational opportunity equal to that provided by the white suburban public school. Thus children compelled by state compulsory attendance laws to attend the segregated Negro school are deprived of equal protection of the law. The fact that the classification to attend the school is based on geography,[64] and not on race, does not necessarily make the school less segregated or less inferior. Nor does it make the classification less illegal unless it can be shown that no reasonable classification will alleviate the inequality.[65]

The touchstone in determining equal protection of the law in public education is equal educational opportunity, not race. If classification by race is used to achieve the invidious discrimination, the constitutional insult is exacerbated. But the focus must remain on the result achieved. If the untoward result derives from racial classification, such classification is per se unconstitutional. Where the result is segregation, and therefore un-

---

59. Board of Educ. v. Barnette, 319 U.S. 624, 656 (1943) (dissenting opinion).
60. 347 U.S. 483, 493 (1954).
61. Ibid.
62. Id. at 495.
63. Brown v. Board of Educ., 347 U.S. 483 (1954).
64. Compare the reapportionment cases: Reynolds v. Sims, 377 U.S. 533 (1964); Wesberry v. Sanders, 376 U.S. 1 (1964); Gray v. Sanders, 372 U.S. 368 (1963). See also Barksdale v. Springfield School Comm., 237 F. Supp. 543 (D. Mass. 1965).
65. McLaughlin v. Florida, 379 U.S. 184 (1964). Compare Sherbert v. Verner, 374 U.S. 398, 406-09 (1963).

equal educational opportunity, the classification used, whatever it is, is constitutionally suspect and a heavy burden is placed on the school board and the state to show, not only innocent intent, but also lack of a suitable alternative.[66] In short, since segregation in public schools and unequal educational opportunity are two sides of the same coin, the state, in order to provide equal educational opportunity, has the affirmative constitutional obligation to eliminate segregation, however it arises.

Our experience with the cases involving racial segregation in Southern schools has blurred the issue presented by de facto segregation. In the Southern school cases the classification was on the basis of race. It was this classification that achieved the segregated, and therefore unequal, schools. What made the classification invidious, and therefore unconstitutional, was the inequality it produced. When the same invidious result is achieved by another classification, that classification likewise must be tested by the Constitution.

Perhaps the clearest statement of the principle involved in adventitious de facto segregation has been made by Chief Judge Sweeney of the United States District Court for the District of Massachusetts in the only case to date, state or federal, squarely holding that a state may be required to relieve racial imbalance in the public schools. In ordering the city of Springfield to file a desegregation plan for its schools by April 3, 1965, Judge Sweeney wrote:

> The defendants argue, nevertheless, that there is no constitutional mandate to remedy racial imbalance. . . . But that is not the question. The question is whether there is a constitutional duty to provide equal educational opportunities for all children within the system. While *Brown* answered that question affirmatively in the context of coerced segregation, the constitutional fact—the inadequacy of segregated education—is the same in this case, and I so find. It is neither just nor sensible to proscribe segregation having its basis in affirmative state action while at the same time failing to provide a remedy for segregation which grows out of discrimination in housing, or other economic or social factors. Education is tax supported and compulsory, and public school educators, therefore, must deal with inadequacies within the educational system as they arise, and it matters not that the inadequacies are not of their making. This is not to imply that the neighborhood school policy per se is unconstitutional, but that it must be abandoned or modified when it results in segregation in fact.[67]

66. McLaughlin v. Florida, supra note 65.

67. Barksdale v. Springfield School Comm., 237 F. Supp. 543, 546 (D. Mass. 1965).

There can, of course, be no mathematical formula[68] to determine at what point the unequal educational opportunity inherent in racial imbalance and de facto school segregation rises to constitutional dimension. A judgment must be made in each case based on the substantiality of the imbalance under the particular circumstances. Once substantial racial imbalance is shown, however, no further proof of unequal educational opportunity is required. What may be substantial imbalance in Boston, where the Negro school population is relatively small, may not be in Washington, where the Negro school population is approaching 90 per cent. Numbers alone do not provide the answer. The relevant population area is an important consideration. Is the relevant area the city alone or the suburbs as well? A variety of other circumstances may also be important in answering this sometimes difficult question.

The judicial process is equipped to develop the necessary evidence and to make the judgment as to substantial racial imbalance. The word "substantial" does not provide a certain or mechanical guide to decision, but judicial judgments based on similar guides are made routinely. The test for negligence in every case is whether the party charged acted "reasonably" or as "the reasonably prudent person would have" under the circumstances. In every jury case, civil and criminal, the judge decides whether the evidence against the defendant is "substantial" before he allows the case to go to the jury. The examples can be multiplied, but the point is already made. The determination as to substantial racial imbalance, and therefore unequal educational opportunity, is clearly within the competence of the judiciary. As in other areas involving due process and equal protection of the law, the guidelines will have to be staked out on a case-by-case basis.[69] Once substantial racial imbalance is shown, however, the case for relief is complete and the burden of going forward with the evidence falls on the state.[70]

V

Assuming the constitutional question is answered affirmatively in favor of the Negro, the question of appropriate remedy arises. What can a state do—what can a court require a state to

---

68. For example, a school, though mathematically racially imbalanced as compared with other schools in the area, ordinarily would not be racially segregated in the constitutional sense unless the Negro population of the school outnumbered the white.

69. Davidson v. New Orleans, 96 U.S. 97, 104 (1877).

70. See note 65 supra.

do—to relieve racial imbalance? In short, what, if any, remedies are available?

Initially, public school authorities must be cured of the neighborhood school syndrome. The neighborhood school, like the little red school house, has many emotional ties and practical advantages. The neighborhood school serves as the neighborhood center, easily accessible, where children can gather to play on holidays and parents' clubs can meet at any time. But twentieth-century education is not necessarily geared to the neighborhood school. In fact, the trend is definitely in the opposite direction. Educational parks, each consisting of a complex of schools, science buildings, libraries, gymnasiums, auditoriums and playing fields, are beginning to replace the neighborhood school. Although the development of the educational park idea in education is unrelated to the question of racial segregation, its use in relieving racial imbalance in public schools is obvious. Instead of having neighborhood schools scattered through racially homogeneous residential areas, children of all races may be brought together in the educational parks.

In many areas where the educational park is not feasible, simple changes in the existing school district lines may relieve racial imbalance. For example, the homogeneous character of a school in a segregated neighborhood may be changed by redrawing its district lines along with the district lines of the nearest white school so as to include Negro and white pupils in both schools. Also, under the well-known Princeton Plan, where the district lines of two racially diverse schools are contiguous, the racial imbalance can be relieved by limiting the grades in one school from kindergarten to third and in the other from fourth to sixth. And where new schools are to be built to accommodate the expanding school population, the sites for those schools should be, not in Negro or white residential areas, but near the dividing line so that the children living in both areas may be included in each school district. These plans, alone or in combination, when properly used, may well suffice to eliminate the inequality arising from the segregated school in most areas. But in some sections of our large cities, because of the density of the residential segregation, Negro schools are back to back. Princeton Plans and the like are not geared to this problem, but educational parks do provide the answer to Harlem-type residential situations. And pending the construction of the educational parks, open enrollment may be used as a temporary expedient.

An even more difficult problem is presented by the flight of the white population to the suburbs. The pattern is the same all over the country. The Negro child remains within the political boundaries of the city and attends the segregated slum school in his neighborhood, while the white children attend the vastly superior white public schools in the suburbs. The situation is accurately described in the 1964 Advisory Panel Report to the Board of Education of the City of Chicago:

> Finally, it cannot be too strongly stressed that programs to effect school integration must reckon with the fact that the white elementary school child is already in the minority in the public schools of Chicago and the time is not far off when the same will be true of the white high school student. Unless the exodus of white population from the public schools and from the City is brought to a halt or reversed, the question of school integration may become simply a theoretical matter, as it is already in the nation's capital. For integration, in fact, cannot be achieved without white students.[71]

While a court, in proposing or approving a plan of desegregation, may find no great difficulty in ordering the local school authorities to use the Princeton Plan, or one of its variants, or, under the authority of *Griffin v. School Board*[72] in ordering the local taxing authority or the state to levy taxes to raise funds to build an educational park, relieving the inequality between the suburban public school and the segregated city slum public school presents a greater challenge. Obviously, court orders running to local officials will not reach the suburbs. Nevertheless, when political lines, rather than school district lines, shield the inequality, as shown in the reapportionment cases,[73] courts are not helpless to act. The political thicket, having been pierced to protect the vote,[74] can likewise be pierced to protect the education of children.

Education, as stated in *Brown*, is "the most important function of the state." And, as shown in *Hall v. St. Helena Parish School Board*,[75] and *Griffin v. School Board*,[76] that important function must be administered in all parts of the state with an even hand. The state operates local public schools through its agents, the local school boards, it directly supplies part of the money for that operation, it certificates the teachers, it accredits the schools, and, through its department of education, it maintains constant supervision over the entire operation. The involve-

---

71. Advisory Panel on Integration in the Public Schools, Report to the Board of Education of the City of Chicago 12 (1964).

72. 377 U.S. 218 (1964).

73. See note 64 supra.

74. Baker v. Carr, 369 U.S. 186 (1962).

75. 197 F. Supp. 649 (E.D. La. 1961) (per curiam), aff'd, 287 F.2d 376 (5th Cir.), aff'd, 368 U.S. 515 (1962) (per curiam).

76. 377 U.S. 218 (1964).

ment of the state in the operation of its public schools is complete. Indeed, the state is the conduit through which federal money, in increasing amounts, is being funnelled into the public schools. Certainly federal money may not be used to indurate an inequality.[77] Thus no state-created political lines can protect the state against the constitutional command of equal protection for its citizens or relieve the state from the obligation of providing educational opportunities for its Negro slum children equal to those provided for its white children in the affluent suburbs.[78]

When the Supreme Court decided the first reapportionment case, *Baker v. Carr*,[79] just as when it decided *Brown*, it left to the district courts the task of fashioning the remedy. Undoubtedly, if and when the Supreme Court tackles the suburban vis-à-vis the city slum school problem, in the event of a decision in favor of the complainants, it will again remit the remedy to the district courts, with instructions to ignore the state-created political lines separating the school boards and to run its orders directly against state, as well as local, officials.

VI

I am aware, of course, that what has been said here this evening will not find favor with the advocates of judicial restraint—many of whom have already expressed the view that de facto segregation is a political and social matter which requires a political, not a judicial, solution, that the Congress and the states are equipped to remedy any inequality which may exist in the public schools, and that any attempted judicial resolution of the problem would adversely affect the balance of our federalism by trenching on states' rights.

These objections to judicial intervention into de facto segregation all have a slightly familiar ring. The Supreme Court's opinion in *Brown* was subjected to just such criticism. Yet because of that decision definite progress has been made toward the recognition of Negro rights. The Court's action unquestionably moved other branches of government to act. Is there anyone who seriously thinks that the Civil Rights Act of 1964 would be a reality today without *Brown* and other Supreme Court decisions exposing racial injustice? Is it conceivable that the Southern states would have abolished segregation compelled by law without prodding from the federal courts?

---

77. Simkins v. Moses H. Cone Memorial Hosp., 323 F.2d 959 (4th Cir. 1963), cert. denied, 376 U.S. 938 (1964); see Bolling v. Sharpe, 347 U.S. 497 (1954).
78. See note 64 supra.
79. 369 U.S. 186 (1962).

The reapportionment cases are also in point. Does anyone really believe that the state legislatures would have reformed themselves? Legislators elected via the rotten borough system ordinarily would not be expected to vote for its abolition. Perhaps the reapportionment cases do trench on states' rights, but the people who now have a full vote are not complaining.

The advocates of judicial restraint have also been critical of the Supreme Court's work in the field of criminal justice. It is true that the Court has insisted on civilized procedures in state as well as federal criminal courts. An accused in a serious criminal case must now have a lawyer available to represent him, coerced confessions must be excluded from state and federal criminal trials, and state as well as federal police must now respect the fourth amendment. How long should the Supreme Court have waited for the states to civilize their own criminal procedures before it undertook to protect the constitutional rights of persons accused of crime?

The Supreme Court's intervention into these fields of primary state responsibility was not precipitous. The states were given ample opportunity to correct the evils themselves. Before *Brown*, the Supreme Court handed down a series of decisions in the field of education indicating quite clearly that, if the states did not act to eliminate racial segregation compelled by law, it would. The persistence with which reapportionment cases continued to reach the Supreme Court after it had refused to exercise jurisdiction in *Colegrove v. Green*,[80] should have been warning enough to the states that, one way or the other, vote dilution was on the way out. And civilizing of state criminal procedures, under gentle urging from the Supreme Court, has been going on since *Brown v. Mississippi*,[81] in which the Court set aside a death sentence based solely on a confession obtained by hanging the accused from a tree.

There is no indication that the Supreme Court will rush into the de facto segregation arena. Two circuit courts of appeals[82] have already denied relief from de facto segregation and the Supreme Court has stayed its hand. But this is no guarantee that the Court will not act if the problem persists and the states fail to correct the evil. Proper judicial restraint does not include a failure to act where a state has abdicated its responsibility to protect the constitutional rights of its citizens.

80. 328 U.S. 549 (1946).

81. 297 U.S. 278 (1936).

82. Downs v. Board of Educ., 336 F.2d 988 (10th Cir. 1964), cert. denied, 33 U.S.L. Week 3284 (U.S. Mar. 2, 1965); Bell v. School City, 324 F.2d 209 (7th Cir. 1963).

Equal educational opportunity is not the only demand of the Negro Revolution of the 1960's, but it is the most important one. Education is the key to social mobility. Without it the Negro will continue to be tied to the segregated slum where the social, intellectual and educational damage suffered by his children begins the day they are born. Repeated studies have confirmed that the ability of Negro children to learn, given equal conditions, is equal to the white.[83] But, by school age, the segregated slum culture in which they are born and reared has opened an educational gap, as compared with the white child, which not only is never closed, but which actually increases as time goes on.[84]

It is not enough, therefore, simply to provide equal educational opportunity beginning at the age of six. Until society eliminates these segregated slums, cultural and educational enrichment for slum children must begin at birth. To their great credit, some enlightened states, including New York and California, are already planning just such programs. And the President of the United States, in his recent message on education,[85] has asked the Congress for legislation providing financial aid to states undertaking pre-school educational programs for slum children.

The American Negro is a totally American responsibility. Three hundred years ago he was brought to this country by our forefathers and sold into slavery. One hundred years ago we fought a war that would set him free. For these last one hundred years we have lived and professed the hypocrisy that he was free. The time has now come when we must face up to that responsibility. Let us erase this blemish—let us remove this injustice—from the face of America. Let us *make* the Negro free.

In closing this, the sixth James Madison Lecture, it is fitting that we note the passing of the man whose conception and guidance made this series possible. It was Edmond Cahn's dream that America would one day fulfill the constitutional promise of equality before the law and yet maintain, by adherence to the Bill of Rights, the individuality of each human being. To this dream he dedicated this series of lectures. It was to this dream, too, that Edmond Cahn gave so much of himself. His inspirational writings will long serve the cause of equal liberty under law.

Edmond Cahn was a concerned man. Injustice in any of its forms disturbed him deeply. He seemed particularly distressed that, in all the years of history, man appeared incapable of mold-

83. See The Effects of Segregation and the Consequences of Desegregation: A Social Science Statement, 37 Minn. L. Rev. 427 (1953) (Appendix to Appellants' Briefs in the School Segregation Cases).

84. Ibid.

85. 111 Cong. Rec. 499-500 (daily ed. Jan. 12, 1965).

ing a just society. But the events of the recent past had given him reason to hope. For in the concluding paragraph of his last published work he wrote:

> The condition of democratic man is something new and young on the face of the earth, and his work of political creation is only beginning. In all the sad stages of human history, his is the first that, by the grace of intelligence, can actually will the elements of a just society into practical existence. Now that he has commenced to discover his capacities and flex his desires, the work is visibly accumulating power and momentum. I see a world where no man is accounted strong except in justice, rich except in compassion, nor secure except in freedom and peace.[86]

I trust that my friend Edmond Cahn proves as great a prophet as he was a human being.

---

86. Cahn, The Predicament of Democratic Man 187 (1961).

7

Color-Blind Theories and Color-Conscious Remedies

This article is a direct consequence of Judge Wright's views on de facto segregation set forth in Chapter 6. Here, he undertakes a systematic analysis of the question of "affirmative action" plans that are designed to help black Americans (and other disadvantaged citizens) to better their status. Often called "reverse discrimination," affirmative action is one of the most controversial developments of the process started by the Supreme Court in 1954 when it began the process of maintaining that blacks are entitled to be treated decently by government. Those plans are, as Judge Wright says, "now firmly entrenched in our public law as a means of eradicating the gross disparities in opportunity between the white majority and the nonwhite minorities."

Judge Wright approves such programs. To him, they are a necessary extension of his fundamental judicial philosophy of the pre-eminence of equality under the law. It is to be noted, however, that Wright speaks of equality of opportunity. He is not a Leveller, and does not advocate equality of condition except insofar as individuals are able to attain a better condition through improved opportunities. The failure to guarantee equality of opportunity among the races of America is, to Wright, a tragedy—not only for the victims of discrimination but also for the nation at large. Unless racial discrimination is extirpated, once and for all, further troubles are to be expected. It is one thing, he says, to be color-blind but quite another to be color-conscious. "Color-blind is a meaningless abstraction," Wright maintains, because certain groups in society—Wright uses black Americans as his chief example but notes that others exist—require help from government in the form of affirmative remedies to reduce the impact of centuries of neglect and discrimination.

Whether affirmative action programs will long continue as American public policy is by no means certain. There is much opposition to them, an opposition that rejects the basic arguments of this aricle. Which will prevail is, at this juncture, an unanaswered question. Despite Judge Wright's eloquent presentation, it may well be that the tide of history is running against his beliefs in this area.

Color-blind theory has proven to be the main tribute inequality pays to the principle of equality in our national life. At the nation's founding, the assertion that "all men are created equal" was used to justify establishment of a regime in which enslavement of the black population was given constitutional sanction.[1] In 1857 the Supreme Court managed to harmonize the principle of equality of all citizens with the continued existence of slavery by simply declaring that black persons are not citizens.[2] In 1896 the Supreme Court placed its imprimatur on a ghastly system of apartheid, but in doing so, felt it necessary to declare the policy "separate but equal."[3] It is a tribute to the American ideal of equality that the High Court was driven to *lie* rather than to admit what it was doing.[4]

Today, many decry affirmative attempts to remedy the continued social and economic deprivation of blacks and other minority group members. Once again, people tip their hats in tribute to the principle of equality and insist that their sole object is to ensure that everyone is treated equally without regard to race. I suggest

---

[1] Slavery was not merely permitted under the original Constitution; it was protected. *See, e.g.*, U.S. CONST. art. IV, § 2, cl. 3 (fugitive-slave clause).

[2] Dred Scott v. Sandford, 60 U.S. (19 How.) 393 (1857).

[3] Plessy v. Ferguson, 163 U.S. 537 (1896).

[4] Lest there be any doubt that "separate but equal" was a wholly inaccurate description of the post-*Plessy* practice, see Cumming v. Richmond County Bd. of Educ., 175 U.S. 528 (1899) (Board of Education allowed to close black high school for economic reasons, even though black students not admitted to white high school).

that this version of equality, which permits the continuation, indeed the exacerbation, of grave disparities in the opportunities and advantages available to persons of different races, ignores the context in which the problem of inequality has persisted in this country, and ultimately endangers our democratic institutions.

I do not suggest that everyone who opposes affirmative action on behalf of persons of disadvantaged background[5] is motivated by racism or ill will. Quite the contrary: many are sincere and idealistic. Moreover, it is easy to understand the distaste many feel for programs that allocate burdens or benefits on the basis of race. Nevertheless, I believe that such persons focus too narrowly on the importance of formally neutral rules, and thereby inhibit achievement of the equality necessary to our political system. No one can deny that race is, and has always been, the most serious, the most divisive, and the most persistent problem in the United States. To paraphrase—and I believe to correct—Professor Alexander Bickel's famous statement: the lesson of race relations in this country has been the same since the Founding; inequality between the races is "illegal, immoral, unconstitutional, inherently wrong, and destructive of democratic society."[6] If we come to understand why this is so, then it may become more clear what we must do about it.

I

Equality and egalitarian justice have animated political movements in countries around the globe through much of recent history. Yet nowhere is the principle of equality so central to the proper functioning of the political system as it is in the United States. This is partly the product of historical and geographical circumstance: the United States—more than most nations—comprises a profusion of races and ethnic groups. It is not surprising that racial equality is a vital issue to so heterogeneous a

[5] For purposes of this essay, I will write primarily about black Americans. To a large extent, however, the black race is a paradigm for other disadvantaged groups. This analysis should be understood as applying to those other groups as well, except where the context indicates otherwise.

[6] Professor Bickel's actual words were: "The lesson of the great decisions of the Supreme Court and the lesson of contemporary history have been the same for at least a generation: discrimination on the basis of race is illegal, immoral, unconstitutional, inherently wrong, and destructive of democratic society." A. Bickel, The Morality of Consent 133 (1975). This statement has recently provided the inspiration for a sharp attack on affirmative action programs. Van Alstyne, *Rites of Passage: Race, the Supreme Court, and the Constitution,* 46 U. Chi. L. Rev. 775 (1979).

people. But in saying that racial equality is central to our political institutions, I am referring not to historical happenstance, but rather to political theory and practice.

People often assert that equality is antithetical to liberty, and that promotion of equality is antidemocratic. Properly understood, these concepts are in harmony. This understanding is best captured by the ideal of self-rule, by which I mean a system of government in which a large measure of control is vested in each citizen over his own life, and in which social control is exercised with the consent of, and through the representatives of, the citizens. Equality, far from being antithetical to this understanding of liberty, is indispensable to it. The essential equality of the citizens is a fundamental precondition to the operation of the liberal democratic regime as established in this country.

The genius of the American system has been to mold out of the conflicting private interests of its individual citizens a common interest of the community. The system requires a particular type of citizen, and it emphasizes a particular type of interest. The citizen must have a stake in his country: he must feel that his country's prosperity is his prosperity, that his country's woe is his woe. Unless he feels this bond of community, he will—no matter what his legal status—consider himself an alien in his own land. Moreover, the individual citizens must pursue interests that are flexible and open to compromise, lest they be unable to reach mutually advantageous agreements with citizens who have conflicting interests. Thus, our politics must be based upon the shifting alliances of economic and social interest, rather than the immutable and uncompromising lines of race, clan, or religion. With respect to each of these requirements, racial inequality destroys the operation of the political system.

How can we expect blacks and other members of disadvantaged minority groups to feel they have a stake in the present system? They are denied the fruits of the nation's bounty. They are crowded together in the nation's slums; they suffer widespread unemployment; they receive the worst of most social services; they bear the brunt of the nation's brutalities. As they survey our white legislatures and congresses, our white courtrooms and bureaucracies, must they not feel that their citizenship is second-rate—that, no matter what the Constitution may say about their equality as citizens, they are unequal and ruled from above? And if this *objective* inequality undermines the bonds of community felt by black Americans, the fact that it was the *deliberate* product of oppression by the white majority should make white Americans marvel at the continued patience and patriotism of their black countrymen. Plainly, the disadvantaged position of blacks and members of other minority groups is a structural flaw in our political system, and an abomination.

Moreover, so long as the disadvantaged groups of the United States remain outside of the mainstream of our social and economic life, they will be driven to the very race-based politics feared by many opponents of affirmative action.[7] A poor black man will often vote for black candidates espousing black causes, just as any other citizen may sometimes vote on the basis of racial or ethnic identity. But unlike his more prosperous fellow citizens, whose ethnic identity is diluted and usually overwhelmed by interests grounded in economic or other concerns, the poor black man often has no faction to support other than one based on race. Because he plays no other role in the economy or society, he has no conflicting allegiance. Hence, affirmative action may be the only way to dismantle racial politics in the long run. Only when the divisions of race and ethnicity cease to correspond, and begin to conflict, with divisions along economic, social, and other shifting lines will racial politics be subordinated. When there are large numbers of black doctors, shopkeepers, corporate executives, developers, engineers, shareholders, and so on, the problem will be solved. This must be the goal of the United States, if the clash of private interests is to continue to serve as our means of approaching the common good.

II

America's tragedy has been her failure to guarantee the equality among the races so manifestly required by the structure and theory of her government. The country has paid a price. It took a bloody civil war to extirpate slavery, and an acrimonious Reconstruction to attempt, unsuccessfully, to eradicate the gross inequality that remained. More recently there has been disorder in our cities and elsewhere, which has subsided into squabbling among races and ethnic groups for larger shares of an economic pie now perceived by many to be shrinking. Obviously, the problem of inequality has not been solved, and we can expect further racial troubles in the future until its solution. A nation preconditioned on

---

[7] *See, e.g.*, Van Alstyne, *supra* note 6, at 778.

equality among its major groups cannot function with such a contradiction in its midst.

Unfortunately, inequality among the races is extraordinarily difficult to eradicate. Many persons expected that, once formal discrimination had been curbed, members of deprived minorities would have little difficulty in entering into the mainstream of American economic and social life. It has not been so—even assuming optimistically that most formal discrimination has now ceased. We should have known that inequality would continue until we took active steps to end it. As de Tocqueville predicted long before slavery was abolished, "[a] natural prejudice leads a man to scorn anybody who has been his inferior, long after he has become his equal; the real inequality . . . is always followed by an imagined inequality rooted in mores."[8] This "imagined inequality rooted in mores" plagues our civic life with a vengeance, and will continue to do so until experience proves that blacks can serve competently in all levels of society.

Inequality and disadvantage do not end simply because we pass laws against them. For a member of a deprived minority group to succeed, he must develop the discipline, drive, and skills demanded by the marketplace. Unfortunately, schools and job training programs cannot effectively impart such attributes, or our task would be relatively easy. Rather, the most basic education needed by a person entering the economic and social mainstream of this country must usually be provided in the home. And although many disadvantaged parents try very hard to train their children for productive lives, they succeed too rarely. A black mother and father, deprived by past discrimination of an adequate education, and inured because of past experience to second-class status, may often be unable to help their children to develop their academic skills and self-confidence. Their despair, compounded by the cruelties of the welfare system as it is administered, may indeed cause a breakdown in the family structure altogether—to the severe detriment of their children's chances to take advantage of opportunities now open by law to them. Discrimination, having once taken its toll, can in this manner perpetuate its effects long after the society has adopted formal equality in its racial practices.[9]

---

[8] A. DE TOCQUEVILLE, DEMOCRACY IN AMERICA 341 (J. Mayer ed. G. Lawrence trans. 1969).

[9] National economic statistics prove beyond doubt that inequality continues unabated, and even indicate that it may be increasing. The ratio of the unemployment rate of black

Moreover, poverty and race, acting in conjunction, tend to produce prejudice. So long as most blacks are poor, they will continue to exhibit the work habits and other characteristics of the poor that often impede success in the employment and society of middle class America. And so long as white persons associate being black with being poor, they will tend to discriminate against blacks, no matter how open-minded they may imagine themselves to be. This places the poor black in a situation far more desperate than that of his poor white counterpart. Both must overcome severe educational handicaps, but the black must in addition overcome the obstacles of racial prejudice.[10]

It has become increasingly evident that this cycle of discrimination, deprivation, inadequate education, and renewed discrimination must be broken if a genuine equality is to emerge. Doing nothing—or doing nothing but prohibiting the more obvious forms of racial discrimination—will avail little against the momentum of poverty and discrimination that we have allowed to build. To break this cycle requires, as a matter of common sense, special treatment for the victims of past discrimination. Such special treatment may appear unnatural—even unfair in the short run—but the only alternative is to allow the effects of our history of discrimination to plague our civic life in perpetuity.

Oddly, affirmative efforts designed to remedy the effects of past racial or ethnic discrimination have aroused far more heated opposition, both in the public and in the Supreme Court, than have efforts to remedy other forms of discrimination. Even though it is now well established, as a matter of either constitutional or statutory law, that discrimination *against* older persons, handicapped persons, and women is illegal, we find that private and governmental efforts *on their behalf* are largely considered unobjectionable. Who doubts that Social Security for the aged and special programs for the handicapped are legal and constitutional? Affirmative action on behalf of women is more controversial, at least in

---

males to that of white males was 2.2 in 1977 and 2.7 in 1979. The ratio of the unemployment rate of Hispanic males to that of white males was 1.7 in 1977 and 1.6 in 1979. U.S. COMM'N ON CIVIL RIGHTS, THE STATE OF CIVIL RIGHTS: 1979, at 21 n.2 (1980). In business, progress has been almost as scant. In 1972, minority-owned businesses generated 0.7% of all American business receipts. In 1977 this figure had increased to only 2.1%. *Id.* at 26 (citing U.S. DEP'T OF COMMERCE, A NEW STRATEGY FOR MINORITY BUSINESS ENTERPRISE DEVELOPMENT (1979)).

[10] The persistence of racial prejudice is well documented. *See, e.g.*, *id.* at 1-2 (housing discrimination).

some settings,[11] but the Supreme Court—with the acquiescence of some opponents of racial affirmative action[12]—has sustained special benefits to women on the ground that such benefits are needed to remedy the relative economic deprivation of women caused by economic discrimination.[13] Readers of Justice Rehnquist's dissent in *Weber*[14] must surely be surprised to read his dissent in *Califano v. Goldfarb,*[15] in which he urged the Court to uphold a provision of the Old Age, Survivors, and Disability Insurance Benefits program that favored widows over widowers.[16] Justice Rehnquist called this difference in treatment "scarcely an invidious discrimination,"[17] and explained: "The differentiation in no way perpetuates the economic discrimination which has been the basis for heightened scrutiny of gender-based classifications, and is, in fact, explainable as a measure to ameliorate the characteristically depressed condition of aged widows."[18] Of course, this logic is equally applicable to race-based affirmative action, which in no way perpetuates the economic or other discrimination that was the basis for strict scrutiny, and which in fact serves to ameliorate the depressed condition of blacks and other deprived minority group members. Since the "depressed condition" of minority persons in the United States is more intractable, and arguably more severe and politically divisive, than that of women, what supports the proposition that it is legitimate to help the latter, but not the former, to overcome past discrimination?

---

[11] One major concern is that programs ostensibly for the benefit of women may actually be predicated on outmoded stereotypes about the role of women in society, and thus may serve to impede the efforts of women to obtain genuine equality. *See, e.g.,* Weinberger v. Wiesenfeld, 420 U.S. 636 (1975).

[12] *Compare* Kahn v. Shevin, 416 U.S. 351 (1974) (Douglas, J.) *and* Schlesinger v. Ballard, 419 U.S. 498 (1975) (Stewart, J.) *with* Regents of the Univ. of Cal. v. Bakke, 438 U.S. 265, 408 (1978) (Stevens, J., joined by, *inter alia,* Stewart, J., concurring in the judgment in part and dissenting in part) *and* DeFunis v. Odegaard, 416 U.S. 312, 320 (1974) (per curiam) (Douglas, J., dissenting from finding of mootness).

[13] Califano v. Webster, 430 U.S. 313 (1977) (per curiam); Schlesinger v. Ballard, 419 U.S. 498 (1975); Kahn v. Shevin, 416 U.S. 351 (1974).

[14] United Steelworkers v. Weber, 443 U.S. 193, 219 (1979) (Rehnquist, J., dissenting).

[15] 430 U.S. 199, 224 (1977) (Rehnquist, J., dissenting).

[16] Strictly speaking, Justice Rehnquist's dissents in *Goldfarb* and *Weber* are not contradictory, since the former concerned a constitutional and the latter a statutory issue. Nevertheless, the Justice's recognition of the noninvidious nature of the discrimination in *Goldfarb* stands in sharp contrast to his description of affirmative action in *Weber* as "a creator of castes, a two-edged sword that must demean one in order to prefer another." 443 U.S. at 254.

[17] 430 U.S. at 242 (Rehnquist, J., dissenting).

[18] *Id.*

III

Rarely do opponents of affirmative action on behalf of racial or ethnic minorities squarely confront the undeniable need of those minorities for special assistance, or the grave consequences of continuing to deny such assistance. Rather, they immediately retreat to the abstract ground of high principle. They assert the necessity of strict neutrality between the races, and urge the courts to adopt what they invariably describe as a "color-blind" theory of the Constitution and laws. They argue that such neutrality is required by the equal protection clause, thereby giving a new twist to Justice Holmes's disparaging characterization of equal protection claims as "the usual last resort of constitutional arguments."[19] In fact, strict "color-blindness" of a sort was frequently urged by opponents of the Civil Rights Act of 1964. This strict neutrality would require that the government not interfere with the decisions made by its citizens, whatever their basis. Just as the government has no business telling its citizens that they should treat ballet the same way that they treat roller derby, so also should it permit its citizens to prefer whites to blacks, blacks to whites, or whatever. In this way, the government could remain aloof from the matter of color; it would treat all citizens exactly alike.[20]

Whether or not we fully realize it, this nation has irrevocably rejected the strict "color-blind" theory of government. Now it is agreed and solemnly enacted into law that racism—both governmental and private—is wrong, and that the government should employ its power to eradicate it. The purpose of this legislation cannot be denied: to help blacks and members of other minority groups overcome the prejudice that oppresses them. Its effect is to give special advantage to those minority groups. To call such legislation

---

[19] Buck v. Bell, 274 U.S. 200, 208 (1927).

[20] Even this limited position of strict neutrality of the government toward matters of racial preference would be preferable to the mandatory apartheid approved in Plessy v. Ferguson, 163 U.S. 537 (1896). The challenged state statute in *Plessy* required railway companies to segregate their passengers by race, depriving members of the public of the right to choose an integrated setting for their travels. That this type of legislation impeded good-spirited voluntary efforts to promote racial harmony and equality is clear from Berea College v. Kentucky, 211 U.S. 45 (1908). Berea College was and is a private religious college in the Appalachian region of Kentucky dedicated to the education of white and black students without segregation or discrimination. This commendable practice was outlawed by passage of a criminal statute in Kentucky, which was sustained by the Supreme Court, *id.* at 58, over an eloquent dissent by Justice Harlan, *id.* Presumably, under the strict color-blind theory of the Constitution, such odious legislation would be struck down.

"color-blind" is a meaningless abstraction. Legislation against invidious discrimination helps one race and not the other because one race and not the other needs such help. Blacks and members of other minority groups receive special protection against the irrational or malevolent decisions of states, schools, or employers, because they need it. *Equal* protection for them is not the *same* protection accorded others.

Two Supreme Court cases nicely illustrate this point. In *Reitman v. Mulkey,*[21] the voters of California approved by referendum a new provision in the state constitution guaranteeing to residential property owners the right to refuse to sell their property to any person, on any ground, including race. In *Hunter v. Erickson,*[22] the voters of Akron, Ohio approved a city charter amendment that prevented the passage of any open housing ordinances without approval by referendum. The Supreme Court did not deny that the challenged provisions were neutral on their face, and did not deny that cities and states have the right to decline to enact fair housing laws. The Court nevertheless struck down both provisions because they made it more difficult for minority groups that suffer discrimination to obtain political redress. In short, minority groups have been given special consideration for their interests, and special protections against the majoritarian political process, because of the reality that otherwise they will continue to be oppressed by an unsympathetic and often hostile majority. They require *greater assistance* to receive *equal protection.* As Justice Blackmun has said, "[i]n order to get beyond racism, we must first take account of race . . . . And in order to treat persons equally, we must treat them differently. We cannot—we dare not—let the equal protection clause perpetrate racial supremacy."[23]

This paradox has not discouraged some persons from insisting that it is possible to protect minority groups against discrimination—and indeed to remedy past instances of discrimination—without racial preference. It should be evident by now that no such course is available; the "color-blind" theorists are either deluding themselves, or are insincere in their commitment to equality. Instead of debating the abstract merit of the proposition that the government may not "regulate or allocate by race,"[24] we

---

[21] 387 U.S. 369 (1967).

[22] 393 U.S. 385 (1969).

[23] Regents of the Univ. of Cal. v. Bakke, 438 U.S. 265, 407 (1978) (Blackmun, J.).

[24] Van Alstyne, *supra* note 6, at 777.

must ask two simple, practical questions. First, how can we detect the effects of racial or ethnic discrimination? Second, how can we remedy them? If we neither detect nor remedy invidious discrimination, then obviously we have no antidiscrimination policy. But if we do, we will discover that we have begun to "regulate or allocate by race."

A

Professor Philip Kurland has recently written to decry the "new egalitarianism,"[25] which he describes as a perversion of the equal protection clause so as "not to require equality under law for select minorities, but to afford them preferences."[26] To Professor Kurland, the "new egalitarianism" is no venial constitutional aberration:

> My principal personal complaint about the new egalitarianism is that its goal seems to be homogenization of the human race, nay, that it already assumes homogeneity as the fact. My creed is different. With Judge Learned Hand, I have a "faith in the indefectible significance of each one of us." I think that the question posed by the egalitarianism of today is "whether the ultimate value shall be this wistful cloudly, errant You or I, or that Great Beast, Leviathan." And for me the choice is easy.[27]
>
> It is not too late to turn back from the new egalitarianism to the old equality. It is not too late to turn back from Leviathan. But it soon may be.[28]

While Professor Kurland's attention is riveted on the apocalypse, he loses interest in the practical problem of solving racial discrimination. Federal judges cannot be so lofty; they must detect and remedy specific instances of discrimination. Professor Kurland offers this comment:

> It is one thing to say that if A has been excluded from a job or a place in school because he is black, . . . [he] should be and is now entitled by law to the place that should have been his were it not for his race . . . , and to monetary compensation

---

[25] Kurland, *Ruminations on the Quality of Equality*, 1979 B.Y.U.L. Rev. 1, 18.

[26] *Id.*

[27] *Id.* at 20 (quoting L. Hand, The Spirit of Liberty 173, 82 (Phoenix ed. 1977)) (footnotes omitted).

[28] *Id.* at 23.

> for the period of deprivation . . . . It is another thing, however, to say that one becomes entitled to a place not because he has been discriminated against, but simply because he is black . . . .[29]

But is it so clearly "another thing"?

If all racial discrimination were blatant, it might be possible to apply Professor Kurland's simple rule of justice. But we have come to recognize that discriminators do not always announce themselves clearly: more often they employ ostensibly neutral criteria to accomplish their desired end. Unfortunately, direct proof of discriminatory motivation is usually difficult, often impossible, to obtain.[30] Thus, experience has proven what common sense would otherwise suggest: to establish evidence of illegal racial discrimination, the courts must employ reasonable presumptions about causes and results. If a member of a minority group is qualified for a job opening, but is denied the job, then—in the absence of a legitimate, nondiscriminatory explanation—racial discrimination may be presumed.[31] This is hardly a radical way of evaluating a charge of discrimination: given the pervasive, subtle, and persistent history of racial discrimination in this nation's workplaces, it is not unreasonable to presume that a black applicant rejected for no apparent legitimate reason is a victim of discrimination. But by this mode of analysis, have we not given the black applicant preferential treatment—"simply because he is black"? In effect, the qualified black applicant is given an entitlement to employment, denied to similarly qualified white applicants. The qualified white applicant, denied a job on the basis of some irrational or bigoted decision of the employer, is relegated to his luck. Given the subjective nature of the employment decision, the law must prefer the black applicant

---

[29] *Id.* at 18.

[30] *See* B. Schlei & P. Grossman, Employment Discrimination Law 16 (1976).

[31] *See* McDonnell Douglas Corp. v. Green, 411 U.S. 792 (1973). The prima facie case to be borne by the Title VII plaintiff alleging unlawful failure to hire consists of four parts:

> (i) that he belongs to a racial minority; (ii) that he applied and was qualified for a job for which the employer was seeking applicants; (iii) that, despite his qualifications, he was rejected; and (iv) that, after his rejection, the position remained open and the employer continued to seek applicants from persons of complainant's qualifications.

Id. at 802. This showing shifts the burden of proof to the employer to "articulate some legitimate, nondiscriminatory reason for the employee's rejection." *Id.* The plaintiff then has a final opportunity to prove that the asserted reason for rejection was a "pretext" for discrimination. *Id.* at 804. Statistics showing underemployment of the plaintiff's racial group are relevant to that inquiry. *Id.* at 805.

because he is black in order to ensure that employers do not discriminate against him because he is black.

Moreover, in the absence of direct evidence of discriminatory intent, it seems reasonable to presume that an actor intends the natural consequence of his deeds. As Justice Stevens has pointed out, this implies that "[f]requently the most probative evidence of intent will be objective evidence of what actually happened rather than evidence describing the subjective state of mind of the actor."[32] In the employment area, we should evaluate personnel policies and practices not solely on the basis of their purposes, but also on the basis of their consequences.[33] If an employer's practices consistently cause the disproportionate hiring of members of the majority race, and if the employer can show no legitimate business purpose for those practices, then—again given the pervasive, subtle, and persistent history of racial discrimination—we can presume that the challenged practices are discriminatory. Nine years after the decision in *Griggs v. Duke Power Co.,*[34] few persons would dispute this. But the same proposition, restated, is: absent legitimate business reasons, employers must adopt employment practices that result in the hiring of minority workers roughly in proportion to their availability in the pool of qualified laborers.

To some, this looks like "reverse discrimination." Before they condemn it, however, they should provide some credible explanation of why allegedly neutral employment practices[35] should produce rankly unneutral results. Can anyone believe that low hiring

---

[32] Washington v. Davis, 426 U.S. 229, 253 (1976) (Stevens, J., concurring).

[33] *See* Griggs v. Duke Power Co., 401 U.S. 424, 432 (1971) ("Congress directed the thrust of the Act to the *consequences* of employment practices, not simply the motivation.") (emphasis in original).

[34] *Id.* The Court held: "If an employment practice which operates to exclude Negroes cannot be shown to be related to job performance, the practice is prohibited." *Id.* at 431.

[35] Not all employment practices that cause the disproportionate hiring of white employees are illegitimate, of course. Only practices that erect "artificial, arbitrary, and unnecessary barriers to employment" are proscribed by Title VII. *Id.* at 431. "Congress did not intend by Title VII . . . to guarantee a job to every person regardless of qualifications." *Id.* at 430. I believe that much of the opposition to affirmative action among employers is the product of a misunderstanding on this point. To allay such misunderstanding—and also to enforce Title VII faithfully—the courts and the EEOC should be careful to respect the legitimate business needs of employers, even where those needs cannot be precisely documented or quantified. But they must be vigilant as well to ensure that discriminatory practices do not intrude into the nation's workplaces in the guise of legitimate business practices. *See generally* Comment, *The Business Necessity Defense to Disparate-Impact Liability Under Title VII,* 46 U. CHI. L. REV. 911 (1979); Note, *Business Necessity Under Title VII of the Civil Rights Act of 1964: A No-Alternative Approach,* 84 YALE L.J. 98 (1974).

rates for blacks are the product of chance?[36] Unless there is a legitimate explanation for the disparities, a fair-minded person should not be reluctant to conclude that something is amiss. In short, a serious commitment to removing race barriers from the nation's workplaces requires steps to remove racial disparities in hiring. If this be "reverse discrimination," make the most of it: I know of no other way to enforce the antidiscrimination laws.

B

Racial discrimination must not only be detected, but it must also be remedied. In practice, this requires that the courts and other institutions engaged in remedying past discrimination begin to prefer minority groups to the majority. Even if they adopt a "color-blind" theory, they will find that preferential methods are the only effective means of executing it.

This much seems to be admitted by most critics of affirmative action. Professor William Van Alstyne, for example, recently argued that "regulation and allocation by race are wrong," no matter what the purpose of the regulation or allocation may be.[37] Nevertheless, he was willing to agree with Supreme Court decisions that "paired racially identifiable schools, redrafted attendance lines, or mandated busing"[38] strictly on the basis of race. His justification is suggestive: "In each instance, the fulcrum of judicial leverage was an *existing governmental* race line, which the particular judicial order sought to remove. The object was thus to disestablish particular, existing uses of race, not to establish new ones."[39] Apparently, therefore, Professor Van Alstyne makes an exception to his otherwise categorical condemnation of "regulation and allocation by race" and would permit such regulation and allocation if it is useful to "disestablish particular, existing uses of race."

Professor Van Alstyne's principle is subject to a wider construction than he may expect. He seems to be thinking of a situa-

---

[36] *Cf.* Alexander v. Louisiana, 405 U.S. 625, 629-31 (1972) (inference of discrimination from disproportionate selection of white grand jurors).

[37] Van Alstyne, *supra* note 6, at 792. In fact, Professor Van Alstyne stated that the message of the Supreme Court civil rights decisions is "commendably even stronger." *Id.* He said that "[l]aws that divide and index people to measure their civil rights by race are unconstitutional. Laws that encourage others to do so are similarly invalid. And laws attempting to advance either policy even in disguise will likewise be struck down whenever it is within the capacity of conscientious courts to see beneath their cellophane wrappers."

[38] *Id.* at 784.

[39] *Id.* (emphasis in original) (footnote omitted).

tion in which race lines were established by the very instrumentality of government now attempting to disestablish them. An example might be a school board that once operated a dual system, and that now is required to integrate pupils and teachers so as to eradicate the vestiges of the dual system. But may an instrumentality of government seek to remedy the effects of a race line drawn not by it but by a separate agency? For example, may a housing agency employ color-conscious criteria in selecting new housing sites in order to compensate for the residential segregation caused in the past by zoning regulations or other practices of governmental agencies? The answer must surely be "yes," since the various governmental agencies are merely instrumentalities of a single responsible actor.[40] And why should not a governmental agency be permitted to take steps to disestablish the race lines wrongfully erected by its citizens?[41] In a sense, all civil rights law is an attempt by government to correct the injustices created by privately imposed slavery. Government is little more than the organized arm of society. If concerted action by the citizenry is needed to correct past abuses committed by the citizens as individuals, there is no apparent reason why it cannot democratically choose to take that action through its organized arm. If race lines are wrong, then they are wrong no matter who was responsible for their establishment. It makes little sense to hamstring those in a position to fashion remedies in the way Professor Van Alstyne seems to suggest.

The principle of disestablishing race lines may also be extended to the private sector. There is no reason to confine its operation to "*governmental*" race lines. If a corporation or other private

---

[40] The Court in Milliken v. Bradley, 418 U.S. 717 (1974), may have held that one state governmental entity cannot be required to remedy the effects of another's discriminatory decisions. It reversed a lower court order requiring 53 school districts in suburban Detroit to participate in cross-district busing, stating that cross-district remedies for the segregation of a single district could not be required unless *interdistrict* segregative effects had been proved. *But cf.* Hills v. Gautreaux, 425 U.S. 284 (1976) (upholding a plan requiring the U.S. Department of Housing and Urban Development to build public housing in Chicago suburbs even though the plan would involve separate local governments apparently innocent of past discrimination). Even so, nothing in *Milliken* detracts from the power of separate governmental entities to participate voluntarily in cross-jurisdictional affirmative action if they so choose.

[41] *Cf.* Swann v. Charlotte-Mecklenburg Bd. of Educ., 402 U.S. 1, 16 (1971) ("School authorities . . . might well conclude, for example, that in order to prepare students to live in a pluralistic society each school should have a prescribed ratio of Negro to white students reflecting the proportion for the district as a whole.").

association is motivated to eradicate race lines in its organization, it should be encouraged to do so—and permitted to do so without making admissions about past illegal action that would precipitate costly lawsuits against it.[42] Surely Professor Van Alstyne, who nearly twenty years ago pointed out the fallacies in the application of the "state action" requirement,[43] would not now decree a "state action" limitation on affirmative remedies.

Thus, the principle of disestablishing race lines, stripped of its artificial restrictions, would justify a large range of affirmative action programs: race-conscious public housing construction, in order to erase the race line of segregated housing; race-conscious special admissions programs in professional schools, to erase the race line of segregated professions and student bodies; race-conscious hiring or training programs, to erase the race lines in employment. Indeed, it is difficult to think of a reasonable affirmative action program that could not be justified on the basis of the need to "disestablish particular, existing uses of race."

Other practical concerns make some form of racial regulation useful. Without it, the courts would be unable to monitor compliance with their decrees effectively.[44] Congress would be unable to determine whether federal contracts are being granted to firms in compliance with its desire to eradicate racial disparities in contracting, minority group members would be reluctant to waste their time applying for jobs withheld from them in the past without some clear indication of change, employers or admissions officers would be unable to correct the pernicious effects of culturally biased testing,[45] businesses would be left uncertain about their obli-

---

[42] *See* United Steelworkers v. Weber, 443 U.S. 193 (1979).

[43] Van Alstyne & Karst, *State Action,* 14 Stan. L. Rev. 3 (1961).

[44] Professor Alan Freeman has propounded a telling example of this:

> Suppose a municipality has gerrymandered its districts so that the entire black population is in one district, and every other district is white, and you have evidence of purposeful discrimination. If you go to court and get the practice declared illegal, what's the remedy? Suppose the court simply issues an order to the municipality that says "stop doing that." And then a redistricting follows, with most of the black population still in the one district, and a handful of people shifted elsewhere. Assume there is no further evidence of "purposeful" discrimination. How do you know if the new scheme is a violation or not?

A. Freeman, School Desegregation Law: Promise, Contradiction, Rationalization (Oct. 25, 1978) (to be published in a collection of essays edited by Professor Derrick Bell tentatively entitled Alternative Visions: Revisionist Essays on School Desegregation (Teachers' College Press 1980)).

[45] *See* Sexton, *Minority-Admissions Programs after* Bakke, 49 Harv. Educ. Rev. 313, 324-27, 333-34 (1979).

gations under the law, society would be unable to address those subtle forms of discrimination not yet detected or proved, and civil rights, religious, and other public-spirited groups would be unable to discover the proper objects for application of moral pressure. Without objective evidence of result based on a rough element of racial proportionality, discriminators would be able to mask the motives for their decisions behind their unchallengeable discretion. In short, only clear, easily monitored goals and timetables are likely to make a real difference.

IV

Few parties in litigation now question the broad discretion of courts to remedy proven past discrimination, even using preferential goals and quotas, however controversial the practice may still be in academia or among the public. Although the Supreme Court has never authoritatively approved racial hiring or promotion quotas imposed by court decree, the lower federal courts have uniformly done so.[46] But controversy still rages over the seemingly subsidiary issue of *who* may determine when race-conscious remedies are needed. Some argue that such remedies are appropriate *only* when particular acts of past discrimination have been proven in some authoritative public forum: by court decree if possible, or maybe by administrative or congressional determination.

On the surface, this purported limitation on the freedom of institutions to remedy the effects of past misdeeds seems curious. It seems to suggest that affirmative action is forbidden unless it is required: an unusual proposition under our jurisprudence. Moreover, in an age when moderates and conservatives are usually heard to praise the virtues of voluntarism and to decry coercion, it is surprising that on this issue they should forbid uncoerced acts to remedy injustice. In an age when moderates and conservatives are quick to point out the inefficiencies and perversities of decision making by bureaucrats, politicans, and judges, it is peculiar to hear them say that *only* such officials have the ability accurately to discern racial discrimination. In an age when moderates and conservatives frequently express concern that businesses are unfairly throttled by unclear and inconsistent governmental pronouncements, it is odd that they should be willing to impose an-

[46] *See* B. Schlei & P. Grossman, *supra* note 30, at 1199-1200. The decision in *Weber* presumably lays this question to rest, at least by implication.

tidiscrimination laws on employers and unions, but deny them the only clear and manageable way of ensuring compliance with the law.

The decision in *Weber* settled the most important aspect of this dispute: "that Title VII's prohibition in §§ 703(a) and (d) against racial discrimination does not condemn all private, voluntary, race-conscious affirmative action plans."[47] At least in the case of private employers, therefore, reasonable affirmative action plans are permissible despite the absence of any judicial, administrative, or congressional finding of discrimination.

Were it not for Justice Powell's opinion in *Regents of the University of California v. Bakke,*[48] I would have thought the matter settled in other statutory[49] or constitutional areas as well. In *Bakke,* however, Justice Powell said that a racially based classification cannot be upheld on the ground that it "aids persons perceived as members of relatively victimized groups at the expense of other innocent individuals in the absence of judicial, legislative, or administrative findings of constitutional or statutory violations."[50]

Does Justice Powell really mean to limit constructive efforts to remedy the effects of past discrimination to those aimed at specific discriminatory acts identified by a governmental tribunal? In the face of the past treatment of this nation's black citizens by the white majority, it takes no special expertise to see that the present disadvantaged position of blacks can be traced directly to that unfair treatment. Why is a governmental tribunal needed to tell us what we already know? The only effect such a requirement could have would be to slow the process by preventing persons of goodwill from helping to remedy this pressing inequality. If we must wait for governmental tribunals, we may wait forever.

The appeal to the expertise of a governmental tribunal seems especially strained in the context of *Bakke.* Justice Powell stated that the University of California at Davis was "not competent"[51] to

---

[47] 443 U.S. at 208.

[48] 438 U.S. 265 (1978). There was no opinion of the Court in *Bakke,* but most scholars and lawyers treat Justice Powell's opinion, *id.* at 269, as if it were controlling, even though his *constitutional* holding in favor of Bakke was joined by no other Justice.

[49] In *Weber,* Justice Brennan indicated that Titles VI and VII of the Civil Rights Act of 1964, 42 U.S.C. §§ 2000d-2000e (1976), "cannot be read *in pari materia.*" 443 U.S. at 206 n.6. Thus Title VI, at issue in *Bakke,* may not allow for voluntary affirmative action efforts at least to the same extent as does Title VII.

[50] 438 U.S. at 307.

[51] *Id.* at 309.

make findings concerning past discrimination. The "broad mission" of the University, the Justice said, "is education, and not the formulation of any legislative policy or the adjudication of particular claims of illegality."[52] Were it not for this pronouncement, most persons probably would think that education professionals are the most "competent" to judge the effects of various causes on the educational attainments of students—certainly in a better position than judges or bureaucrats. One would also think that education professionals are the most "competent" to decide what sort of remedial program would be most effective in counteracting past discrimination. Moreover, as an agency receiving federal funds, the University was explicitly authorized by HEW regulations to "take affirmative action to overcome the effects of conditions which resulted in limiting participation by persons of a particular race, color, or national origin."[53] Apparently HEW did not think any special "competence" necessary to perceive that blacks and members of other minorities have suffered discrimination in the past; the Regents of the University of California obviously were not disabled on that score.[54] So long as the remedial purpose of the program was clear, what difference did it make that the need for it was perceived by the University and not by the courts? Allan Bakke is equally disadvantaged either way, and there is no reason to suppose that one way of making the necessary determinations is more or less accurate than the other. The primary effect of imposing the hurdle of "judicial, legislative, or administrative findings" is to make affirmative action programs rarer by making them procedurally more complicated to obtain.

In short, vigilance in the detection and remedy of racial discrimination requires race-consciousness, and such race-consciousness can be legitimate in a variety of circumstances, on the part of a variety of institutions. In the last few years the Supreme Court, albeit haltingly, has approved the use of race-conscious remedies by both public and private institutions on the basis of a number of

---

[52] *Id.*

[53] 45 C.F.R. § 80.3(b)(6)(ii) (1979). Justice Powell disregarded this explicit delegation of authority to the University of California by the federal department most closely associated with enforcement of equal educational opportunity.

[54] The only disagreement Justice Powell expressed with the University's substantive conclusions about the need for remedial assistance was that Asians were included in the program, in spite of the large numbers of Asians admitted through the regular admissions process. 438 U.S. at 309 n.45.

rationales.[55] In my view, this means that a significant victory against discrimination has been won, a victory that "color-blind" theory could never have achieved.

V

Difficult questions remain. Just as it is clear that courts should not overturn affirmative action programs simply because they are "discriminatory," so also is it clear that the courts must be vigilant to ensure that new forms of invidious discrimination are not approved in the guise of remedial affirmative action. In this the critics of affirmative action are correct: by rejecting a clear line against remedial racial preferences, the courts have taken on an oversight task of great subtlety and difficulty. So far, the courts have been faced with cases challenging the *principle* of affirmative action, not with cases difficult to decide on their *facts*. *Weber*[56] was essentially an easy case on its facts because the affirmative hiring program was plainly temporary, and because no workers were deprived of a right to advancement that they previously had considered theirs. *Bakke*[57] was easy because the program employed fixed, undisguised numerical quotas. *United Jewish Organizations*[58] might have been hard had the Court focused on the discrimination against Hasidic Jews—clearly a discrete and insular minority—rather than treating the disadvantaged voters as "white." Under the Court's approach, however, the case was easy because "whites" are well represented in the New York legislature, and because the redistricting was overseen by the Attorney General under the explicit mandate of the Voting Rights Act. The *principles* of these cases were of course difficult and controversial; but once the principle had been decided upon, the cases themselves presented few problems.

Not so cases in the future. As Professor Van Alstyne has pointed out, the courts must inevitably face "numerous" and "rank"[59] decisions about: "*which* races; *how much* to each race; *by*

[55] United Steelworkers v. Weber, 443 U.S. 193 (1979); Regents of the Univ. of Cal. v. Bakke, 438 U.S. 265 (1978); United Jewish Organizations v. Carey, 430 U.S. 144 (1977); Franks v. Bowman Constr. Co., 424 U.S. 747 (1976); Lau v. Nichols, 414 U.S. 563 (1974). *See also* Califano v. Webster, 430 U.S. 313 (1977).

[56] United Steelworkers v. Weber, 443 U.S. 193 (1979).

[57] Regents of the Univ. of Cal. v. Bakke, 438 U.S. 265 (1978).

[58] United Jewish Organizations v. Carey, 430 U.S. 144 (1977).

[59] Van Alstyne, *supra* note 6, at 808.

what test is each of us to be assigned 'our' race?"[60] He is, I think, overly pessimistic when he suggests that the courts will be without constitutional bases for the decisions and will be "overwhelmed" by the task, or will instead abdicate oversight to executive or administrative bodies.[61] Such pessimism may be the result of an overly punctilious standard for evaluating affirmative action programs: many apparent problems are less serious when affirmative action is evaluated in a more flexible and generous spirit. Nevertheless, Professor Van Alstyne is quite correct that there are difficult problems of adjudication ahead, and there is little in our jurisprudence to date that will guide us in the project.[62]

The common-law method of case-by-case adjudication may well serve us better in this area than any overarching theories or principles. As the courts sift through affirmative action programs, upholding some, striking down others, the proper grounds for distinction will in time appear. This apparently is the approach decided upon by the Supreme Court. In *Bakke,* the Court struck down one plan and, in dictum, praised another. In actuality, the lower courts are left with broad discretion to judge such plans in the future.[63] The much-lamented confusion of the *Bakke* opinion may thus be its jurisprudential strength: by deciding little, and providing less than clear reasons, *Bakke* keeps the future open for us. *Weber* was more explicit on this score: "We need not today define in detail the line of demarcation between permissible and impermissible affirmative action plans."[64] This gives little guidance to the lower courts in the short run; in the long run, however, it

---

[60] *Id.* at 804 (emphasis in original). *But see* Regents of the Univ. of Cal. v. Bakke, 438 U.S. 265, 359 n.35 (1978) (Brennan, White, Marshall, and Blackmun, JJ., concurring in the judgment in part and dissenting in part) (citations omitted):

> But, were we asked to decide whether any given rival group . . . must constitutionally be accorded preferential treatment, we do have a "principled basis" . . . for deciding this question, one that is well established in our cases . . . . [T]he only question is whether it was rational for Davis to conclude that the groups it preferred had a greater claim to compensation than the groups it excluded. . . . Thus, claims of rival groups, although they may create thorny political problems, create relatively simple problems for the courts.

[61] Van Alstyne, *supra* note 6, at 808. *See also* Regents of the Univ. of Cal. v. Bakke, 438 U.S. 265, 303 (1978) (Powell, J.).

[62] I doubt that the question "by what test is each of us to be assigned 'our' race?" will realistically be in dispute in most cases. I am content to leave most racial identification to the persons involved, except in cases of outright fraud.

[63] *See generally* Edwards, *Preferential Remedies and Affirmative Action in Employment in the Wake of* Bakke, 1979 Wash. U.L.Q. 113; Sexton, *supra* note 45.

[64] 443 U.S. at 208.

makes less likely the adoption of rigid and inapt distinctions that might prove difficult to correct.

It is therefore with some trepidation that I put forth several considerations that I believe may help to distinguish permissible from impermissible affirmative action plans. No one consideration should be dispositive; rather the court should decide, based on all relevant considerations, whether the challenged discrimination is invidious. Some of these proposed considerations may prove unworkable or wrongheaded; surely the list will be proven incomplete. Nevertheless, now that the principle of affirmative action has been essentially upheld, I think it is time to begin to think about the next step.[65] The following are in no particular order:

What is the relation between the decisionmaker and the burdened and preferred groups? One of the hallmarks of invidious discrimination has been that the decisionmaker—whether government, school, business, union, or whatever—acts out of ignorance or dislike of a racial or ethnic group he does not belong to. Because he is unfamiliar with members of a different and isolated group, he may predicate his decisions on stereotypes and bigoted misconceptions. The fundamental purpose of the equal protection clause is to ensure that governmental decisionmakers treat other groups the same way they treat their own, so as to prevent them from harming—either wittingly or unwittingly—an unrepresented minority. Thus, discrimination by the white majority against discrete, insular, and powerless minorities is considered "invidious" and subjected to "strict scrutiny" because we are suspicious that the ends sought by the majority may be illegitimate or the means irrational.[66] Even where there may be a legitimate basis for treating groups differently, a discriminatory law must be struck down under

[65] This is not, of course, the first attempt to marshal the considerations necessary for deciding affirmative action cases in the future. *See, e.g.*, United Jewish Organizations v. Carey, 430 U.S. 144, 171-78 (1977) (Brennan, J., concurring in part); EEOC, Affirmative Action Appropriate Under Title VII of the Civil Rights Act of 1964, 29 C.F.R. § 1608 (1979).

[66] *See* United States v. Carolene Products Co., 304 U.S. 144, 152 n.4 (1938) (dictum) ("prejudice against discrete and insular minorities may be a special condition, which tends seriously to curtail the operation of those political processes ordinarily to be relied upon to protect minorities, and which may call for a correspondingly more searching judicial inquiry"). *Cf.* San Antonio Independent School Dist. v. Rodriguez, 411 U.S. 1, 28 (1973) ("the class is not saddled with such disabilities, or subjected to such a history of purposeful unequal treatment, or relegated to such a position of political powerlessness as to command extraordinary protection from the majoritarian political process").

the equal protection clause if it is based on outmoded perceptions that certain groups are weak or inferior.

But when a decisionmaker chooses to disadvantage members of *his own* racial or ethnic group, it may hardly be supposed that he is acting out of prejudice, ignorance, or hostility.[67] Such decisions should not be considered "suspect" in the usual sense. As Professor John Hart Ely put it:

> When the group that controls the decision making process classifies so as to advantage a minority and disadvantage itself, the reasons for being unusually suspicious, and, consequently, employing a stringent brand of review, are lacking. A White majority is unlikely to disadvantage itself for reasons of racial prejudice; nor is it likely to be tempted either to underestimate the needs and deserts of Whites relative to those of others, or to overestimate the costs of devising an alternative classification that would extend to certain Whites the advantages generally extended to Blacks.[68]

Many affirmative action programs will be of this sort, and should, in general, be upheld by the courts. *Weber*[69] is a good example. The decision to prefer blacks to whites for the training program at Kaiser Aluminum was negotiated by the company and the union. Since the union membership is made up primarily of persons like Brian Weber, the decision was not likely to be "invidious"—that is, not likely to be predicated on prejudice or hostility toward the disadvantaged group.[70] When the majority group acts to disadvantage

---

[67] Castaneda v. Partida, 430 U.S. 482 (1977), may be an exception to this general rule. In *Castaneda,* the Court found that the grand jury selection system of Hidalgo County, Texas, was invidiously discriminatory against Mexican Americans, even though the judge, the majority of the jury commissioners, and the majority of the elected officials of the county were Mexican Americans. Justice Marshall, concurring, stated that:

> Social scientists agree that members of minority groups frequently respond to discrimination and prejudice by attempting to disassociate themselves from the group, even to the point of adopting the majority's negative attitudes towards the minority. Such behavior occurs with particular frequency among members of minority groups who have achieved some measure of economic or political success and thereby have gained some acceptability among the dominant group.

Id. at 503 (Marshall, J., concurring) (footnote omitted). One might add that members of the *majority* group sometimes adopt the *minority's* negative attitude toward the majority, but surely such reactions are comparatively rare in both situations.

[68] Ely, *The Constitutionality of Reverse Racial Discrimination,* 41 U. Chi. L. Rev. 723, 735 (1974).

[69] United Steelworkers v. Weber, 443 U.S. 193 (1979).

[70] In two respects, however, *Weber* might be considered slightly more troublesome.

itself for the benefit of the minority, there should be a strong presumption of legality.[71]

As Professor Ely points out, however, not all affirmative action plans are genuinely benign in this sense.[72] Sometimes, the non-"suspect" facade of white-black decisions will obscure a subtler, and less innocuous, form of discrimination. In particular, a group of whites in power may establish a remedial program for the benefit of blacks, to the detriment of a discrete and powerless subgroup of whites. Indeed, it may be "the natural consequence of our governing processes that the most 'discrete and insular' of whites often will be called to bear the immediate, direct costs of benign discrimination."[73] One troubling instance of this may have been the *United Jewish Organizations*[74] decision. In that case, legislative district lines in New York City were redrawn under the pressure of the Voting Rights Act so as to increase the representation of nonwhite voters. To do so, a compact district of predominantly Hasidic Jewish voters, which had traditionally sent a representative to Albany, was split in two. The Hasidim lost their legislative seat. The Supreme Court upheld the districting plan, because it treated the Hasidim as merely "white" voters. As the concurring opinion indicates, however, the increase in nonwhite representation could have been accomplished in other ways. The state officials chose to split the Hasidic community in half rather than to redistribute a "more varied and diffuse range" of white voters into predominantly non-

---

First, the union officials who negotiated the contract with Kaiser Aluminum might not be representative of their members: they might constitute a type of white ruling class willing to sacrifice the interests of the workers. Second, the union might have a conflict of interest with its members. Because the union might face lawsuits alleging racial discrimination, it might have chosen to adopt the affirmative action program to protect the union's coffers, with little concern for the consequences on its membership. In general, however, we can safely presume that an elected leadership will adequately defend the interests of its constituency—or at least that it will harbor no prejudice against, or hostility toward, them.

[71] Special deference may be due a congressional determination that certain forms of affirmative action are necessary to effectuate the substantive provisions of the fourteenth amendment: "§ 5 is a positive grant of legislative power authorizing Congress to exercise its discretion in determining whether and what legislation is needed to secure the guarantees of the Fourteenth Amendment." Katzenbach v. Morgan, 384 U.S. 641, 651 (1966).

[72] Ely, *supra* note 68, at 736-39.

[73] United Jewish Organizations v. Carey, 430 U.S. 144, 174 (1977) (Brennan, J., concurring in part). It is possible that many upper-class whites, professionals, and academics derive personal satisfaction and approbation from others by appearing to be "liberal" and "progressive." To sacrifice the interests of less advantaged whites for this reason may be less "benign" than affirmative action may generally be presumed to be.

[74] 430 U.S. 144 (1977).

white districts.[75] I am not saying that, given the state of the record, the plan necessarily should have been struck down; perhaps, however, the Court should have remanded the case for a consideration of the issue.[76]

One consequence of this approach to affirmative action programs is that the courts must scrutinize somewhat more carefully those programs instituted by decisionmakers of the minority race. When black decisionmakers, for example, choose to disadvantage white persons, there is no *a priori* reason to assume that they are not acting out of prejudice or hostility. This does not mean, however, that all minority-instituted affirmative action programs must be struck down: such programs should merely be denied the presumptive validity granted programs instituted by the groups disadvantaged by them. We may no more assume that minority preference programs are "invidious" when members of a minority are in control than we may assume that policies *disadvantaging* members of minorities are necessarily benign on account of such control.[77] Still, the courts may in some circumstances need to protect powerless white persons from invidious discrimination at the hands of black majorities.

Will the classification tend to stigmatize members of a group? Ever since the Court in *Brown v. Board of Education*[78] declared school segregation unconstitutional on the ground that it "generates a feeling of inferiority as to [black children's] status in the

---

[75] *Id.* at 174-75 (Brennan, J., concurring in part). Some evidence suggests that if an alternative districting plan had been adopted, leaving the Hasidic district intact, the desired nonwhite majority in the adjoining district would have fallen from 65% to 63.4%. State officials apparently perceived that the Attorney General required no less than a 65% nonwhite majority. *Id.* at 181-82 (Burger, C.J., dissenting).

[76] The district court ruled that the petitioners had no constitutionally protected rights as Hasidic Jews, *id.* at 153, and petitioners apparently did not pursue this claim. *Id.* at 178 (Brennan, J., concurring in part). This partially explains why the majority blandly discussed the issues of the case as if the Hasidim were indistinguishable from the other whites of New York.

A second problem in the case that received no attention from the majority was the claim by Puerto Rican voters that they were disadvantaged by the redistricting plan. *Id.* at 173 (Brennan, J., concurring in part). The Puerto Ricans were classified with the blacks as "nonwhites," *id.* at 150 n.5 (White, J.), and thus were treated as if they benefited from the plan. This exemplifies a potential problem of affirmative action programs: they may tend to benefit primarily the most vocal and politically powerful of the minority groups. If the courts are not sensitive to this problem, no one will be.

[77] *See* Castaneda v. Partida, 430 U.S. 482 (1977) (leaders from minority groups may act out of prejudice towards their own group).

[78] 347 U.S. 483 (1954).

community that may affect their hearts and minds in a way unlikely ever to be undone,"[79] the courts have recognized that a key aspect of invidious discrimination is its tendency to stigmatize persons of particular groups. This stigma may take the form of stamping the group as inferior, venal, weak, or whatever, depending on the popular prejudice and the nature of the discrimination. Any evaluation of the legality of an affirmative action plan must include a serious search for a stigmatizing purpose or effect, for "[s]tate programs designed ostensibly to ameliorate the effects of past racial discrimination obviously create the same hazard of stigma, since they may promote racial separatism and reinforce the views of those who believe that members of racial minorities are inherently incapable of succeeding on their own."[80] Any affirmative action program that would label a class of persons as innately inferior should therefore be struck down.

That the Supreme Court has been misled on the subject of stigma can be seen in the gender-based discrimination cases such as *Kahn v. Shevin.*[81] In *Kahn,* the Court upheld a statute granting widows, but not widowers, a $500 property tax exemption, stating that it was "reasonably designed to further the state policy of cushioning the financial impact of spousal loss upon the sex for which that loss imposes a disproportionately heavy burden."[82] Under the circumstances, however, that ostensibly benign purpose was likely predicated on the stereotype of the helpless and dependent widow. As Justice White stated in dissent, "[t]he presumption is that all widows are financially more needy and less trained or less ready for the job market than men."[83] Such demeaning presumptions should not be the basis for public policy. More hopeful was the later case of *Craig v. Boren,*[84] in which the Court struck down a law permitting the sale of 3.2% beer to females, but not males, between the ages of 18 and 21. The Court recognized that the law was predicated on the "social stereotype" that young men are more likely to be "reckless."[85] Even when there may be some statistical evidence

---

[79] *Id.* at 494.

[80] Regents of the Univ. of Cal. v. Bakke, 438 U.S. 265, 360 (1978) (Brennan, White, Marshall, and Blackmun, JJ., concurring in the judgment in part and dissenting in part).

[81] 416 U.S. 351 (1974).

[82] *Id.* at 355.

[83] *Id.* at 360-61.

[84] 429 U.S. 190 (1976). *See also* Stanton v. Stanton, 421 U.S. 7 (1975).

[85] 429 U.S. at 202 n.14.

tending to support such stereotypes, it is not permissible for the state to reinforce them so as to perpetuate the stereotype.[86]

I do not expect that many racial affirmative action programs would be struck down on a theory of "stigma." Members of the majority group are rarely if ever stigmatized by the existence of a minority preference program: did anyone conclude on the basis of Allan Bakke's rejection from medical school that whites are not very intelligent? The more serious danger is that the minority, which is apparently being helped by the program, may suffer because of an appearance that its members are unable to "make it" on their own. Such challenges should be rejected, so long as the programs are grounded in the need by minority group members for special treatment to redress the effect of past discrimination. It is not "stigmatizing" to need help for such a reason. And in the long run, as blacks and members of other minority groups assume responsible positions in the economy and government, and display their ample abilities to function effectively, the stigma of minority status will tend to decline. The absence—not the presence—of affirmative action produces the true stigma, for it would perpetuate the disadvantage of minority persons and the stereotypes that accompany it. Moreover, the courts should cast a skeptical eye on the claims of white plaintiffs who seek to strike down a program because of an alleged stigmatizing effect on minority persons. Even if they have standing in a technical sense to mount such a challenge, their assertions on that score carry little weight. For an Allan Bakke to win a place in medical school by purporting to defend the interest of an uncomplaining and unidentified "stigmatized" minority person would be ironic. "What's Hecuba to him or he to Hecuba, [t]hat he should weep for her?"[87]

Does the program take away vested rights? In evaluating a program that benefits certain persons at the expense of others, the courts must inquire whether the vested rights of members of the latter group are disturbed. Programs that take away the vested rights of innocent persons—as opposed to those that affect only the possibility of future benefits—may require a more substantial justification. I think this may explain the tension between such deci-

---

[86] "[P]roving broad sociological propositions by statistics is a dubious business, and one that inevitably is in tension with the normative philosophy that underlies the Equal Protection Clause." *Id.* at 204 (footnote omitted).

[87] W. Shakespeare, Hamlet, II, 2, 562-63.

sions as *Weber*[88] and *International Brotherhood of Teamsters v. United States.*[89] In *Teamsters,* the Supreme Court held illegal under Title VII a remedy granting retroactive seniority rights to black workers who had been discriminated against prior to enactment of Title VII. In *Weber,* the Court approved a plan admitting less senior blacks into a job training program ahead of more senior whites, thereby diluting the value of the whites' seniority rights. In *Teamsters,* the retroactive seniority would have denied the white workers the benefits of seniority that they already had, and thus would have disrupted their settled expectations.[90] In *Weber,* on the other hand, the white workers never had any right or expectation to be admitted into the job training programs, because prior to the adoption of the affirmative action plan, all of Kaiser's skilled craftsmen were hired from outside the plant. Thus, Brian Weber himself was better off after adoption of the challenged plan than he was before: now he has at least some chance of receiving the training, whereas before he had none.[91]

Often, employers and other persons in authority attempt to reallocate the vested rights of innocent persons in order to cover their own misdeeds. The courts should insist where possible that affirmative remedies be at the expense of the wrongdoer, rather than at the expense of innocent bystanders. Back-pay remedies, special training, damages, and the like place the onus for correcting past injustice on the employer-perpetrator rather than on the innocent employee, and should therefore be preferred. Of course, where the employees had participated in the past instances of discrimination, it matters little whether their settled expectations are defeated; we should apply the traditional rule of justice that a person should not

---

[88] United Steelworkers v. Weber, 443 U.S. 193 (1979).

[89] 431 U.S. 324 (1977).

[90] *But cf.* Franks v. Bowman Transp. Co., 424 U.S. 747 (1976) (holding that an award of retroactive seniority is an appropriate remedy for racial discrimination occurring after passage of Title VII). *Franks* serves as a reminder that even the established seniority rights of innocent persons may sometimes be disturbed if the public interest is sufficiently compelling. As the Court noted, denying retroactive seniority to victims of discriminatory hiring would completely "frustrate the central 'make whole' objective of Title VII." *Id.* at 774. And "employee expectations arising from a seniority system agreement may be modified by statutes furthering a strong public policy interest." *Id.* at 778 (footnote omitted).

[91] Both the majority and the concurring opinions in *Weber* stress this point. *See* 443 U.S. at 208 (Brennan, J.) ("At the same time the plan does not necessarily trammel the interests of the white employees."); *id.* at 215 (Blackmun, J., concurring) ("Here seniority is not in issue because the craft training program is new and does not involve an abrogation of pre-existing seniority rights.").

profit from his own misdeeds. Yet, when essentially innocent persons are asked to bear the brunt of remedying injury inflicted by someone else, or by society as a whole, the courts should attempt to protect their interest, so far as it is consistent with justice.[92]

Most affirmative action plans do not disturb vested rights, and thus do not require this special degree of justification. Affirmative hiring goals, preferential admissions processes, minority contracting provisions, and the like only affect the opportunities for future benefits. Important as these opportunities may be, their adjustment for the purpose of promoting racial equality is ultimately not as serious as the reallocation of vested rights.

Is the program reasonably designed to achieve a remedial purpose articulated by the decisionmaker? Perhaps the most important mode of analysis the courts may employ to determine whether a race-conscious remedial program is legal or constitutional is to insist that the purpose of the program be articulated, and that the program be reasonably designed to accomplish that purpose. The Brennan group in *Bakke* said that to justify a racial classification established for ostensibly benign reasons, "an important and articulated purpose for its use must be shown."[93] We need not indulge in the largely meaningless quest for a verbal formulation that expresses the appropriate level of "scrutiny" to be applied in such cases: both the Brennan group and Justice Powell appeared *in fact* to employ ends-means scrutiny stricter than that applied to economic legislation, but less strict than that applied to invidiously

---

[92] One commentator has criticized the view that some persons are innocent of racial discrimination, and that discrimination can be attributed to particular deeds of particular actors, calling this the "perpetrator perspective." Freeman, *Legitimizing Racial Discrimination Through Antidiscrimination Law: A Critical Review of Supreme Court Doctrine*, 62 MINN. L. REV. 1049 (1978). To a certain extent, this criticism is valid. In a society where racial discrimination has been so pervasive, most white persons have both contributed to and benefited from discrimination to some degree. I cannot agree, however, that we should abandon the view that discriminatory acts are unjust and immoral, and that the wrongdoers should bear the consequences of their misdeeds. To place the blame generally on social institutions relieves us all, individually, of responsibility, and it postpones the achievement of racial justice until the coming of a new social, political, and economic order that may not prove desirable. I believe that racial equality is demanded by our liberal democratic system as it is now, and I hope that it can be attained without abandoning the fundamental structure of that system. Even within our present system, moreover, a nonperpetrator who has been unjustly enriched in an ascertainable way by discrimination may have to contribute to remedying the injury from such discrimination. *See* note 90 *supra*.

[93] Regents of the Univ. of Cal. v. Bakke, 438 U.S. 265, 361 (1978) (Brennan, White, Marshall, and Blackmun, JJ., concurring in the judgment in part and dissenting in part).

discriminatory legislation.[94] This seems sensible: given the long history of misuse of racial classifications in this country, the variety of abuses that have occurred, and the danger to our democratic institutions inherent in governance by race, the courts cannot abdicate to the political branches their responsibility to enforce the equal protection clause, even when a challenged discrimination is purportedly "benign." But to treat efforts to remedy past injustice with the same disfavor as we treat invidious discrimination itself would be equally improper. A middle level of scrutiny, therefore, seems best.

The reasonableness of the racial classification may be judged from the viewpoint of whether it is overinclusive or underinclusive. For example, if the purpose of the program is to help persons from deprived backgrounds, we must ask whether the persons advantaged by the program in fact come from such backgrounds, and whether the persons disadvantaged by it come from an affluent background. Moreover, we must ask whether other persons, equally or more deprived than those of the preferred class, have been excluded from the program. The danger is ever-present that affirmative action programs will be set up for the benefit of only the strongest and most politically powerful of the minority groups.

Similarly, if the purpose of the program is to promote cultural diversity at a university, we must inquire whether inclusion of the preferred ethnic groups particularly promotes such diversity or whether preferment of other groups might do so as well or better. If the purpose of the program is to correct for errors in the testing process, we must ask whether the correction to the applicants' scores bears a relation to the groups' differences in testing accuracy. The courts need not engage in these inquiries de novo, but should ensure that the decisionmakers acted reasonably and conscientiously.

The principal result of this inquiry probably will not be to strike down many affirmative action programs. Rather, once the courts begin to scrutinize programs in this way, the universities,

---

[94] The Brennan group did so explicitly. *See id.* at 361-62. Although Justice Powell purported to employ "strict scrutiny," *see id.* at 305, he concluded that the promotion of diversity in education is a sufficiently compelling governmental objective, and that an admissions program that deems minority status a "plus" can be considered necessary to achieve that objective, *id.* at 315-19. This approach obviously falls shy of the "fatal in fact" scrutiny usually called "strict." *See* Gunther, *The Supreme Court, 1971 Term—Foreword: In Search of Evolving Doctrine on a Changing Court: A Model for a Newer Equal Protection*, 86 HARV. L. REV. 1, 8 (1972).

governments, and employers of this country should respond by being more careful in the design of their affirmative action programs. Instead of designing them to placate the demands of the most vocal and powerful of the minorities, they may seek to assist those persons and groups most in need of help. A serious ends-means analysis by the courts should promote more rational decisions by other institutions.

What other characteristics are used as criteria for selection? Much of the opposition to affirmative action programs is based on the view that such programs displace persons of *more ability* in favor of persons of *less ability,* with race as the determining factor. This opposition carries great weight, because in our meritocratic society, we believe that persons should advance on the basis of their ability and effort, both as a matter of efficiency and as a matter of justice. The American dream of equal opportunity is that all arbitrary barriers to advancement on the basis of personal worth can be eliminated, to the benefit of us all.

Affirmative action is not necessarily in conflict with this ideal, for two reasons. First, for many decisions, ability is not the sole or the principal criterion. Entrance to competitive universities may serve as an example. The number of qualified applicants to most such schools far exceeds the number of places available. To select among the pool of qualified applicants, the schools may use a variety of criteria: geographic balance, diversity of experience, relationship to alumni, athletic talent, sincerity or friendliness during an interview, or whatever. What is lost when membership in a disadvantaged race is added to such a list of factors? So long as members of the minority groups given preferential treatment possess the qualifications reasonably necessary to profit from education at the school, then their selection is no more arbitrary or invidious than is the selection of the son or daughter of a distinguished alumnus.

Second, in many contexts, "ability" is difficult, perhaps impossible, to define. Quantitative scores, such as standardized test results or grades, may not by themselves be reliable indicators of future success.[95] The meritocratic ideal does not mean that the person *predicted* to be the most worthy on the basis of incomplete or possibly faulty information deserves to advance the farthest; rather, it means that every person is entitled to the opportunity to attain the highest result he can, given his talents, dedication, and

[95] *See* Sexton, *supra* note 45, at 324-27, 333-34.

luck. A minority person admitted to a law school receives only the *chance* to make it in his profession. He is subjected to the same academic requirements, must pass the same tests, must attract the same clients, must win the same cases, as his white fellow classmates. His success in those endeavors is the true mark of his ability, not his LSAT scores and college grades. Unfortunately, the history of discrimination in this country has distorted the indicators of ability for persons of disadvantaged groups; now, special recognition of that distortion is needed so that genuine meritocratic selection can proceed fairly.

These considerations suggest that courts should consider what other characteristics are used as criteria for selection. If race is used as a supplement to other arbitrary, non-ability-related criteria, then there is little reason to object to it. Even if race is considered along with predictors of ability, the courts should be aware that such predictors may operate unfairly, and that a genuine commitment to equality of opportunity is often consistent with at least some consideration of race.

Are all applicants for the privilege granted equivalent procedural treatment? Behind the semantic dispute over the difference between "quotas" and "goals" is a fundamental point about procedural fairness: there is a difference between a system that accords members of a minority group an advantage in an otherwise competitive process, and a system that removes certain positions or privileges from competition altogether.[96] As Justice Powell saw the preferential admissions program at the University of California at Davis, its "principal evil" was the denial to Allan Bakke of his "right to individualized consideration without regard to his race."[97] It is appropriate for the courts to insist, as Justice Powell did in *Bakke,* that an affirmative action program guarantee to all applicants the right to compete—even as it recognizes the legitimacy of using race as one criterion for decision.

In his dissent from that portion of Justice Powell's *Bakke* opinion, Justice Brennan rejected the suggestion that there is a constitutional distinction between "adding a set number of points to the admissions rating of disadvantaged minority applicants as an expression of the preference . . . and setting a fixed number of places

---

[96] *See generally* Tribe, *Perspectives on* Bakke: *Equal Protection, Procedural Fairness, or Structural Justice?,* 92 Harv. L. Rev. 864, 867-73 (1979).

[97] Regents of the Univ. of Cal. v. Bakke, 438 U.S. 265, 318 n.52 (1978).

for such applicants."[98] He insisted that the excluded white applicant under the fixed-quota system "receives no more or less 'individualized consideration' " than under Justice Powell's preferred alternative.[99] It cannot be denied, however, that Allan Bakke received no consideration at all for the sixteen reserved minority slots at the Davis medical school; nor can it be denied that this difference *seems* important. It is the difference between process and result, akin to the requirement of a hearing independent of the prospect of eventual success on the merits. We may therefore expect that in the post-*Bakke* world, the question whether applicants are accorded equivalent procedural treatment, or whether certain applicants are eliminated *en masse,* may determine the permissibility of the program.

Is the program temporary or permanent? It may seem a simple point, but an affirmative action program that will terminate is more defensible than one that may persist in perpetuity. Since affirmative action is principally designed to provide temporary assistance now that will enable minority group members to compete on an equal basis in the future, such a program will appear better suited to its ends if it is scheduled to end upon achievement of the intended outcome. Moreover, members of the public are more likely to cooperate with a plan that they see as temporary: part of the opposition to affirmative action can be understood as arising from the fear that whites are to be subject to disadvantage for all time. The demands by minority group members for redress would surely be treated with greater sympathy if the majority were assured that the need for affirmative action will end in the conceivable future.

This is one reason why the hiring program at issue in *Weber* was particularly meritorious. As Justice Blackmun noted in his concurring opinion, Kaiser Aluminum's affirmative action plan was "a moderate one":

> [I]t ends when the racial composition of Kaiser's craftwork force matches the racial composition of the local population. It thus operates as a temporary tool for remedying past discrimination without attempting to "maintain" a previously achieved balance. . . . Because the duration of the program is

---

[98] *Id.* at 378 (Brennan, White, Marshall, and Blackmun, JJ., concurring in the judgment in part and dissenting in part).

[99] *Id.* at 378 n.63.

finite, it perhaps will end even before the "stage of maturity when action along this line is no longer necessary."[100]

Conclusion

Affirmative action programs are now firmly entrenched in our public law as a means of eradicating the gross disparities in opportunity between the white majority and the nonwhite minorities. Recent decisions upholding affirmative action still receive strident criticism. But the permissibility—the necessity—of race-conscious remedies did not begin with *Weber* or *Bakke,* but was impliedly established at least by the time of *Griggs* and *Swann.*[101] Indeed, such remedies are the necessary result of this nation's belated decision to cease its course of racial discrimination in favor of a regime of equality among the races. That principle, in turn, can be traced to the Civil War, and still farther to the Founding itself. The task now is not to justify remedies for the centuries of oppression of blacks by whites, but rather to ensure that the remedies we choose will create a nation of genuine equality in the future. For who are we to accept the bounty that this country presents us, if we do not seek to share that bounty with our fellow citizens?

It is time for the legal community to stop its squabbling: to admit that the Constitution and the Civil Rights Act permit us to remedy the wrongs of the past. It is time to abandon the abstractions of "color-blind" theory and admit that there can be no such thing as a "color-blind" approach to achieving racial equality. It is time now to concentrate our efforts on ensuring that the remedies we construct are humane and effective, that they respect, so much as is possible, the rights of all. Most important, we must be sure that—for the first time in history—we do the job right, so that succeeding generations will not still be faced with the odious sight of institutionalized racial injustice.

---

[100] United Steelworkers v. Weber, 443 U.S. 193, 216 (Blackmun, J., concurring) (quoting *Bakke,* 438 U.S. at 403). *See also id.* at 208 (Brennan, J.) ("Moreover, the plan is a temporary measure; it is not intended to maintain racial balance, but simply to eliminate a manifest racial imbalance.").

[101] Swann v. Charlotte-Mecklenburg Bd. of Educ., 402 U.S. 1 (1971).

8

The Courts and the Rulemaking Process: The Limits of Judicial Review

The final two chapters of this volume address different questions from those that preceded them. Heretofore the focus has been on constitutional matters and how Judge Wright perceives them. Their principal emphasis has been equality. Chapter 8 turns attention toward judicial scrutiny of the decisions of public administrators, of those hundreds of thousands of individuals who make up the bureaucracy—sometimes called a "headless fourth branch of government."

Chapter 8 is a generalized discussion of the posture that Wright believes federal judges should take when scrutinizing "rulemaking" decisions of administrators. In general, administrators either "adjudicate"—that is, act rather like courts in settling a specific claim or dispute—or issue "rules"—that is, act rather like a mini-legislature in promulgating norms of more than specific applicability. This essay, published in 1974, to some extent anticipates Wright's later views that were set forth in Chapter 5. Here, he condemns what he calls the "ad hoc approach" to judicial review because it "lacks those foundations in law and reason which an activist posture requires."

Underlying this presentation, which is cast in rather orthodox legal terms, may be detected Judge Wright's concern about corporate power and how it can manipulate the administrative process. He plumps for fairness and believes that is satisfied when people and groups are accorded the opportunity to make their views known to administrators before rules are promulgated. A "dialogue, not a trial" is the fundamental requirement. There is no need for full-dress adversary proceedings, conducted in an "ad hoc" manner.

Judge Wright is mainly concerned with "informal" rulemaking, sometimes called "notice-and-comment rulemaking." His views have been accepted by the Supreme Court. On this question, but on few others, he and Justice William Rehnquist see eye to eye. Not everyone, however, agrees with Wright; and he has not been able to convince all of his colleagues on the Court of Appeals.

> [T]hat the judiciary should presume to impose its own methods on administrative or executive officers is a usurpation. And the assumption that the methods of natural justice are ex necessitate those of Courts of justice is wholly unfounded.
>
> Lord Shaw in
> Local Government Board v. Arlidge
> [1915] A.C. 120, 138.

Administrative law has entered an age of rulemaking. Administrators who once acted on whim and instinct have been judicially constrained to promulgate and adhere to consistent guidelines.[1] Agencies which once generated policy in a piecemeal fashion through adjudication are now adopting prospective standards of action valid in a number of different settings and against a wide variety of "parties."[2] And the new agencies established by Congress to deal with contemporary environmental, economic, and energy problems have relied heavily on the promulgation of general regulations.[3] These are healthy and welcome developments.

---

[1] *See, e.g.*, United States v. Bryant, 439 F.2d 642 (D.C. Cir. 1971); Environmental Defense Fund, Inc. v. Ruckelshaus, 439 F.2d 584 (D.C. Cir. 1971); Holmes v. New York City Housing Authority, 398 F.2d 262 (2d Cir. 1968); Hornsby v. Allen, 326 F.2d 605 (5th Cir. 1964).

[2] For instance, the Federal Power Commission (FPC), overwhelmed by the task of setting rates in case-by-case adjudications, has begun to establish area-wide rates. *See, e.g.*, Permian Basin Area Rate Cases, 390 U.S. 747 (1968). The FPC has also started to establish maximum rate rules covering a number of parties. *See, e.g.*, Mobil Oil Corp. v. FPC, 469 F.2d 130 (D.C. Cir. 1972), *cert. denied*, 412 U.S. 931 (1973). The Federal Trade Commission (FTC), in a major change of position, may also be ready to exercise some rulemaking powers. *See* National Petroleum Refiners Ass'n v. FTC, 482 F.2d 672 (D.C. Cir. 1973).

[3] For example, the Environmental Protection Agency (EPA), in partnership with state governments, is authorized to establish air quality standards governing many major indus-

Arguably, some areas of the economy should be deregulated to give fuller play to competitive market forces;[4] and one may doubt that Congress is always wise to delegate to the executive branch and to administrative agencies the responsibility for making fundamental decisions about the economy and the environment.[5] But when Congress *has* adopted a regulatory solution, and when the Delegation Doctrine does not bar that solution, the case for making administrative policy through rules, rather than adjudicatory decisions, is overwhelming.

Trial-like adjudication is extremely costly in time, staff, and money. Before an adjudicatory common law can acquire coherence, conditions typically will have overtaken it. As a consequence, industries subject to adjudicatory regulation are left in a state of perpetual uncertainty, and agencies assume the dangerous power to create new law affecting parties selected at random, or in a discriminatory manner. Orderly innovation is difficult, and emergencies often go unmet. To discern basic agency policy, the public must wade through volumes of scarcely relevant testimony and findings. The technicalities of adjudication allow lawyers to minimize the input of experts and to frustrate agency consideration of relevant scientific and economic perspectives. Regulation becomes an advocate's game. Especially in the rapidly expanding realms of economic, environmental, and energy regulation, the policy disputes are too sharp, the technological considerations too complex, the interests affected too numerous, and the missions too urgent for agencies to rely on the ponderous workings of adjudication.

---

tries and most areas of the United States. Clean Air Act of 1970, 42 U.S.C. §§ 1857c-3 to -7 (1970). The four "phases" of the current round of wage-price control have involved rulemaking of an even more farreaching character. The extent to which "legislative" power has been delegated to the Executive to allow him to manage the economy may be gleaned from the language of the seminal Economic Stabilization Act of 1970:

> The President is authorized to issue such orders and regulations as he deems appropriate, accompanied by a statement of reasons for such orders and regulations, to
>
> (1) stabilize prices, rents, wages, and salaries . . .
>
> (2) stabilize interest rates and corporate dividends and similar transfers at levels consistent with orderly economic growth . . . .

Act of Dec. 22, 1971, Pub. L. No. 92-210, §§ 203(a)(1), (2), 85 Stat. 744, *amending* 12 U.S.C. § 1904 (1970). *See also* S. 2176, 93d Cong., 1st Sess. (1973).

[4] For a lively debate on this issue, see Green & Nader, *Economic Regulation vs. Competition: Uncle Sam the Monopoly Man,* 82 YALE L.J. 871 (1973); Winter, *Economic Regulation vs. Competition: Ralph Nader and Creeping Capitalism, id.* at 890; Green & Moore, *Winter's Discontent: Market Failure and Consumer Welfare, id.* at 903.

[5] Elsewhere, this author has expressed uneasiness at the demise of the Delegation Doctrine as a tool for judicial review of administrative action. Wright, Book Review, 81 YALE L.J. 575, 582-87 (1972).

These observations are not novel,[6] and judges have not failed to recognize them. A Supreme Court majority recently suggested that agencies may not use an adjudicatory forum to announce new legal standards which will have only prospective effect.[7] A quarter century ago, the Court advised the agencies that "[t]he function of filling in the interstices of [an act] should be performed, as much as possible, through this quasi-legislative promulgation of rules to be applied in the future."[8] Judge Friendly has persuaded the Second Circuit to take the next logical step, requiring that the National Labor Relations Board promulgate standards of general application only by means of proper rulemaking procedures.[9] The converse claim—that regulated parties have some "right" to an adjudicatory promulgation of general policies merely because these policies affect important interests or preexisting licenses—has been decisively rejected.[10] And when agencies have asserted long dormant rulemaking powers, the courts have been quick to sustain the change of heart.[11]

[6] There is abundant literature criticizing the administrative agencies for excessive reliance on adjudicatory procedures. *See, e.g.,* R. FELLMETH, THE INTERSTATE COMMERCE OMISSION 11-12 (1970); PRESIDENT'S ADVISORY COUNCIL ON EXECUTIVE ORGANIZATION, A NEW REGULATORY FRAMEWORK: REPORT ON SELECTED INDEPENDENT REGULATORY AGENCIES 5, 21, 59 (1971) ("ASH COUNCIL" REPORT); Peck, *The Atrophied Rule-Making Powers of the National Labor Relations Board,* 70 YALE L.J. 729 (1961). *See also* 1 K. DAVIS, ADMINISTRATIVE LAW TREATISE § 6.06 (1958). For a comprehensive analysis of the relative merits of rules and adjudicatory orders in the making of general policy, see Robinson, *The Making of Administrative Policy: Another Look at Rulemaking and Adjudication and Administrative Procedure Reform,* 118 U. PA. L. REV. 485 (1970); Shapiro, *The Choice of Rulemaking or Adjudication in the Development of Administrative Policy,* 78 HARV. L. REV. 921 (1965). Professor Davis has forcefully argued that arbitrary administrative action can be effectively curbed only by requiring agencies to formalize their policies in clear rules of prospective application. *See generally* K. DAVIS, DISCRETIONARY JUSTICE—A PRELIMINARY INQUIRY (1969). Absent promulgation of rules, administrative adjudications are often chaotic and unfair, for neither the parties nor the administrators have any clear notion of what legal standards are being applied. *See generally* Friendly, *The Federal Administrative Agencies: The Need for Better Definition of Standards,* 75 HARV. L. REV. 863, 1055, 1263 (1962).

[7] NLRB v. Wyman-Gordon Co., 394 U.S. 759 (1969). Splitting seven-two on the outcome, the Court in *Wyman-Gordon* upheld an NLRB order which the Board purported to base on a "rule" adopted at the close of an earlier adjudication and not applied to the parties to that adjudication. But only three justices thought that this "rule" had any legal force. *Id.* at 769-75. The four remaining justices in the majority agreed with the minority that the rule was invalid, but concluded that the NLRB had other legal authority to issue the order in question. *Id.* at 765-66.

[8] SEC v. Chenery Corp., 332 U.S. 194, 202 (1947).

[9] Bell Aerospace Co. v. NLRB, 475 F.2d 485, 495-97 (2d Cir. 1973).

[10] *See, e.g.,* FPC v. Texaco, Inc., 377 U.S. 33 (1964); United States v. Storer Broadcasting Co., 351 U.S. 192 (1956); American Airlines, Inc. v. CAB, 359 F.2d 624 (D.C. Cir.), *cert. denied,* 385 U.S. 843 (1966); Air Line Pilots Ass'n Int'l v. Quesada, 276 F.2d 892 (2d Cir. 1960).

[11] *See, e.g.,* Permian Basin Area Rates Cases, 390 U.S. 747 (1968); National Petroleum Refiners Ass'n v. FTC, 482 F.2d 672 (D.C. Cir. 1973).

But a general background of judicial applause is not enough. In rulemaking, no less than in adjudication, Congress has fastened the courts and agencies into an intimate partnership,[12] the success of which requires a precarious balance between judicial deference and self-assertion. In passing on administrative adjudications, the courts over the years have learned to maintain that balance, but judicial review of rulemaking is presenting a new and troublesome question. Some courts have recently shown an inclination to force rulemakers to adopt trial-like procedures—formal hearings, interrogatories, oral argument, cross-examination, and the like—which clearly are not required by the Administrative Procedure Act (APA).[13] Should this tendency become general, rulemaking will lose most of its peculiar advantages as a tool of administrative policymaking, and the merits of the many rulemaking experiments now under way will be denied a fair opportunity to be tested. The trend in agencies toward over-proceduralization arose largely because reviewing courts were hostile to regulation and were uncritically fond of adjudicatory methods for resolving social controversies.[14] From the general paralysis of administration which resulted, the agencies are only now emerging. Before throwing history into reverse, we in the judiciary should at least pause for thought.

---

[12] *See* Greater Boston Television Corp. v. FCC, 444 F.2d 841, 850-52 (D.C. Cir. 1970), *cert. denied,* 403 U.S. 923 (1971).

[13] 5 U.S.C. §§ 551-706 (1970).

[14] No doubt American regulators adopted trial-like procedures for many reasons. Our government is peculiarly lawyer-ridden at all levels, and "judicial" habits of thought and practice thus often dominate other possible perspectives. *See generally* Reich, *The Law of the Planned Society,* 75 YALE L.J. 1227 (1966). That the first chairman of the ICC was a judge no doubt helped Congress and the public to view agencies as quasi-courts. *See* M. BERNSTEIN, REGULATING BUSINESS BY INDEPENDENT COMMISSION 29 (1955); R. CUSHMAN, THE INDEPENDENT REGULATORY COMMISSIONS 65 (1941). But judicial review of agency actions has also played a part. When the courts claimed that ratemaking was "eminently a question for judicial investigation" (Chicago, M. & St. P. Ry. v. Minnesota, 134 U.S. 418, 458 (1890)), and insisted on weighing de novo the evidence supporting agency actions, administrators naturally felt called upon to mimic courtroom procedures and to provide regulated industries the full inventory of "adversary" rights. *See* R. CUSHMAN, *supra* at 66. Early judicial attempts to impose adjudicatory procedures on the agencies were motivated by a generally conservative social philosophy. A contemporary observer protested that "the attempt to read the procedural predilections of judges into the due process clause is as much to be condemned as the similar attempt to read economic predilections into the same constitutional provision." Feller, *Administrative Procedure and the Public Interest—The Results of Due Process,* 25 WASH. U.L.Q. 308, 315 (1940). Chief Justice Stone noted that the legal

> profession of our day, like its predecessors who saw in the pretensions of the chancellor but a new danger to the common law, has given little evidence that it sees in this new method of administrative control any opportunity except for resistance to a strange and therefore unwelcome innovation.

Stone, *The Common Law in the United States,* 50 HARV. L. REV. 4, 17 (1936).

I

"Fairness" in Rulemaking and the APA's Procedures

While procedures for rulemaking, like those for adjudication, should no doubt promote "fairness," that slippery term has very different meanings in the two contexts. An adjudication applies a preexisting legal standard to a small set of controverted facts to determine whether a particular individual should receive a benefit or a penalty. An adjudication is fair to the individual only if the facts are accurately found, and Anglo-American jurisprudence assumes that accuracy is best served by traditional adversary procedures. But it makes no sense to speak of a rule as being fair or unfair to an individual in this objective sense of accuracy. A rule allocates benefits and penalties among large classes of individuals according to a specific normative standard, and the fairness of such an allocation is ultimately a political or philosophical question.[15] Thus, in the rulemaking context, fairness is not identified with accuracy, and procedures designed to maximize accuracy at the cost of all other values are simply inappropriate.

Nor can adjudicatory procedures be justified on the theory that fairness affords parties some basic right to participate in the formulation of rules which may affect them. Administrative agencies derive their sovereignty from Congress, not from the consent of parties potentially affected by agency rules. Moreover, trial-like procedures are a thoroughly illogical vehicle for democratically weighting the views of the interested parties. Such weighting would require instead the election of administrative policy makers or the establishment of some formal system by which interest groups might be represented in the agencies' higher councils.

But there is one sense in which the notion of "fairness" may be applied to administrative rulemaking. Put simply, the *public* is treated unfairly when a rulemaker hides his crucial decisions, or his reasons for them, or when he fails to give good faith attention to all the information and contending views relevant to the issues before him. To this notion of fairness—that rulemaking must be openly informed, reasoned, and candid—there is a two-fold logic. First, if administrators rule in obscurity, Congress cannot intelligently de-

[15] Although a rulemaker may make use of empirical conclusions, these are so dependent on predictions, and on inherently uncertain estimates, that objective terms such as "accurate" and "inaccurate" will typically have little application. Further, because a rulemaker must make and coordinate many empirical and normative judgments, the ultimate shape of the rule seldom "follows from the facts."

legate power or police the exercise of power already delegated. Second, although the "public interest" cannot be objectively defined, one can safely conclude that administrators who ignore relevant facts and who take the counsel of blind prejudice will serve the "public interest" only by the operation of chance. Therefore, although a rulemaker's decisions cannot be "accurate" in the conventional sense, and although regulated parties have no fundamental "right" to participate in rulemaking, the administrator owes a duty to the public to give serious consideration to all reasonable contentions and evidence pertinent to the rules he is considering.

The APA provides rulemaking procedures which directly enforce this duty. The procedures are uncluttered by inappropriate references to the ways of the courtroom or the world of electoral politics. Section 553 imposes a three-fold obligation on a rulemaker. First, the rulemaker must give public notice of "the legal authority under which the rule is proposed" and of "either the terms of substance of the proposed rule or a description of the subjects and issues involved," at least thirty days before its effective date. Second, he must "give interested persons an opportunity to participate in the ruling making through submission of written data, views, or arguments with or without opportunity for oral presentation." Finally, "[a]fter consideration of the relevant matter presented," the rulemaker must "incorporate in the rules adopted a concise and general statement of their basis and purpose."[16]

If accorded a properly expansive reading, section 553 provides a fully adequate scope for judicial review of rulemaking. Certainly, the courts have not felt cramped by the section's brevity. Recent cases, for instance, have put useful teeth into the step one notice provision. If an agency's empirical predictions constitute a substantial basis for its rule, the methodology of prediction should be made public so that interested parties have an opportunity to study and criticize it.[17] If a flat rate is to be set for allocating costs between two industry services, the agency should specifically inform the public of this result and not merely report that *some* method of allocation is contemplated.[18] If an agency wishes to base its rulings on facts developed in a corollary adjudication, the agency must say so, and interested parties must be allowed to contest the relevance of the adjudicatory record to the contem-

---

[16] 5 U.S.C. § 553 (1970).

[17] *See* Portland Cement Ass'n v. Ruckelshaus, No. 72-1073 (D.C. Cir., June 29, 1973) 31-37; *cf.* International Harvester Co. v. Ruckelshaus, 478 F.2d 615, 649 (D.C. Cir. 1973).

[18] *See* Mobil Oil Corp. v. FPC, 483 F.2d 1238, 1251 n.39 (D.C. Cir. 1973).

plated rulings.[19] It is the common spirit of such decisions that the agency must make continuous disclosure of the facts and assumptions on which it intends to rely in promulgating its rule. Obviously, this philosophy of candor must also characterize the "basis and purpose" statement issued by the agency in step three. It cannot be so "concise" and "general" that the court is faced with merely conclusory assertions; the agency must show that it truly has given serious consideration to possible alternative rulings.[20] Although detailed findings of fact are unnecessary, the reviewing court may demand reasoned explanations for controversial normative and empirical determinations made by the agency.[21] At a minimum, the statement should refer to relevant submissions by interested parties and should rebut or accept these submissions in an orderly fashion.[22]

Section 553 contemplates that rules will be made through a genuine dialogue between agency experts and concerned members of the public. In policing the three-step procedure, the reviewing court must satisfy itself that the requisite dialogue occurred and that it was not a sham.

II

THE AD HOC APPROACH TO PROCEDURAL REVIEW OF RULEMAKING

There is an important difference between interpreting section 553 creatively and simply disregarding it. That section mandates a dialogue, not a trial. Nothing in section 553 says that a rulemaker must give individual answers to critical interrogatories, provide oral hearings, allow cross-examination of experts, or develop a testimo-

---

[19] *See* Texas Gulf Coast Area Natural Gas Rate Cases, No. 71-1828 (D.C. Cir., Aug. 24, 1973) 51-52; Mobil Oil Corp. v. FPC, 483 F.2d 1238, 1251 n.39 (D.C. Cir. 1973). Compare Chicago v. FPC, 458 F.2d 731, 746 (D.C. Cir.), *cert. denied,* 405 U.S. 1074 (1972).

[20] Pillai v. CAB, No. 73-1408 (D.C. Cir., Aug. 22, 1973) 18-24.

[21] *See* National Air Carrier Ass'n v. CAB, 436 F.2d 185, 198-99 (D.C. Cir. 1970); Automotive Parts & Accessories Ass'n v. Boyd, 407 F.2d 330, 338 (D.C. Cir. 1968). In Kennecott Copper Corp. v. EPA, 462 F.2d 846, 849-50 (D.C. Cir. 1972), the court, in an opinion which this author joined, reached similar results, but suggested that it was requiring more than the APA minimally demanded. This caveat may have been unnecessary. Both the notice and the "basis and purpose" requirements of § 553 are obviously very flexible, and should be adapted to the particular rules and issues in the case. Such flexibility may also be appropriately exercised to reflect intensified standards of substantive review contained in particular agency statutes. *See* note 34 and accompanying text *infra.*

[22] Portland Cement Ass'n v. Ruckelshaus, No. 72-1073 (D.C. Cir., June 29, 1973) 35. Obviously, the agency's duty to rationalize its decisions is not met by post hoc rationalizations offered for the first time by counsel during judicial review of those actions. Burlington Truck Lines v. United States, 371 U.S. 156, 167-69 (1962).

nial record. Section 553 does not prevent agencies from adopting such procedures if they wish to do so, and in establishing a new rulemaking authority or agency, Congress may, of course, carve out exceptions to section 553 or impose procedures beyond those listed there. Indeed, the APA itself permits Congress to invoke the full panoply of adjudicatory procedures, set out in sections 556 and 557, simply by stating that rulemaking by a particular agency must be preceded by a "hearing on the record."[23] But if Congress remains silent, the APA clearly contemplates that reviewing courts will insist on neither more nor less than section 553 requires.

Some recent lower court decisions, however, have urged upon rulemaking agencies a variety of procedures not found either in section 553 or in the particular agency statutes under review. Consider *International Harvester Co. v. Ruckelshaus,*[24] an exceptionally thoughtful decision rendered last term by a panel of our court. There the Environmental Protection Agency (EPA) had decided not to suspend for one year the Clean Air Act's 1975 standards for auto emission control. The Act permitted a suspension only if the EPA Administrator determined that the technology necessary to meet the 1975 standards was not "available."[25] Because the Administrator had determined the availability of such technology by means of a complex "prediction methodology" never revealed to the auto companies, the court remanded the case to the EPA to give "the parties . . . [an] opportunity . . . to address themselves to matters not previously put before them."[26] Arguably, this conclusion followed directly from the notice requirement in section 553 of the APA, for the methodology itself was an important "issue" which the Agency should have publicized for comment and criticism before announcing its final decision.

The court went further, however, stating that

> [i]n the remand proceeding . . . we require reasonable cross-examination as to new lines of testimony, and as to submissions previously made to EPA in the hearing on a proffer that critical questions could not be satisfactorily pursued by procedures previously in effect.[27]

It is true that the opinion permits the EPA to "confine cross-examination to the essentials, avoiding discursive or repetitive

[23] 5 U.S.C. § 553(c) (1970); *see id.* §§ 556, 557.

[24] 478 F.2d 615 (D.C. Cir. 1973).

[25] 42 U.S.C. § 1857f-1(b)(5)(D)(iii) (1970).

[26] 478 F.2d at 649.

[27] *Id.*

questioning."[28] But the fact remains that neither section 553 nor the Clean Air Act requires *any* cross-examination procedure for rulemaking. The court rested its order simply on "the interest of providing a reasoned decision."[29]

Similarly, in *Mobil Oil Corp. v. FPC,*[30] the court questioned a Federal Power Commission rule under the Natural Gas Act[31] which established flat-rate cost figures for transporting various fuels by pipeline. While acknowledging that the Natural Gas Act did not require a "hearing on the record" and that the adjudicatory procedures of sections 556 and 557 of the APA were not required, the court nevertheless held that the FPC could not "proceed with only the guidance of the . . . standards of section 553."[32] The court reasoned that "artificial distinctions based upon the language of the APA should be avoided in determining what procedure should be followed."[33] The APA's language was disregarded here because the Natural Gas Act requires "substantial evidence" as support for agency actions.[34] The court did not dictate any particular proce-

---

[28] *Id.* The majority held that these procedures were required on remand in the case, but did not hold that the EPA had erred in neglecting to use them in its initial disposition of the case. In his concurring opinion, Judge Bazelon labelled this approach a "bit of judicial legerdemain"; he would have held such procedures necessary in the agency's original action. *Id.* at 652.

[29] *Id.* at 649.

[30] 483 F.2d 1238 (D.C. Cir. 1973).

[31] 15 U.S.C. §§ 717(c), (d) (1970).

[32] 483 F.2d at 1251.

[33] *Id.* at 1252.

[34] *Id.* at 1257-58. Ignoring the APA in this manner reads too much into the term "substantial evidence." Although the term obviously has its roots in the history of adjudicatory proceedings, it literally establishes a standard of substantive review, not a procedural requisite. There is no logical impediment to associating this standard of review with the rulemaking procedures of § 553. *See* Texas Gulf Coast Area Natural Gas Rate Cases, No. 71-1828 (D.C. Cir., Aug. 24, 1973) 49-50 & n.59; Phillips Petroleum v. FPC, 475 F.2d 842 (10th Cir. 1973); *cf.* Chicago v. FPC, 458 F.2d 731, 744-45 & n.62 (D.C. Cir.), *cert. denied,* 405 U.S. 1074 (1972). Rulemaking procedures generate an "administrative record," which may be searched for substantial evidence to support the rule decided on. *See* text accompanying notes 90-92 *infra.* This is not to say that the standard of review is wholly unrelated to "procedural" questions. If a particular rule rests on an extensive analysis of data or on a complex prediction—which may well be the case with rules subjected to the "substantial evidence" test by Congress—courts should require the agency to operate the three-step procedure of § 553 in a manner sensitive to the empirical complexities at stake. The step-one notice should, for instance, include all the important details of the factfinding methods and research sources which the agency intends to utilize. And the step-three "basis and purpose" statement should make detailed reference to all the factual disputes raised by the submissions of interested parties. Most important, the agency should not rely on any research methods or data which were not presented to the interested parties for comment and criticism. *See* Texas Gulf Coast Area Natural Gas Rate Cases, *supra* at 50. The rulemaking process established by § 553 is not inflexible; it can vary with the issues involved. The mere

dures for use on remand, concluding only that "some sort of adversary, adjudicative-type procedures" would be necessary.[35] Cross-examination and written interrogatories were suggested "by way of illustration."[36]

Although *International Harvester* and *Mobil Oil* depart from the APA with diffidence, dicta in other cases do so rather bluntly. We are told that the APA's distinctions between informal rulemaking procedures[37] and full adjudicatory procedures[38] have been "discarded . . . as criteria for determining the type of hearing to which the parties affected by administrative action are entitled."[39] Courts are to devise mandatory procedures according to the "kind" or "importance" of the issues in the proceeding.[40] Hearings, for instance, are deemed necessary whenever "a genuine and substantial issue of fact" has been raised by means of an offer of proof,[41] or at least when "the issue presented is one which possesses great substantive importance, or one which is unusually complex or difficult to resolve on the basis of pleadings and argument."[42] The underlying theory of these cases has been accurately conveyed by Professor Claggett:

> In *any* case where a rulemaking proceeding involves a contested issue of fact which has a vital bearing on the reasonableness of the rule and which is readily susceptible to taking of evidence, an agency may well abuse its discretion if it fails to conduct an evidentiary hearing even in an area where no statutory right to an adjudication is involved.[43]

Thus, after an agency has fully completed its consideration and promulgation of a rule, the reviewing court may demand reconsideration under any procedures which, in retrospect, strike the court as being appropriate to the issues raised. This curious "ad hoc" approach to procedural review is not authorized by the APA or by any other statute; nor should it become the law by judicial fiat.

presence of factual questions in a rulemaking or of a "substantial evidence" standard of review is thus no reason to substitute formal, adjudicatory procedures for the expeditious routine of agency notice-comment by parties-agency decision.

[35] 483 F.2d at 1259.

[36] *Id.* at 1262-63 & n.91.

[37] 5 U.S.C. § 553 (1970).

[38] *Id.* §§ 556, 557.

[39] Appalachian Power Co. v. EPA, 477 F.2d 495, 500 (4th Cir. 1973) (dictum).

[40] *See* Walter Holm & Co. v. Hardin, 449 F.2d 1009, 1015 (D.C. Cir. 1971); Marine Space Enclosures, Inc. v. FMC, 420 F.2d 577, 585-86 n.22 (D.C. Cir. 1969).

[41] Upjohn Co. v. Finch, 422 F.2d 944, 955 (6th Cir. 1970).

[42] National Air Carrier Ass'n v. CAB, 436 F.2d 185, 191 (D.C. Cir. 1970).

[43] Claggett, *Informal Action—Adjudication—Rulemaking: Some Recent Developments in Federal Administrative Law,* 1971 DUKE L.J. 51, 78.

III

A Critique of the Ad Hoc Approach to Procedural Review

A. *Legal Infirmities*

The ad hoc approach contravenes recent, authoritative interpretations of the APA. These interpretations make clear that an agency does not "abuse its discretion" by declining to utilize procedures more formal than those set out in section 553.[44] In *United States v. Allegheny-Ludlum Steel Corp.*[45] and *United States v. Florida East Coast Ry.*,[46] courts examined Interstate Commerce Commission (ICC) regulations aimed at alleviating the nation's chronic freight car shortage. The Commission had formulated these regulations through section 553 procedures, taking only written submissions on its proposals before issuing final rulings. Noting that the Interstate Commerce Act itself requires a "hearing" prior to Commission action,[47] the petitioners in both cases claimed that more formal procedures should have been followed by the ICC. But in *Allegheny-Ludlum,* the Supreme Court held that the term "hearing" in the Interstate Commerce Act is insufficiently close to the APA's term "hearing on the record" to indicate any congressional desire to impose on the ICC the adjudicatory procedures of sections 556 and 557.[48] In *Florida East Coast Ry.*, the Court held that the ICC's receipt of written submissions adequately met the "hearing" provision of the Commerce Act.[49] The message of these cases is clear. Courts are not to impose on agencies the formalities of sections 556 and 557 unless Congress has unmistakably so provided, and courts are not to spin their own procedural requirements from statutory catch-phrases of uncertain meaning.

If the APA precludes the ad hoc approach, then that approach can survive only if the Constitution requires it. But there is not even a colorable claim to this effect. Of course, the due process clause often confers trial-like procedural rights on an individual who becomes the focus of a government action.[50] However, in the

[44] *See* notes 45-49 and accompanying text *infra.*

[45] 406 U.S. 742 (1972).

[46] 410 U.S. 224 (1973).

[47] 49 U.S.C. § 1 (14)(a) (1970).

[48] 406 U.S. at 756-58; *see* 410 U.S. at 234-38.

[49] 410 U.S. at 238-46.

[50] *See, e.g.,* Goldberg v. Kelly, 397 U.S. 254 (1970); Sniadach v. Family Fin. Corp., 395 U.S. 337 (1969); Willner v. Committee on Character & Fitness, 373 U.S. 96 (1963); *cf.* Greene v. McElroy, 360 U.S. 474 (1959).

rulemaking context, the constitutional touchstone remains Mr. Justice Holmes's opinion for a unanimous court in *Bi-Metallic Investment Co. v. State Board of Equalization,*[51] holding that a hearing was unnecessary before Colorado tax officials could substantially increase the valuation of all property in Denver. *Bi-Metallic* is nearly sixty years old, but just last term, the Supreme Court cited it with approval and reemphasized that the due process clause embodies the "recognized distinction in administrative law between proceedings for the purpose of promulgating policy-type rules or standards, on the one hand, and proceedings designed to adjudicate disputed facts in particular cases on the other."[52] This need not mean that the due process clause has *no* application to rulemaking. Arguably, all government actions must be surrounded by procedures representing a reasonable balance between fairness and efficiency. For rulemaking, however, the fairness is owed to the public generally, not to particular individuals, and there is consequently no reason to doubt that the procedures of section 553 strike other than a reasonable balance.

B. *Infirmities of Logic and Policy*

Having no foundation in the Constitution or the APA, the ad hoc approach to procedural review of rulemaking should be rejected as a violation of statutory law. But two general arguments have been advanced in support of the ad hoc approach: (*1*) that it promotes "procedural inventiveness,"[53] and (*2*) that it somehow facilitates judicial review of the substance of administrative rules.[54] These arguments sound rather good as slogans, but they do not withstand close scrutiny.

1. *"Procedural Inventiveness"*

No one can deny that the ad hoc approach would allow courts to be "procedurally inventive." Judges could custom tailor procedural requirements to each distinct administrative action and could thus discontinue what Professor Claggett calls the "unprofitable exercise" of trying to "draw general and abstract lines separating areas especially appropriate for formal adjudication from those more appropriate for rulemaking."[55] But if judges now

[51] 239 U.S. 441 (1915).

[52] Florida East Coast Ry. v. United States, 410 U.S. 224, 244-46 (1973).

[53] Claggett, *supra* note 43, at 70.

[54] *See* text accompanying notes 71-72 *infra*.

[55] Claggett, *supra* note 43, at 68.

have trouble inscribing a clear line between "legislative" and "adjudicatory" actions,[56] how could they reach a consensus on the appropriate procedures to govern the thousands of actions issuing annually from the federal bureaucracy? On occasion, an agency may make a "rule" which applies to only one regulated party,[57] or it may adopt a new legal standard in an adjudication.[58] Such administrative perversions obviously raise problems of fairness with which the courts should deal.[59] But this is no reason to disregard section 553 when reviewing the vast majority of agency actions which are indisputably valid exercises of rulemaking power. If reviewing courts ignored the guidance of section 553 and instead operated under a vague injunction to find those procedures "best" suited to *each* agency action presented, judicial review of rulemaking would become totally unpredictable.

The administrative response would, however, be completely predictable. Fearing reversal of his substantive initiatives, each administrator would clothe his agency's actions in the full wardrobe of adjudicatory procedure. By demanding procedural refinements on an ad hoc basis, reviewing courts would inadvertently induce

---

[56] The problem is discussed in 1 K. Davis, *supra* note 6, § 5.01, at 285. *See also* American Airlines, Inc. v. CAB, 359 F.2d 624 (D.C. Cir.), *cert. denied,* 385 U.S. 843 (1966).

[57] The problem is mentioned in American Airlines, Inc. v. CAB, 359 F.2d 624, 631 (D.C. Cir.), *cert. denied,* 385 U.S. 843 (1966). It should be noted, however, that the APA's definition of a "rule" includes "an agency statement of . . . particular applicability." 5 U.S.C. § 551(4) (1970). Professor Davis reads the legislative history of the Act as suggesting that an agency action which applied expressly to only one or several named parties might nevertheless be a "rule." 1 K. Davis, *supra* note 6, at § 5.02. Such a rule might, however, have considerable trouble surviving an equal protection challenge or the constitutional prohibition against bills of attainder. *See* United States v. Brown, 381 U.S. 437 (1965).

[58] *See, e.g.,* NLRB v. Wyman-Gordon Co., 394 U.S. 759 (1969); SEC v. Chenery Corp., 332 U.S. 194 (1947); Bell Aerospace Co. v. NLRB, 475 F.2d 485 (2d Cir. 1973).

[59] The fairness problems may be simply articulated; they are not so prolix or multifaceted as to cast a shadow over the basic distinction between rules and adjudicatory orders. Consider first the making of new rules in an adjudication. The possible unfairness here is two-fold. If the rule is applied to the parties in the adjudication, the rule is retroactive; the parties have been denied fair notice of what the law expects of them. Even if the rule's application is only prospective, its formulation without the participation and comment of all interested parties constitutes a violation of the public's right to open and informed rulemaking. When a rule applies to only a single party, there are also several problems. Generally, discrimination between parties is fair only if (*1*) a rational theory underlies the distinction, and (*2*) the theory has been accurately applied to the behavior or empirical traits of the parties. A rule singling out one party for special treatment will often be invalid for lack of a rational and permissible basis for the discrimination, a problem which no amount of adjudicatory procedure will cure. The agency may, however, cite a rational underlying theory and claim that application of that theory to the world of possible regulated parties in fact selects out a single party. This is an empirical proposition which is so unlikely, and so dependent on detailed, fine grain factual determinations, that courts can justifiably demand that the agency subject the proposition to the test of traditional adjudicatory procedures.

agencies to adopt maximum procedures in all cases. Seeking administrative variety, we would obtain administrative paralysis. The inherent virtues of rulemaking—expedition, flexibility to experiment, a sensible balance between expertise and broad public participation—would be forfeited. Like adjudicatory regulation today, rulemaking would become a lawyer's game.

There is a clear need for procedural innovation in many new areas of administrative rulemaking.[60] But such innovation can only come, as the APA contemplates, from Congress or from the agencies themselves. To the extent that oral argument and cross-examination are genuinely useful in illuminating the empirical questions that course through some rulemaking, it is hardly utopian to rely on Congress and the agencies for a proper response. In the past decade, most of the major grants of rulemaking authority made by Congress have specified procedures that exceed in one way or another those required by section 553.[61] The excessive fondness of the agencies for adjudicatory methods is a matter of historical record.[62] Therefore, lawyer-like procedures in the rulemaking context simply do not need the services of an extra-statutory judicial crusade.

2. *Procedural Review vs. Substantive Review*

In this "new era"[63] of environmental, economic, and energy regulation, there would be great attraction to any approach which genuinely facilitated substantive review of agency rules. In the past year, this author has personally received a compulsory education in the intricacies of nuclear breeder reactor development,[64] the difficulties of pipeline construction through the Alaskan tundra,[65] the effect of different gasoline grades on auto engine performance,[66] the economics of air transport between small cities

---

[60] *See generally* Boyer, *Alternatives to Administrative Trial-Type Hearings for Resolving Complex Scientific, Economic, and Social Issues,* 71 MICH. L. REV. 111 (1972); Hamilton, *Procedures for the Adoption of Rules of General Applicability: The Need for Procedural Innovation in Administrative Rulemaking,* 60 CALIF. L. REV. 1276 (1972).

[61] For a useful listing and analysis of recent rulemaking grants containing procedural guaranties beyond the requirements of § 553, see Hamilton, *supra* note 60, at 1315-30.

[62] *See* notes 6 & 14 *supra.*

[63] Environmental Defense Fund, Inc. v. Ruckelshaus, 439 F.2d 584, 597 (D.C. Cir. 1971).

[64] Scientific Institute for Pub. Information v. AEC, No. 1131 (D.C. Cir., June 12, 1973).

[65] Wilderness Soc'y v. Morton, 463 F.2d 1261 (D.C. Cir. 1972), *aff'd on rehearing en banc,* 479 F.2d 842 (D.C. Cir.), *cert. denied,* 411 U.S. 917 (1973).

[66] National Petroleum Refiners Ass'n v. FTC, 482 F.2d 672 (D.C. Cir. 1973).

in New England,[67] and the differing methods of producing sulphuric acid.[68] This is a rather rich diet for a "generalist" decisionmaker who feels more comfortable with a volume from West Publishing Company than with a computer print-out. Furthermore, these new rulemaking cases raise questions of the utmost political urgency. In the Alaskan pipeline litigation,[69] for instance, the environmental integrity of our largest state was pitted against the immediate economic needs of its citizens, against the huge investments of several oil companies, and against the acute energy and fuel requirements of the entire nation. In the auto emissions case, the court recognized it was dealing with perhaps "the biggest industrial judgment that has been made in the United States in this century."[70]

But how exactly do the difficulties of substantive review justify adopting the ad hoc approach to procedural review? Two suggestions have been advanced. Reasoning that agency use of adjudicatory procedure would guarantee the substantive adequacy of agency rules, Judge Bazelon has argued that the ad hoc approach could—and should—virtually replace substantive review.[71] He fears that in many of the new areas of rulemaking, the exercise of substantive review dangerously taxes the competence of courts, converting them into superagencies charged with second guessing the technological, scientific, and economic judgments of rulemakers. The other suggestion accepts the need for a wide ranging

---

[67] Eastern Air Lines v. CAB, No. 72-1703 (D.C. Cir., Oct. 3, 1972) (unpublished).

[68] Essex Chem. Corp. v. Ruckelshaus, No. 72-1072 (D.C. Cir., Sept. 10, 1973).

[69] Wilderness Soc'y v. Morton, 463 F.2d 1261 (D.C. Cir. 1972), *aff'd on rehearing en banc,* 479 F.2d 842 (D.C. Cir.), *cert. denied,* 411 U.S. 917 (1973).

[70] International Harvester Co. v. Ruckelshaus, 478 F.2d 615, 633 (D.C. Cir. 1973), *quoting* remarks of Senator Baker during debate on the Clean Air Act of 1970. *See* 116 CONG. REC. 33,085 (1970) (remarks of Senator Baker).

[71] *Id.* at 650-53 (Bazelon, J., concurring); *cf.* Texas Gulf Coast Area Natural Gas Rate Cases, No. 71-1828 (D.C. Cir., Aug. 24, 1973). Writing for the majority in the *Texas Gulf Coast* case, Judge Bazelon stresses that an agency, in settling rates, must meet a statutory test of being "just and reasonable," and should "set forth with clarity the grounds for its rejection of opposing views and the reasons it has arrived at its results." *Id.* at 108-11. This author is in full sympathy with that position; indeed the "basis and purpose" requirement of the APA's § 553 should be read to demand no less. *See* text accompanying notes 20-22 *supra.* But there is a difference between asking an agency lucidly to justify its actions and requiring the agency to take action only through *adjudicatory procedures.* Judge Bazelon finds *both* requisites necessary to provide "a framework for principled decision-making." Texas Gulf Coast Natural Gas Rate Cases, *supra* at 109; International Harvester Co. v. Ruckelshaus, 478 F.2d 615, 651 (D.C. Cir. 1973). Judge Bazelon's "framework" fails, in my judgment, to take sufficient account of the distinction between the kinds of "principled decision-making" required for fairness to an individual, on the one hand, and fairness to the public generally on the other. *See* text accompanying notes 15-22 *supra.*

substantive review and argues that rulemakers must be forced to embrace adjudicatory procedures so that an adequate "record" will be developed for such review.[72]

To both of these suggestions, there is a threshold objection: each tries to facilitate substantive review at the cost of paralyzing agencies with procedures otherwise irrelevant to sound rulemaking. Surely the court's task can be rendered tolerable without rendering rulemaking a practical impossibility. Furthermore, both suggestions misconceive the role of substantive review. Since the APA not only disallows the ad hoc approach to procedural review,[73] but also requires substantive review, Judge Bazelon's proposal is doubly doubtful. It is also unnecessary. Substantive review under the APA does not convert the reviewing court into a superagency. The APA standard of review is singularly undemanding, and it allows adequate play to Judge Bazelon's perception that courts can often better assess the way rules are made than the merits of the rules themselves. By the same token, courts do not need an adjudicatory record to undertake the necessary task of substantive review. Rather, they can and should review the legally sanctioned record of rulemaking which must be generated as a matter of course by section 553 procedures.

a. *The APA Requires Substantive Review.* Under section 706 of the APA, the reviewing court must strike down not only those agency rules which are "in excess of statutory jurisdiction, authority, or limitations, or short of statutory right," but also those actions which are "arbitrary, capricious, an abuse of discretion, or otherwise not in accordance with law."[74] Presumably, the first standard means that an agency rule must conform to the agency's delegated power, just as a statute must conform to the Constitution. However, unless the Act's drafters committed a redundancy, the "arbitrary, capricious" standard goes beyond this. It applies to the factfinding, fact-predicting, and factual reasoning processes which led the agency to adopt the rule. As Judge MacKinnon has pointed out, a contrary interpretation would reduce review under the "arbitrary, capricious" standard to "a relatively futile exercise in formalism," because a "regulation perfectly reasonable and appropriate in the face of a given problem may be highly capricious if that problem does not exist."[75] This is the precise teaching of the

[72] *See, e.g.,* Mobil Oil Corp. v. FPC, 483 F.2d 1238, 1259-60 (D.C. Cir. 1973). Compare Superior Oil Co. v. FPC, 322 F.2d 601, 619 (9th Cir. 1963), *cert. denied,* 377 U.S. 922 (1964).

[73] *See* notes 44-52 and accompanying text *supra.*

[74] 5 U.S.C. §§ 706(2)(C), (A) (1970).

[75] Chicago v. FPC, 458 F.2d 731, 742 (D.C. Cir. 1971), *cert. denied,* 405 U.S. 1074 (1972).

Supreme Court's important decision in *Overton Park v. Volpe.*[76] There, the Secretary of Transportation had approved construction of an interstate highway through a public park, even though applicable legislation allowed such approval only if no "feasible and prudent" alternative route existed. Although the Secretary's action was not a "rule" in the APA sense,[77] the Court nevertheless applied the "arbitrary, capricious" standard of section 706 and ordered a "searching and careful" review by the district judge of all the facts, studies, and expert views which had provided the basis for the Secretary's action. The purpose of review was to determine "whether the decision was based on a consideration of the relevant factors."[78] After *Overton Park,* it is highly doubtful that courts can simply avoid substantive review of rulemaking, no matter how many "procedures" are imposed on the rulemaking agency.

b. *The Standard of Review Is Undemanding.* While the converse of arbitrariness and caprice is rationality, the APA authorizes a reviewing court to demand of rulemakers only the most basic, minimal sort of rationality. A judge cannot strike down a rule merely because it seems to him "unreasonable," in the sense of being unwise or wrong, any more than he could upset congressional legislation for that reason.[79] Rather, the APA has been interpreted by the Supreme Court to require only that "th[e] inquiry into the facts . . . be searching and careful, [and] the ultimate standard of review [be] a narrow one. The court is not empowered to substitute its judgment for that of the agency."[80] The reviewing court is not even authorized to examine whether a rulemaker's empirical conclusions have support in substantial evidence. The APA reserves the substantial evidence test for review of adjudications and of rules which must be made after a "hearing on the record."[81] This exemption of conventional rulemaking from the substantial evidence test is very important, because that test is not itself terribly demanding. Exercising review under it, a court cannot disturb a factfinder's weightings of conflicting evidence merely because these seem "clearly erroneous"; only those determinations which are patently unreasonable can be upset.[82] Finding

[76] 401 U.S. 402 (1971).

[77] *Id.* at 414.

[78] *Id.* at 416.

[79] *See* 1 K. Davis, *supra* note 6, § 5.03, at 299.

[80] Overton Park v. Volpe, 401 U.S. 402, 416 (1971).

[81] 5 U.S.C. § 706(2)(E) (1970).

[82] Appellate courts use the "clearly erroneous" test in reviewing the factual determinations of a trial judge, sitting without a jury, but the less demanding test of "substantial evidence" is used in reviewing a jury's findings or in determining whether to direct a verdict

words to formulate a standard of review which is less demanding than substantial evidence is no easy task.[83] It must be conceded that the cases applying the "arbitrary, capricious" test have not approached this problem with great vigor.[84] Simple logic, however, suggests a rough answer. If weightings on conflicting evidence need be only "reasonable" to pass the substantial evidence test, it follows that they can be less than reasonable and still survive the "arbitrary, capricious" test. If this is so, the latter standard subjects a rulemaker to only the most rudimentary command of rationality. In drawing empirical conclusions, he must give actual, good faith consideration to all relevant evidentiary factors. If he has in fact given serious attention to a factor, the weight which he assigns to it in his final judgments is of virtually no concern to the reviewing court.

This is not quite so radical as it sounds. Final empirical conclusions never flow directly or mechanically from the weights assigned to raw items of evidence. In between, there are typically several steps of inferential reasoning and, even under the "arbitrary, capricious" test, these presumably must be something more than exercises in whimsy or free association. Nevertheless, the "arbitrary, capricious" standard seems to require not an evaluation of the rulemaker's empirical conclusions, but rather an inquiry into the basic orderliness of the process by which evidence and alternative rulings were considered. Thus, *Overton Park* requires that agency action be "based on a consideration of the relevant

---

in a jury case. For a cogent discussion of this familiar distinction, see 4 K. DAVIS, *supra* note 6, § 29.02, at 118-22.

[83] Indeed, Professor Davis thinks the task an impossible one. *Id.* § 29.07, at 149. He believes that the "substantial evidence" test itself is made of "rubber" rather than "wood" and is therefore capable of supporting de facto standards of review with widely differing degrees of rigor. *Id.* § 29.02, at 126. This view is not necessarily inconsistent with the suggestions in the text. In speaking of the "reasonableness" or "rationality" of an agency's empirical determinations, we may obviously mean many different things. While these differing meanings may constitute a continuous spectrum which cannot be neatly broken into discrete segments, it may nevertheless be possible to give a rough characterization of that end of the spectrum represented by the "arbitrary, capricious" standard of review.

[84] For example, the court in Chicago v. FPC, 458 F.2d 731, 744 (D.C. Cir. 1971), *cert. denied,* 405 U.S. 1074 (1972), contented itself with pointing out that the "arbitrary, capricious" test and the "substantial evidence" test both derive from the "general principle" that "the object of review is to determine whether a reasoned conclusion from the record as a whole could support the premise on which the Commission's action rests." In Overton Park v. Volpe, 401 U.S. 402, 416 (1971), the Court actually suggested that the "arbitrary, capricious" test authorizes a reviewing judge to upset "a clear error of judgment" by the agency. Such language contains inappropriate echoes of the "clearly erroneous" standard of review and is inconsistent with *Overton Park*'s own admonition that a reviewing court "is not empowered to substitute its judgment for that of the agency." *Id.*

factors,"[85] and a later case mandates that rulemakers conduct "a considered evaluation of the presently available alternatives."[86] These phrases mark out a realistic approach to substantive review. The empirical judgments at stake in rulemaking necessarily rest on prediction, for a rule has prospective application only, and agency rules typically involve issues of great technical complexity. Reviewing judges can make a valuable contribution to the rationality of rulemaking by asking questions such as: "Did you take this factor into account?" "What about this possibility?" But once the court is satisfied that the administrator did touch all the bases, absent obvious irrationality, there is little more a court can accomplish. Judges lack the special skills to evaluate sensibly the weightings assigned to technically abstruse evidence; only future historians can assess the merits of a rulemaker's predictions.

This analysis of substantive review undermines Judge Bazelon's proposal that substantive review be replaced by the ad hoc approach to procedural review. Substantive review, properly understood, is too modest an enterprise to convert courts into superagencies, and the standard of substantive review itself incorporates Judge Bazelon's underlying, and correct, perception that courts can more competently assess the rationality of the rulemaking process than the merits of the resultant rules. The problem with the ad hoc approach to procedural review is that it goes well beyond this sound perception. The ad hoc approach mandates that the courts prescribe precise and formal methods for bureaucratic policymaking. This mandate assumes an expertise in administrative science which duty on the bench simply does not confer. By contrast, the "arbitrary, capricious" standard of substantive review authorizes courts merely to scrutinize the actual making of a rule for signs of blind prejudice or of inattention to crucial evidence—a task of straightforward detective work which is well within the capacities of generalist judges.

Replacing substantive review with the ad hoc approach to procedural review would make sense only if adjudicatory formalities constituted both a necessary and a sufficient condition for the rulemaking process to be rational. Neither branch of this proposition is sound. Rulemaking is adequately rational, under the APA, so long as the administrator is presented with all relevant evidentiary factors, gives serious consideration to those factors, and

---

[85] Overton Park v. Volpe, 401 U.S. 402, 416 (1971).

[86] Pillai v. CAB, No. 73-1408 (D.C. Cir., Aug. 22, 1973) 3.

uses reason rather than whim to progress from initial assumptions to final conclusions. Let us take these requisites in turn.

For purposes of presenting evidence, formalized adjudicatory methods are clearly inessential: The three-step procedure of section 553[87] is expressly designed to provide the administrator access to all data, criticisms, suggestions, alternatives, and contingencies relevant to his decisions. Adjudicatory methods are in fact insufficient to this task. A rulemaker must typically make and coordinate many empirical conclusions dependent on raw material outside the conventional evidentiary categories of "testimony" and "exhibits." For example, the rulemaker must often draw upon prior experience, expert advice, the developing technical literature, ongoing experiments, or seasoned predictions.

As for the consideration given to these factors, a rulemaker can surely demonstrate his seriousness and good faith without allowing interested parties to cross-examine him or quarrel orally before him. He can, for instance, through the "basis and purpose" statement,[88] detail for the court the actual attention he gave to the factors, and explain his final disposition with respect to each of them. It would indeed be insufficient for him to listen passively to the contentions of the best financed and most skillfully represented formal "parties." An agency is not a judge or a sequestered juror. It cannot "act as an umpire blandly calling balls and strikes for adversaries appearing before it; the right of the public must receive active and affirmative protection at the hands of the Commission."[89] Further, an administrator's attendance at an adjudicatory hearing does not guarantee that he has given good faith attention to all the disparate factors bearing relevantly on his decisions. Indeed, mere attendance does not even ensure attention to factors raised in the hearing itself.

Finally, *no* form of procedure can ensure the minimal rationality of a rulemaker's inferences. These after all occur within his head! To see whether he has kept the counsel of reason, the reviewing court must in each instance demand an orderly explanation of the rulemaker's inferences. For such an explanation, logic suggests no procedural substitute.

c. *Substantive Review Operates on an "Administrative" Record.*

---

[87] *See* notes 16-22 and accompanying text *supra.*

[88] *See* text accompanying notes 20-22 *supra.*

[89] Scenic Hudson Preservation Conference v. FPC, 354 F.2d 608, 620 (2d Cir. 1965), *cert. denied,* 384 U.S. 941 (1966); *cf.* Office of Communications of the United Church of Christ v. FCC, 425 F.2d 543, 546 (D.C. Cir. 1969).

That rulemakers should use adjudicatory procedures merely to provide courts with a "record" of those procedures is an argument which may charitably be termed circular. If courts adopt this curious theory, their partnership with the agencies will be transformed into a quaint minuet. Substantive review is an inquiry into the realities of the rulemaking process, not an occasion for pretending that agencies are some species of lower court.[90] Consequently, a proper record must reflect all of the relevant views and evidence considered by the rulemaker, from whatever source, and—like a mini-history—it must reveal if and how the rulemaker considered each factor throughout the process of policy formation. Such is the "full administrative record" adverted to in *Overton Park* and its progeny.[91] To provide such a record is one of the functions of the three-step procedure in section 553. If that provision receives the broad interpretation and strict enforcement which it merits,[92] the reviewing court will be provided the following record:

Step one of section 553 will yield the agency's initial proposal, its tentative empirical findings, important advice received from experts, and a description of the critical experimental and methodological techniques on which the agency intends to rely. Step two will produce the written or oral replies of interested parties to the agency's proposals and to all the other "step one" materials. And step three will furnish the final rule, accompanied by a statement both justifying the rule and explaining its normative and empirical predicates through reference to those parts of the record developed in steps one and two.

Section 553 thus opens a broad window on the rulemaking process, surely broad enough to reveal any unfairness to the public committed by the rulemaker. At the same time, the window is not so large as to invite a judicial breaking and entering. By generating a unique sort of "record," the APA's procedures simultaneously facilitate and carefully channel the exercise of substantive review. Upsetting those procedures would almost certainly disturb the appropriate balance between skepticism and deference in substantive review itself.

---

[90] The Supreme Court has said that:

> [T]o assimilate the relationship of these administrative bodies and the courts to the relationship between lower and upper courts is to disregard the origin and purposes of the movement for administrative regulation and at the same time to disregard the traditional scope, however far-reaching, of the judicial process.

FCC v. Pottsville Broadcasting Co., 309 U.S. 134, 144 (1940).

[91] Overton Park v. Volpe, 401 U.S. 402, 420 (1971). *See also* Automotive Parts & Accessories Ass'n v. Boyd, 407 F.2d 330, 336-37 (D.C. Cir. 1968).

[92] *See* text accompanying notes 17-22 *supra*.

IV

The Mechanics of Restraint

When based on a proper administrative record, the mechanics of review are quite straightforward. If the subject matter of a rule falls within an agency's delegated authority, there are only two grounds for a court upsetting it. First, the "basis and purpose" statement given by the agency may include no reasons, or merely conclusory reasons, for adopting the rule or for rejecting evidence, criticisms, or alternatives submitted by outsiders. In this instance, the agency has violated the third procedural step of section 553 and simultaneously has violated the "substantive" standard of review by failing to show good faith consideration to all relevant factors. No matter how the agency's default is labelled, the remedy is of course to remand the rule. But such remand is only to allow the agency, through fuller explanation, to show that the rulemaking process was actually animated by reason rather than blind instinct.[93] Since the "basis and purpose" statement is part of the "record," as well as a "procedure," this is in essence a remand "for a fuller record." But there should be no suggestion that the agency need take more submissions from outsiders, and certainly no suggestion that adjudicatory procedures are required.[94]

Second, remand will be proper when the agency has relied on important findings, assumptions, or techniques not made public prior to the rule's promulgation. In this instance, the agency has violated step one of the section 553 procedures. Since the unfairness here is to the public and not to an individual "party," the remedy is to instruct the agency to return to step one, *not* to order a legally impermissible adjudicatory consideration of issues theretofor unrevealed by the agency.

Compared to this simple routine, the ad hoc approach to procedural review assigns to the judiciary a relentlessly "activist" role. In some other areas of law, this author has not found such a

---

[93] Courts often remand agency actions with the understanding that the action need not be changed so long as the agency can supply a satisfactory legal justification for the action. *See, e.g.,* FTC v. Sperry & Hutchinson Co., 405 U.S. 233, 249-50 (1972); SEC v. Chenery Corp., 332 U.S. 194 (1947); Essex Chem. Corp. v. Ruckelshaus, No. 72-1072 (D.C. Cir., Sept. 10, 1973) 23 n.40.

[94] Of course, the basis supplied for an action must not be simply a post-hoc rationalization for action that was essentially arbitrary when taken. *See, e.g.,* Burlington Truck Lines v. United States, 371 U.S. 156 (1962). And it cannot be based on evidence or methods of which the regulated public received no prior notice. *See* text accompanying notes 17-19 *supra.*

role uncongenial.[95] But the ad hoc approach to administrative review lacks those foundations in law and reason which an activist posture requires. The approach has no statutory underpinnings; indeed, it flies in the face of the APA. It can claim no constitutional mandate, and it certainly protects no minority interests which the political system would otherwise ignore. Furthermore, the approach draws on no talents peculiar to the judiciary. Although we judges may have a professional attachment to cross-examination and oral argument, we have no special expertise in the procedure appropriate to bureaucratic policymaking.

What reviewing courts can realistically do to improve rulemaking is just what the APA asks them to do—open the agencies to outside information, challenge, and scrutiny. Before dismissing this as a demeaning or trivial task, we should recall how many agencies have become captives of private interests, closed to new methods or regulation and planning, and dedicated to obscuring their policies from the public and Congress. In sections 553 and 706, the APA provides the courts with powerful tools to attack these abuses. We should learn to use these tools and give up playing arcane procedural games authorized by neither statute nor common sense.

---

[95] *See* Wright, *Professor Bickel, the Scholarly Tradition, and the Supreme Court,* 84 Harv. L. Rev. 769 (1971); Wright, *The Role of the Supreme Court in a Democratic Society—Judicial Activism or Restraint,* 54 Cornell L. Rev. 1 (1968).

9

Beyond Discretionary Justice

How much discretion should public administrators have? To what extent should their decisions be subjected to scrutiny and possible reversal by federal courts? These are the questions that Judge Wright discusses in this essay. It complements his more generalized disquisition on judicial review in Chapter 8.

Judge Wright bases the discussion in this chapter on Professor Kenneth Davis's book, Discretionary Justice *(1969). He agrees with Davis that government is shot through with unnecessary discretion in the "police, prosecutors, and petty bureaucrats." The consequence is an "intolerable situation" of untrammelled discretion. Judge Wright would not do away with all administrative discretion but would guide and channel it so as to ensure that individual decisions are not arbitrary or capricious. He calls for more rules, rather than ad hoc decisions, and believes that federal judges have the power to require administrative agencies to formulate general rules.*

In addition, Judge Wright maintains that Congress should re-examine the ancient principle of "delegation of legislative powers," and through narrower delegations seek to keep the bureaucracy in adequate check. "We are now surrounded with agencies that are in fact laws unto themselves." Congress and the courts, working together, can rectify that parlous situation.

Judge Wright's views about administrative law and the role of judicial review in administrative matters are particularly important since he sits on what has been called "the second most important court" in the nation. Furthermore, the U.S. Court of Appeals for the District of Columbia Circuit, the bench upon which he sits, is far and away the most important administrative law court in the nation, outshadowing even the Supreme Court in that respect. Many of the problems of the courts and the bureaucracy sooner or later come before the Court of Appeals, the decisions of which are usually final because of the number of cases. Judge Wright has been a leading spokesman, both on and off the bench, on the relationship of federal judges to the bureaucracy.

In his little book *The Morality of Law,* Lon Fuller relates an allegory about a King Rex who sets out to reform the legal system of his kingdom. Upon assuming the throne, King Rex repeals all existing law and, lacking the confidence to write a new code, begins the process of developing new rules on a case-by-case basis.

> In this way under the stimulus of a variety of cases he hoped that his latent powers of generalization might develop and, proceeding case by case, he would gradually work out a system of rules that could be incorporated in a code. Unfortunately the defects in his education were more deep-seated than he had supposed. The venture failed completely. After he had handed down literally hundreds of decisions neither he nor his subjects could detect in those decisions any pattern whatsoever. Such tentatives toward generalization as were to be found in his opinions only compounded the confusion, for they gave false leads to his subjects and threw his own meager powers of judgment off balance in the decision of later cases.[1]

In the allegory, King Rex eventually dies, "old before his time and deeply disillusioned with his subjects."[2] In the real world, the King is still with us, enthroned in the legal department of a federal regulatory agency.

But although the King may feel secure for the present, his subjects are getting restless. Consumer groups are no longer so certain that

---

1. L. Fuller, The Morality of Law 34 (rev. ed. 1969) [hereinafter cited as Fuller].
2. *Id.* at 38.

the Federal Trade Commission acts in the public interest when it grants and denies secret merger clearances according to no ascertainable standards. Welfare mothers are beginning to wonder about the life and death power which a single social worker wields over them without any realistic possibility of restraint or review. Poor people no longer believe that something about the natural order makes it inevitable that the criminal laws be enforced against them, but not against white collar criminals who daily victimize them. There is the smell of revolution in the air.

I

Now Professor Davis, in his powerful manifesto *Discretionary Justice*,[3] has proposed that we modify King Rex's powers, turning him into a constitutional monarch. Davis argues that the administrative system in this country is shot through with unnecessary discretion. The police, prosecutors, and petty bureaucrats in our local and national governments are free to run loose in an Alice-in-Wonderland of unchannelled, unreviewable, untrammelled discretion. The result, unsurprisingly, is a crazy quilt of secret, ad hoc decisions which are essentially lawless, because they are presently beyond the power of law to control. Professor Davis has the temerity to suggest that this is an intolerable situation in a country theoretically dedicated to equal justice under law. He then proceeds to provide a series of specific suggestions for how administrative discretion can be checked or channelled and made subject to binding, prospective rules. This is not to say that he argues for complete elimination of discretionary decision-making. He would not exchange Lewis Carroll's fantasy for Franz Kafka's nightmare. A tyranny of petty bureaucrats who lack power to change the rules even an iota in order to do justice is at least as bad as a tyranny of petty bureaucrats who make up the rules as they go along.

But the need for some discretion in no way justifies the vast scope of unnecessary discretionary authority which is harbored in our present administrative apparatus. While an agency is new and unfamiliar with the subject matter with which it is dealing, it may have to feel its way around for a while on a case-by-case basis. But from the very beginning, the agency should concentrate considerable attention on

3. K. Davis, Discretionary Justice—A Preliminary Inquiry (1969) (paper ed. 1971) [hereinafter cited to page number only].

the problem of developing coherent general principles to guide its decisions. As soon as such principles can be formulated, they should be publicly discussed and, if found satisfactory, set down in the form of binding rules. If the agency is still too uncertain to issue a complete set of rules, it should promulgate them for areas which have become well settled. If general rules to cover all cases are impossible, specific rules to cover identifiable sub-categories of cases should be issued. If the agency feels unable to do even this much, then it should be compelled to explain publicly the reasons for its inability to formulate prospective rules in a specific class of cases, and it should utilize other devices such as fair informal procedures, effective review by superior officers, and nonbinding policy statements to ensure that individual decisions are not arbitrary and capricious. The underlying tone of *Discretionary Justice* is optimistic: although there may be a hard core of decisionmaking which must remain discretionary, there is nothing intractable about most of the problem. If we have the will to create an effective system of law to guide and channel administrative decisionmaking, then the monster can be tamed.

II

The real question, of course, is whether we have the will. Professor Davis subtitles his book "A Preliminary Inquiry," and that caveat should be taken seriously. Davis has brilliantly and systematically laid bare the soft underbelly of the American legal system. Moreover, he has tentatively outlined means by which the most important abuses of discretionary power can be curbed. He is at his most convincing when he argues that "the procedure of administrative rule-making is . . . one of the greatest inventions of modern government,"[4] and his solution follows plainly: "the chief hope for confining discretionary power . . . [lies] . . . in much more extensive administrative rule-making."[5] An interlocking network of rules, laid out in advance, can serve as a bulwark which strengthens the agency and prevents co-optation by the forces which it is attempting to regulate. The absence of rules has too often meant that the agency is at the mercy of the pressures brought to bear on it, its decisions little more than the resulting vector produced by conflicting political and economic forces.[6]

4. P. 65.
5. P. 55.
6. *See* Shapiro, *The Choice of Rulemaking or Adjudication in the Development of Administrative Policy,* 78 HARV. L. REV. 921, 952 (1965).

But while Professor Davis' perception of the problem is clear, when it comes to outlining methods by which agencies can be forced to make rules and to obey the rules they do make, he barely scratches the surface. This is a shortcoming which leaves Davis' work seriously flawed. He seems to suppose that many agencies will suddenly see the error of their ways. In his view, "the chief hope for confining discretionary power" lies in voluntary agency rule-making. If that is true, there may be no hope at all. For the sad fact is that powerful forces are at work which incline agencies toward an ad hoc, case-by-case mode of operation. The first of these is simply the bureaucratic imperative of keeping the wheels turning. As Professor Jaffe has written,

> [t]ime has corrected one dearly held illusion. It was thought in the heyday of the New Deal that an operating administrative agency, because of its continuous exposure to the problems of an area, was ideally fitted for progressive planning and programming. We have found that such is not the case. The agency is so deeply, so anxiously involved in solving the problems of the moment that most of its effort goes out in keeping astride of its operating agenda. Furthermore, buffeted by strong, opposing forces, it looks for compromise, expediency, and short-term solutions. After its first strenuous years of conflict with those whom it must regulate, it may arrive at a modus vivendi which it looks upon and pronounces to be good.[7]

Once this accommodation is reached, the agency is sheltered from the scrutiny of Congress, the courts, and the public. It seems clear that the amorphous, ad hoc mode in which most agencies operate has made them resistant to congressional control. Of course, some agencies are notoriously vulnerable to a well-timed telephone call from a congressman or a threat from a powerful committee chairman. But these are essentially ad hoc devices to deal with ad hoc decisions. Most of the time they reflect the sort of constituent pressure from private interest groups which has too much effect on agency decisions already.[8] In the aggregate, all of the individual calls from congressmen and threats at appropriations time do not add up to systematic congres-

7. L. Jaffe, Judicial Control of Administrative Action 51 (1965).

8. The late Senator Dirksen's intervention in administrative affairs for the benefit of individual constituents, and his vociferous defense of this practice, are notorious. He once remarked, "I have been calling agencies for 25 years. . . . Are we to be put on the carpet because we represent our constituents, make inquiries, and find out what the status of matters is, and so serve our constituents?" 105 Cong. Rec. 14057 (1959).

sional control at the policy level. The ineluctable fact is that all too often there can be no congressional supervision of agency policy because the agency has no policy to supervise. Congress will never be able to influence the directions in which agencies are heading until the agencies begin to head in *some* direction and stop floundering in the morass of case-by-case litigation.

Moreover, ad hoc decisions tend to leave the agency freer to change direction at will and allow it to avoid the risks inherent in advance commitments.[9] As Professor Shapiro has pointed out, a reviewing court which might declare invalid a clearly promulgated regulation may well affirm the application in a particular case of a principle of adjudication based on past agency decisions.[10] In addition, an agency will be more readily permitted to ignore its past principles of adjudication than to depart from its regulations.[11]

Given this historical and legal context, it is unrealistic to suppose that many agencies will dramatically move to confine their own discretion. Fortunately, however, there are other strategies available to implement Professor Davis' plans for administrative reform of executive agencies. The publication of *Discretionary Justice* coincides with the culmination of a number of trends in American thought—trends which can be utilized to make the Davis solution something more than an unrealizable ideal. On the one hand, there has been a growing sense of disillusion with the role which regulatory agencies play in the political and economic processes of the country. Credit for the genesis of these critiques must go to conservative economic theoreticians who yearn for a return to a free market economy and view administrative intervention as officious intermeddling.[12] But the sense of disillusion has spread throughout the political spectrum, and critics from the right and left now generally agree that many regulatory agencies are inept, inefficient, and overly protective of the interests which they are supposed to regulate.[13]

9. There may also be something to Professor Jaffe's observations: "The question may be asked whether there is not an essential conflict of attitude between the task of adjudication and long-range planning. The former may be thought to intensify the sense of the particular to a degree which makes planning appear inexact, insensitive, Utopian, and futile." JAFFE, *supra* note 7, at 20.

10. Shapiro, *supra* note 6, at 944-47.

11. *Id.* at 947-52.

12. *See, e.g.,* M. FRIEDMAN, CAPITALISM AND FREEDOM 119-60 (1962).

13. *See, e.g.,* Moss v. CAB, 430 F.2d 891, 893 (D.C. Cir. 1970); F. COX, R. FELLMETH, & J. SCHULZ, "THE NADER REPORT" ON THE FEDERAL TRADE COMMISSION (1969); Meyers, *The Root of the FTC's Confusion,* in PUBLIC POLICIES AND THEIR POLITICS 104-09 (R. Ripley ed. 1966).

On the other hand, we have seen in the last few years a dramatic, if still incipient, reassertion of congressional power which poses the first serious challenge to the practical supremacy of the executive branch since the early days of the New Deal. This movement began with congressional frustration over the inability of the legislature to affect the conduct of the Vietnam war. It has quickly spilled over, however, into numerous other areas. The right of the executive to impound appropriated funds and to impose sweeping wage-price controls without congressional guidance has recently come under challenge. More and more legislators have come to realize that the so-called "expertise" of the executive branch is in reality no more than a cloak which hides the raw exercise of untrammelled power. Whereas once it was believed that administrative "experts" could magically provide a "scientific" solution to public policy problems,[14] many congressmen now realize that most questions of policy are questions of values, and that the people must determine for themselves the values which they favor. In time, the movement for greater balance between the legislature and the executive promises to bring about the first substantial reallocation of power in almost two generations.

III

It is possible that these overlapping movements toward a reassertion of congressional power and away from blind trust in administrative competence will, of their own force, produce voluntary reform. Indeed, there is some evidence that a few agencies—notably the Federal Trade Commission[15]—are already responding to public pressures and changing their ways. But for the reasons outlined above, I think it would be foolish to rely too heavily on voluntary conversion. Fortunately, such reliance is unnecessary. A side effect of the trends toward congressional power and distrust of administrative activity has been the discovery of a counter-tradition which favors close supervision of administrative agencies. This counter-tradition—long overshadowed by the mainstream infatuation with administrative expertise—is supported by a number of legal doctrines which could serve to force reluctant administrators to conform their actions to prospective, publicly promulgated rules and standards.

14. *See* J. LANDIS, THE ADMINISTRATIVE PROCESS 9-12 (1938) [hereinafter cited as LANDIS].

15. *See* Osborne, *The Nixon Watch: Reform at the FTC,* THE NEW REPUBLIC, Oct. 2, 1971, at 13-15; Osborne, *The Nixon Watch: Reform at the FTC—II,* Oct. 16, 1971, at 10-11.

The reform of administrative procedure is a large task, and Congress, the agencies, and the courts all have roles to play. Congress should control discretion by reassuming its rightful role as the architect of fundamental administrative policy. Its current discontent with the consequences of excessive delegation could best be translated into a practice of approving only those statutes which set standards sufficiently precise to ensure that the relevant agency receives clear signals regarding the policy it is expected to carry out. Congressional insistence on such clarity would also give the courts a workable standard for review, and—of great importance—enable congressmen to monitor more effectively the performance of executive agencies. Administrators should take their cue from Congress and the courts and move to confine their own discretion. The courts should control discretion by vigorously reasserting their inherent role as the interpreters of legislative enactments and guardians against invidious and irrational exercises of governmental power. They must repudiate the dictum of *Gray v. Powell,* which still seems to satisfy the Supreme Court: "Where, as here, a determination has been left to an administrative body, this delegation will be respected and the administrative conclusion left untouched."[16] This attitude has led to the practice of sustaining any order of an agency which colorably has kept within the bounds of the statute[17]—an unjustifiable abdication of the responsibility of judicial review.

But while all branches of government must join in the fight to limit discretion, I believe it is the courts which will have to bear the primary burden. Not only must the courts, on occasion, formulate rules of their own which will limit discretion. They must also resuscitate the legal principles which will force sometimes reluctant congressmen and administrators to take action. The courts cannot bear the burden alone; they are not equipped to act as super-administrators, formulating individual rules to govern the thousands of cases heard daily by agencies. But they can reestablish the doctrines which were

16. 314 U.S. 402, 412 (1941).

17. *See, e.g.,* Brooks v. NLRB, 348 U.S. 96 (1954); NLRB v. Seven-Up Bottling Co. of Miami, Inc., 344 U.S. 344 (1953); NLRB v. Gullett Gin Co., 340 U.S. 361 (1951); FCC v. WOKO, Inc., 329 U.S. 223 (1946); Republic Aviation Corp. v. NLRB, 324 U.S. 793 (1945); SEC v. Chenery Corp., 318 U.S. 80 (1943). Of course, there is also a counter-tradition that favors active judicial review of agency decisionmaking. *See, e.g.,* Burlington Truck Lines v. United States, 371 U.S. 156, 167 (1962); Secretary of Agriculture v. United States, 347 U.S. 645, 653 (1954); Ohio Bell Tel. Co. v. Public Utilities Comm'n, 301 U.S. 292 (1937). In fact, it is the thesis of this piece that this counter-tradition can be used to build an effective system of constraints against administrative arbitrariness. The only point I wish to make here is that in recent years the requirements of administrative consistency and rationality, while not abandoned, have been frequently observed in the breach.

designed to compel or encourage other branches of government to assume their parts of the task. Some of these doctrines are outlined below.

A. *The Congressional Role: The Delegation Doctrine*

It is a commonplace that, in its entire history, the Supreme Court has invalidated only two statutes on the ground of improper delegation of power.[18] Today, most scholars rank the delegation doctrine together with substantive due process, nullification, and common law forms of action as arcane notions which inexplicably fascinated an earlier generation but which were given the decent burials they deserved long ago. Indeed, even Professor Davis rejects the delegation doctrine as a realistic means of subjecting agencies to the rule of law. "What Congress says in some such statutes is, in effect: 'We the Congress don't know what the problems are: find them and deal with them.' In many circumstances this is sound government. And the determination of whether or when it is sound government is primarily for Congress to decide."[19]

Yet, at the risk of seeming antiquarian, I think the reported demise of the delegation doctrine is a bit premature. To be sure, we can all join in rejecting broad formulations of the doctrine, such as the famous statement in *Field v. Clark*: "That Congress cannot delegate legislative power to the President is a principle universally recognized as vital to the integrity and maintenance of the system of government ordained by the Constitution."[20] But one can reject this extreme position without conceding that Congress should be permitted, in effect, to vote itself out of business. There must be some limit on the extent to which Congress can transfer its own powers to other bodies without guidance as to how these powers should be exercised.

No judge of any federal court has specifically disavowed the delegation doctrine in its entirety,[21] and numerous decisions can be cited

18. Panama Refining Co. v. Ryan, 293 U.S. 388 (1935); A. L. A. Schechter Poultry Corp. v. United States, 295 U.S. 495 (1935). *See also* Carter v. Carter Coal Co., 298 U.S. 238 (1936).

19. P. 48.

20. 143 U.S. 649, 692 (1892). *See also* United States v. Shreveport Grain & Elevator Co., 287 U.S. 77, 85 (1932).

21. Even Professor Davis, while correctly arguing that de facto standardless delegations have been permitted, concedes that "[t]he courts keep repeating and repeating that the exercise of delegated power must be guided by meaningful safeguards even when the delegated power is carefully circumscribed and even when the intent to delegate is based upon a fully-considered judgment that the delegation is necessary and desirable . . . ." K. Davis, Administrative Law Treatise 50 (1970 Supp.).

which reaffirm it as at least a theoretical check on standardless shifts of power.[22] As recently as 1963, three Supreme Court Justices found that

> [t]he delegation of . . . unrestrained authority to an executive official raises, to say the least, the gravest constitutional doubts. . . . The principle that authority granted by the legislature must be limited by adequate standards serves two primary functions vital to preserving the separation of powers required by the Constitution. *First,* it insures that the fundamental policy decisions of our society will not be made by an appointed official but by the body immediately responsible to the people. *Second,* it prevents judicial review from becoming merely an exercise at large by providing the courts with some measure against which to judge the official action that has been challenged.[23]

In 1967, a fourth Justice argued: "Because the statute contains no meaningful standard by which the Secretary is to govern his designations, and no procedures to contest or review his designations, [it] is constitutionally insufficient to mark 'the field within which the [Secretary] is to act so that it may be known whether he has kept within it in compliance with the legislative will.' "[24]

Moreover, the delegation doctrine continues to be applied—albeit in somewhat erratic fashion—by numerous state courts,[25] and it has even proved a useful tool in some special situations in recent federal cases.[26] I think the delegation doctrine retains an important potential as a check on the exercise of unbounded, standardless discretion by administrative agencies. At its core, the doctrine is based on the notion that agency action must occur within the context of a rule of law previously formulated by a legislative body. That concept is as im-

22. *See, e.g.,* Arizona v. California, 373 U.S. 546, 585, 593 (1963); Lichter v. United States, 334 U.S. 742 (1948); Woods v. Cloyd W. Miller Co., 333 U.S. 138 (1948); Yakus v. United States, 321 U.S. 414 (1944).

23. Arizona v. California, 373 U.S. 546, 626 (1963) (Harlan, J., with Stewart and Douglas, JJ., dissenting) (citations and footnotes omitted: original emphasis).

24. United States v. Robel 389 U.S. 258, 272-73 (1967) (Brennan, J., concurring), *quoting from* Yakus v. United States, 321 U.S. 414, 425 (1944). It must be conceded that Mr. Justice Brennan would apparently restrict his application of the delegation doctrine to cases where protected freedoms and criminal sanctions are involved. *See* 389 U.S. at 276.

25. *See, e.g.,* City of Chicago v. Pennsylvania R. R., 41 Ill.2d 245, 242 N.E.2d 152 (1968); Bologno v. O'Connell, 7 N.Y.2d 155, 164 N.E.2d 389, 196 N.Y.S.2d 90 (1959). *But see, e.g.,* Kugler v. Yocum, 69 Cal.2d 371, 445 P.2d 303, 71 Cal. Rptr. 687 (1968); Warren v. Marion County, 222 Ore. 307, 313-14, 353 P.2d 257, 261 (1960).

26. Thus, on occasion, the Supreme Court has been willing to imply a standard in order to save the statute from an unconstitutionally broad delegation. *See, e.g.,* Kent v. Dulles, 357 U.S. 116 (1958). *Cf.* Shuttlesworth v. Birmingham, 394 U.S. 147 (1969); Schneider v. Smith, 390 U.S. 17 (1968).

portant now as it was a century and a half ago when it was first propounded.[27]

In the end, Professor Davis rejects the delegation doctrine as a means of controlling administrative discretion because, in his view, it is impractical. He reads the long history of the doctrine as conclusively demonstrating that the legislature either cannot or will not impose meaningful standards on administrative discretion. "[T]he emphasis," he says, "should not be on legislative clarification of standards but on administrative clarification, *because that is where the hope lies*."[28] Moreover, he contends, legislative standards might not be desirable even if the legislature could be persuaded to provide them. There are times, Davis argues, when the legislature does not really know what it wants or when political pressure makes it impossible for it to accomplish its objectives. In these situations, if the job is to be done at all, it will have to be done by an agency under a broad delegation of discretionary authority.[29]

It seems to me both of these arguments are open to serious question. When Davis complains that the delegation doctrine has not solved the problem of discretionary power, he is heaving boulders from the none-too-safe haven of a rather fragile glass house. *Discretionary Justice* would not have been written if agency rule-making—"where the hope lies"—had provided a solution. As argued above,[30] there are substantial reasons why agencies are unlikely to be persuaded that they should make fuller use of their rule-making power. Congress, on the other hand, seems to be in a mood to reassert some of its long dormant prerogatives. There is every reason to believe that, with a slight nudge from the courts, Congress would eagerly reassume its rightful role as the author of meaningful organic charters for administrative agencies.

Davis is not quite so vulnerable when he argues that at times the congressional will may not be clear enough to permit formulation of a specific set of standards under which the agencies should operate. When Congress is too divided or uncertain to articulate policy, it is

27. I am thus in accord with Judge Friendly's view that "[w]e still live under a Constitution which provides that 'all legislative Powers herein granted shall be vested in a Congress of the United States, which shall consist of a Senate and House of Representatives'; even if a statute telling an agency 'Here is the problem: deal with it' be deemed to comply with the letter of that command, it hardly does with the spirit." H. FRIENDLY, THE FEDERAL ADMINISTRATIVE AGENCIES 21-22 (1962).

28. P. 50 (original emphasis).

29. Pp. 46, 49. In this respect, Davis seems to be in agreement with some of the strong advocates of administrative discretion. *See, e.g.*, LANDIS, *supra* note 14, at 51.

30. *See* pp. 578-79 *supra*.

no doubt easier to pass an organic statute with some vague language about the "public interest" which tells the agency, in effect, to get the job done. But while this observation is no doubt correct, it seems to me to argue for a vigorous reassertion of the delegation doctrine rather than against it. An argument for letting the experts decide when the people's representatives are uncertain or cannot agree is an argument for paternalism and against democracy.[31] As Justice Brennan has argued,

> [f]ormulation of policy is a legislature's primary responsibility, entrusted to it by the electorate, and to the extent Congress delegates authority under indefinite standards, this policy-making function is passed on to other agencies, often not answerable or responsive in the same degree to the people.[32]

The whole reason we have broadly based representative assemblies is to require some degree of public consensus before governmental action occurs. To be sure, we pay a price for awaiting such consensus. Sometimes desirable action is delayed or becomes impossible altogether because the representative organs of government are too fragmented or uncertain to formulate a coherent policy. But our experience with broad delegations such as the Tonkin Gulf Resolution makes clear that there is a price to be paid for congressional abnegation as well.

Ultimately, the arguments for broad delegation rest on the illusion that problems are solved by conflict avoidance. Congress, for one reason or another, cannot deal with a problem, so it passes some "soft" statutes which throw the mess into the lap of an administrative agency. Such a broad delegation can yield only two possible results, both of which are unfortunate. On the one hand, if the problem is really intractable, it is unlikely that the agency, with all its expertise, will do any better with it than Congress. Indeed, if there is political opposition to any contemplated action, the agency may actually be more vulnerable than Congress.[33] In this situation, the agency is likely to act like King Rex—blundering along on a case-by-case basis without any discernible direction or purpose. Alternatively, it is possible that

31. "'[T]aking things out of politics' [means] taking things out of popular control. This is a frequent device of special-interest groups to effect the transfer of governmental power away from the large public to the special-interest small publics." J. Appleby, Policy and Administration 162 (1949).

32. United States v. Robel, 389 U.S. 258, 276 (1967) (Brennan, J., concurring).

33. "Where Congress has not been able to formulate a consensus, we cannot expect the politically weaker agency to do much better." Jaffe, *supra* note 7, at 25.

the agency will be able to deal with the problem forcefully. It may be that the agency is sufficiently insulated from political pressure so that it can take action which would have been unavailable to Congress, or that Congress is badly split while the agency is united.[34] In this situation, a strong agency will be able to formulate prospective rules, develop a clear sense of purpose, and minimize unnecessary discretion. But these goals will have been accomplished at the expense of democratic decisionmaking. The putatively substantial portion of the electorate which opposes the agency action, or which is merely uncertain as to its wisdom, is likely to believe—and with some justification—that Congress has done through the back door what it could not accomplish in direct, democratic fashion.[35]

We have recently seen enough evidence of what happens when a substantial number of people come to believe that major decisions have been made without their consent. If the social fabric is to survive, the politics of manipulation and delegation simply must be replaced by a politics of informed consent. It is perfectly natural for congressmen to attempt to avoid or delay substantial conflict by any device available, including broad delegations of power to the executive branch. But it is time we came to realize that in a democracy conflict over basic policy cannot be avoided and that when too long delayed it may, like Langston Hughes' dream deferred, explode.

None of this is to argue that a revitalized delegation doctrine is likely to emerge easily and completely. There are severe problems involved in the development of a coherent, principled, and meaningful

34. *See* Landis, *supra* note 14, at 51-55.

35. It is ultimately impossible to talk sensibly about administrative law outside the framework of a theory of democratic government. Such a theory would determine how loud a voice the citizenry should have in various kinds of decisions. Using criteria derived therefrom, one could then go about labelling certain decisions as properly legislative, others as administrative, judicial, and so forth. I do not propose, even if I could do so, to put forth such a theory, for it would sweep far broader than this review requires. But the core of the argument may be stated. I have argued elsewhere that the Constitution deliberately places certain decisions—notably those affecting minority rights—outside the domain of the majority and its elected representatives. Wright, *Professor Bickel, the Scholarly Tradition, and the Supreme Court,* 84 Harv. L. Rev. 769, 787-88 (1971). Precisely because of this restriction, it is all the more necessary that those matters reserved for majority decision be done through majoritarian process. It is in this sense that legislative decisions are democratic: unlike a judge, whose decisions purport to be "principled," a legislator may trade off a vote on one question for the support of a colleague on another issue of greater importance to his constituents; decisions are made by vote, with the winning side presumably representing a greater number of citizens. Most important, legislators are subject to electoral control. The justification for the very existence of a bureaucracy, whose members go about their jobs regardless of who wields elective power, is that legislators simply lack the time and expertise to administer the laws they have made. Civil servants are supposed to give effect to the legislators' decisions, not make those decisions for them. Thus their only legitimate policymaking role is the interstitial application of the always imperfectly defined legislative will.

theory of delegation. Delegation is, after all, a matter of degree, and the amount of power which it is permissible to delegate to an agency varies with the problem involved.[36] As Professor Davis points out, some decisions, by their very nature, are more subject to control by prospective rules and standards than others. It would be a fairly simple matter, for example, for Congress to specify with a great deal more precision what exactly it wishes the Federal Communications Commission to do in order to equalize access to the electronic media. Yet it is hard to imagine how Congress could go beyond the vaguest sort of standards to control ratemaking by the Interstate Commerce Commission. It will be necessary to do some systematic thinking about the degree to which various categories of problems are subject to prospective congressional control. We need, in short, some standards for when we should require standards. To be sure, the overall standard is clear enough: Congress should channel its delegations of power with prospective guidelines and standards to the greatest extent possible. But ironically, the courts may have to work out the precise contours of the requirement of prospective standards on an empirical, case-by-case basis, and this process is likely to be time-consuming. In the meantime, I am convinced that Congress can be persuaded to do a great deal more than it is doing now, as a matter of constitutional morality if not constitutional compulsion.

B. *The Administrative Role: A Rule-making Requirement*

If the courts are able to formulate a coherent delegation requirement or if Congress proves willing to assume a more active supervisory role voluntarily, many of the problems of unnecessary discretion will be resolved. But this proposition should not be taken to derogate from Professor Davis' thesis. Even if Congress assumed its full responsibility and began writing meaningful organic charters for administrative agencies, those bodies would still have to be given substantial power

36. I am thus in basic agreement with Dean Landis when he says: "Generalization as to the allowable limits of administrative discretion is dangerous, for the field is particularly one where differences in degree become differences in substance. It is possible to say, on the one hand, that the responsibility for fashioning a policy, not only of great economic importance but also one that has divided the faith and loyalty of classes of people, cannot appropriately be intrusted to the administrative; on the other, that the scope of administrative power should not be so narrowly defined as to take away from the administrative its capacity to achieve effectively the purposes of its creation. Such corollaries, however, are meaningless in the abstract. It is problems alone that can give them content, but the content that they should possess must have reference to situations seen in the light of the weaknesses and strength of administrative responsibility." LANDIS, *supra* note 14, at 55.

to resolve individual controversies. The problem, as Professor Davis correctly perceives it, is to force the agencies to exercise that power through purposeful and coherent prospective rules rather than in the random, ad hoc, and secret manner in which they all too frequently operate at present. Once again, it seems to me the legal tools which could be utilized to reach this goal have already been fashioned. All we need do is bring those tools to bear on the problem in a forceful and determined manner.

Chief among these tools is the due process clause of the Constitution. It should be obvious that to have due process of law it is necessary for the decision involved to be subject to law. Yet when we say a decision is ad hoc, random, or unreviewable we mean in effect the decision is lawless. As Professor Fuller has stated with admirable directness: "The first desideratum of a system for subjecting human conduct to the governance of rules is an obvious one: there must be rules."[37]

It is time, then, we came to recognize that in at least some circumstances there is a due process right to have one's conduct governed by rules which are stated in advance.[38] Moreover, these rules must be clearly formulated and publicly promulgated. These requirements have been recognized for centuries in the area of criminal law. No one would contend that a man could be arrested, tried, and convicted of a "crime" for acts which were perfectly legal at the time they were committed.[39] Moreover, it has long been recognized that a criminal statute must be publicly promulgated and written precisely enough to give fair warning.[40] Similarly, when noncriminal regulation borders on constitutionally protected conduct, the courts have repeatedly held that the statutes involved must be precisely drawn so as to make clear what is lawful and what is not *before the conduct in question takes place.*[41]

37. FULLER, *supra* note 1, at 46.

38. *See, e.g.,* Holmes v. New York City Housing Authority, 398 F.2d 262 (2d Cir. 1968); Hornsby v. Allen, 326 F.2d 605 (5th Cir. 1964); United States v. Atkins, 323 F.2d 733, 742 (5th Cir. 1963). *Cf.* Landman v. Peyton, 370 F.2d 135, 139-41 (4th Cir.), *cert. denied,* 385 U.S. 881 (1966); Jackson v. Bishop, 268 F. Supp. 804, 815-16 (E.D. Ark. 1967), *vacated on other grounds,* 404 F.2d 571 (8th Cir. 1968). *See generally* DAVIS, *supra* note 21, at 58-62.

39. *See, e.g.,* Burgess v. Salmon, 97 U.S. (7 Otto) 381 (1879); *cf.* Rosenberg v. United States, 346 U.S. 273, 290, *reconsideration denied,* 346 U.S. 324 (1953).

40. *See, e.g.,* Connally v. General Const. Co., 269 U.S. 385, 391 (1926); Cline v. Frink Dairy Co., 274 U.S. 445, 465 (1927). *See generally* Note, *The Void-For-Vagueness Doctrine in the Supreme Court,* 109 U. PA. L. REV. 67 (1960).

41. *See, e.g.,* Cantwell v. Connecticut, 310 U.S. 296 (1940); Schneider v. State, 308 U.S. 147 (1939); Hague v. CIO, 307 U.S. 496 (1939). *See generally* Note, *The First Amendment Overbreadth Doctrine,* 83 HARV. L. REV. 844 (1970).

As an abstract proposition, few would argue that these requirements are limited to the areas of criminal law and constitutional rights. Imagine, for example, a system where individual social workers are given the unfettered right to grant and deny welfare benefits to whomever they please on whatever basis they please. Or imagine a system under which a man's right to pursue his chosen occupation depends upon his ability to get approval from a board which gives no hint of when it will give such approval and when it will withhold it. Is it really open to question that such schemes would be unconstitutional? Regulatory systems which operate without rules are inherently irrational and arbitrary. The purpose of such a system is presumably to bring primary conduct into conformance with agreed upon societal norms. Yet a system operating without rules cannot possibly achieve this goal, since the people being regulated are not informed of what the societal norms are. Unless they are prescient, they cannot possibly be expected to mold their conduct in accordance with rules which, if they can be said to exist at all, are created after the conduct occurs.[42]

Moreover, it should be apparent that *any* system which operates without rules chills the exercise of constitutional rights. When a court strikes down a vaguely worded statute providing for licensing of public demonstrations, it presumably does so because the statute permits those charged with administering it to make decisions on the basis of criteria which are forbidden by the First Amendment.[43] Yet precisely the same flaw is inherent in the statutory schemes described above. A social worker administering a standardless public assistance program might deny benefits because the applicant is a Black Panther. The medical board described above might withhold a license to an otherwise qualified physician because he belongs to the Republican Party. It might be argued that these possibilities do not in themselves make the schemes unconstitutional but rather only demonstrate that they are subject to abuse. When the individual abuses come to light, the argument goes, they will be corrected. But the trouble with a standardless regime is that the abuses may never come to light. In a system under which government officials do not have to act in accordance with publicly stated rules, it is very difficult to know when they are acting in accordance with secret, illicit rules.[44]

42. *See* FULLER, *supra* note 1, at 46-65.
43. *See* Note, *supra* note 41, at 857.
44. The slaughter at Attica and the series of prison revolts which followed in its wake—notably at prisons in Norfolk and Walpole, Massachusetts and Rahway, New

When these propositions are baldly stated, they seem obvious to the point of triteness. Yet the sad fact is that we have barely begun to apply these fundamental due process precepts to the millions of discretionary decisions made by government officials every day. Welfare workers *do* exist who possess the de facto power to grant or deny benefits as they choose.[45] Government boards *do* control access to various professions without reference to any discernible criteria.[46] Indeed, even in the area of criminal law, where the necessity for prospective rules is most widely recognized, police, prosecutors, judges, and parole officers continue to arrest and incarcerate people on the basis of standards which are apparent only to themselves.[47] Under a criminal justice system which makes such conduct as petty gambling, possession of marijuana, statutory rape, and abortion criminal offenses, a large proportion of the population becomes criminal. When the law enforcement establishment picks and chooses on an ad hoc basis which of these "criminals" are to be arrested and prosecuted, they are in effect making up the criminal law as they go along, in a manner which suits the whims and prejudices of individual policemen and prosecutors.[48] Similarly, when a judge decides to impose a maximum sentence or a parole board denies release without a statement of reasons, they make the degree of punishment subject to considerations which were not publicly explicated at the time the offense was committed.[49]

There is simply no reason why we should go on pretending this sort of ex post facto lawmaking by administrative fiat is constitutional. It cannot be doubted that most agencies possess the lawful authority to decide most of the cases which they in fact handle. But the fact that an agency is within the bounds of the relevant statutes in acting

Jersey—have focused public attention on the governance of prison institutions. In no area is the need for public ventilation and public rule-making more compelling. A few recent cases indicate that the courts are aware of this need. *See* Nolan v. Fitzpatrick, 451 F.2d 545 (1st Cir. 1971); Landman v. Royster, 333 F. Supp. 621 (E.D. Va. 1971); Smith v. Robbins, 328 F. Supp. 162 (D. Me. 1971); Landman v. Peyton, 370 F.2d 135, 139-41 (4th Cir.), *cert. denied,* 385 U.S. 881 (1966); Jackson v. Bishop, 268 F. Supp. 804 (E.D. Ark. 1967), *vacated on other grounds,* 404 F.2d 571 (8th Cir. 1968).

45. Pp. 180-83. *Discretionary Justice* was written before the Supreme Court decided that welfare recipients were entitled, under the due process clause, to an evidentiary hearing according them "rudimentary due process" before their benefits could be taken away. Goldberg v. Kelly, 397 U.S. 254, 267 (1970). But neither *Goldberg* nor any subsequent decision does anything to check the abuses Professor Davis describes.

46. P. 38.

47. For an argument that the police have a constitutional duty to formulate rules, see Amsterdam, *The Supreme Court and the Rights of Suspects in Criminal Cases,* 45 N.Y.U. L. REV. 785, 813-15 (1970). *Cf.* United States v. Bryant, 439 F.2d 642 (D.C. Cir. 1971).

48. *See* Pp. 188-91.

49. *See* Pp. 126-41.

has never been thought sufficient, by itself, to insulate its decision from judicial review. The decision must not only be lawful—it must be lawfully made as well.[50] Indeed, that is what the due process clause is all about. As argued above, one element of a lawfully made decision is that it accords with previously stated and clearly articulated rules. Thus, in a proper circumstance, it is clearly within the power of a reviewing court to insist as a matter of constitutional law that the agency state prospective rules and standards before its decision will be enforced.[51]

Moreover, even if the reviewing court is not willing to go this far, there are several subconstitutional devices available to force administrative agencies into rule-making. In some circumstances, for example, it may be possible to extrapolate a rules requirement from the statute under which the agency operates. When Congress sets up an administrative agency, it provides guidelines which concern not only what decisions the agency is to make but also how those decisions are to be arrived at. True, Congress rarely states explicitly that the agency must act through rule-making rather than adjudication. But, as argued below,[52] reviewing courts need not be reticent about putting meat on vague congressional language concerning the "what" of agency decisions. In proper circumstances, I believe, a court can construe congressional intent as to the "how" of these decisions as well. In a situation where an agency is capable of proceeding by rule-making rather than adjudication and where ad hoc decisionmaking is not a rational means of tackling the problem, a court would be justified in concluding that this mode of proceeding was not in accord with the purpose of the statute which the agency is administering.[53] Indeed, given the strong constitutional considerations outlined above,[54] such a conclusion fits neatly with the more general maxim that courts should construe congressional enactments so as to avoid serious constitutional question.[55]

50. *See, e.g.,* Ohio Bell Tel. Co. v. Public Utilities Comm'n, 301 U.S. 292 (1937); Londoner v. Denver, 210 U.S. 373 (1908); Folkways Broadcasting Co. v. FCC, 375 F.2d 299 (D.C. Cir. 1967).

51. *See* note 47 *supra.*

52. *See* pp. 595-96 *infra.*

53. *See* Camp v. Herzog, 104 F. Supp. 134 (D.D.C. 1952), holding that, while the Labor Board had the power to disbar an attorney from practice, Congress did not intend for this power to be exercised on a case-by-case basis. *Cf.* NLRB v. Insurance Agents' Int'l Union, 361 U.S. 477 (1960), holding that Congress intended for the Board to determine the requirements of good faith bargaining on a case-by-case basis rather than by formulating per se rules.

54. *See* pp. 588-91 *supra.*

55. *See, e.g.,* Welsh v. United States, 398 U.S. 333 (1970); Gutknecht v. United States, 396 U.S. 295 (1970); United States v. Rumely, 345 U.S. 41, 45 (1953).

Finally, even if the reviewing court rejects both the constitutional and the statutory theories for a rules requirement, there remain some situations in which the court can exercise its own inherent supervisory powers to force the agency to write rules governing its conduct. Thus if the police are destroying evidence, or preserving it, only in a random fashion, the courts can require police authorities to formulate rules governing the precise disposition of potential evidence in a variety of situations.[56] Similarly, when an agency handles a recurring problem on an ad hoc basis despite the fact that a normative standard could easily be devised, courts can and should require rule-making on the basis of their inherent supervisory powers.[57] These powers are derived from the underlying power of the courts to protect the integrity of judicial review. No one has ever questioned the authority of a court sitting in equity to issue orders designed to preserve a *res* which is *sub judice*.[58] I believe courts have a similar power to require analogous measures which make judicial review of agency action possible. Since it is obvious that judicial review cannot exist unless there is a standard against which agency action can be measured, the courts have the authority to demand that such a standard be erected. As Judge Bazelon has argued,

> judicial review alone can correct only the most egregious abuses. . . . When administrators provide a framework for principled decision-making, the result will be to diminish the importance of judicial review by enhancing the integrity of the administrative process, and to improve the quality of judicial review in those cases where judicial review is sought.[59]

It is clear, then, that when agencies refuse to make use of their rule-making powers, the courts need not take "no" for an answer. Under well established principles of law, the courts have the authority to demand that agency action be subject to rules. This is true because it is what the Constitution requires, because it is what Congress often intends, and because it is what the courts must do if they are to preserve their reviewing function. But, whatever theoretical pigecnhole is chosen, it is ultimately true because fair procedures are impossible without rules which guide agency action. We cannot have a

56. *See* United States v. Bryant, 439 F.2d 642, 652 (D.C. Cir. 1971).
57. *Cf.* Environmental Defense Fund, Inc. v. Ruckelshaus, 439 F.2d 584 (D.C. Cir. 1971).
58. *See, e.g.*, Continental Ill. Nat. Bank & Trust Co. v. Chicago, Rock Island & Pac. Ry., 294 U.S. 648 (1935); Kline v. Burke Const. Co., 260 U.S. 226 (1922).
59. Environmental Defense Fund, Inc. v. Ruckelshaus, 439 F.2d 584, 598 (D.C. Cir. 1971).

society under law without first having laws. The judiciary fulfills its highest obligation when it insists not only that the laws be obeyed but also that there *be* laws to be obeyed.

C. *The Judicial Role: Review Without Rules*

Having said all this, I should hasten to add a caveat. I do not intend to adopt what Professor Davis has called the extravagant version of the rule of law.[60] Advocates of discretionary decisionmaking can argue with some force that there is a value in flexible, empirical growth of the law and that the rules for resolving some problems are for one reason or another simply not susceptible to neat codifications.

My view is that these arguments are correct as far as they go, but that they are essentially incomplete. While I do not wish to dispute the proposition that in some situations comprehensive prospective rule-making is impossible or undesirable, I share Professor Davis' view that a great deal more can be done. The criminal justice system provides an excellent example. It is doubtless true that the decision to prosecute or not to prosecute a suspected offender is a complex one and it would be a mistake to require the determination to be made in accordance with totally inflexible rules.[61] But this is not to say that prosecutorial discretion cannot be significantly narrowed without interfering with the sort of individualized justice that empirical decisionmaking is designed to protect. Studies of prosecutorial decisionmaking reveal that the decision to prosecute is based at least in part on a number of factors which are quite readily generalizable, such as the amount of evidence available and the likelihood of conviction.[62] I see no reason why these relatively straightforward considerations cannot be stated in the form of prospective rules so that they can be judicially enforced and fairly applied.

Of course it is true that even after this has been done there will remain aspects of prosecutorial decisions which cannot be put in the form of binding, prospective rules. Some of these considerations will be too individual in nature to be generalized beyond the one case to which they apply. Others are more general in nature, but involve decisions as to allocation of prosecutorial resources which, if publicly

60. Pp. 28-33.

61. *Cf.* Goldstein, *Police Discretion: The Ideal versus the Real,* 23 PUB. AD. REV. 140 (1963). *But see* pp. 162-70.

62. *See* F. MILLER, PROSECUTION—THE DECISION TO CHARGE A SUSPECT WITH A CRIME 24-43 (1970).

announced, might encourage criminal conduct.[63] But the important point to be made is that, although in some situations it may be impossible to formulate prospective rules governing official conduct, it does not follow that unbridled discretion should reign supreme. Although publicly announced prospective rules should be the preferred method of limiting agency discretion, there are other methods as well.

These alternative methods once again derive from basic notions about what courts are supposed to do in a constitutional democracy. One of their underlying functions is to ensure that official action is not irrational or invidious. The Administrative Procedure Act clearly empowers courts to set aside agency action which is "arbitrary, capricious, an abuse of discretion, or otherwise not in accordance with law,"[64] or which is "contrary to constitutional right, power, privilege, or immunity."[65] Thus even in situations where the agency cannot articulate a rule in advance, the courts should still oversee agency action to ensure that the agency is following *some* rational and permissible rule of decision. While it is sometimes inevitable that the rule of decision be developed on a case-by-case basis, this development should not be confused with a system under which decisions are made without rules.[66] When the prosecutor chooses to press charges in one case but not in another, for example, he should be able to point to some distinction between the two cases which it is permissible for him to consider. While he may not be able to articulate in advance what all the distinguishing factors in all cases will be, he must at least be able to show later that cases treated differently were in fact different in some relevant respect—that is, that he is following some sort of rational, non-discriminatory rule. If he cannot make such a showing, his different treatment of the two cases is irrational or invidious, and hence violative of equal protection.[67]

Moreover, there are certain evidentiary principles which guard this

63. *Cf.* Shapiro, *supra* note 6, at 928-29.

64. 5 U.S.C. § 706(2)(A) (1970).

65. 5 U.S.C. § 706(2)(B) (1970). It is, of course, true that the Administrative Procedure Act also precludes from review "agency action [which] is committed to agency discretion by law." 5 U.S.C. § 701(a)(2) (1970). But in my view Congress should not be taken as having given agencies discretion to act in an arbitrary, irrational, or unconstitutional fashion. *See* Balanyi v. Local 1031, International Bhd. of Elec. Wkrs., 374 F.2d 723, 726 (7th Cir. 1967). *Cf.* Saferstein, *Nonreviewability: A Functional Analysis of "Committed to Agency Discretion,"* 82 HARV. L. REV. 367, 370 (1968).

66. "It should . . . be emphasized . . . that the choice between rulemaking and adjudication is not necessarily the choice between the articulation of a rule and an *ad hoc* approach in which each case is governed only by a general statutory provision. Agencies, like courts, frequently evolve detailed and precise rules in the course of adjudication." Shapiro, *supra* note 6, at 926.

67. *Cf., e.g.,* Morey v. Doud, 354 U.S. 457 (1957).

requirement of rationality. For example, if the prosecutor has, over a period of time, been charging only blacks with certain crimes despite the fact that white violators are also brought to his attention, this means that his basis for prosecution, however stated, is inherently suspect[68] and that courts will scrutinize the reasons offered for the apparently invidious discrimination with particular care.[69]

To be sure, none of these notions is particularly new or revolutionary. Indeed, they are the core concepts upon which equal protection doctrine is built. I offer them here only to demonstrate that methods are available to control agency discretion even in cases where prospective rule-making is impossible. Nor need these methods always involve constitutional adjudication. Even in situations where the agency is able to offer plausible reasons for distinguishing between different cases, it is still possible for the courts to limit the scope of agency choice. The administrative agencies, after all, derive all of their delegated power from statutes passed by the legislative body, and it is the task of the courts to interpret those statutes in cases which are properly brought before them.

Once again, the Administrative Procedure Act is quite explicit: "To the extent necessary to decision and when presented, the reviewing court shall decide all relevant questions of law, interpret constitutional and statutory provisions, and determine the meaning or applicability of the terms of an agency action."[70] If the agency acts beyond its statutory authority as the relevant statute is interpreted by the courts, the agency action must be reversed.[71]

> The construction put on a statute by the agency charged with administering it is entitled to deference by the courts, and ordinarily that construction will be affirmed if it has a 'reasonable basis in law.' . . . But the Courts are the final authorities on issues of statutory construction . . . and 'are not obliged to stand aside and rubber-stamp their affirmance of administrative decisions that they deem inconsistent with a statutory mandate or that frustrate the congressional policy underlying a statute.' . . . 'The deference owed to an expert tribunal cannot be allowed to slip into a judicial inertia . . . .'[72]

68. *Cf.* Loving v. Virginia, 388 U.S. 1 (1967); McLaughlin v. Florida, 379 U.S. 184 (1964).
69. *See, e.g.,* Yick Wo v. Hopkins, 118 U.S. 356 (1886).
70. 5 U.S.C. § 706 (1970).
71. *See, e.g.,* Greater Boston Television Corp. v. FCC, 444 F.2d 841, 850-52 (D.C. Cir.), *cert. denied,* 403 U.S. 923 (1971); Mary Carter Paint Co. v. FTC, 333 F.2d 654 (5th Cir. 1964).
72. Volkswagenwerk Aktiengesellschaft v. FMC, 390 U.S. 261, 272 (1968), *quoting from* NLRB v. Hearst Publications, 322 U.S. 111, 131 (1944). *See also* NLRB v. Brown, 380 U.S. 278, 291 (1965); American Ship Building Co. v. NLRB, 380 U.S. 300, 318 (1965).

Of course many congressional delegations are phrased in extremely broad terms and, literally read, they permit an exceedingly wide range of agency choice. But the very breadth of such statutes provides an argument for a narrowing judicial construction in accordance with congressional intent.[73] Advocates of administrative discretion seem to forget that the courts construe broad statutory mandates all the time —that indeed, the courts have no choice but to do so when faced with the problem of applying a vaguely worded statute to a specific set of facts. As Professor Jaffe has said,

> [t]he scope of judicial review is ultimately conditioned and determined by the major proposition that the constitutional courts of this country are the acknowledged architects and guarantors of the integrity of the legal system. . . . An agency is not an island entire of itself. It is one of the many rooms in the magnificent mansion of the law. The very subordination of the agency to judicial jurisdiction is intended to proclaim the premise that each agency is to be brought into harmony with the totality of the law; the law as it is found in the statute at hand, the statute book at large, the principles and conceptions of the 'common law' and the ultimate guarantees associated with the Constitution.[74]

It may nonetheless be true that in situations where the agency sets out to limit and define its own mandate by adopting prospective rules to guide it in consideration of individual cases, the courts have some obligation to respect agency expertise. But when the agency has defaulted—when it purports to do no more than follow the vague statutory mandate without additional prospective rules of its own—the courts have no obligation to respect undemonstrated or hypothetical expertise. Instead, the reviewing court should look at the statute on its own and determine for itself whether the agency decision is within the congressional purpose. In this way, judges can narrow the scope of agency discretion even if the administrators are unwilling to narrow its scope themselves.

IV

Justice Jackson argued years ago that

> administrative experience is of weight in judicial review only to this point—it is a persuasive reason for deference to the Commission in the exercise of its discretionary powers under and within

73. *See* Burlington Truck Lines v. United States, 371 U.S. 156, 166-68 (1962).
74. JAFFE, *supra* note 7, at 589-90.

> the law. It cannot be invoked to support action outside of the law. And what action is, and what is not, within the law must be determined by courts, when authorized to review, no matter how much deference is due to the agency's fact finding. Surely an administrative agency is not a law unto itself . . . .[75]

Mr. Justice Jackson wrote those words in a dissenting opinion. His warning was not heeded in that case, and it has gone largely unheeded to the present day. Because of that neglect, we are now surrounded with agencies that are in fact laws unto themselves. The well-intentioned reformers of another generation have created a monster which threatens to destroy our very system of law.

And yet, although the danger is real, I cannot help sharing the underlying optimism of Professor Davis. Administrative discretion was created by law, and there is no inherent reason why the law should be unable to control it. The legal devices which we could use for this purpose were all formulated years ago and remain perfectly serviceable. Professor Davis and others have alerted us to the peril, and a broad public consensus is beginning to coalesce in favor of doing something about unbridled and arbitrary administrative power. If that consensus is properly marshalled and the legal tactics carefully planned, King Rex can indeed be turned into a constitutional monarch. Failing that, we may still be able to pull off a bloodless *coup d'etat* and send the King packing to a land that does not purport to govern its affairs by rules of law.

75. SEC v. Chenery Corp., 332 U.S. 194, 215 (1947) (Jackson, J., dissenting).

Bibliography

This bibliography lists all 55 of Judge J. Skelly Wright's nonjudicial writings in chronological order. Those marked with an asterisk are reproduced in this volume.

Pre-Trial on Trial, 14 Louisiana Law Review 391 (1954).

Opening Remarks (in *Open Forum: Evaluation of a Personal Injury Case for Settlement Purposes),* 23 Insurance Counsel Journal 267 (1956).

Jurisdiction in the Tidelands, 32 Tulane Law Review 175 (1958).

Act 85-554 of 1958 and the Disposal of the Judicial Power of the United States, 6 Louisiana Bar Journal 147 (1958).

The Pretrial Conference, 28 Federal Rules Decisions 37 (1960).

Sentencing the Income Tax Violator, 30 Federal Rules Decisions 302 (1961).

The Role of the Courts: Conscience of a Sovereign People, The Reporter, Sept. 26, 1963, at 27.

The Mentally Disabled: Stepchildren of the Law, The New Republic, May 9, 1964, at 24.

The Judge Evaluates the Insanity Plea, 36 Postgraduate Medicine No. 4 (Oct. 1964).

A Judge's View: The News Media and Criminal Justice, 50 American Bar Association Journal 1125 (1964).

**Public School Desegregation: Legal Remedies for De Facto Segregation,* 40 New York University Law Review 285 (1965).

Law School Training in Criminal Law: A Judge's Viewpoint, 3 American Criminal Law Quarterly 166 (1965).

Crime in the Streets and the New McCarthyism, The New Republic, Oct. 9, 1965, at 10.

Let the Lawyers Try the Lawsuit, 71 Case & Comment 11 (1966).

Free Press and Television, 5 Publishing Entertainment, Advertising and Allied Fields Law Quarterly 419 (1966).

Fair Trial—Free Press, 38 Federal Rules Decisions 435 (1966).

Review: Radio, Television, and the Administration of Justice, 15 American University Law Review 414 (1966).

The Renaissance of the Criminal Law: The Responsibility of the Trial Lawyer, 4 Duquesne Law Review 213 (1966).

Federal Habeas Corpus for State Prisoners: The Allocation of Fact-Finding Responsibility, 75 Yale Law Journal 895 (1966) (co-author).

The Right to Counsel: Fact or Fiction? Trial, Aug.-Sept. 1966, at 15.

The New Role of Defense Counsel under Escobedo *and* Miranda, 52 American Bar Association Journal 1117 (1966).

Justice at the Dock: The Maritime Worker and Mr. Justice Black, 14 University of California at Los Angeles Law Review 524 (1967).

The Federal Courts and the Nature and Quality of State Law, 13 Wayne Law Review 317 (1967).

The Supreme Court As I See It Today, Trial, April-May 1967, at 14.

Review of Newman, Conviction: The Determination of Guilt or Innocence Without Trial, 40 Southern California Law Review 176 (1967).

The Need for Education in the Law of Criminal Correction, 2 Valparaiso Law Review 84 (1967).

Defamation, Privacy, and the Public's Right to Know: A National Problem and a New Approach, 46 Texas Law Review 630 (1968).

In Memory of Dr. Martin Luther King, 68 Columbia Law Review 1046 (1968).

**The Role of the Supreme Court in a Democratic Society—Judicial Activism or Restraint?* 54 Cornell Law Review 1 (1968).

Review of Tigar, Selective Service Law Reporter, 78 Yale Law Journal 338 (1968).

Criminal Correction and the Law, Trial, Feb.-March 1969, at 27.

The Courts Have Failed the Poor, New York Times Magazine, March 9, 1969, at 26.

Poverty, Minorities, and Respect for Law, 1970 Duke Law Journal 425.

**Professor Bickel, the Scholarly Tradition, and the Supreme Court,* 84 Harvard Law Review 769 (1971).

The Scholars and the Supreme Court, 26 Record of the Association of the Bar of the City of New York 567 (1971).

No Matter How Small, 2 Human Rights 115 (1972).

**Beyond Discretionary Justice,* 81 Yale Law Journal 575 (1972).

Court of Appeals Review of Federal Regulatory Agency Rulemaking, 26 Administrative Law Review 199 (1973).

**The Courts and the Rulemaking Process: The Limits of Judicial Review,* 59 Cornell Law Review 375 (1974).

Promises to Keep, 3 Black Law Journal 106 (1974).

A Colleague's Tribute to Judge David L. Bazelon on the 25th Anniversary of His Appointment, 123 University of Pennsylvania Law Review 250 (1974).

Are the Courts Abandoning the Cities? 4 Journal of Law & Education 218 (1975).

Oral Argument and the Appellate Process, Litigation, Fall 1975, at 5.

**Politics and the Constitution: Is Money Speech?* 85 Yale Law Journal 1001 (1976).

New Judicial Requisites for Informal Rulemaking: Implications for the Environmental Impact Statement Process, 29 Administrative Law Review 59 (1977).

Rulemaking and Judicial Review, 30 Administrative Law Review 461 (1978).

Foreword, 16 American Criminal Law Review 1 (1978).

David L. Bazelon—A Tribute to My Colleague, 1979 Annual Survey of American Law xvi.

*_Judicial Review and the Equal Protection Clause,_ 15 Harvard Civil Rights-Civil Liberties Law Review 1 (1980).

Musings on Administrative Law, 33 Administrative Law Review 177 (1980).

Law and the Logic of Experience: Reflections on Denning, Devlin, and Judicial Innovation in the British Context, 33 Stanford Law Review 179 (1980).

*_Color-Blind Theories and Color-Conscious Remedies,_ 47 University of Chicago Law Review 213 (1980).

Thurgood Marshall: A Tribute, 40 Maryland Law Review 398 (1981).

The Bill of Rights in Britain and America: A Not Quite Full Circle, 55 Tulane Law Review 291 (1981).

*_Money and the Pollution of Politics: Is the First Amendment an Obstacle to Political Equality?_ 82 Columbia Law Review 609 (1982).

Index

Abrams v. United States, 78 n.17, 122, 124-26
Adams, John, 183
Adderley v. Florida, 84 n.41
Adjudication, 231-81
Administrative law, 231-81
Administrative Procedure Act, 142, 236-55
Administrative record, 241 n.34, 252-53
Administrative rulemaking, 233-55; fairness in, 237-40
Affirmative action plans, 195-229
American Bar Association, 152-53
American Medical Association, 108 n.58
Auerbach, Carl, 24
Avery v. Midland County, 68 n.108

Bachrach, Peter, 55 n.68
Bacon, Lord Chancellor, 159
Bailey v. Drexel Furniture Co., 30 n.128
Baker v. Carr, 22, 190
Bakke, Allan, 214, 222, 227
Barron, Jerome, 127 n.168, 128 n.176
Bazelon, David, 247-48, 251, 276
Bell, Derrick, 211 n.44
Berea College v. Kentucky, 204 n.20
Berg, Larry, 108 n.59
Berle, Adolf A., 6, 17
Bernstein, Marver, 236 n.14
Bickel, Alexander, 12, 16, 24, 33-71, 198. Works: *The Least Dangerous Branch,* 41-42, 46, 51; *The Supreme Court and the Idea of Progress,* 33-71
Biddle, Francis, 139-40
Bill of attainder, 148
Bill of Rights, 14, 17, 50, 60, 99, 126, 149, 154
Bi-Metallic Investment Co. v. State Board of Equalization, 244
Black, Charles, 11, 17, 36 n.6, 37 n.8, 43, 95, 155
Black, Hugo L., 3, 125-27, 154, 164, 166, 184
Blackmun, Harry, 205, 228
Bork, Robert, 124 n.149
Bradley, Joseph, 150, 161
Brandeis, Louis D., 17, 62, 65, 122, 124 n.149, 128, 179
Brennan, William J., 125, 224, 227
Brest, Paul, 126 n.164
Bridges, Harry, 140
Brown v. Board of Education-I, 19-21, 38, 167, 172-80, 220
Brown v. Board of Education-II, 8-9
Brown v. Mississippi, 191
Buckley v. Valeo, 73-133
Buck v. Bell, 204
Bullock v. Carter, 118
Burger, Warren, 120

Cahn, Edmond, 192-93
California v. Goldfarb, 203
Campaign costs, 110-12
Campaign financing reform, 73-95
Carrington v. Rash, 26
Centralization, 59-60
Chafee, Zechariah, Jr., 124, 126
Chambers v. Florida, 166

Chase, Salmon, 150
Choper, Jesse, 19, 31 n.128
Civil Rights Act of 1866, 161, 170
Civil Rights Act of 1964, 8, 173-74, 190, 204
Civil Rights Cases, 20, 161
Claggett, Bruce, 242, 244
Clark, Tom, 164
Clean Air Act, 240
Colegrove v. Green, 22, 191
Constitution, 148
Constitutional duty, 12, 17, 19
Constitutional interpretation, 51
Constitutional scholarship, 33-71
Continental Congress, 183
Cooley, Thomas, 184. Work: *Constitutional Limitations,* 184
Corporations, 73-135; and pollution of politics, 97-135
Cox, Archibald, 17, 36 n.6, 131
Cox v. Louisiana, 84 n.41
Craig v. Boren, 221
Cramton, Roger, 31 n.128
Criminal procedure, 26-29

Dahl, Robert, 94 n.72
Daniel, John A., 149-50
Davis, Kenneth Culp, 245 n.37, 250 n.82, 257-81. Work: *Discretionary Justice: A Preliminary Inquiry,* 257-81
Declaration of Independence, 116
De facto segregation, 167-93
Delegation of powers, 266-71
Democracy, 13
Deutsch, Jan, 9, 44
Dirksen, Everett M., 262 n.8
Discretionary justice, 257-81
Dixon, Robert, 44 n.33
Douglas, William O., 3, 26, 30, 164
Douglas v. California, 27
Dred Scott v. Sandford, 63
Due process of law, 151
Dworkin, Ronald, 155

Economic due process, 8
Education, need for, 184-85
Ely, John, 155, 218
Emerson, Thomas, 52, 127, 132
Environmental Protection Agency, 240
Equal employment opportunity, 208
Equality, 19, 22, 25, 29, 115-21, 132, 171
Equal protection, 137-66, 185
Ervin, Sam J., 100 n.4
Ex post facto laws, 148

Fair Labor Standards Act, 139
Fairness doctrine, 130, 134
Federal Communications Commission, 271
Federal Election Campaign Act, 100-104
Federal Election Commission, 112
Federalism, 28
Federalist No. 10, 89, 94 n.72
Federalist No. 57, 116
Federal Power Commission, 233 n.2
Federal Trade Commission, 109, 260
Feller, Abe, 236 n.14
Field v. Clark, 266
First amendment, 77-135
First National Bank v. Bellotti, 97-135
Foote, Caleb, 36 n.6
Founding Fathers, 95, 128, 134, 144
Fourteenth amendment, 24, 29, 149
France, Anatole, 121, 160, 166
Frankfurter, Felix, 3, 15, 41, 46, 144, 164-65, 185
Franks v. Bowman Transportation Co., 223 n.90
Freeman, Alan, 211 n.44
Freund, Paul, 24
Friendly, Henry J., 235, 268
Fuller, Lon, 259, 272. Work: *The Morality of Law,* 259
Fuller, Melville, 20
Full faith and credit, 148

Gideon v. Wainwright, 27-28
Gitlow v. New York, 124 n.149
Gray v. Sanders, 23
Griffin v. Illinois, 27, 160, 162
Griffin v. School Board, 189
Griggs v. Duke Power Co., 208, 229
Gunther, Gerald, 225 n.94

Habeas corpus, 148
Hahn, Harlan, 99 n.3, 108 n.59, 111 n.78
Hall v. St. Helena Parish School Board, 189
Hammer v. Dagenhart, 30 n.128
Hand, Learned, 16-18, 39, 206
Harlan, John M., I, 24, 171, 181, 204 n.20
Harlan, John M., II, 24, 160
Harper v. Board of Elections, 26
Harvard Law Review, 36
Harvard Law School, 141
Hayes, Rutherford B., 170
Hills v. Gautreaux, 210 n.40
Hill v. Wallace, 30 n.128
Hobson v. Hansen, 167
Holmes, Oliver Wendell, 17, 44, 77 n.17, 124 n.149, 126, 156, 184
Hunter v. Erickson, 205

Initiatives, 112-15
Interest groups, 59
International Brotherhood of Teamsters v. United States, 223
International Harvester Co. v. Ruckelshaus, 240

Jackson, Robert, 140, 280-81
Jackson v. Pasadena City School District, 176
Jaffe, Louis L., 262, 280
Jefferson, Thomas, 146, 183
"Jim Crow" laws, 163
Judicial activism, 3-32, 158
Judicial restraint, 3-32, 158
Judicial review: and administrative law, 229-81; and equal protection, 137-65; in general, 3-31; by Supreme Court, 73-95
Judicial value choices, 42

Kafka, Franz, 260
Kahn v. Shevin, 221
Kaiser Aluminum Co., 228
Kalven, Harry, 83 n.39
Karst, Kenneth, 132, 155
Katzenbach v. Morgan, 31 n.129, 59
Kennedy, Robert, 63
Kirkpatrick v. Preisler, 67 n.105
Kovacs v. Cooper, 84 n.41, 121
Kurland, Philip, 19, 24, 61-62, 69, 206

Landis, James, 271 n.36
Law School Admissions Test, 227
Least Dangerous Branch, The, 41-42, 46, 51. *See also* Bickel, Alexander
Legalization, 60
Legal realism, xiii-xvi
Legal reasoning, 55
Legislative reapportionment, 22-26
Legitimacy, 11
Leventhal, Harold, 101 n.18
Leviathan, 206
Lewis, Anthony, 35
Liberty, 199
Liberty of contract, 151
Llewellyn, Karl, xv
Local Government Board v. Arlidge, 233
Lochner v. New York, 8, 151, 154, 158
Lowi, Theodore, 94 n.72

McCarthy, Eugene, 63
McCulloch v. Maryland, 31 n.128
MacKinnon, George, 248
Madison, James, 31 n.128, 62, 89, 94 n.72, 116-17, 183
Magna Carta, 151
Majority rule, 16, 58
Mapp v. Ohio, 28
Marbury v. Madison, 51 n.59
Marshall, John, 37
Marshall, Thurgood, 84 n.40, 218 n.67
Marshall Court, 37 n.8
Mass media, 110
Meiklejohn, Alexander, 52, 73, 75, 92, 95, 122, 125, 128-29
Mendelson, Wallace, 20
Meritocracy, 226
Michelman, Frank, 58
Miller, Arthur S., 36 n.6
Milliken v. Bradley, 210 n.40
Minersville School District v. Gobitis, 11-12
Miranda v. Arizona, 9, 28, 46

Mobil Oil Co. v. Federal Power Commission, 241
Money: and pollution of politics, 97-133; as speech, 75-95
Mosk, Stanley, 176

NAACP v. Alabama, 122
National Association for the Advancement of Colored People, 174
National Automobile Dealers Association, 109
National Labor Relations Board (NLRB), 139
Natural Gas Act, 241
Neutral principles, 42, 45, 49. *See also* Wechsler, Herbert
New York Times v. Sullivan, 122, 124-25
Nine Old Men, 5, 18
NLRB v. Wyman-Gordon Co., 235 n.7
Northwest Ordinance, 183

Olmstead v. United States, 17
Orwell, George, 61
Overton Park v. Volpe, 249

Peckham, Rufus, 151
Philip Morris, Inc., 113
Plessy v. Ferguson, 20, 65, 134, 160, 163, 170-71, 172, 182, 197, 204 n.20
Pluralism, 49, 55, 87-95
Political Action Committees (PACs), 104-10, 128, 133
Political equality, 99-135. *See also* Equality
Political question, 157
Political spending, 73-135
Pollak, Louis, 36 n.6
Popular responsibility, 10-13
Powell, Lewis, 213, 224, 227
Privileges and immunities, 148
Progressive realists, 37, 39-40, 46
Public interest, 94 n.72, 238, 260

Railway Express Agency v. New York, 26-27, 30
Rawls, John, 119-20
Reason, 57
Red Lion Broadcasting Co. v. Federal Communications Commission, 130
Referenda, 112-15
Regents of the University of California v. Bakke, 159, 213, 216, 224, 229
Rehnquist, William, 203
Reich, Charles, 126 n.164
Reitman v. Mulkey, 205
Representative government, 118
Republican form of government, 25
Result orientation, 39
"Revolt against formalism," 39
Reynolds v. Sims, 23, 38, 118
R. J. Reynolds Tobacco Co., 113
Roosevelt, Franklin D., 139, 157
Roosevelt, Theodore, 119
Rosenthal, Albert, 112, 119, 120 n.130
Rostow, Eugene V., 15
Rousseau, Jean-Jacques, 116-17

San Antonio Independent School District v. Rodriguez, 217 n.66
Schmidhauser, John, 108 n.59
Scholastic mandarins, 43-44
Securities Exchange Commission v. Chenery Corp., 281 n.75
Segregation, racial, 167-93
Shapiro, David, 263
Skinner v. Oklahoma, 27
Slaughterhouse Cases, 150, 165
South Carolina v. Katzenbach, 31 n.129
Standard Oil Co., 114
States rights, 30 n.128
Sterilization, 27 n.111
Stone, Harlan Fiske, 17, 236 n.14
Stromberg v. California, 82 n.36
Substantive due process, 151-54
Suffrage, 117
Supreme Court, 3-32; effect on popular responsibility, 10-13; institutional competence of, 7-10; post-Civil War, 170; as "revolutionary committee," 17; as undemocratic institution, 13
Supreme Court and the Idea of Progress, The, 33-71. *See also* Bickel, Alexander

Swann v. Charlotte-Mecklenburg Board of Education, 210 n.41, 229

Taney, Roger, 63
Taylor v. Board of Education, 177
Thayer, James Bradley, 10-11
Thornhill v. Alabama, 122
Tilden, Samuel J., 170
Tocqueville, Alexis de, 89, 117, 201
Tribe, Laurence, 155, 161
Truman, David, 94 n.72

Unconstitutional conditions, 77 n.11
United Jewish Organizations v. Carey, 215, 219
United States v. Allegheny-Ludlum Steel Corp., 243
United States v. Butler, 30 n.128
United States v. Carolene Products Co., 217 n.66
United States v. Darby, 31 n.128, 139
United States v. Florida East Coast Railway, 243
United States v. Guest, 31 n.129
United States v. Jefferson County Board of Education, 9
United States v. MacDaniel, 143
United States v. O'Brien, 80-82
United Steel Workers v. Weber, 203, 218, 229

Van Alstyne, William, 77 n.11, 209-15
Vested rights, 222-24
Voting Rights Act of 1965, 8, 26, 161, 215

Warren, Earl, 3, 5, 164, 172
Warren Court, 3-32; as "revolutionary committee," 6. *See also* Bickel, Alexander
Washington, George, 183
Watergate, 77, 100
Weber, Brian, 223
Wechsler, Herbert, 41-42, 44-46, 49, 51
Weeks v. United States, 29
Wells v. Rockefeller, 67 n.105
Wesberry v. Sanders, 14, 23, 118
West Publishing Co., 247
West Virginia State Board of Education v. Barnette, 11, 24
White, Byron, 102, 130 n.188, 131
Whitney v. California, 17, 122, 124-25, 127
Wilderness Society v. Morton, 247
Williams, Bernard, 120 n.129
Wolff, Robert, 55 n.68
Wolf v. Colorado, 28-29
Wright, J. Skelly, 3, 33, 73, 97, 137, 142, 167, 195, 227, 257

About the Editor

Arthur Selwyn Miller is Leo Goodwin, Sr., Distinguished Professor of Law at Nova University Center for the Study of Law and Professor Emeritus of Law at George Washington University. His previously published books include *Toward Increased Judicial Activism: The Political Role of the Supreme Court* (Greenwood Press, 1982), *Democratic Dictatorship: The Emergent Constitution of Control* (Greenwood Press, 1981), *Social Change and Fundamental Law: America's Evolving Constitution* (Greenwood Press, 1979), *The Supreme Court: Myth and Reality* (Greenwood Press, 1978), and *The Modern Corporate State: Private Governments and the American Constitution* (Greenwood Press, 1976). He has also written many articles in legal, political science, and economics journals.

Recent Titles in
Contributions in American Studies
Series Editor: Robert H. Walker

Business and Its Environment: Essays for Thomas C. Cochran
Harold Issadore Sharlin, editor

Sources for American Studies
Jefferson B. Kellogg and Robert H. Walker, editors

A New World Jerusalem: The Swedenborgian
Experience in Community Construction
Mary Ann Meyers

Musical Nationalism: American Composers'
Search for Identity
Alan Howard Levy

The Dilemmas of Individualism: Status, Liberty, and
American Constitutional Law
Michael J. Phillips

Sons of Liberty: The Masculine Mind
in Nineteenth-Century America
David G. Pugh

American Tough: The Tough-Guy Tradition and American Character
Rupert Wilkinson

Uncle Sam at Home: Civilian Mobilization, Wartime Federalism, and the
Council of National Defense, 1917-1919
William J. Breen

The Bang and the Whimper: Apocalypse and Entropy in American Literature
Zbigniew Lewicki

The Disreputable Profession: The Actor in Society
Mendel Kohansky

The Formative Essays of Justice Holmes: The Making of an
American Legal Philosophy
Frederic Rogers Kellogg

A "Capacity for Outrage": The Judicial Odyssey
of J. Skelly Wright
Arthur Selwyn Miller